Hemingway: The Paris Years

CVCA Royal Library
4687 Wyoga Lake Road
Stow, OH. 44224-1011

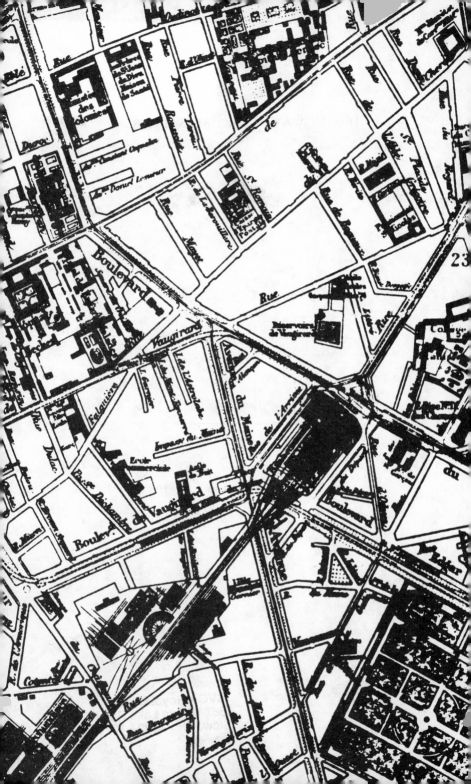

By Michael Reynolds

The Young Hemingway

Hemingway: The Paris Years

Hemingway: The Homecoming

Hemingway: The 1930s

Hemingway: The Final Years

HEMINGWAY:

THE PARIS YEARS

Michael Reynolds

W. W. NORTON & COMPANY

New York • London

B
Hemingway

T-21188

Copyright © Michael Reynolds 1989

First published as a Norton paperback 1999

All rights reserved
Printed in the United States of America

Library of Congress Cataloging in Publication Data

Reynolds, Michael S., 1937–
  Hemingway, the Paris years / Michael Reynolds.
    p.   cm.
  Includes index.
    1. Hemingway, Ernest, 1899–1961—Homes and haunts—France—Paris.
2. Hemingway, Ernest, 1899–1961—Biography.   3. Authors,
American—20th century—Biography.   4. Americans—France—Paris—
History—20th century.   5. Paris (France)—Intellectual life—20th
century.   I. Title.
PS3515.E3727547   1989
813′.52—dc19
[B]   89 – 30910
                                                                        CIP

ISBN 0-393-31879-6

W. W. Norton & Company, Inc.
500 Fifth Avenue, New York, N.Y. 10110
www.wwnorton.com

W. W. Norton & Company Ltd.
10 Coptic Street, London WC1A 1PU

CVCA Royal Library
4687 Wyoga Lake Road
Stow, OH. 44224-1011

3 4 5 6 7 8 9 0

C. 1   9-14-01   1595

This book is for the Supper Club

Let the ritual begin, for I bring garlic, herbs and oil to hold the night in place.

"The story of your life is not your life. It is your story."

John Barth

Contents

CONTENTS

ACKNOWLEDGEMENTS

No biography is ever written alone, and to be finished is to be thankful to many who helped.

I am grateful to John, Patrick and Gregory Hemingway and the Hemingway Foundation for their generosity to scholars, and in particular for their permission to print previously unpublished material from the manuscripts and letters of Ernest Hemingway. Excerpts from *Dateline: Toronto* by Ernest Hemingway, ed. W. White, are reprinted by kind permission of Charles Scribner's Sons, an imprint of Macmillan Publishing Company (copyright © 1985 Mary Hemingway, John Hemingway, Patrick Hemingway and Gregory Hemingway), and The Hemingway Foreign Rights Trust. Excerpts from *Ernest Hemingway: Selected Letters*, ed. Carlos Baker, are reprinted by kind permission of Charles Scribner's Sons, an imprint of Macmillan Publishing Company (copyright © 1981 Mary Hemingway), Grafton Books, a division of William Collins and Sons, and The Hemingway Foreign Rights Trust. The detailed maps of part of Paris on pages ii and iii appear by kind permission of the Map Division of the Library of Congress.

I give special thanks to: the National Endowment for the Humanities whose grant made possible the free year to write the book; John Bassett and the English Department of North Carolina State University whose encouragement and financial support were there when I needed them; the English Department of the University of New Mexico for visiting privileges. I should also like to thank the libraries and staffs who did their jobs well: the Stanford University Library and the Field Collection; the Bancroft at University of California, Berkeley; the Lilly Library at the University of Indiana; the Beinecke Library at Yale; the Firestone Library at Princeton; the Humanities Research Center at the University of Texas; the Alderman Library at the University of Virginia; Interlibrary Loan at D. H. Hill Library, North Carolina State University; and the

Library of the University of New Mexico, Albuquerque. Special thanks are due to Megan Desnoyers, curator of the Hemingway Collection at the John F. Kennedy Library, Boston, for help early and late.

To be thanked as well are all the members of the Hemingway Society who, over the years, have given me much heart and always kept a place for me at the bar.

In Santa Fe, there are these to thank: David Salazar and his Santa Fe restaurant El Farol for sustaining us with good tapas and Fundador; Sharon Zaccari and Bob Keesing for good housing; Marcia Cate and her Los Llanos Book Store, a writers' haven; Samuel Adelo for his translations; Ann Brady for being a good neighbor; C.J. and Dierdre for helping out.

Closer to home, I thank Ann Reynolds, who listened to every word of it, corrected every page, insisted on important additions, remembered rare connections, went to all the research centers, took excellent notes, and seldom lost her patience. This woman, my wife, who composes only Miltonic sentences, assisted in every phase except the actual writing of this book. I also thank Paul Smith who shared everything – his insights and information, his house and pool, his own manuscript, and even gave up his balcony room at Caux. No better friend or critic could I find. Also, Patsy and Hal Hopfenberg, Jen and George Bireline: good readers and good friends whose comments made this a better book, whose interests have made me a better writer. Almost everything important begins in the kitchen. Thanks too to Bob and Esther Fleming whose close reading picked a good many nits out of this book, and whose questions were always on the mark; Don Junkins whose poet's eye forced me to my revisions, and for whose dialogue I am indebted; Charlene Turner for logistical support; Maury and Marcia Neville for sharing; Bernice Kert for helping at short notice; Noel Riley Fitch and Jerry Kennedy for helping me keep the streets in place; Lu Brennan for mapping the territory when there wasn't a moment to lose; Brad Dismukes and "Jake" Martin for always providing over the years a warm bed and a full plate. Old friends indeed.

Thanks are also due to Russ and Katie Boone for photographic assistance and moral support; and the Tourist Information Center in Rapallo, Italy, for help with translation, photographs and historical material. Special gratitude goes to Claire Andrews for her patience and diligence in editing this book.

And, as always and forever, Carlos Baker. Even in death his files support the living: honey from the belly of the dead lion.

Chronology

1921

December
20   Hemingways arrive in Paris.

1922

January
9   Move into Paris apartment, 74 rue du Cardinal Lemoine.
10   Leave for Switzerland: Chamby sur Montreux.

February
2   Return to Paris. Mid-February meet Ezra Pound.

March
8   Hemingways meet Gertrude Stein.

April
6   Ernest leaves for Genoa Conference.
27   Ernest returns from Genoa.

May

       Double Dealer publishes "A Divine Gesture."

24   Ernest, Hadley and Chink Dorman-Smith at Chamby. Hike over St. Bernard pass into Italy.

June

11   Hemingways in Milan.
18   Return to Paris.

August

4   Hemingways begin Black Forest walking tour.
25   In Triberg, Germany.

September

2   Back in Paris.
25   Ernest departs Paris to cover the Greco-Turkish war.
29   Ernest arrives Constantinople.

October

18   Ernest departs Constantinople.
21   Ernest arrives Paris.

November

21   Ernest enters Switzerland for Lausanne Conference.

December

3   Hadley loses MSS. Ernest returns to Paris.
4   Ernest takes night train back to Lausanne.
16   Hemingways at Chamby with Chink Dorman-Smith.

1923

January

1   Isabel Simmons arrives Chamby.
*c.*15   Simmons departs. Hadley becomes pregnant.
17–20 Ernest in Paris.

CHRONOLOGY

February

7   Ernest and Hadley to Rapallo, Italy.

12   Ezra Pound leaves Rapallo for Rome.

15   Robert McAlmon arrives Rapallo.

March

10   Hemingways in Milan on way to Cortina.

23   Ernest in Paris enroute to Germany. Hadley waits in Cortina.

30   Ernest in Germany for ten days.

April

12   Ernest arrives back in Cortina.

May

2   Leave Italy to return to Paris.

June

1   Ernest goes to Spain with McAlmon, joined by Bird.

July

6   Hemingways go to first Pamplona festival.

17   Back in Paris from Pamplona; reading proofs of *Three Stories & Ten Poems*.

August

13   *Three Stories & Ten Poems* published in Paris.

17   Due to sail on *Andania*; ship delayed ten days.

26   Sail for Canada.

September

4   Dock in Montreal.

10   Ernest begins regular work at *Star*.

18   Trip to Sudbury to cover coal story.

October

4   Sent to New York to cover Lloyd George trip.

10   Hadley delivers son. Ernest arrives late.

December
20   Galley proofs of *in our time* arrive.
23   Ernest goes to Oak Park alone for Christmas visit.
25   Arrives back in Toronto Christmas morning.

1924

January
10   Hemingways leave Toronto.
19   Sail on *Antonia* for France.
30   Dock in Cherbourg, two days late.

February
8   Sign lease at 113 rue Notre-Dame-des-Champs.
17   Working for Ford on *transatlantic review*.
20   "Cat in the Rain," "The End of Something" done and
        starting "Indian Camp."

March
16   John Hadley Nicanor Hemingway baptized.

April
        "Indian Camp" appears in *transatlantic*.
7   First draft of "Doctor and Doctor's Wife" finished.
25   Finished "Soldier's Home," "Mr. and Mrs. Elliot," "Cross
        Country Snow." Ernest takes trip to Provence alone.

May
2   Ernest returns from Provence.
c.15   Begins "Big Two-Hearted River."
c.21   Ford goes to New York; Ernest edits *transatlantic*.

June
25   Hemingways leave for second Pamplona.

July
6   Pamplona begins: Dorman-Smith, Stewart, McAlmon, Birds,
        Dos Passos are there.

13   Last bullfight. Group goes to Burguete.
19   Ernest starts working on "Big Two-Hearted River" again.
27   Hemingways return to Paris.

August
      Writes "Pamplona Letter" for *transatlantic*.
3   Conrad dies. Ernest writes his Conrad "Homage."
*c.*15   Finishes "Big Two-Hearted River."

September
30   *In Our Time* sent to Don Stewart in New York to find a
      publisher.

October
5   *Der Querschnitt* appears with poems: "The Soul of Spain"
      and "Earnest Liberal's Lament."

November
1   *transatlantic* publishes "Doctor and Doctor's Wife." *Der
      Querschnitt* publishes part II of "Soul of Spain" and "Lady
      Poets With Footnotes."
23   Has finished "The Undefeated."

December
      "Cross Country Snow" in *transatlantic*.
20   Hemingways leave Paris for Schruns, Austria.
22   Ernest's review of Anderson's *A Story Teller's Story* in
      Tribune.

1925

January
12   Sends "Big Two-Hearted River" to *This Quarter*.
17–19   Three-day ski trip to Lech.
30   Writes "A Banal Story."

CHRONOLOGY

February

21   Perkins writes first letter of enquiry. Wrong address.

26   Two cables saying *In Our Time* accepted by Boni &
      Liveright.

March

4   "Mr. and Mrs. Elliot" appears in *Little Review*.

5   Liveright telegrams acceptance of *In Our Time*.

6   Ernest accepts offer.

8   Writes "Homage to Ezra" for *This Quarter*.

13   Hemingways exit Austria enroute back to Paris.

c.16 Liveright contract arrives.

31   Mails signed contract including "The Battler."

April

10   *The Great Gatsby* published in New York.
      End of April meets Scott and Zelda Fitzgerald.

May

      "Big Two-Hearted River" and "Homage to Ezra" in *This
      Quarter*.

15   Ernest reading *The Great Gatsby*.

c.20 Receives galley proofs of *In Our Time*.

22   Mails back galleys.

June

      "The Undefeated" first half in *Der Querschnitt*.

12   Contracts to buy Miró painting "The Farm."

26   Hemingways leave for third Pamplona.

28–30 Fishing in Burguete.

July

2   Return to Pamplona.

6   San Fermin festival begins: Bill Smith, Pat Guthrie, Duff
      Twysden, Don Stewart, Harold Loeb, and Hemingways.

12   Ernest apologizes to Loeb by letter.

13   Hemingways depart Pamplona for Madrid. Begins story that
      becomes novel.

21   Ernest's 26th birthday. Travels to Valencia.

23   Begins first blue notebook of *The Sun Also Rises*.

August
3   Has six chapters done. Valencia.
4   Returns to Madrid.
5   Has eight chapters done.
7   Hemingways travel to San Sebastián.
10 Move to Hendaye.
11 Hadley returns to Paris.
15 Has ten chapters done.
18 Ernest returns to Paris.

September
5   Loeb and Bill Smith sail for U.S.
15 First draft of *The Sun Also Rises* finished.
27 Ernest's trip to Chartres: begins "Fifty Grand" and "Ten Indians."
30 Completes purchase of Miró's "The Farm."

October
5   *In Our Time* published in New York.

November
23 Begins *Torrents of Spring*.

December
2   Finishes *Torrents of Spring*.
7   Sends *Torrents of Spring* to Liveright.
11 Hemingways leave for second Schruns.
c.25 Pauline Pfeiffer arrives Schruns.
30 Liveright rejects *Torrents* by cable.

1926

January
4   Hemingways and Pauline in Gaschurn for four days.
14 Pauline back in Paris.
28 Ernest in Paris enroute to New York; Hadley in Schruns.

CHRONOLOGY

February

3   Ernest leaves Cherbourg on the *Mauretania* for New York.

9   Ernest arrives New York.

10   Breaks contract with Horace Liveright.

11   Approaches Perkins at Scribner's.

17   Scribner's contract ready and Ernest signs.

20   Sails for France on the *Roosevelt*.

MAPS

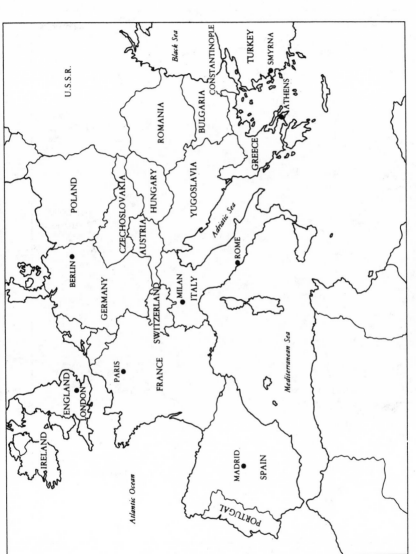

Map 1 Hemingway's Europe 1922–26
(copyright © Adrienne Louise Brennan)

Map 2 France
(copyright © Adrienne Louise Brennan)

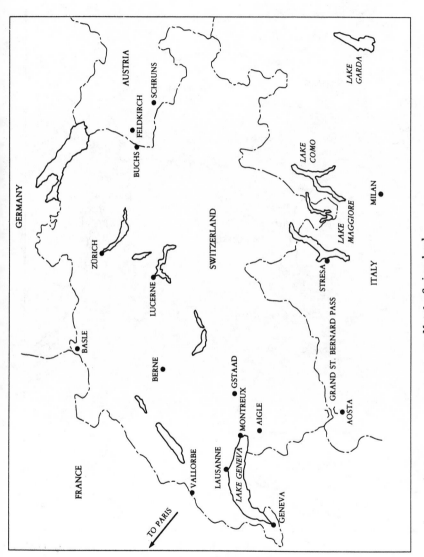

Map 3 Switzerland
(copyright © Adrienne Louise Brennan)

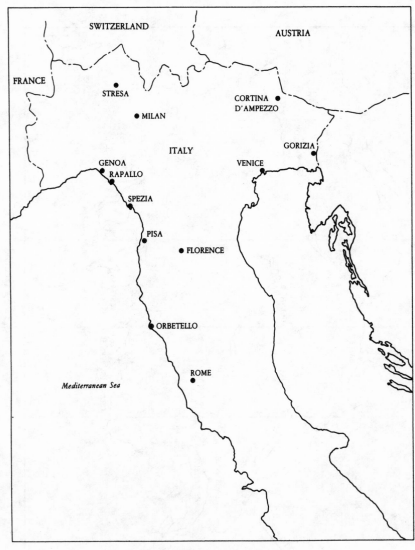

Map 4 Italy
(copyright © Adrienne Louise Brennan)

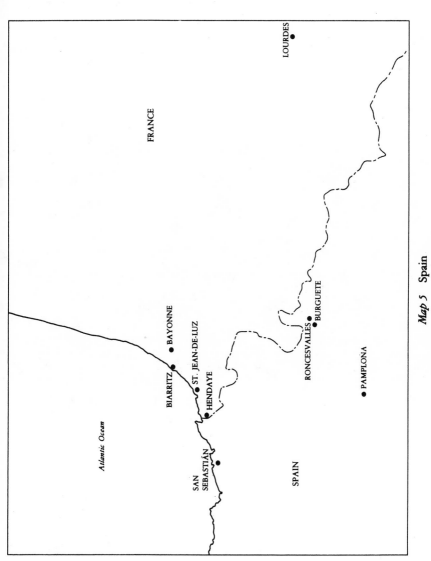

Map 5 Spain

(copyright © Adrienne Louise Brennan)

Part One

1922

Chapter One

LOSSES

He had twelve hours before the Express reached Paris, twelve hours to feel sorry for himself, to find someone to blame for his losses. At Lausanne, it did not seem possible that his wife packed all of his fiction, that she trusted a porter with the valise, that it was stolen from her compartment before the train even left the station. The closer he got to rainy, grey, cold Paris the more he was sure it happened just like that. It was the sort of thing he expected of Paris in winter. Pick up the paper almost any day and read about thieves at train stations, stolen bags, stolen jewelry, but never stolen manuscripts that no one wanted to print. It was almost funny. He could imagine the thief's disgust on forcing the lock: bloody nothing, not even a suitcase worth selling. The whole lot was probably down the sewer or in the Seine; still, he had to be certain. At Vallorbe he filed through the station with other travelers to have his joint passport checked. Yes, he was Ernest Hemingway. No, Mrs. Hemingway was elsewhere, losing things no doubt. No, he was taking nothing out of the country worth mentioning. The uniformed official stamped his papers: December 3, 1922.[1]

It was the same return train to Paris he and Hadley had taken the previous February, still fresh from busting loose from Chicago. They were so certain the year would be wonderful, full of adventure, a year to finish the novel begun in Chicago. They cuddled shamelessly in the compartment, talking their private love-talk that made strangers turn away, embarrassed to intrude. That was then. Now he returned alone, thinking all the way. The year had been departures and returns; sometimes together, sometimes alone. This time alone was different.

Usually he left Paris with Hadley on his arm or left her behind to wait for him; this time he left her in tears at Lausanne. Usually she met him at Gare de Lyon or was waiting in their small apartment with bed and body warmed. This time the apartment would be as cold as all of winter Paris. He really did not care for the Paris of winter rain, did not like its touristy summers, its pushy women nor its fairies flitting among the cafés.

Barely a year ago Sherwood Anderson urged Ernest and Hadley to connect with Paris, promising the writing would improve and they would meet important people. They met the people – Joyce, Stein, Pound, Sylvia Beach – but Hemingway's writing did not fulfill the promise. The autobiographic war novel which he pecked at during the year was unfinished. If Hadley had packed the carbons with the manuscripts, it might never be finished. No one had seen the novel since he showed it to Gertrude Stein in March. She read only enough to say, "Begin over again and concentrate." She was right. Part of him now knew the novel was a bust, but that did not mitigate the hurt of its likely loss. Writing seemed so easy in Chicago, imitating slick fiction out of *Saturday Evening Post*. That was then – poor imitations boxed in Oak Park and best forgotten. When his models changed so did his style, which meant the war novel needed to be rewritten from scratch, but that did not stem the anger rising in his throat. He was a man who kept everything – to-do lists, tickets to boxing matches, notes made on the backs of old letters. To lose that much of his writing was to lose a part of himself, a piece of his identity. This grey day would be there between himself and Hadley always as something painful and unspoken.[2]

Part of him knew that all was not lost. Before going to Lausanne he sent Greg Clark, his old buddy on the Toronto *Star*, a typescript of "My Old Man" and he left another copy of it with Lincoln Steffens in Lausanne. It was as good a story as he knew how to write, and he was proud of it. He did not show them any of the stories written before he read Joyce or understood how Sherwood did it. He now had Sherwood down pat. "My Old Man" was as good as anything of Sherwood's. Later, when it was published, critics would say that here was another of Anderson's boys, just another imitator. They missed the point. "My Old Man" was a form of thank-you, a sort of homage, but also a challenge match with Anderson that was at least a draw. Ernest knew that Sherwood would understand it when he read it. The year was not wasted; it only felt that way as night fell and the Express clicked on toward Paris. Grey and dead countryside disappeared into darkness past

Dijon, and there were only the rain streaks on the window and passing lights.[3]

At twenty-three, Ernest Hemingway was closer than he knew to becoming the writer he envisioned. All he lacked was the confidence to commit himself totally to his profession. After a rushed and ragged year spent in and out of Paris, he could not see himself clearly. Since his 1919 return from the war in Italy, he told everyone he was a writer: four years later his only publications were a short, satirical fable and a poem, both written before he left Chicago and both printed in an arty little magazine in New Orleans. John McClure, the editor of *The Double Dealer*, was a friend of Sherwood's, who opened the door there for Hemingway. That hardly counted. He had not yet made it on his own merit, not even an encouraging rejection. He did not count the news stories with his by-line in the *Star*, the stories that left him so little time for fiction.[4]

One of the earliest features he sent back to the *Star* told how cheaply two people could live in Paris. "Exchange," he said, "was a wonderful thing." Their room at Hotel Jacob came to thirty dollars a month. Breakfast was only "two francs and a half," or about six dollars a month. One could, he confided, spend vast sums at swank Right Bank hotels and restaurants charging whatever the traffic would bear, but the smart visitor, like their correspondent, was not taken in by the glitter or robbed by inflated bills and taxi overcharges. Already Hemingway prided himself on knowing how to get the most for his money.

> . . . there is a splendid restaurant where the prices are a la carte. . . . My wife and I have an excellent meal there . . . for fifty cents a piece. . . . There are several hundred small hotels . . . where an American or a Canadian can live comfortably, eat at attractive restaurants and find amusement for a total expenditure of two and one half to three dollars a day.[5]

They did not need Hemingway's income from *Star* feature stories, for Hadley's several trust funds provided them with almost $3000 a year, more than enough money to live well in Paris. Their first apartment came furnished for only 250 francs a month, or less than $20. If he wished, Hemingway could have spent the entire year working on his fiction without selling a single line to the *Star*. Partly out of male pride, partly from lack of confidence, he could not take that step beyond the edge of middle-class life. No man he knew in Oak Park lived off his wife's income; even Sherwood Anderson wrote advertising copy for tractors. In Paris he fell in readily with the Anglo-American Press Club where a handful of professional newsmen accepted him as Hemingway of the *Star*. When the fiction would not write, it was easier to fall back on journalism than to face the blank page.[6]

There were a lot of blank pages to face that year. He came to Paris knowing, he thought, what he was going to write. He had the war novel going and several stories on his mind. But Paris changed all of that. For the first time, he read the Russians, Turgenev and Dostoievsky; he read the French, Stendhal and Flaubert. In Paris, he read James Joyce and T. S. Eliot, and his reading changed everything. For the first time, he saw the difference between slick fiction and master craftsmanship. At sixteen his favorite authors were O. Henry, Kipling and Stewart Edward White. Part of their influence remained with him forever, but in Paris they were neither the competition nor the models for 1922. In Paris writing was a new game with Left Bank rules; even the playing field was changed. Hemingway needed time to absorb what amounted to his college education.[7]

That was part of his problem, but only part. John Bone, his editor at the Toronto *Star*, bought anything Ernest sent, even the less than well-written pieces, paying at space rates. Hemingway could not turn down the easy money, for part of him worried about money the way his father did in Oak Park. In that affluent suburb of Chicago, where other boys got reasonable allowances, Ernest, at sixteen, received sixteen cents a week. In Oak Park, his father periodically forced his children to keep a detailed weekly accounting of expenditures. No matter how hard the children tried, they could not please Clarence Hemingway, for by the time Ernest was twelve, his father was beyond being pleased. As his perplexed children watched, Dr. Hemingway slipped gradually into deeper depressions accompanied by estranging paranoia and moodiness that could change direction with scary speed. The children did not understand the medical reasons for their father's behavior, but they lived with his daily fears, one of which was that the family might become penniless, the same fear that later put him into a suicide's grave.

Dr. Hemingway, whose medical practice produced less income than his wife's voice lessons, was never a player in the Oak Park money game. Watching his father accept Grace's earned money, Ernest sensed the advantage his mother assumed, and he suspected her money might have contributed to his father's strange behavior. Ernest was born in her father's house, where the Hemingways lived until Ernest was seven. Then his mother's inherited money built their North Kenilworth house and later her private cottage at Walloon Lake. Her money paid for her separate vacations taken each year to California or Nantucket. Ernest Hemingway saw exactly what his mother's money did to her marriage. In Paris at the Guaranty Trust Bank, Ernest set up a checking account, but not a joint one. Hadley could not make withdrawals, and only he knew how much money they had on deposit. Into the account went Hadley's quarterly trust fund checks and Ernest's payments from the *Star*, which amounted to less than half of Hadley's income.[8]

Thus it was, during those first two months in Paris before he met Gertrude Stein or started his educative reading, Ernest Hemingway spent most of his creative energy writing articles for the Toronto *Star*. In the first sixty days he mailed John Bone thirty feature stories. While he was learning the new literary game, journalism toughened and educated him and laid in a stock of far-flung images and short-takes that would later feed his fiction. But that December night, as the train pulled into the domed and darkened Gare de Lyon, he knew only that his year was gone with little to show for it even if the carbons of his fiction remained. He stepped down to the damp platform, breathing in the familiar sulfuric odor of damp coal smoke, vaguely urinous: the inescapable smell of winter Paris. It was late. Rain continued to fall outside the station. He walked past the few remaining taxi cabs without pausing. He was too depressed to indulge in a taxi, and he was not eager to face the possibly empty drawer.[9]

It was a short walk across the Austerlitz bridge, then through the Jardin des Plantes with the chestnut trees cropped close for winter and on up the hill to where rue Mouffetard ran into one side of Place de la Contrescarpe and came out the other side rue Descartes. The small square, now empty of drunks, led him to the front door where he banged awake the smelly concierge. He climbed the twisted stairs passing at every level the urinous stench of the W.C. In their small rented rooms, the odor of Hadley's perfume hung faintly in the air. Sheet music lay open on her piano. He must have stopped for a moment before moving to the dining room cupboard – a moment to focus and taste the anger welling up inside. He could see so clearly the three folders as he left them: manuscripts in one, typescripts in another; carbons in the third. He opened the drawer.

Nothing.

Empty.

Put out the light.

From the *bal musette* below the sound of an accordion drifted up through the light rain falling.[10]

Chapter Two

MAKING CONNECTIONS
PARIS, WINTER, 1921–2

I

The apartment, dark and winter cold, was less charming than it first appeared the previous winter when he and Hadley found it. On December 21, 1921, they cleared customs at Cherbourg: escapees from Chicago out to discover the world. Almost the first thing he did in Paris was to write Sherwood Anderson, the man who sent them there armed with introductory letters and notes on where to stay and eat, what to see and how to get about. He told Anderson about the Atlantic voyage, the brief stop in Spain and the train trip to Paris:

> villages with smoking manure piles and long fields and woods with the leaves on the ground and the trees trimmed bare of branches way up their trunks and a roll of country and towers up over the edge. Dark stations and tunnels and 3rd class compartments full of boy soldiers and finally everyone asleep in your own compartment leaning against each other . . .

One literary man to another, Hemingway was writing Anderson in the best prose he knew, using images appropriate to Anderson's taste but the precise images that were later so crucial to his fiction. Before he read any of the modernists or listened to the dictums of Ezra Pound or Gertrude Stein, Hemingway knew the importance of place, the look of the land, sharp, singular details marking a place forever in the reader's mind. Paris had much to teach the young writer, but not how to observe detail. He arrived with that skill sharply honed.[1]

He also arrived aware of his limitations – he did not know much about Paris and could not speak the language – limitations he was determined to disguise until they could be removed. The language problem was not serious, for Hadley with eight years of schoolgirl French had visited Paris in 1910. She was not fluent in the street idioms that Ernest grew to love, but she managed most conversations and situations. Ernest's quick ear, able to imitate most sound patterns, picked up phrases before he knew their meanings. Later he would claim he learned French from reading French newspapers: "They were all written the same way. You did not have to look up the word; you learned the French word by reading the dispatch copied from an American or British [wire service]. You were familiar with the subject or you easily saw what the dispatch was about and you learned the words." Grammar, he claimed, "was a matter of the ear, not something to be studied." Perhaps it happened just that way, but he never did learn the grammar, and to the end of their marriage, Hadley wrote the letters in French to their landlord.[2]

As soon as they arrived in the French capital, Hemingway bought a copy of Hilaire Belloc's *Paris*, a general guide to the city's historic past. In his letter to Anderson, Ernest said almost too casually, as if it were information he had always known, "when it's a cold night in the streets of Paris and we're walking home down the rue Bonaparte we think of the way the wolves used to slink into the city and François Villon and the gallows at Montfaucon." He may have remembered the gallows from *A Tale of Two Cities*, but Villon and the wolves were new details from Belloc's book. All his writing life he had a way of taking things out of books, making them his own. Ernest Hemingway, who despised amateurs no matter what the situation, quickly created in his correspondence and journalism the persona of an experienced American in Paris, street wise and supremely confident. Whatever the game, Ernest wanted an edge on it, inside knowledge. When around truly experienced Americans in Paris, like Lewis Galantière, Hemingway would listen with an intensity that flattered the speaker. Absorbing all for his own, Ernest would use it as first-hand knowledge in his writing or in the presence of less experienced tourists. He himself could not bear to be taken for a tourist, a person who learned French, as his wife had, by studying it in a book. Four years later he could see it both ways. In *The Sun Also Rises*, his narrator tells us that Robert Cohn got his ideas out of books, as if books were an untrustworthy source. At the same time, Ernest knew his own ideas came frequently from his reading. It was a joke on himself.[3]

Barely two days in Paris, he told Anderson he was working at his typewriter to earn the family living. The first feature story he sent back to the *Star* described tuna fishing in the Spanish bay at Vigo where, after the Atlantic crossing, the *Leopoldina* stopped long enough for him to see the great fish jumping in the almost landlocked harbor and long enough for him to gather information to write the story. He described how the giant tuna were caught:

> It is a back-sickening, sinew-straining, man-sized job even with a rod that looks like a hoe handle. But if you land a big tuna after a six-hour fight, fight him man against fish until your muscles are nauseated with the uneasing strain, and finally bring him up alongside the boat, green-blue and silver in the lazy ocean, you will be purified and will be able to enter unabashed into the presence of the very elder gods and they will make you welcome.

Maybe that's how "you" felt, but Hemingway imagined it all, extrapolating from his first-hand knowledge of trout fishing, from watching fishermen in the bay and from inspecting gutted fish in the market place. For his readers he created an impression of first-hand experience. Their correspondent was not a mere tourist watching professional fishermen; he was a brother to them, his back aching with theirs at their heavy trade. Hemingway became so proficient in creating this kind of illusion that later readers and critics were certain he lived the experiences described in his fiction. "That is natural," he said, "because while were making them up, you had to make them happen to the person who was telling them. If you do this successfully enough you make the person who is reading them believe that the things happened to him too."[4]

Having registered in Paris at Hotel Jacob et l'Angleterre where Anderson stayed the previous fall, Ernest and Hadley were soon sitting beside a charcoal brazier outside Café du Dôme where Sherwood said the right people drank. Across the street, the Rotonde was closed for redecoration – Montparnasse was beginning to change under the pressure of monied Americans moving to Paris. Ernest and Hadley arrived just before their countrymen changed the Left Bank completely. The Dôme remained the bohemian artist's retreat that it always was, but within two years the old café would be a memory, changed irrevocably by

American spenders. Within two years the young Hemingway would also have disappeared, replaced by the stockier, mustached, more experienced writer of the mid-Twenties.

That day in front of the Dôme a casual observer would have seen a smooth-faced, young American in a dark suit, muffled against the cold and hair askew, sipping his hot rum punch by the charcoal fire and watching everything and everyone with quick, dark eyes. Beside him was a woman with chestnut hair and wire-rimmed glasses. She looked older than the man. When the waiter came to the table, the woman spoke to him in textbook French. The young man listened. He had a quick ear, and the next time he would order for himself. Other than the age difference, there was nothing particularly remarkable about the American couple so obviously in love. Along Montparnasse and Boulevard Raspail, natives, hurrying along on the last Friday before Christmas, paid the young lovers little attention. It was too cold to be sitting out at the Dôme.

Less than two blocks from Hemingway's table, what was left of Charles Baudelaire and Guy de Maupassant lay beneath stone memorials in the Montparnasse cemetery. A five-minute walk down Boulevard Raspail, Gertrude Stein and Alice Toklas were planning their Christmas meal. Close by Ezra Pound was reading through a bit of manuscript left him by his young friend with exhausted nerves, Tom Eliot, on his way to a rest cure in Lausanne. Eventually Eliot would call it *The Waste Land*. Less than two blocks from the Hemingways' hotel, James Joyce was dressing to attend a party at Sylvia Beach's bookstore, Shakespeare and Company, where he would celebrate the final revisions to his manuscript *Ulysses*. None of these literary giants knew that Ernest Hemingway was in town, but before the year was out they would know him well. A conjunction of literary influences was about to take place which would forever change the topography of American literature.

II

The conjunction began on December 28, 1921, when Hemingway entered for the first time the bookshop, Shakespeare and Company. Inside he met the postmistress and den mother of Left Bank Americans, Sylvia Beach, soon to be the publisher of James Joyce's *Ulysses* and later to be the one woman besides Gertrude Stein whom every writer remembered from his youth in Paris. Almost forty years later, Hemingway said of her:

> Sylvia had a lively, sharply sculptured face, brown eyes that were as alive as a small animal's and as gay as a young girl's, and wavy brown hair that was brushed back from her fine forehead and cut thick below her ears and at the line of the collar of the brown velvet jacket she wore. She had pretty legs and she was kind, cheerful and interested, and loved to make jokes and gossip.[5]

Without makeup and with little pretense, dear Sylvia, as Hemingway later called her, was the gatekeeper. She collected and forwarded mail for steady customers on vacation, loaned books and money to those in need, helped the helpless to find rooms, mediated arguments and kept track of where her customers were and what they were doing. From the already crowded walls of her bookshop and lending library stared the writers, living and dead, who were the founders of modernism. Eventually Hemingway's own picture would be there with those of Joyce, Pound, Conrad, Lawrence and others. But on that late December day, Hemingway had only his introductory letter from Sherwood Anderson as entree. The letter was unnecessary, for he had only to say that he was in Paris to write fiction to gain Sylvia's sympathy.

In his half-fictive memoir, *A Moveable Feast*, Hemingway put his meeting with Sylvia two months after it actually occurred, remembering it right in spirit. He told us that he "started with Turgenev and took the two volumes of *A Sportsman's Sketches* and an early book of D. H. Lawrence, I think it was *Sons and Lovers*, and . . . the Constance Garnett edition of *War and Peace*, and *The Gambler and Other Stories* by Dostoyevsky." His one month, twelve franc subscription to Sylvia's lending library allowed him only two volumes at a time. The following Monday, the first working day of the new year, Hadley came in to subscribe at thirty francs for three months and two volumes. The pair of them could then keep out four volumes at once, although Sylvia gave the Hemingways large leeway.[6]

The Hemingways' check-out cards from 1921–25 are, unfortunately, lost. However, both were avid, voracious readers. Ernest typically kept two and sometimes three books in progress. Except for remarks in their correspondence, we can only speculate on what the Hemingways read. On the day he first subscribed, Sylvia also sold a copy of Joyce's *Dubliners*; she does not say to whom. If Hemingway did not buy that particular copy, we know that he read all of Joyce – *Dubliners, Portrait of the Artist, Pomes Penyeach, Chamber Music* and *Ulysses* – during the next eighteen months. Shakespeare and Company kept a good stock of all Joyce's works on the shelves, for winter friends and summer tourists depended on the shop for the Irish author's work largely unavailable elsewhere. Whenever asked to suggest reading, Sylvia was sure to mention Joyce; not only was she his friend, benefactor and money-raiser, she also sold more of Joyce's works than of any other single author's.[7]

Sylvia was also a Paris outlet for most literary and intellectual magazines of the period. At any time Hemingway could stop in to browse through *Vanity Fair*, Harold Loeb's short-lived *Broom*, *The English Review*, *Chap Book*, *Little Review*, the *Times Literary Supplement*, *Gargoyle*, *Tyro*, *S4N*, *The Double Dealer*, *Dial*, *Contact*, *Nation* and *Criterion*. Without spending a cent, Hemingway remained current on the literary scene. If Sylvia loved literary gossip, she found a willing ear with the young man from Oak Park, where gossip was an art form. Within two years Hemingway would be writing his own gossip column for the *transatlantic review*.[8]

Another magazine regularly appearing at Sylvia's was the much-banned *Birth Control Review* which Hemingway might have thumbed through with some interest. He and Hadley, joke as they might about the raising of their young, were not interested in a child just yet. The periodical must have disappointed him, for its pages argued the need for disseminating birth control information while, in fact, saying little if anything about the specifics of preventing conception. The review's presence at Sylvia's was, however, part of a pattern. When Joyce's *Ulysses* in serial form caused the *Little Review* to be confiscated, banned, taken to trial in New York and judged obscene, no reputable publisher would touch the book. In March of 1921, Sylvia, without understanding exactly the difficulties involved, agreed to Joyce's suggestion that Shakespeare and Company become the publisher of *Ulysses*. A banned periodical and a banned novel: daring action for a single, American woman trying to make her Paris living selling English books.[9]

For a minister's daughter, Sylvia Beach was less than religious and more than daring. Sexual matters held no particular taboo for this woman whose only apparent sexual relationship was with another woman, Adrienne Monnier, fellow bookseller, neighbor and patron of the arts. At Shakespeare and Company, the summer tourist could find the sort of books not sold in America. During the Twenties, Sylvia carried all of Havelock Ellis' work, including the multi-volume *Psychology of Sex* and *Erotic Symbolism*. When Lawrence's *Lady Chatterley's Lover* was banned, Sylvia sold it. She also carried Oscar Wilde's *De Profundis* and his *Salome* with Beardsley's decadent illustrations. John Cleland's eighteenth-century bawdry, *Fanny Hill*, sold regularly at the bookshop, as did Frank Harris' *My Life and Loves*, even the illustrated edition which was offensive enough to be banned in Paris. Pretty, dear Sylvia was unashamedly selling erotic books to any who asked for them, and these sales, not always reported to the French tax man, contributed significantly to her economic survival during this period when she was always on the edge of insolvency.[10]

Shakespeare and Company also carried the cheap Modern Library and Tauchnitz lines of classics, contemporary fiction and murder mysteries. Major British authors – Shaw, Kipling, Conrad – sold steadily. H. G. Wells and Henry James were always available, as were Theodore Dreiser and Jack London. Hemingway's Paris reading probably followed the same pattern which developed over his lifetime: 50 percent British, 25 percent European and 25 percent contemporary American. After 1924, he read widely in literary biography, literary and military history, travel books of all kinds, short story collections, poetry, murder mysteries and contemporary novels. Some books he bought. By the time he returned to the states in 1928, he owned $1200 worth of books – about 450 volumes. Between 1922 and 1928, he checked out twenty to thirty books a year from Sylvia's lending library. Hadley, alone much of their first year in Paris, probably used the lending library even more than Ernest. When he was still reading Belloc's *Paris*, Hadley checked out Lytton Strachey's *Queen Victoria* and D. H. Lawrence's *Lost Girl*. A crucial part of Hemingway's literary education, Hadley came to their marriage better read than he and with more formal education – a year at Bryn Mawr. Although both Ezra Pound and Gertrude Stein would tell Hemingway to read Henry James, Hadley was the first and closest person to tell him about the "Master."[11]

Whomever else Hemingway might have read those first days in Paris, he must have checked out Gertrude Stein's *Three Lives* and *Tender Buttons* and some of Ezra Pound's poetry. Arriving as he had with Anderson letters to Pound and Stein, Hemingway would have immediately read their work. He knew that Pound was his connection to most of the little magazines, including the *Dial*, the most prestigious literary magazine in America. Ezra Pound was crucial to his future, but about Gertrude Stein, Hemingway was less sure. Sherwood's insistence that her experiments with words were tremendously important left Hemingway a little puzzled. He did not share Sherwood's romantic response to Stein's enigmatic and surreal experiment, *Tender Buttons* (1914). When Gertrude wrote "To dine is west," Anderson knew "a great revolution in the art of words had begun." Hemingway's foundation in Kipling and O. Henry simply did not prepare him for dealing with statements like,

THIS IS THIS DRESS, AIDER

Aider, why aider why whow, whow stop touch, aider whow, aider stop the muncher, muncher munchers.
A jack in kill her, a jack in, makes a meadowed king, makes a to let.

Hemingway must have puzzled a good deal over such use of the language. Was it a joke? Should he laugh? What was the proper response? If he had read the lines out loud, he might have gotten a sense of the word play and punning that Stein used long before Joyce immortalized it. Perhaps it said: "This is distress. Aid her. Aid her, why aid her, why, how?" But who was the muncher? A jack in killer? And how would such a killer make a meadowed king, or create a vacancy to be let? Or was it a toilet being made? Perhaps he caught the sexual jokes that ran through *Tender Buttons*, but it seems unlikely. This was a new world that took getting used to. If at Sylvia's Hemingway was hesitant to use his Anderson letter for introduction, he was even more intimidated by the prospect of facing Pound and Stein. [12]

III

The new year in Paris, which began overcast and chilly, turned bleak, cold and rainy wet with snow flurries in the evenings that did not stick to the wet cobblestoned streets and left only a wisp of white on the roofs at morning. With the help of Lewis Galantière, another of Anderson's contacts, the Hemingways spent the first week of January searching for an apartment. The *Tribune*, complaining about the rising cost of Paris life, said that a nicely furnished apartment should cost 1000 francs or 85 dollars a month. The place Hemingway found was only 250 francs a month. Galantière first directed the couple toward

15

CVCA Royal Library
4687 Wyoga Lake Road
Stow, OH. 44224-1011

the Luxembourg Gardens and Montparnasse, but those addresses did not appeal to Hemingway, whose first impression of the Montparnasse artsy crowd was negative. Perhaps because of Belloc's romantic descriptions of the Latin Quarter but partly because the price was right, Hemingway took, instead, a fourth-floor walk-up in the oldest part of the Left Bank: 74 rue du Cardinal Lemoine, just off Place de la Contrescarpe. Only four months earlier, James Joyce moved out of a borrowed apartment across the street, taking with him his almost finished *Ulysses*. Close by was the cavernous Halle aux Vins where bonded wines were stored, and the Jardin des Plantes, seventy-eight acres of botanic gardens, menagerie and museum reminding him of Chicago's Field Museum of Natural History where he first saw African animals. On Thursdays and Sundays one could roam through the reptile or the monkey house, the bear pits, the museum or the gardens for free. Around the corner from Cardinal Lemoine, the Ecole Polytechnique was training military engineers for the next war. Two blocks away, dominating the highest point of the Left Bank, loomed the classic form of the Panthéon with its strangely mixed murals and its dark, cold vaults where lay the bones of Voltaire, Rousseau, Victor Hugo and Emile Zola.[13]

No one who visited the Hemingways on Cardinal Lemoine quite understood why they lived as they did. The apartment was not convenient to a Metro stop; only the wandering green autobus gave transportation. It was in a working-class neighborhood without great charm or decent restaurants. From the blue collar *bal musette* at street level came accordion music and easy laughter from locals – quaint perhaps but not always desirable. Their fourth-floor walk-up consisted of only two rooms with a tiny kitchen appended. The dining room was so small that when Hadley put her rented piano into it, the table had to be moved to the bedroom. Visitors concluded that Ernest and Hadley were truly as poor as Ernest said they were. One visit to the toilet concealed by curved doors in the bend of the stairs confirmed the impression: it was a French two-footer known as "Turkish." It consisted "of an enamelled metal crater in the floor with a circular hole four inches in diameter in the not-exact center." One placed both feet firmly on the raised footholds and squatted. From the flush box hung a chain that, when pulled, deluged the floor of the compartment to the depth of two inches. Those adept at its use were able to get out of the door before their feet got wet. Those who did not were tourists.[14]

He told his parents, the apartment was

16

the jolliest place you ever saw. We rented it furnished for 250 francs a month, about 18 dollars . . . Bones [Hadley] has a piano and we have all our pictures up on the walls and an open fire place and a peach of a kitchen and a dining room and big bed room and dressing room and plenty of space. It is on top of a high hill in the very oldest part of Paris. The nicest part of the Latin Quarter.[15]

To Katy Smith, his old girl friend in Chicago, he said the apartment was

directly above a fine place called the Bal au printemps . . . The noise of the accordion they dance to you can hear if you listen for it, but it doesn't intrude. We have a Femme du Menage . . . who comes in and gets breakfast and cleans and empties in the morning and then goes away and comes back and cooks and serves dinner at night. She can cook the best meal you ever put in your mouth and I make out the menus, me and Bones, for all the things we've ever heard of or eaten and she does them all wonderfully.[16]

Both of these letters, written after only two days in the apartment, were special kinds of fiction. With a little imagination, the large closet with its slop jar, bowl and water pitcher could be called a dressing room. The black-manteled fireplace was indeed open, for its coal fire was their only source of winter heat. The tiny kitchen with its two-burner gas stove admitted only one person at a time. The "fine place" next door was filled with sailors and working-class men from the area, a dime-a-dance place. The nightly slop jar was emptied in the closet at the end of the hall, and the garbage was carted down four flights of stairs. In the surrounding streets, drunks frequently slept in doorways, undisturbed by the housewives arguing with vendors for the best price. To Oak Park he wrote what his parents needed to hear without telling them how intense and interesting he found this new Paris life that they could never understand.[17]

No matter what he wrote or to whom, Ernest Hemingway found it impossible to transmit bare facts uncomposed. To the artist's eye, painter or writer, the physical world continually poses, arranging itself here, disposing itself there. Whenever Hemingway put words on paper, he was creating fiction. That was his trade, his art, his calling. He was born to it. Later he would say:

It is not *un-natural* that the best writers are liars. A major part of their trade is to lie or invent and they will lie when they are drunk, or to themselves, or to strangers. They often lie unconsciously and then remember their lies with deep remorse. If they knew all other writers were liars too it would cheer them up.[18]

But that judgement was too harsh. In the post-Newtonian universe reality became subjective and truth relative. The world was what one believed it to be, and a man like Hemingway, with a strong imagination, created fictions so believably well-wrought that his world became permanently ours.

IV

After a week of wet feet and cold ears, Ernest and Hadley found their apartment, but paid the price with winter sniffles. The first week of the new year in Paris was rain and cold, cold and more rain, day after day. One night, horse urine in the gutters would turn to frozen slush; the next day would be 50 degrees and showers. They signed the lease on Saturday the 7th and moved in the following Monday but with train tickets already in their pockets for immediate departure to Switzerland. As they stood in the rain, watching the porter lug their trunks up the winding stairs, they were happy to be getting out of Paris as quickly as possible. The rain was too depressing, and Ernest's throat was beginning to get sore, as it would, chronically, most of his life. In the papers they read that St. Moritz enjoyed a week of "picnic and excursion in brilliant weather." At Chamonix, snow, not rain, was falling. Boat friends staying at Hotel Jacob told them about an inexpensive pension at Chamby sur Montreux which a quick telegram reserved.

More than the rain, however, drove the couple out of Paris. Europe was suffering another of its periodic outbreaks of influenza or grippe, as the papers called it. They were already at Chamby, clear of the flu belt, when the *Tribune* told Paris:

AMERICANS WARNED AGAINST GRIPPE SPREAD

Immediate attention to any indication of a bad cold accompanied by a cough and dry nostrils was advised last night . . . to Americans in Paris as a safe-guard against the grippe epidemic which has been severely felt in England and which is spreading to the continent. More cases of the grippe are being reported daily at the Paris hospitals.

Ernest's well-grounded fear of the flu would, at the slightest inflamed throat, take him to bed. The 1917–18 epidemic of Spanish influenza killed more Americans than died in World War One. Bullets or trench mortar shells in a random chance universe were certainly to be feared, but the idea of drowning in his own mucous truly frightened Hemingway. Although he did not see anyone die of the Spanish flu during his recuperation from wounds in the Milan hospital, he wrote an unpublished sketch about such a death later. "At the end of the last war," the narrator, hospitalized for a reopened foot wound, develops a sore throat, while down the ward a young aviator is dying of the flu. The narrator is furious with the incompetent, cowardly doctor who is needlessly risking the narrator's life. As the nauseating sounds of the aviator's flu-filled lungs grow worse, nurses raise isolating screens around the dying man's bed: a terminal case. All his life Ernest Hemingway was prone to sore, inflamed throats, and always the once imagined sounds came to haunt him.[19]

The snows of Switzerland were only twelve hours from Paris by train. First there was a supper at the upstairs restaurant at Gare de Lyon and then a seven dollar ticket, second-class, on the night train to Montreux. Sitting up all night was bearable, almost fun. At the Dijon stop, they bought sandwiches and a bottle of wine. In the dark at Vallorbe, the porter shook them awake to pass through Swiss customs; Ernest watched as the sleepy official stamped their joint passport, before the year's end to be filled with more official ink than they ever planned. By nine that morning they were in Montreux getting directions to the electric train to take them up the mountain to the Gangwisches' small pension at Chamby, a thousand feet above Lake Geneva. The two-story chalet, perched on a slope within a stone's throw of the railway, looked out across the lake far below to the snowy peaks of the Dent du Midi. There, in the mountains, they felt free, reading at night beneath the feather comforter and by day bob-sledding down the mountain. Two miles up the mountain and seven hundred feet higher at Les Avants, the young lovers rented a bob-sled named Theodore. Ernest wrote: "The roads are like iron with two feet of packed snow and you shoot down with a shriek . . . when you put on the brakes and lean way out you go round the turns in a slither of ice dust." On an all-day pass, they could train up the mountain and then zoom down the icy roads as long as the light held. Together in a good place, Hadley and Ernest were alone, a confederacy of two. This was the time he remembered most fondly, the time before he gathered the winter bunch of friends for the slopes and sleds. But no matter how idyllic the setting or how bracing the sports, it was never enough for Ernest to be there alone with Hadley. Always he missed the rowdy comradeship he had known at Walloon Lake after the war; he particularly missed Bill Smith and his green-eyed sister Katy, missed the unstructured and carefree life of the summer people, as he called them. For the next thirty years he would try to reassemble some vestige of the lake life, cajoling and arranging new and old friends to gather and be free again.[20]

Jutting out into the lake below them, moored like some great stone ship to the rocky shore, stood the Castle of Chillon, with its picturesque turrets and battlements. Beneath the carved stone windows of the great hall, a pair of red hawks fished silently past the ancient walls. For Ernest, whose interest in the romantic medieval past was never far beneath the surface hardness he sometimes affected, the icy castle was more interesting than some women might have appreciated. But Hadley never faltered. Of all the women in his many lives, she best understood his romantic streak, his admiration of Chaucer's medieval knight. Down in the dungeon, among the graffiti of forgotten tourists, the name Byron was carved into the third stone pillar where once Bonivard, the Prisoner of Chillon, was chained. There in the winter keep, Ernest could just imagine how it had been for Bonivard.[21]

Letters went back to friends and family, and feature stories for the *Star* were beaten out on a borrowed typewriter. Hemingway's knack of turning whatever he was doing into a story made his bob-sledding days fodder for Toronto.

> The bob is rushing along with a steely lisp from the runners . . . There is a great snowy valley on the left with huge saw-toothed bulks of mountains on the other side, but you only get rushing glimpses of it out of the corner of your eye as the bob shrieks around a turn . . . the road swoops into a forest and you roar through it on the iciness of the road . . . you slow . . . wipe the wind tears out of your eyes and look back at the sunset that is turning the white shoulders of the mountain pink. . . . the road dips into another stretch of timber and you roar down the last steep slope to the railway station.[22]

Catching the intensity of action in a specific place, what one sees, feels, hears roaring down the mountain – no matter where he took his readers, to what foreign country or strange experience, he always gave them what he later called "the way it was": the people, the weather, the look and feel of a place, the small detail capturing on paper the intense moment forever fresh. Twelve years later he would say, "For we have been there in the books and out of the books – and where we go, if we are any good, there you can go as we have been." That was always his gift, taking us along for the ride: Italy, Spain, Africa, the Gulf Stream, any place but home. When he became the public writer with substantial books on the shelf, many would come forward to claim *they* taught him all that he knew, *they* formed his style, *they* critiqued his early work: Anderson, Stein, Fitzgerald, Pound each helped him at crucial points, but his gifts were already there; the talent, in place; the ambition and energy, unlimited.[23]

Back to the *Star* Hemingway sent stories about German export taxes along the Swiss border balancing the disparity between the two economies, about proper Englishmen in their colony near Vevey, about the lack of winter tourists and the hazards of lugeing. Whatever he wrote carried his personal touch. His article "Clemenceau Politically Dead" claims to take the reader behind the official political statements to those candid remarks of the man on the street. He tells us:

> In the cafés the Frenchmen have nothing to gain or lose by the things they say, so they consequently say the things they believe. . . . And if you catch enough Frenchmen in different parts of France, you will have the national opinion; the real national opinion, not the shadow of the national opinion that is reflected in elections and newspapers.[24]

Hemingway wrote this article unable to speak more than a few words of French and having been in the country less than two weeks.

What began as a short trip for the winter sports lingered on at Chamby, probably because the flu epidemic in Paris continued. Between January 11 and 20, 136 Parisians died of the grippe, and 846 others were in hospital beds. On January 23, the *Tribune*'s banner headline announced the death of Pope Benedict XV, a victim of the grippe and pneumonia, a common complication of flu. During the next ten days, the sickness declined in Paris, as only fifty-one victims died and hospital cases decreased. After three weeks, when Paris seemed safe and there were no more sledding stories to write for the *Star*, the Hemingways packed their bags to return to their new and unused apartment.[25]

On the morning of February 2, while Ernest and Hadley were eating their farewell breakfast at the Gangwisches' pension, the Cardinals of the Catholic Church entered their secret conclave in Rome to elect a new pope. At that same moment in Paris, Sylvia Beach was pacing the concrete platform at Gare de Lyon, waiting impatiently for the train to bring the first two copies of James Joyce's *Ulysses* from the Dijon printer. By mid-morning the Montreux to Paris train carried Ernest and Hadley through Lausanne, where Tom Eliot, less than a month before, welded together the scraps he would call *The Waste Land*. By late afternoon the Hemingways were in Dijon and by evening in Paris, arriving on the same platform that delivered *Ulysses*. There was no one to meet them, and Joyce's outrageous text left no traces in the air. Quite without their knowing it, the new literary age was being born about them.[26]

V

Ezra Pound, literary talent scout, carpenter, self-taught musician, writer of poems and midwife to the new age, received Anderson's introduction of the Hemingways as soon as they returned to Paris. Among his shelves of books and sturdy homemade furniture, they found him and his lovely, soft-spoken, English wife Dorothy. "Eccentric, querulous, egocentric, grandiose, expansive, and exuberant," Ezra left clear impressions of himself stamped into the clay of others. Hadley remembered him drinking endless cups of tea and talking and talking, his hands moving nervously through his sandy red hair.

> We were asked to a tea in their big, rather gloomy (to me) studio on Notre Dame des Champs. It was very quiet there, so that even the low-voiced words seemed a little presumptuous. . . . Ernest listened at E.P.'s feet, as to an oracle, and I believe some of the ideas lasted all through his life. Ezra was very kind and helpful to the young, oncoming talents, at least those he liked or believed

in. Quite cantankerous in temperament . . . not to me a lovable person, though we did have some good times together.

Harold Loeb remembered Ezra's predilection for half-baked economic theories and his black velvet jacket with fawn-colored pants, the same jacket Sylvia Beach recalled. "His costume – the velvet jacket and open-road shirt – was that of the English aesthete of the period. There was a touch of Whistler about him; his language, on the other hand, was Huckleberry Finn's." Scofield Thayer found the poet "a queer duck . . . like most people he means well and unlike most people he has a fine imagination. . . . He wears a pointed yellow beard and elliptical pince-nez and an open Byronic collar and an omelette yellow bathrobe." His golden red hair, two shades brighter than Hadley's, tended to stick up in the air, and his pointed, sometimes ragged goatee bobbed and wagged, emphasizing the import of his words. He could not sit properly or still. When he was not moving about the room, feline and restless, he was sprawled carelessly in one of his sturdy chairs, his legs propped on the closest table. The last time Ezra sat down at Gertrude Stein's apartment, he managed to break one of her delicate chairs, accustomed as he was to the sturdy plank chairs of his own construction. The village explainer, as Gertrude called him, was not invited back.[27]

At first meeting, Hemingway found Ezra a strange mixture of pomposity and twitter, far too affected and far too much the *Artist* for the young man from Oak Park. Barely two months in Europe, Hemingway had not yet developed a tolerance for this kind of public posturing. Impatient with literary manifestos and Oh-Art-Oh-Beauty café discussions, repulsed by Ezra's poetic costume, Hemingway's initial impulse was to satirize Pound in a slight sketch which he proposed sending to the *Little Review*. Only after Lewis Galantière told him that Ezra was the talent scout for that literary magazine did Hemingway destroy the piece, but the urge to satirize was basic to Hemingway's nature. Whenever he needed to assert himself, whenever at a disadvantage among more experienced men, whenever cornered, he might respond with satire. Throughout the Twenties, indeed, throughout his life, the satiric impulse initiated much of his writing and more than a few of his problems.[28]

For Hemingway, there was something effete, something too precious to go unpricked in Ezra's role as Poet. He would have the same initial trouble after meeting James Joyce and Gertrude Stein. The problem lay not in those writers but in himself, in the values he brought with him to Paris, values that increasingly would not sustain him there. Like a hundred other young Americans in Paris, Hemingway, too, had his sheaf of poetry, but unlike the others, he did not wish to be thought of as a Poet. He wanted to write, but not to be a Writer, for that public role was far too passive to satisfy his Oak Park dreams. Of all the young men who came to Paris to write – Malcolm Cowley, e. e. cummings, William Faulkner, John Dos Passos, Archibald MacLeish and a myriad others since forgotten – Ernest Hemingway was perhaps the only one who initially despised the literary life of the Left Bank. No sooner was he back from Switzerland than he sent to the *Star* his scathing article, "American Bohemians in Paris."

In Left Bank cafés like the Rotonde, he told his readers,

> the scum of Greenwich Village, New York, has been skimmed off and deposited in large ladles . . . They have all striven so hard for a careless individuality of clothing that they have achieved a sort of uniformity of eccentricity. . . . You can find anything you are looking for at the Rotonde – except serious artists . . . for the artists of Paris who are turning out creditable work resent and loathe the Rotonde crowd. . . . They are nearly all loafers . . . talking about what they are going to do and condemning the work of all artists who have gained any degree of recognition.[29]

Hemingway wrote this article knowing next to nothing about artists in Paris or how they used the cafés as social clubs. He was angered by grown men as unkempt and ill dressed as he would appear within two years.

His Rotonde broadside, the product of more than one evening's observations, also satirized a large, rich woman "making jokes and laughing hysterically. The three young men laugh whenever she does. The waiter brings the bill, the big woman pays it . . . she and the three young men go out together." In an earlier *Star* feature on Swiss hotels, Hemingway did a satiric sketch of "utterly charming young men, with rolling white sweaters and smoothly brushed hair, who make a living playing bridge. . . . They are usually playing with women who are old enough to be their mothers." The women, we are told, can apparently afford to lose. In both pieces, Hemingway resents men who live off older rich women, but when he wrote these words, he was paying his bar tab at the Rotonde and the pension bill at Chamby with his older wife's money. Contradictions, always contradictions and always the ability to see in others what he most disliked, feared or resented in himself. He resented loafers, the ones talking about work but never working. He was always working, always telling someone he was working. Two years later Hemingway, without visible means of support and his collar as open as Ezra's or Walt Whitman's, was sitting in Paris cafés, nursing his drink and conspicuously writing.[30]

On the one hand, he desperately wanted to be a writer of fiction, living on his earned income. However, the contemplative role of writer did not satisfy a deeply embedded need in Hemingway to be a man of action. Back in Oak Park at sixteen, he promised to become an explorer in Africa, South America or north of Hudson Bay. His hero was the most public of Americans, Theodore Roosevelt, a man whose every exploit was newsworthy: bad lands rancher, San Juan Hill military hero, President, killer of dangerous game, maverick politician and writer of books. With Roosevelt as role model, Hemingway was never completely satisfied with being merely a writer, for no one saw a writer at his work. All his life he was in search of America's mythical west, the land of heart's hard desire, where a man stood alone, physical and self-reliant. Because writing was not physically demanding, it simply did not fulfill Hemingway's ideal of Roosevelt's strenuous life. Thus, during those early years in Paris, Hemingway was a man divided against himself. He was destined to be a writer, but he was equally destined never to be completely at ease with that identity.[31]

To gratify that deeper need, he fished, skied, hiked, sledded, went to bullfights, boxing matches and bike races so frequently and wrote about them so much that everyone from those years remembered his physical prowess. Within a month of their first meeting, Ernest was giving Ezra boxing lessons: the physical, pragmatic man trying out the resolve of the classically trained mind. How a man behaved in physical situations was always Hemingway's acid test of character.

To Anderson, Hemingway described afternoons at Ezra's:

He habitually leads wit[h] his chin and has the general grace of the crayfish or crawfish. He's willing but short winded. . . . I have to shadow box between rounds to get up a sweat. Pound sweats pretty well, though, I'll say that for him. Besides it's pretty sporting of him to risk his dignity and his critical reputation at something that he don't know nothing about. He's really a good guy, Pound, wit[h] a fine bitter tongue onto him.[32]

Three years later in his "Homage to Ezra," Hemingway described the

poet as a tall man, with "fine eyes, strange haircuts and . . . very shy."
Then, using his own first-meeting reaction to Ezra as his source material,
Hemingway wrote condescendingly about young Americans coming to
Ezra's door.

> Young men in the years after the war, coming over from America
> where Pound was a legendary person, to Paris where they found
> him with a patchy red beard, very accessible, fond of tennis and
> occasionally playing the bassoon, decided there could not be
> anything in the Pound legend and that he was probably not a
> great poet after all.[33]

Ezra's "fine bitter tongue" was laced with the same irony that became
Hemingway's hallmark in the Twenties. Irony and understatement,
which he honed to a fine edge, Hemingway did not learn from Pound,
but Ezra certainly encouraged him in their practice.

As with so many of his learning experiences, Hemingway's relationship
with Pound was brief and intense, and its effects long lasting. They
shared less than six Paris months together in 1922, a brief visit at Rapallo
in 1923 and two more months in the fall of 1924. The remainder of
their relationship was largely by correspondence. Hemingway's timing
was perfect. His luck held. Had he come to Paris six months later, he
might never have met Pound. Within a week of their meeting, Ezra was
reading Hemingway's stories and poetry, giving advice and directing his
reading. We do not know which stories Pound saw in February, possibly
a version of "Up in Michigan" begun in Chicago the previous summer.
Whatever stories he read, Pound was not enthusiastic enough to tout
them for publication as he had when he first read Joyce's *Dubliners*.
Six of Hemingway's poems, however, Pound thought well wrought
enough to submit to Scofield Thayer's *Dial*, for which Pound was the
paid European talent scout.[34]

On February 20, Hadley, to whom the task fell, wrote Hemingway's
mother that "Ezra Pound has sent a number of Ernest's poems to
Thayer of the 'Dial' and taken a little prose thing of his for the *Little
Review* also asked him to write a series of articles for the 'Dial' on
American magazines. It is all surely most flattering. . . . The 'Dial' if
they take his stuff is such a wonderful place for a young writer to
appear . . . at the start." At the start, or any other time, the *Dial* was,
in 1922, *the* place to be published in America. A month earlier its
$2000 annual literary award went to Sherwood Anderson, and its

July–December 1922 list of authors included D. H. Lawrence, Kenneth Burke, Jean Giraudoux, William Butler Yeats, Hart Crane, e. e. cummings, Marianne Moore and William Carlos Williams. None of Hemingway's slight poems, mostly written in Chicago the previous year, came close to the quality expected by the *Dial*'s owner and editor, Scofield Thayer.

On March 5, Thayer wrote Pound: "I was interested to see the poems by Ernest Hemingway. I am however of the opinion that The Dial has enough young blood already to make it decidedly rough reading. I have therefore been unable to accept even those examples of Mr. Hemingway's art which you as always so perceptively point out to be the better ones." Thayer sent the manuscripts back to Hemingway directly, but no record of his rejection letter survives. Whatever he said hurt Hemingway deeply and left him embittered against the magazine. This rejection grew large in his mind which tended, as he grew older, toward paranoia. In 1925, he could joke with Scott Fitzgerald that his ideal house "would be fitted up with special copies of the Dial printed on soft tissue and kept in the toilets on every floor." As late as 1930, he was irrationally demanding of Marianne Moore an explanation of the magazine's treatment of his work.[35]

That first year in Paris was a year of rejections, but the *Dial*'s hurt Hemingway most, for Sherwood Anderson was the magazine's pet. Three years as a professed writer with no publications to show for his effort, Ernest deeply needed to see his name in print alongside Anderson's. If Ezra filled him with false expectations, Hemingway does not seem to have blamed the poet. Pound, who was probably not surprised by Thayer's response to Hemingway's poetry, wanted merely to encourage the young writer. It was easier for him to let the editor write the rejection letter than to tell Hemingway himself that the poems were minor league.

VI

Hemingway's failure with the *Dial* was a momentary setback, which did not dim his growing friendship with Pound, from whom he had more to learn about the business and politics of literature than about its writing. When the boxing lessons paled, tennis matches began. A loose-knit tennis club was formed around a hired court and Pound's enthusiasm for the sport. Ernest, slow on his feet, brought more vitality than skill to the game, but he took his losses easily – tennis was not his speciality. Pound continued to use his influence to push Hemingway's literary future; at every chance he introduced Hemingway as a rising literary star. That June when John Peale Bishop asked to see new talent, Ezra took him directly to 74 Cardinal Lemoine to introduce him to Ernest. Within six months of having met Pound and with nothing in print, Hemingway was recognized on the Left Bank as a promising young writer, one of Ezra's discoveries. It was no bad thing to be discovered by Ezra, whose earlier finds included Joyce and Eliot. Hemingway's rejected poems were eventually published in Harriet Monroe's *Poetry* magazine in Chicago where Pound's name still commanded attention. Hemingway's other early Paris publications – *Three Stories & Ten Poems* (1923) and *in our time* (1924) – depended heavily on his relationship with Pound, who was also responsible for Hemingway's later association with the *transatlantic review*.[36]

Once Hemingway got past Ezra's aesthete street mask, he found the father he most needed that year and next, a sensible man who enjoyed the physical life, a frank, sexual man. Theory was interesting but the art was in the artist who must do his work, theory or no. Like Whitman, his forefather, Pound stated his position broadly and often:

> I would much rather lie on what is left of Catullus' parlour floor and speculate the azure beneath it and the hills off to Salo and Riva with their forgotten gods moving unhindered amongst them, than discuss any processes and theories of art whatsoever. I would rather play tennis. I shall not argue.[37]

Hemingway did not recognize the Whitman touch, but one of his major talents, much exercised in Paris, was his ability to listen. Pound required and rewarded intense listening.

Besides helping Hemingway into print, Pound's greater service was in Hemingway's literary education, particularly his reading. Ernest, browsing through the crowded bookshelves at Pound's apartment, found there many names he had not read, some he had never heard of. Pound gave Hemingway the same advice he gave to everyone: read Joyce and Eliot. Twenty years later Hemingway's library still contained everything written by both writers, including obscure publications and all of Eliot's essays. Reading *The Waste Land* with Ezra Pound at one's elbow is no bad way to pick up a thing or two. Whatever else Pound told Hemingway about the poem, he must have drilled home the necessity of cutting, revising, eliminating the dross. (His own blue pencil reduced Eliot's original draft by at least a third.) "Use no superfluous words," he preached, "no adjective which does not reveal something. . . . Go in fear of abstractions." In his endless *Cantos*, Pound may seem to make mockery of his earlier dictums, but that year in Paris young Hemingway listened intently and began to re-evaluate his own work. Pound said, "Be influenced by as many great artists as you can, but have the decency either to acknowledge the debt outright, or try to conceal it." Pound's lessons were not easily or quickly learned, but within a year their effect was apparent. Within two years, Hemingway fulfilled Pound's prediction of coming greatness with some of the most tightly, precisely written stories of our time. Five years after meeting Pound, Hemingway jotted the following note to himself:

> Imitating everybody, living and dead, relying on the fact that if you imitate someone obscure enough it will be considered original. Education consists in finding sources obscure enough to imitate so that they will be perfectly safe.

It was Pound who told Hemingway that symbols first must be natural objects, their symbolic function not obtruding into the work: at the primary level the hawk must first and solidly be a hawk before it could function as symbol. A lifetime later, Hemingway would say more simply that symbols were not like raisins to be stuck into the bread dough wherever the artist wished. They had to arise naturally out of the story. Anybody can write, he told Lincoln Steffens' wife; all it took was hard work. That first year in Paris he was working hard, but no one could see the results, not even himself. All the while he was learning faster than Pound, his tutor, imagined. With his rat-trap mind, Hemingway held on to whatever he needed that floated to the surface of Pound's cluttered conversations.[38]

Pound probably gave Hemingway the same list of required reading he gave to all novices. He sent Ernest to those ancient authors who formed what he and Eliot called the Tradition: Homer, Catullus, Ovid, Chaucer, Dante, Villon, and the Metaphysical poets, particularly Donne. Eventually most of these writers would contribute to Hemingway's own work, sometimes in strange and unexpected ways. More immediately important to Hemingway's education was Pound's insistence that he read Flaubert and Stendhal: *The Red and the Black*, the first half of

The Charter House of Parma, Madame Bovary, Sentimental Education, Three Stories and *Bouvard and Pecuchet*. This amount of reading, Pound said, "would not overburden the three-or-four-year student. After this inoculation he could be 'safely exposed' to modernity or anything else in literature. . . . He would have the axes of reference and . . . would find them dependable." Hemingway completed the course in three years. From Flaubert he learned to be detached, ironic, precise. From Stendhal he learned how to deal with panoramic movement; seven years later, when he was writing of Frederic Henry's retreat from Caporetto, Hemingway would use Stendhal's description of Waterloo as a general model. These were valuable lessons, but ones not quickly turned to practice: for the novice writer, theory will always exceed reach.[39]

Pound's most important advice sent Hemingway into the cobwebs and labyrinths of Henry James, an author with whom Hemingway's affinity is less than obvious. Pound gave Hemingway a map to James, a list of the readable books including *The American*, *Daisy Miller*, *Washington Square*, *Portrait of a Lady*, "The Pupil," *The Finer Grain*, *What Maisie Knew* and *The Awkward Age*. To see the James influence at work, one need only compare the terse dialogue of the two American writers, dialogue which seldom conveys direct meaning. In both writers, the significance of the dialogue appears frequently in the white space between the lines; it is what the characters do not say that is highlighted by their conversation. From James, Hemingway inherited the American-in-Europe theme which he played in various keys throughout the 1920s and to great effect.

Much of what he heard from Ezra or read in the poet's didactic essays remained with Hemingway always. It was Pound who told him that bad art was "inaccurate art . . . art that makes false reports." Good art "bears true witness, I mean the art that is most precise." Bearing true witness that year in Paris changed Hemingway's idea of his art, allowing him to see how false his Chicago fiction rang to the ear. A year earlier, he was able to begin a story: "In a former unenlightened time there was a saying 'In vino veritas,' which meant roughly that under the influence of the cup that queers a man sloughed off his dross of reserve and conventionality and showed the true metal of his self." Never again would he be able to write that way. The war novel, upon which he placed so much hope, now must have sounded like a school boy's tall tale.[40]

By the middle of 1922, Hemingway returned to basics – the simple, declarative sentence – trying to gain control of first elements first. In

A Moveable Feast he said, "All you have to do is write one true sentence. Write the truest sentence that you know. . . . If I started to write elaborately . . . I found that I could cut that scrollwork or ornament out and throw it away and start with the first true simple declarative sentence I had written." This technique, advocated by Pound, was simple yet demanding: let action speak for itself. Without telling readers how to respond, what to feel, how to judge, let images convey meaning. If action is presented truly, precisely, using only its essential elements, then readers, without being told, will respond emotionally as the writer intended. The technique had been in the air since early 1912 when, in London, Pound helped form the Imagist Manifesto. Hemingway arrived in Paris, using some of the technique unconsciously; Pound and, a little later, Stein made him see clearly what he was doing. At first he responded self-consciously, intimidated by his new knowledge as a self-taught pianist who learned by ear might lose some of his confidence after a few serious music lessons. Later, when simplicity, understatement and irony were his perfected tools, he called this style of rendering "the way it was."[41]

Chapter Three

RITES OF PASSAGE
PARIS, SPRING, 1922

I

In March, when the afternoon temperature warmed into the fifties and the horses were running, Ernest and Hadley would sometimes treat themselves to the steeplechase at the Auteuil, Enghien or Maisons-Laffitte tracks, all within an easy train or bus ride. On race days, special trains ran straight through to the tracks, where the rich, dapper and diamonded strolled past the paddocks for a thirty franc fee and sipped champagne in the grandstand. The Hemingways, for only six francs, slipped into the open field circled by the track, where they could eat their picnic lunch and drink the good, cheap wine they brought from the cooperative in rue Mouffetard.

During his recovery from war wounds in Milan, Hemingway had played the San Siro track, meeting a number of the American and British jockeys who lived permanently in Europe. The honesty of those races was sometimes questionable, but Ernest learned his way around the track, listened to touts spiel and mastered the betting game. On the *pelouse* at Auteuil, where bets were laid on in five franc increments, for less than a dollar Ernest and Hadley could get the thrill of winning or losing without risking serious money. Hemingway approached this new game with the same vital enthusiasm he focused on all of his interests. The jocks, swipes and trainers lived in a special world, a place apart with unwritten rules of behavior. They were their own society, separate from the grandstand crowd and living on the outskirts of respectability.

The young man from Oak Park loved it all, loved the long ripple of muscle moving beneath smooth flanks, the smell of horse piss on fresh hay, the jocks dandy in their bright silks. He had to know everything about the track: the slang, the gimmicks, the stories that got told but not written down. American jocks and trainers working the Paris tracks were another part of his education.

Everywhere he turned there was something new to learn, and turning with him was Hadley, always close, eager to move in whatever direction his interests led: piano concerts, gallery openings, late night spots drinking and early morning breakfasts afterwards among the fresh produce at Les Halles. It was all a rush of sensations, sharp tastes down ancient streets, vintage wines and new friends. Everywhere there were games playing – the race track and prize fight games, the literary game, the newspaper game – each with its special rules and inside operators. In, among and around them, of course, was the oldest game of all, the sex game played by Paris rules.

"Nothing was simple there," he told us much later. Certainly relationships were never simple. A bisexual named McAlmon married a lesbian named Winifred who called herself Bryher. As long as they remained married, McAlmon received a handsome allowance from Bryher's father. All the while, Bryher lived very quietly at Territet, Switzerland with Ezra's old girl friend Hilda Doolittle, who had a child fathered perhaps by D. H. Lawrence. Sometimes they all came to Paris to confuse everyone even further. It was easy to be confused in Paris where seemingly responsible adults did not behave as they did in Oak Park, where gender and sexual preferences were not always obvious, and where the rules Hemingway inherited had little bearing on the games being played in the cafés and salons. In Oak Park, he probably never met a homosexual; in Italy, he was propositioned by an older man and tested by a younger one, but both were well mannered and discreet, taking his rejection with good grace. In Paris it was different. In 1925, he wrote but did not publish Jake Barnes' gut reaction to the blatant, swishy and strident homosexuals on the Left Bank:

> This Paris is a very sad and dull place and it has few permanent inhabitants. It seems as though the Fairies lived there permanently but this is a mistake because they take flight like the birds and go off to Brussels or London or the Basque coast to return again even more like the birds. . . . It is interesting that they go away and quite pleasant but the pleasure is diminished by the fact that

one can not count on it and many times they are gone for several days and one does not notice it and so can not enjoy it. Once I remember they were all gone to Brussels for a week and were back before I noticed they were gone away and a week's enjoyment of their absence was lost.[1]

Wherever he turned that first year in Paris, Ernest met men and women whose sexual roles were beyond the paling of the Oak Park barricades. His initial response of anger or disgust was a knee jerk reaction, a part of his essentially conservative nature. The longer he was in Paris, the more tolerant he became, and with the tolerance came an erosion of his Oak Park values, and in the end Paris was Paris still, but Hemingway was changed.

The change began the first time he met Gertrude Stein and her wife, Alice Toklas. After two months of priming himself for the meeting, Hemingway finally mailed to her Anderson's letter of introduction. On March 7, Gertrude responded, inviting the Hemingways to tea the following day. Before the war she would have invited them to her salon to meet her painters, but those days were over. Life on rue de Fleurus was more settled now, less intense socially. Gertrude Stein and Alice still had people to tea and cakes, but in small groups and only after four in the afternoon. As an Oak Park wife would do, Hadley sent their immediate acceptance: "Mr. Hemingway and I are delighted at hearing from you so soon and will come in to tea with you tomorrow with pleasure. Sherwood has told us so many nice things that we are glad to come right away to see you."[2] Hadley's so polite "delight" was short lived, for she never felt comfortable in Gertrude Stein's presence, and Alice with her light mustache, sharp eyes and sharper tongue did nothing to help.

The Stein–Toklas apartment at 27 rue de Fleurus was, in 1922, legendary for its pre-war salon, its collection of modernist paintings and its curiously matched pair of women: Gertrude the garrulous and Alice the caretaker. No one who afternooned with the pair ever forgot the paintings or the ladies, and all the young writers made, sooner or later, their obligatory visit. Scofield Thayer wrote:

Gertrude Stein is five feet high and two feet wide and has a dark brown face and small, wise old Jewess' eyes. She curls up in the corner of a divan and falls over like a doll in trying to receive editors. She possesses the homely finish of a brown buckram bean bag.[3]

Of his first visit, Robert McAlmon remembered they shared "a mutual passion for Trollope's novels, for documentary, autobiographic, and biographic things." In his parodic sketch, McAlmon portrays Stein as an ancient elephant wallowing in the mud of her own ideas. To Sisley Huddleston, she resembled a Cistercian monk with her mannish face and clothes. Mary Berenson remembered only Gertrude's enormous bulk, "a round waddling mass . . . fatter than ever." To tiny Alice, Gertrude was husband, lover and entirely beautiful. Beneath the surface of Gertrude's frequently enigmatic prose was the love story of their life at rue de Fleurus.[4]

Throughout the Twenties, far from home, Ernest needed surrogates to replace his parents and provide the support he required. His father, the Doctor, was replaced by Pound, the surgical poet. Of all Hemingway's Paris friends, none escaped as unscathed as Ezra from Ernest's satiric pen, for Pound was the father with whom Hemingway was not competing. Unlike most male children, Ernest Hemingway rebelled against his mother's creative energy, not his father's stoic suffering. At age twenty-one, he forced his mother to throw him out of their summer cottage: a rite of passage usually reserved for father and son. Grace Hemingway, a large woman driven to perform as musician, singer and painter, was the genetic source of her son's creativity and a disturbing presence in his early Oak Park years. She championed women's rights, marched for the vote and was constantly in the public eye or ear. No one who knew her ever forgot her sometimes eccentric but always commanding presence, for she filled whatever stage was available. Grace Hemingway may have been the "all-American bitch," as Ernest later called her, but he was undoubtedly her son.[5]

Thus on that March afternoon when he first met Gertrude Stein, Hemingway found the Paris mother he needed. Like Grace Hemingway Gertrude was imperious, headstrong, talented and over-weight. Both women dominated conversations and lived as they pleased. Years later Hemingway remembered Gertrude with an understanding he was never able to find for his first mother:

Miss Stein was very big but not tall and was heavily built like a peasant woman. She had beautiful eyes and a strong German–Jewish face that also could have been Friulano and she reminded me of a northern Italian peasant woman with her clothes, her mobile face and her lovely, thick, alive immigrant hair which she wore put up the same way she had probably worn it in college. She talked all the time and at first it was about people and places.[6]

That was before Gertrude bobbed her hair and began her Roman empress phase. Within a month Gertrude thanked Anderson for sending Hemingway to see her: "He is a delightful fellow and I like his talk and I am teaching him to cut his wife's hair." Alice, whose crow's eyes quickly assessed the sexual politics of each new face in her drawing room, was less enthusiastic about the Hemingways, but for the moment, kept her judgements veiled. With Hadley she played her role as ferret: "with her brown eyes brightly glittering, she would dart questions like arrows, and in three minutes, would know your place of birth, your environment, your family, your connections, your education, and your immediate intentions. And she never forgot what she acquired." Each new arrival in the house required her attention, for she did not harbor rivals lightly and rivalry could appear in strange quarters. Alice had survived any number of Gertrude's attachments: her brother Leo, Mable Dodge, and others. When the bickering was done, Alice always remained more firmly entrenched than ever and the intruder gone.[7]

On March 9, the day after his first visit to Stein's apartment, Hemingway wrote Sherwood Anderson: "Gertrude Stein and me are just like brothers and we see a lot of her." One meeting does not make a brotherhood, but knowing how enthusiastic Anderson was about Gertrude, Ernest exaggerated without a blush. Perhaps there was a double edge to their being "like brothers," perhaps a comment on Gertrude's sexuality, but probably not. She was, after all, forty-eight years old, only two years younger than his mother, and he was well trained in being polite to older women. Not that Gertrude's relationship with Alice was a secret; after fifteen years of living together, Gertrude and Alice were no mystery to the Left Bank of Paris.

Lesbian relationships quickly became, for Hemingway, an interesting part of his Paris life. Arriving, as he did, a generation too late to participate in the pre-war revolution in the arts, Hemingway missed the gaudiest period of lesbians in Paris. By 1922, strong and lasting lesbian relationships were woven permanently into the social fabric of the Left Bank. Loving couples like Gertrude and Alice, Sylvia Beach and Adrienne Monnier, Djuna Barnes and Thelma Wood were neither ostentatious nor threatening; except for their sexual choice of partner, these relationships were modeled on and mirrored the heterosexual world. Only Natalie Barney, long past the dazzling beauty of her youth, continued to make a public issue of her sexual preference. Hemingway was, as his later fiction shows, aroused by the idea of two women in love. He remembered when his father banished young Ruth Arnold, their live-in governess, from the Oak Park house. Gossips said that Ruth came between the Doctor and the Doctor's wife. Although the actual cause of the crisis was probably a case of tuberculosis in the Arnold family heightened by Dr. Hemingway's growing nervous instability, the incident left residual effects on Ernest, sixteen at the time and sexually curious. In Paris his curiosity was renewed. By the time he met the *Little Review*'s editor Margaret Anderson in the company of singer Georgette LeBlanc and co-editor Jane Heap, he did not flinch at Jane's masculine clothes, at her hair cut shorter than his own, or at her cigars. He closed his letter to Anderson, "We love Gertrude Stein."[8]

Within the month, Gertrude and Alice returned the visit. In the Hemingways' cramped quarters, Gertrude sat on the bed, skimming through his pile of manuscripts. He wanted approval and help, neither of which were Gertrude's forte. Self-centered, public proclaimer of her own mostly unpublished genius, and secretly less sure than she appeared, Gertrude Stein was not adept at either critical appraisal or lavish praise of others. If she read any of the manuscripts carefully, they were probably the short stories, including "Up in Michigan" which she told Ernest was un-hangable like a painter's private erotica. If the surviving manuscript with its purple ink marginalia is one that Gertrude marked up, then her editorial skills were marginal indeed. Nothing in purple proved at all useful in revising the story. Gertrude, with her reams of unintelligible and unpublishable prose, told him to stop wasting his time writing stories no one would print. Fortunately, he did not listen to this advice; for a young writer, Hemingway had sure instincts: he knew when to listen to Ezra and Gertrude and when to ignore them.[9]

After reading Stein's *Three Lives*, Hemingway knew he could learn something from Gertrude's continuous present tense and her steady repetition of key phrases that created meanings larger than the words themselves. It was a technique Hemingway had first used in his Chicago journalism for the *Star*, but in Paris, for the first time, he analyzed what he was doing and how his prose worked. His unpublished and uneven juvenilia, left behind in Oak Park, lacked critical self-awareness. Before Paris, he was quite capable of writing a splendid paragraph without understanding its elements or how to repeat it. Ezra forced him to become self-critical, to make revisions. Gertrude's advice was almost the opposite. As she told another young writer in the Twenties:

> I have never understood how people could labor over a manuscript, write and rewrite it many times, for to me, if you have something to say, the words are always there. And they are the exact words and the words that should be used. If the story does not come whole, *tant pis*, it has been spoiled. [10]

From talking with Stein and from reading her first-draft work, Hemingway learned about automatic writing. Gertrude claimed that she never wrote in that way, but her manuscripts from 1922 make her protest vain. Using the blue notebooks of school children, she began, with huge strokes, to fill pages as rapidly as possible, letting words flow freely:

> Mildred's thoughts are where. There with pear, with the pears and the stairs Mildred's thoughts are there with the pear with the stairs and the pears. Mildred will be satisfied with tomatoes, apples, apricots, plums and peaches, beets and ever greens, peas and potatoes. Mildred cares for us and Kitty Buss, what a fuss what a happy surprise. We only expected you last night and you have come again. When. It is very hot and no one knows what is the reason. [11]

Free association, verbal connections, puns, alliteration – it was all there and moving. Sometimes it worked well; sometimes it even made sense.

It was, Hemingway understood, a way of short circuiting the brain, a way of preventing the critical apparatus from interfering with the creative flow. One did not need to know where or how the sentence or the story was going to turn out in order to begin. Sometimes, when the well went dry, he would switch to Gertrude's automatic technique to prime the pump. In 1923, he wrote:

> Down through the ages. Why is it down through the ages? Down through the ages. Down and out through the ages. Out through the ages. No not that. Down through the ages. Way down through the ages. Down on the ages. Go down on the ages. And the sages.

Down down down through the ages. He rages at the ages. Down through the ages. That will be about enough of that.[12]

It was also an excellent way of taking notes. Soon he was using Gertrude's technique for capturing scenes quickly and pinpointing elements that gave an event its impact. He was learning something from Gertrude Stein that she did not completely understand herself. Soon, others would see what he learned and it would become the style for his time. But it did not happen that first year in Paris.

II

What Hemingway learned from Gertrude Stein he learned quickly. He was one who always learned quickly, one who could seize anyone's gift and make it his own. Sometimes the gifts were freely given and later regretted when he took them to the market place. When she saw his first work, Gertrude Stein told him to start over again, and Gertrude, as Alice loved to say, was never wrong. Hemingway began to write, as Gertrude did, in blue notebooks, imitating her style with a surprising adeptness. Sometimes he wrote quickly by ear, letting the words fall on to the paper in their right order. About that same time a young apprentice very like Ernest appears in Stein's "Objects Lie On A Table." The tyro and tutor speak about the problem of authentic writing:

And he says I am very willing but I have had to invent something to fill in and I say to him you had better really have it and he said I am not able to get it and I say to him I am sorry I have not one to lend you . . . and he replied, I do not doubt that you will be of great assistance to me and as for the result that is still in question.[13]

Once the teacher reprimands her student: "When visiting they had said to him, listen while we are talking." Later she gives him object lessons to carry out, imitations to be written without naming the thing itself. "Imitate a cheese if you please. We are very well pleased with gold coin and ribbons. . . . We were not pleased with the imitation of the lamb." Ernest was neither the first nor the last young man to show up on Gertrude's doorstep, but she had no way of knowing that March how apt and agile this pupil would be. She let him read her new work and look at the paintings on the walls.[14]

At rue de Fleurus he saw paintings of Cézanne, Matisse, Braque, Gris and Picasso. When Gertrude Stein said buy Masson, Hemingway bought Masson. When she said buy Miró, he purchased "The Farm." To have access to Gertrude Stein was better than having a stock broker. "The Farm" cost him less than $200; sixty years later it was worth $2,000,000. Leo Stein, her estranged brother, was the brains behind the art discoveries, but Gertrude knew a good thing when she had it. Maybe she should have kept more of the Matisses, but on average she did well in the market with what Leo left her when they split their lives. In 1922, Gertrude Stein did not have a commercial book to her name; her publications were all vanity press publications paid for out of her own pocket. When Alice decided they should publish *Lucy Church Amiably*, they sold Picasso's *Girl with a Fan* to finance the operation.[15]

Afternoons at Stein's, between the tea and cakes, among the talk of who and where, he could see Picasso's blue period hung high on the wall, and his portrait of Gertrude with the face looking as much like Picasso as Gertrude, and his funny "Homage à Gertrude" with its high breasted angels. There were some fine Matisses left and plenty of Braque and Gris. And always Cézannes, blue and purple, and the portrait of Madame Cézanne with its planes of color, its reds and blue-greys, shaping the Madame exactly forever. Gertrude Stein told Hemingway that she sat in front of the Cézanne while writing *Three Lives*, and that her sentences worked like those planes of color. Hemingway listened and looked and went to the Luxembourg Musée to see more Cézannes, landscapes and bathers, and went to the Louvre to see his card players, the courtyard at Anvers and the house of the hanged man and wherever he could to see the Cézanne work from Arles. Two years later, his Nick Adams would say he "wanted to write like Cézanne painted."

> He could see the Cezannes. The portrait at Gertrude Stein's. She'd know it if he ever got things right. The two good ones at the Luxembourg, the ones he'd seen every day at the loan exhibit at Bernheim's. The soldiers undressing to swim, the house through the trees, one of the trees with a house beyond, not the lake one, the other lake one. . . . He knew just how Cezanne would paint this stretch of river.

Nick got it from Hemingway who learned it from Gertrude Stein in the little Paris time they shared.[16]

In 1922, he saw her frequently in March, but he was out of Paris most of April, half of May, all of June and half of July. When he returned in July, Gertrude and Alice were in the country at St. Rémy, not to return until February 1923. No matter what fictions he told later about his life at Gertrude's, the calendar says he saw her about six weeks of his first nineteen months in Paris, just enough time to learn the lessons he needed. In 1924, when stories began to explode in his head, he no longer needed Gertrude Stein.[17]

That March in Paris snow came late, chilling the buds in the Luxembourg Gardens and sending Ernest with a sore, pussed throat back to his sick bed from whence he saw little of Gertrude Stein before he left for Genoa on April 11.

III

In April, one thing led to another. The Great European War led to the Treaty of Versailles which led, in turn, to the 1922 Economic Conference at Genoa, one of the most important political gatherings of the decade. With his Toronto *Star* press pass, Hemingway was there to watch and learn. Before leaving Paris on the now familiar Simplon–Orient Express, he received a postcard poem from Ezra Pound:

> Ole Cosmo de Medici
> an ornery son[,] a kuss wuz he
> In his hock shops the Florentines
> Hocked their wives & lands
> & vines
> They hocked their coats
> They hocked their shorts
> Old Kus Cos roped in the Jews
> He did the sheenies as he did the Dutch.[18]

A wry comment on Italy past and Genoa present: money. The erratic flow of post-war money was the sickness at Europe's heart, depressing currencies and creating unemployment. France won the war, dictated the peace treaty, but was losing the peace. Germany lost the war but was winning the peace by paying off war reparations with worthless marks and hiding industrial profits in the Ruhr. The Turks, who lost the war, were ready to fight another one with Greece. The British wanted peace in the Middle East to control the enormous Arabian oil deposits. And no one wanted to recognize the Russian revolution as a legitimate power; the disease of bolshevism was more feared than war itself. As if the world were unchanged by the war, England returned to the gold standard and regulated international currencies in pound sterling. Proper British gentlemen continued to behave as if the Empire were not crumbling about them, as if at home two million were not without jobs. All the while, America remained aloof and uncommitted, unwilling to assume the mantle of world leadership that was hers almost by default. The United States sent observers to Genoa but wanted no further entanglements, having just agreed to destroy a significant portion of the war fleet built five years earlier to save the world for democracy. The world, as far as America was concerned, could now save itself. Beneath the bickering lay the one unifying problem: economic recovery from the post-war recession. Ezra's slightly crazed economic view of history was no more bizarre than Europe's economic politics.[19]

Hemingway's first story on Genoa, which appeared in the Toronto *Star* on April 13, was mailed from Paris on March 27 and either written off the wire service or from talk overheard at the Anglo-American Press Club lunches. The story had little to do with the issues, focusing instead on the conflict between Italian reds and fascists. Of the two groups, Hemingway felt more sympathy for the Italian left wing than for the fascists, who "make no distinction between Socialists, Communists, Republicans or members of cooperative societies." He described the sporadic but bloody meetings of reds and fascists, supplying through invention enough specific details to carry the story. Genoa was designed to be an economic conference, not a political one, but Hemingway's instincts were right: no matter what the economic settlements of the decade the real problem was political extremes: the far left and the far right. John Bone ran the Hemingway feature the day after it arrived in the mail, telling Ernest to keep writing human interest stories. By the time Bone's letter reached Hemingway, the conference was essentially finished, but the human interest features arrived as ordered, for Hemingway found them easiest to write.[20]

In Genoa, 750 reporters from everywhere in the world fought for the 200 spaces allotted the press in the Palazzo San Giorgio. Hemingway got one of those spaces, largely because he arrived in knowledgeable company. Traveling on the train with Bill Bird, Guy Hickok, Paul Mowrer and Gilbert Seldes – all old hands at the news game – Hemingway slipped into the madhouse, a crowded "modern Babel with a corps of perspiring interpreters trying to bring the representatives of forty different countries together." In his private notes Gilbert Seldes of the *New York News* caught the scene in terse prose:

> Palace of St. George. Stunted saints in marble. The very great of the world gathered. . . . Troops. Massed formations in the streets. Press gallery, three to a seat. Crowds. Perspiration.
> Long afterwards the Russians. They have actually come, assassins or no. And looking so German. In European clothes too, even if old and a bit shabby. Curiosity remains. The crowd pushes, the sweat is noticeable to eye and nose.[21]

In his coverage of the opening day, Hemingway rightly identified the Russians as important players. All of the West wanted to know how these leaders of the proletariat would behave west of Moscow. These were the men who made the revolution, who brought down the Czar, executed the entire royal family and made a separate peace with Germany that almost defeated the Allies in 1918. The world, afraid of bolshevism, was nonetheless eager to see what these men looked like and how they would act.

The world did not have to wait long to find out. Late on opening day at Genoa, Chicherin, the Russian foreign minister, quite casually split the conference wide open. After agreeing that war debts should not be repudiated and that Russia would not "engage in aggressive operations against other nations," Chicherin said, "All efforts toward reconstruction . . . are vain so long as there remains suspended over Europe and the world the menace of new wars." Russia, he said, was ready to disarm on a reciprocal basis with the West. With that statement, the agenda for the twentieth century was set: the arms race versus disarmament. Lloyd George and the British delegation tried behind the scenes to keep the question of disarmament off the Genoa table; that first afternoon, Chicherin, with the skill of a surgeon, lanced the sore point.

Hemingway's story of Chicherin's bombshell opened with the same kind of significant detail that later characterized his fiction:

> At the left of the statue of Columbus, a marble plaque twelve feet high is set into the wall bearing a quotation from Machiavelli's history, telling of the founding of the Banco San Giorgio, site of the present palace, the oldest bank in the world. Machiavelli, in

his day, wrote a book that could be used as a textbook by all conferences, and from all results, is diligently studied.[22]

The discoverer of America, the oldest bank and political manipulation were a shorthanded way of setting the scene: America's refusal to participate framed the economic heart of the problem which was compounded by devious political self-interest. Some wag suggested that in the birthplace of Columbus it would be fitting if America rediscovered Europe, but America was not playing the game. The *Tribune* headline was good for laughs:

RUSSIANS TO HAMMER ON DISARMAMENT
Have Made Conference
Political, Not
Economic

As most knew and Ernest was learning, everything was political, most especially economics. The next day, Seldes noted: "The conference has become Russia's. The little tiff yesterday [disarmament] is today the question of the world."[23]

After that opening day, the major powers were wary of giving the Russians such a public forum when no one knew what they might say. As pre-planned, the conference went behind closed doors, splitting into commissions and sub-commissions, all meeting simultaneously at separate locations. Newsmen scurried up and down the funicular that connected Palazzo San Giorgio on the bay with the telegraph office at the top of the hill. They were guided in their pursuit of stories by newly created public relations men that some of the delegations employed and by twice-daily news conferences provided by Lloyd George's British delegation. "In this manner," Seldes noted, "the whole world got the British tinge, because no one else is wise enough to offer a rival press conference." Hemingway's stories, largely descriptive and featuring the antics of the Russians, reflected the difficulty of getting real news at Genoa. According to Seldes' notes of April 12:

> The paranoid Russian press representative, Rosenberg, sent us on a fool's errand to Santa Marghrita – their headquarters town near Rapallo. Went with Hemingway only to find that their Imperial Hotel was guarded like the Czar's palace, ourselves suspect, and the birds flown.[24]

Without a news story to report, Hemingway skillfully turned the day into a feature about getting into the Russian compound: the difficulty of obtaining a Russian pass through the Italian police lines, followed by background information on the Russians, all written as if he alone were given access and no mention of the trip's failure to obtain significant information. What Bone encouraged was what Hemingway did best: write about himself in the act of being a reporter. Eventually this technique became a cornerstone of his fiction – the narrator conscious of his act of observation, conscious of his own responses to the event.[25]

That night, George Seldes went "with George Slocum, William Bird and Ernest Hemingway to 'little Genoa,' the poor section, Slocum being the guide and Hemingway the most willing." The chianti flowed freely, leaving tow-headed Max Eastman, from *Masses* magazine, feeling sorry for the poor and proud of the Russians. Hemingway, younger than anyone else around the table, was very much with them, telling his own embellished war stories punctuated with songs he'd learned at the Italian front. For a little while at Genoa, Hemingway found the intense and free life he loved best and missed most from the summer days at Walloon Lake: a group of older, more experienced men who liked to drink and eat and joke around. Up in Draper's room at Hotel de Genes, the nightly poker game did not appear on anyone's expense account.[26]

The conference, continuing into April's weather, became more and more an inquisition of the Russians. Moscow needed capital investment, but without assurances, no one was eager to make the loans. Some wanted their pre-revolution investments secured. Others wanted old debts repaid, old bank accounts unfrozen. The Standard Oil man wanted Russia to open herself to the West, but only if she guaranteed the right to private property, the sanctity of contracts and the rights of free labor. Behind their varied beards, the Russians must have laughed long in private: the Standard Oil man had not yet seen their future. No matter how deep Lloyd George tried to bury the disarmament issue, the Russians kept digging it up again. Rokowsky told the financial commission: "you cannot suppress the disarmament question. If it is barred out of the doors, it will come in by the windows. It is of the utmost importance because it is a large item in all budgets."[27]

With the same self-interest that brought them to a separate peace with Germany in the Great War, the Russian delegation brought Genoa to its knees with another German treaty, violating all the tacit gentlemanly rules of the conference. Germany recognized the legitimacy of the Russian government and agreed to call their war debts even. Each gave the other "most favored nation" status for purposes of trade and agreed to settle any differences "in the most benevolent spirit." This was not on anyone's agenda for the conference: the beaten Germans allied with the rising red menace in economic union. When asked if he had informed Lloyd George of his negotiations, Chicherin replied: "We did not tell Lloyd George of the treaty because we are not a British colony." Germany was expelled from the sub-committee dealing with Russian problems, but it was too late: the damage was done and the conference, for practical purposes, was finished. Russia was not going to pay war debts incurred by the Czar, bringing to question Germany's outstanding debt of reparation. Protests flew back and forth; threats were made, huffs were puffed, but the conference was dead. In his notes, Seldes asked himself, "Is it ending or beginning anew?" – a rhetorical question that needed no answer. Nothing was ending, least of all the Great War.[28]

In early April, when Bone wired Hemingway his press pass to cover Genoa, Ernest's understanding of European politics was general and vague. Two weeks in Genoa began to change that condition. If the Left Bank of Paris was part of his education in the humanities, then the Genoa Conference was his required survey course in political science and economics. During the next twelve months Hemingway completed his social science requirements at Constantinople, Lausanne, Rapallo and in the Ruhr. Whatever political innocence he brought to Europe disappeared; eighteen months of close study left him cynical about all politicians and all political systems.

When he returned to Paris, he borrowed a phrase from Ezra's *Mauberley* and made it his own:

> The age demanded that we sing
> and cut away our tongue.
> The age demanded that we flow
> and hammered in the bung.
> The age demanded that we dance
> and jammed us into iron pants.
> And in the end the age was handed
> the sort of shit that it demanded.[29]

Not a great lyric nor a particularly interesting technique, but the conclusion was a succinct appraisal of his times.

IV

By April 28, with the Genoa Conference stalemated, Hemingway returned to Paris with his throat once more badly inflamed. Hadley gathered him in, bedded him down; nurse and lover, she complained only a little of her three weeks alone in Paris. When Ernest fevered, Hadley was once more his feather cat, he the sick kitten – a game he first played with his mother in her conjugal bed.[30]

April ended and May began in chilly rain. While Jack Dempsey, world heavyweight champion, slept late in his 2000 franc suite at Claridge's Hotel, Ernest and Hadley tried not to irritate each other in their cramped quarters. No matter how one described it, no words could change the fact of its two rooms. With Ernest occupying the bedroom, his typewriter in his lap and newspapers spread about him on the dining table next to the bed, Hadley was left to her piano in the dining room or a book next to the coal fireplace.

As was his habit life long, Hemingway read the Paris papers diligently – the New York *Herald*, the paper of the Right Bank; the Chicago *Tribune* for Left Bankers and Chicago boys far from home; Lord Northcliffe's *Daily Mail*; and the sporting news covering boxing matches and horse racing. Those first two rainy days in May, while bedded down with his raw throat, he read with special attention two stories of violence.

TWO POLICEMEN SHOT AT END OF REDS' MEETING

Two policemen were shot late yesterday afternoon at the close of the "preliminary May Day demonstration" in which several thousand communists took part at Saint-Ouen.

Both men were wounded by one bullet from a revolver fired by Andre Taullette, 25, . . . The crowd began to flow back into the city through the Saint Ouen gate when police found it necessary to halt it for a moment. Immediately a scuffle occurred and several shots were fired. . . . Police then charged the crowd and several of the latter were roughly handled.[31]

It was the sort of story that played to Hemingway's deep-seated distrust of police authority. Since his youthful illegal shooting of a blue heron and his subsequent court appearance, he always distrusted armed authority. (In a satiric piece of high-school writing, he once advocated setting a special hunting season during which no family was allowed to kill more policemen or game wardens than it could consume.)[32]

Ernest Hemingway had never fired a shot at anyone, but he could imagine what it would be like, what the boy's face looked like. He had seen front-line troops, their faces white with strain. He knew the stiff jolt of the pistol's recoil, the odor of burnt powder. He re-read the newspaper story slowly. Just then he was beginning to practise the preachments of Pound and Stein; now, for the first time, he tried out every word, each phrase of a sentence. If he could get a true sentence, then he could build a paragraph. In his notebooks he had begun working on a series of Paris sentences based on observations from the street, conversations and what he read in the papers. The ones he made up were just as good as the ones based on experience, sometimes better. There in his sick bed he played with this new sentence, focusing on the young killer's face and the police charging the crowd. Whatever he wrote that day was lost with the rest of his early Paris manuscripts, but its impression was strong enough for him to later reconstruct it.

The next day the *Tribune* headlined an even better story.

CHILEAN KILLS SELF FOR LOVE OF PEGGY JOYCE

Actress is Prostrated By Champs-Elysées Tragedy

William Errazzuriz, attaché at the Chilean legation . . . committed suicide over unrequited love for Mrs. Peggy Hopkins Joyce, and jealousy of her latest admirer, it was learned yesterday. . . . Peggy is prostrated in her rooms at the Claridge adjoining those in which M. Errazzuriz took his life.

The death of M. Errazzuriz came some time between six and eight o'clock on Sunday morning, following an all night dancing party at which he was present with Peggy and M. Henri Letellier, proprietor of the newspaper *Le Journal*. . . . "Billy pleaded with me to marry him and give up M. Letellier," said Peggy . . . "He reminded me how he had separated from his wife because of me and insisted we become engaged immediately and that I should set a date in the near future when we could be married."[33]

Suicide fascinated Hemingway: "Why did he kill himself, Daddy?"

his fictive Nick Adams will later ask his father about an Indian suicide. "I don't know, Nick. He couldn't stand things, I guess." *Things.* There were lots of things. He turned from the news story to write a letter to his father, the Doctor, in Oak Park. Maybe the lives of the wealthy made him think of home. Hemingway's family was never part of Oak Park's wealth, but during all his early years, money and its attributes dangled before his eyes, just out of reach. His parents pretended they had no use for that kind of money, but Ernest, inside the homes of friends, saw what Oak Park money could buy. It was good and worth having. Relatively poor in Paris they might be, but not forever. Maybe he could not yet afford to register at Claridge's, maybe it was a joke pilfering embossed stationery from the Crillon's writing room, but one day he would sleep at the Ritz, enjoying every expensive touch of it. This day, with the rain in the gutters and his notebook in his lap, he tried out a sentence about Peggy Joyce, seeing what the words would do.

When he was not writing, he got a lot of Hadley's attention: more hot tea, more aspirin, another look down his throat. Less than a year married, she knew his throat by heart. But he would not go to the doctor unless his fever was out of control. He did not have much faith in French physicians, and as a doctor's son he knew far too many diseases, symptoms and complications for his own good. Had not the past president of France, Deschanel, last week died from bronchial pneumonia? Hadley was sympathetic and stoic, knowing they were booked for Switzerland in mid-May along with Ernest's war buddy, Chink Dorman-Smith. The prospect of hiking with the great Chink would get Ernest out of bed and back to writing. On May 6, he felt well enough to walk to Sylvia's bookshop, pick up fresh reading and buy five francs' worth of blue notebooks. Eight days later he, Hadley and Dorman-Smith were waiting on the familiar platform at Gare de Lyon to board the Montreux train.[34]

The three of them left Paris with the city blazing in national flags and the blue and white colors of St. Joan's Day. In the states it was Mother's Day, but Joan of Arc was closer kin to their war stories that day than any discussion of mothers, as Chink, Ernest and Hadley trained toward the mountains. Hadley listened, charmed by Chink's blue eyes, Irish wit, military posture and gentle manners. Eric Edward Dorman-Smith, four years older than Ernest, met Hemingway in Milan at the end of the Great War. Ernest led him to believe that his limp, cane and wound stripes resulted from combat; Chink, a temporary major in the Northumberland Fusiliers, bore three battle wounds of his own and a Military Cross. Years later Dorman-Smith remembered that first meeting quite clearly:[35]

> Hem and I met quite accidentally, on 3rd November 1918 in the Anglo-American Club in Milan. . . . That morning . . . a young American Red Cross officer came in, on crutches. When he sat down I noted that he was wearing an Italian decoration, the Croce di Guerra. . . . He had his wound on him, I had three wounds on record . . . I discovered that this harmless looking Red Cross youngster had been badly wounded leading Arditi storm troops on Monte Grappa.[36]

The wound's truth, which he never told Dorman-Smith, was not heroic and had nothing to do with Monte Grappa. On July 6, 1918, while distributing chocolate, cigarettes and postcards to Italian troops along the Piave river, Hemingway found his way into a forward observation post for the only close look he ever got of the enemy – a glance across the river bottom in the dark, interrupted by an incoming trench mortar shell that killed two Italian soldiers and left Hemingway with a right leg full of shrapnel. That he reinvented his wounding into a more heroic version was typical of the aging boy and the man he became. He must have been slightly apprehensive of Hadley's meeting Chink. With so much of his life invented, there was always the danger that voices from the past might undo him. Fortunately, Hadley was never certain what Ernest's exploits had been. As she twitted him in Chicago, he kept so much of his life dark she was not sure what to tell the papers about her husband then to-be.[37]

Dorman-Smith, on leave from his Rhine-watch duties and visiting his parents in Paris, remembered Hemingway barging in to the flat and demanding that Chink accompany the Hemingways to Montreux.

> He looked more than ever like my youngest brother, a fact which reconciled my mother to allowing me to leave them and Paris at a moment's notice. The Hemingways were living in lodgings in a hamlet on the road between Montreux and Les Avants. Hadley was nice; they were much in love and used to disturb my bachelorhood at breakfast coffee by reciting, blow by blow, the

events of their nights. . . . It was narcissus time and Hem seemed to make up for all the friends I'd lost in the World War. . . .[38]

There was fishing in the Stockalper where the Rhône joined Lake Geneva – fat trout, long hikes and much talk. It was almost like summer days in upper Michigan: two war brothers and one brother's wife: the first and happiest triad of Hemingway's married life – an innocent, joking time, narcissus time. Part of Ernest needed such an audience. As physicists were discovering, an observer altered the results of an experiment: Chink's presence changed Ernest's behavior. Gone were his Paris doldrums and broods; his throat cured and the trout rising to his bait, this was the good time long remembered.

Twelve years later, writing about the green hills of Africa, Hemingway recalled those days:

> when we walked on the mountain road to the Bains de Alliez and the beer-drinking contest where we failed to win the calf and came home that night around the mountain with the moonlight on the fields of narcissus that grew on the meadows and how we were drunk and talked about how you would describe that light on that paleness, and the brown beer sitting at the wood tables under the wisteria vine at Aigle . . . with the horse chestnut trees in bloom and Chink and I again discussing writing and whether you could call them waxen candelabras. God, what bloody literary discussions we had; we were literary as hell then just after the war.[39]

The artist remembering himself: a self-referential, modernist moment. Maybe he learned it from Pound or Stein; maybe it came from reading about the lives of Byron and Lawrence; or maybe he was born knowing it, and all the reading was simply confirmation of what his intuition told him. Hemingway understood early that it was not enough to write to be remembered; he had to act, perform, leave his impression on the photographic plates, on letters and on surrounding minds. Everywhere he left his spoor, his signs, sometimes backtracking to disguise the trail, to rewrite the event to suit later versions.

Chink and Hadley were a good audience. Together the three climbed Cape au Moine and Dent de Jaman and planned to hike over the Grand St. Bernard Pass into Italy. Hadley's fair complexion sprouted freckles in the high-altitude sun; with her chestnut hair even redder now, her breasts full, her waist narrow, she was never more beautiful than that first year in Switzerland. In Paris, she always looked a bit dowdy in clothes that were out of tune with the cafés and boulevards. Ernest insisted she spend no money on clothes. That had been Gertrude Stein's advice: no clothes, cut your own hair, buy paintings. At least that is what he later remembered her to have said, which was a convenient memory, allowing him to blame a woman as old as his mother for the way he dressed his wife. Whatever Gertrude's advice may have been, the Hemingways bought some art that first year, an African fetish and sketches of Tami Koume touted by Ezra; but mostly their money, Hadley's money, paid for travel. Her only new clothes were tweed knickerbockers Ernest had made for her to match his own which came with his new tailored suit. The knickerbockers were daring in America and comfortable in Switzerland, but not much worn in Paris. But no matter what she wore, Hadley shone through, a lovely woman, lush and soft, with a mind of her own and sexually adept at following Ernest's lead. His baby-talk games were a sexual code she understood quite well. She, his feather cat, said it and he wrote it down, a midnight poem:

> Two little animals
> up in the heather
> Snuggling together
> as protection from the weather
>
> Two little animals
> Out on the heath
> One on top
> The other underneath.[40]

On May 20, when the Genoa Conference finally closed amid frustration, hurt national feelings and promises to meet again later in the year, Ernest was fishing the Rhône canal and drinking beer at Aigle. Four days later, his Genoa expense money and three weeks' pay arrived from the *Star*: $465, enough to extend their trip into Italy for as long as they wanted. Bone's letter also contained Hemingway's credentials for a trip into bolshevik Russia. Toronto and the world, just then, were eager for feature stories on the revolution. What was the fate of the royal family? Had none of the children survived? Was Russia the future or merely another form of tyranny? For reasons not completely clear, Toronto never read Hemingway's slant on Russia. He had the necessary passes but never made the trip. Probably the reason was Hadley. His three weeks in Genoa were no fun for her alone in Paris. The prospect of an even longer Russian trip may have triggered the first serious argument of their marriage.[41]

As so often in marriages, the serious is buried, surfacing in trivial arguments. The three friends decided to follow Chink's suggestion of hiking over the St. Bernard pass using rucksacks to carry bare necessities. The bulk of their luggage would go by train to Milan. On the morning of departure for Italy, when Chink went to their room, he found the couple exchanging angry words about Hadley's toilet articles. She refused to ship them ahead; Ernest refused to pack them in the rucksacks: a silly stand-off that may have been more about Ernest's Russian trip than Hadley's beauty aids. For the sake of peace, Chink stuffed the bottles into his rucksack, not certain what the argument was actually about.

Chink remembered the painful day:

> A small railway took us part of the way up the pass, across the Rhône valley; from Bourg St. Pierre we had to walk. The snow-line was low that year; beyond Bourg St. Pierre we soon reached it. Not long afterwards Hem developed a form of mountain sickness and Hadley had to help him on. I took both their packs. The journey became something of a nightmare, with Hem sick, Hadley worried and myself carrying two packs forward at a time and returning for the odd one. . . . eventually we saw the gaunt hospice, like a barracks in a moonscape. Even then I had trouble with a hostile St. Bernard dog who disapproved of visitors at the wrong time of year and at first would not allow me to ring the almoner's bell.[42]

The distance between Bourg St. Pierre and the hospice – eight miles (13 km) – was uphill all the snowy way, climbing from 5358 feet to 8110. On that same path Napoleon crossed the Alps in 1800, and before him centuries of monks, tradesmen and fugitives, all stopped at the hospice of St. Bernard erected in the year 962. Hemingway wrote Gertrude Stein,

> It was a great trek because the pass wasn't open yet and no one had walked up it this year from the Suisse side. It took the combined efforts of the Captain and Mrs. H and a shot of a cognac

every two hundred yards to get me up the last couple of kilometers of snow.[43]

The hospice itself contained two buildings: the monastery with forty-five beds for travelers and a connected inn with eighty more beds. The three travelers spent the night and breakfasted early next morning at no charge as was the custom of the monks. On leaving, they may have followed Baedeker's recommendation: "Travelers . . . should deposit in the alms-box in the church (first pillar on the left) at least as much as they would have paid at a hotel. The offering may also be handed to the Father Almoner personally; gratuities to the servants are not forbidden."[44]

That second day the three walked down hill twenty miles to the village of Aosta, where the hike, supposed to continue to Milan, stopped when Hadley's blistered and swollen feet gave out. She had trekked twenty-eight snowy miles in low-cut saddle oxfords. At Aosta they took the train to Milan, where Chink picked up his pre-shipped baggage and retrained for Paris, his leave almost over. The three made tentative plans to meet again for the Christmas ski season at Chamby. After a last drink in a bar familiar from earlier days, they parted in the Milan station, where, under the same frescoes and sculptures, Ernest was once carried wounded out of the war. Memories flooded back, reinforced by every odor and taste.

Milan was the first of Hemingway's many reprises, returning to places once important in his life. Inevitably the revisit did not match the earlier experience. The only way to capture significant time and place was to write it truly. He learned that first in Italy, only to relearn it again and again. He and Hadley dined at Campari's, at the Cova, and walked the Piazza del Duomo with its black-winged pigeons and its pink stone cathedral, light and airy, glowing to a blush in the sunset, seemingly ready to lift off the ground. In the Galleria, under high, vaulted ceilings, stained glass and mosaics, they strolled before enclosed shops and sipped their drinks at the open tables of Biffi's. Ernest took Hadley past Ospedale Maggiore where he had done physical therapy to recover from his leg wounding and knee operation. He showed her the balcony of what once was the Red Cross hospital; maybe he even told her more about Agnes Von Kurowsky, his American nurse whose blue eyes and long, blonde hair he never forgot. At the San Siro track, where he and Agnes once backed fixed races, Ernest and Hadley worked the field, but it was not the same. Telling old jokes in old places where no one remembered his face and where the war was reduced to statues in the park was not like old times. Old times were irretrievable. The past was just a good-bye unless redeemed with words on paper.[45]

The words he wrote in Milan redeemed nothing, but helped pay the bills. When Hemingway heard that Benito Mussolini was in town, he pulled out his press card to arrange an interview with the newspaper editor turned politician who commanded the strident and armed Fascisti movement. He found him sitting behind his editor's desk, a wolf-hound pup playing beside him – "a big, brown-faced man with a high forehead, a slow smiling mouth, and large, expressive hands." With a quarter of a million armed irregular "black shirts" ready to overthrow any government opposing his fascist movement, Mussolini was sitting on a powder keg of his own making. The question, as Hemingway so clearly saw, was what did Mussolini "intend to do with his 'political party organized as a military force'?" Before the year was out, the newspaper editor would be proclaimed fascist dictator of Italy, answering Hemingway's almost rhetorical question.[46]

From Milan, Ernest took Hadley by bus to Schio up in the Trentino hills, the same hills over which he had briefly driven a Red Cross ambulance in June of 1918. Another mistake. Nothing was the same. The camaraderie of war, intensified by death's close presence, was gone. No one in Schio wanted to remember it. The wool factory spewed muck into the Timonchio river where the "boys" once bathed while waiting for battles to begin. "I wouldn't have recognized it now," he wrote, "and I would give a lot not to have gone." Few of the drivers' names and none of their jokes meant anything to Hadley.[47]

A few days later, after a trip through the hill country, Ernest and Hadley arrived at Sirmione on Lake Garda where they accidentally ran into Dorothy and Ezra Pound, relaxing in the holy place of Catullus and his saffron sandals: blue water in the rock caves and light, silver off the water, "wherein the sun lets drift in on us through the olive trees a liquid glory."

> and the leaves are full of voices
> A-whisper, and the clouds bowe over the lake,
> And there are gods upon them,
> And in the water, the almond-white swimmers,
> The silvery water glazes the upturned nipple.

What better guide into the buried world of the old gods than Ezra under the olive trees of Garda? A moment outside of time, consumed by time. From there down to Mestre by train and then a hired car to Fossalta, the place of his wounding, the dark landscape he walked so often in his dreams. Hadley must have had misgivings; too often she held him in the night, fending off Germans chasing her helpless husband across no man's land.[48]

In Fossalta, the trenches were gone, and the scarred terrain returned to smooth green slopes. With nothing looking as it had, Ernest could not be certain of his wounding's location. A rusted fragment from what might have been a gas shell was all that remained of his night journey into death's domain. Rebuilt, Fossalta lacked the war dignity of its ravagement, bore no resemblance to the dark place he went in his dreams. Back in Paris he wrote it down for the *Star*, trying to exorcise the old ghosts:

> Don't go back to visit the old front. If you have pictures in your head of something that happened in the night . . . do not try and go back to verify them. It is no good. The front is as different from the way it used to be as your highly respectable shin, with a thin, white scar on it now, is from the leg that you sat and twisted a tourniquet around while the blood soaked your puttee and trickled into your boot, so that when you got up you limped with a "squidge" on your way to the dressing station. . . . don't go back to your own front . . . It is like going into the empty gloom of a theater where the charwomen are scrubbing.[49]

Unlike his fictional journalist, Hemingway did not limp back to the dressing station. They had to carry him back, his right leg a bloody mess. In one month at the front he learned all he would ever need to know about war. One did not need years in the trenches to know fear, to dream residual nightmares, to remember always one's brief test of nerve, to smell again the sweet odor of one's own blood. No matter how he wrote it down, his ghosts refused to rest. Time and again he returned to that Fossalta blast zone of his youth where he had crawled out to the forward observation post, excited, stomach tight, a kid barely out of high school. What he found there, he never forgot: courage was not enough to protect him from the roaring blast, nor did it stop the pain. Courage was one thing, fear another. They were separate, and no amount of courage could protect him from the fear if it were strong enough.

Chapter Four

FIRST BLOOD
PARIS, SUMMER, 1922

I

By the time Ernest and Hadley returned to Paris on June 18, the city was filling with summer tourists as quickly as the regulars left for the country. On the grand boulevards mechanical traffic signals were being erected, taking the fun out of Paris free-style driving. Imported yellow cabs from Chicago now challenged home-grown red taxis for fares. (At 32 cents to the mile, Paris was a cabby's dream.) Gertrude and Alice had already departed for St. Rémy, but Ezra was back in town, busy promoting painters but not too busy for tennis. At Sylvia's bookshop everyone wanted a copy of *Ulysses*; Brentano's posh Avenue de l'Opéra store kept Sylvia's assistant in taxis bearing fresh copies of the banned book to the Right Bank for American tourists to smuggle into the states.

His month in the far country produced no new fiction for Hemingway, but he sold a few features to the *Star*, returning to Paris with money in his pocket. The entire month on the road did not exhaust his back pay and expenses from the Genoa trip. With extra money and the horses running every day at one of the five Paris tracks, Ernest and Hadley went as often as possible to Auteuil and Enghien. A cheap bus ride and a picnic lunch on the *pelouse*, Hadley sometimes napping in the sun, Ernest always watching, listening. They had the last six weeks of the summer season before the horses, like most affluent Parisians, left town.

Horse racing and its attendant show were an integral part of Paris life, a fashion parade, an outing, an excuse to bet a few francs. Whenever he could, Ernest talked with the small, tight fraternity of American and British jocks who followed the horses across Europe: Frank O'Neill, Bellhouse, George Garner, MacGee. One could turn a steady profit simply by betting on Frankie O'Neill regardless of his horse. One could also pick up a good deal of information about track life if he listened carefully; with a good ear and sound imagination, he could write a story about insiders at the track.

He began the story on the back of a telegraph form, probably jotted down in early July:

> It is time to write a story. It might be a story about horses. At Enghien where we stood at the water jump and the horses came over the jump so big and so close to you and going fast. And before the races Hadley slept on the grass.[1]

That was how a lot of stories started, short notes to get the juices flowing. The story that evolved had nothing to do with Hadley but the water jump was there. A young boy, Joe Butler, narrates the life of his dad, an over-the-hill jockey who left the racing scene in Italy under ambiguous circumstances: a fixed race or a fix refused. At the Paris St. Cloud track armed with inside information, the father makes enough money on another fixed race to buy a steeplechaser of his own. With a renewed license and hard training, he works the horse and himself into sleek enough shape to place third the first time out. At the next race at Auteuil, Butler and his horse Gilford spill:

> They took off over the big hedge of the water-jump in a pack and then there was a crash, and two horses pulled sideways out of it, and kept on going, and three others were piled up. I couldn't see my old man anywhere.[2]

Joe's father is killed in the fall and the horse, its leg broken, is shot. As the boy, almost in shock, leaves the track, he hears one insider say to another, "Well, Butler got his, all right." The other man replies, "I don't give a good goddam if he did, the crook. He had it coming to him on the stuff he's pulled." The young boy's last words to us are: "Seems like when they get started they don't leave a guy nothing."[3]

In "My Old Man" Hemingway tried, for the first time, themes and techniques he would later perfect. It is his first story in which the father fails the son. In his Chicago juvenilia, he wrote several stories in which the son could not please the demanding father or some other figure whose admiration he sought. After "My Old Man," Hemingway's fictional fathers seldom meet the expectations of their needy sons. As an eleven-year-old on vacation in Nantucket, Ernest, trying to please his father, brought home a two-dollar albatross foot for the Agassiz Club. A year later his father, victim of rising hypertension and depression, abandoned the club, the stuffed animals and the naturalist outings along the river. The ghost of Ernest's albatross hung forever about their necks: the boy never understood his father's depressions. The Doctor, no matter how friendly he tried to be, was never able to renew the closeness that once bound him to his son. It was another story carved off the bone of American life.[4]

Hemingway's narrator, Joe Butler, has the innocence and inside expertise of Huck Finn and much of his disarming appeal. He may not understand his father's shady past, but his knowledge of European race tracks is detailed, specific and highly accurate. Under the guise of the young boy's voice, Hemingway crafted his story from disparate but actual events taken from the Paris racing season of 1922. The two central events – the fixed race and the dead jockey – Hemingway did not actually see, but found ready-made in newspaper accounts.

As any turf man knew in 1922, Ksar and Kircubbin were real horses, who raced as described in "My Old Man" on July 2 at the St. Cloud track, where Hemingway sets his story. In April, the front-page *Tribune* headline had reported: "KSAR ROMPS HOME IN FEATURE," and the sports section said that Ksar was shaping up as the best horse on the continent. Ksar's jockey was Frank Bullock, one of the numerous English riders working the French circuit. On May 8, just before Hemingway left Paris to go to Italy, Bullock rode Ksar, "France's Wonder Horse," to an impressive victory. On June 5, Bullock was taken off the track unconscious after a serious fall from another horse. The next day Kircubbin, an Irish horse who had won the important St. Leger, took the Grand Prix de Temps for his third consecutive win on the continent. When Hemingway returned to Paris, two weeks before the Ksar–Kircubbin race, all the racing sheets and turf enthusiasts were convinced that Ksar would be unbeatable in the prestigious Prix du Président race.

On the day of the Ksar–Kircubbin race, the Paris *Tribune* reported:

> Only an accident can prevent Madame Edmond Blanc's thoroughbred [Ksar] from carrying off the 200,000 francs and the precious soup tureen that goes to the winner.

But there will be two or three gamesters up there in front looking for this break and Kircubbin, Fleçois and Andrea are the most likely looking battlers . . . Trained at St. Cloud, Ksar has never appeared in competition before on that course, while Kircubbin . . . has grabbed off three consecutive victories there.

Ksar went to the starting post a heavy favorite only to lose at the wire to the Irish horse. The payoff on Kircubbin was 65 francs on a 10 franc ticket – almost exactly what Hemingway makes it in the story (67.5 to 10). The winner's share of the 250,000 franc race was 200,000 francs – the same sum Hemingway uses in his story. Joe Butler's father, armed with inside information from Ksar's jockey, knows the fictional race is fixed; he bets 5000 francs on Kircubbin to win and another 1000 francs on him to place, just in case the fix goes wrong. In the real race and in Hemingway's fiction, Kircubbin won at the wire by a nose. The newspapers said nothing about a possible fix.

However, during the 1922 racing season in both Paris and Deauville, there were a number of suspicious races. Three weeks after the Prix du Président race, the *Tribune* reported that the "rumors circulating at the present time regarding several cases of doping all center on the horses of a particular stable, and they tend to be consistent. They concern a stable trained at Maisons-Laffitte, of which one of the veterans recently occupied public opinion by reason of its extremely contradictory performances." (Maisons-Laffitte was where the fictional Butler lived and trained.) Four days later the London *Times* reported that a well-known French trainer had been suspended and fined on charges of doping his horses. Specifically he was charged with administering a "powerful stimulant" to Arcady who won the Prix Antilope at the Tremblay track one day after the Ksar–Kircubbin race. Later that season a winner at the Chantilly track was disqualified after a saliva test, and three cases of doping were charged during the August season at Deauville. Hemingway, who was in Paris from late June until August 1, was well aware of these doping charges.[5]

In his story, which was almost finished by the end of July, Hemingway rearranged the racing season to use an actual steeplechase he witnessed in March, but one which did not have a fatal fall. In fact, Hemingway witnessed several spills that season that killed no one. If a man had seen one serious spill, he could easily imagine the death of the jockey. (Ironically, the same day as the real Ksar–Kircubbin race, a French jockey died in a spill at Marseilles.) Two years later Hemingway said, "The only writing that was any good was what you made up, what you imagined. Like when he wrote 'My Old Man' he'd never seen a jockey killed and the next week Georges Parfrement was killed at that very jump and that was the way it looked."[6]

Hemingway wrote "My Old Man" in the late summer of 1922. Georges Parfrement, the most famous French jockey of the era, died the following April of 1923, not two weeks later as Hemingway said. Hemingway's Butler died at the Auteuil track; Parfrement died at the Enghien track. Moreover, Hemingway was in Cortina, Italy when Parfrement's horse "came down at a stone wall" and fell on the jockey, killing him. Hemingway never saw Parfrement's fatal accident. With Hemingway there is no such thing as non-fiction; there are simply degrees of fiction, some events more fictional than others.[7]

What is most significant in the crafting of "My Old Man" – the only surviving example from his first year's work in Paris – is Hemingway's imaginative ability to interweave first-hand observations with secondary information. He did not learn to do this from Anderson, Pound or Stein, and he would use it again and again throughout his career. After he wrote *The Sun Also Rises*, most of his readers and more than one biographer assumed that all of his fiction was thinly veiled biography, which it almost never was. "My Old Man" clearly demonstrates that Hemingway mastered his craft early in Paris with little tutoring.

Hemingway told Scott Fitzgerald in 1925, "My Old Man" is "a good story, always seemed to me, though not the thing I'm shooting for. It belongs to another category . . . The kind that are easy for me to write." Direct experience, he discovered, was not necessarily the most reliable source of information for a writer: the actor could not observe himself in action, did not have time to analyze his reactions. But the careful observer, the one with an eye steady and detached could imagine what the experience felt like. He mastered that art early in his journalism, and it carried over into his fiction. "My Old Man" shows us a young writer already using the skills and techniques of a seasoned professional. Hemingway had come a long way since leaving Chicago, and his instinct for the sporting life paid off with a story as good as anything Sherwood Anderson ever wrote about horse racing.[8]

II

In Paris Hemingway cultivated the underside of the race track in the same way that he developed expert and inside knowledge about the fight game, quickly and in precise detail. He asked questions, listened intently and read the sporting news and turf sheets religiously. There were always two stories: one on the surface that any tourist or novice could read, and one buried beneath the public display, the insider's story. The fixed race, the thrown prize fight fascinated him. In "My Old Man" the race is fixed; in "Fifty Grand" the championship fight is crossed and double-crossed. In *A Farewell to Arms*, at the heart of the book, is a fixed horse race: the lovers can bet on the fix but win next to nothing because smart money lowered the odds; or they can bet by heart and lose. Either way they lose. He called his third volume of stories *Winner Take Nothing*, and the fixed race was his metaphor for life, the outcome of which was always foreknown: you lose. Life was only a question about dying: how, where, when? It was a small but valuable thing to learn, a truth upon which he built some of his best fiction: "all stories, if continued far enough, end in death, and he is no true-story teller who would keep that from you," he once said. When sophisticated critics became bored with this simple truth, they pretended that it had no great value, but they never did prove it false, and about its lacking value, they were wrong.[9]

That part of Hemingway trained to natural history as a boy in the Agassiz Club never stopped closely observing animal behavior, most particularly that curious animal, himself and his fellow man. How man behaved under stress, in dangerous situations or at the point of death was his life's study found early. He used his own wounding for a benchmark, knowing that alone in the Italian night, with the two dead men splattered over him in the trench and before the stretchers arrived, he felt himself dying and knew fear enough to last his lifetime. At the races, at ring side, at the bull ring, on the battlefield, he would continually check and recalibrate his first readings.

There were other compelling reasons for Hemingway to cultivate the world of jockeys, prize fighters, soldiers, bullfighters and prostitutes. They were the people never admitted into Oak Park, where one could not make, sell or store liquor; where exhibiting bulls inside the city limits was forbidden; where no one could disseminate information on birth control or venereal disease; where one pulled the shades down tight before mixing a cocktail. The underworld that Oak Park acknowledged only by forbidding it was of great interest to Hemingway because it was forbidden. As school boys he and friends played at tough games, intrigued by whatever their parents railed against. They drank when they could get the liquor; played poker on the sly; kidded each other about the whores in Chicago. In Paris and later, he would, on the slightest provocation, trot out the old cliché that a good dose of syphilis or the clap improved the creative mind, implying he had contracted his share of venereal disease. Some in Paris thought that he earned side money giving boxing lessons; others were sure he was buried four days at the front before being rescued. Several were certain he ran away from home early, spending his teen years on the road. Tough talk is only talk, a product of Hemingway's imagined version of himself, the man he wanted to be. He went to many wars, but was never a soldier; saw many bullfights, but never killed a single bull. If he ever fathered an illegitimate child, neither mother nor child has ever pressed claims.

Ernest delighted in dressing down to the level of the working class, taking middle-class visitors to the *bal musette* to dance with the locals. He admired the toughs, the apaches, as much as he despised the tourists upon whom they sometimes preyed. When necessary, he still wore the tweed suit purchased his first week in Paris, but he preferred a fisherman's shirt and the rough pants of the worker. Strange and conflicting identities are endemic to American dreamers, uncomfortable with urban middle-class safety and longing for the lost West: Thoreau pretending to a frontier life long gone; Twain's river days remembered in his Connecticut mansion; Jack London eating his ducks raw. And Ernest, always acquiring costumes and never satisfied with who he was, continued in Paris to create himself anew: Ernest the boxer, the skier, the race track tout, the salty war veteran, the tough reporter, the hard-working Hemingway. None of these guises was exactly true but he gave them great credibility. One can become whatever he pretends to be, even in Paris, where street costumes were nothing strange among Left Bank Americans.

Surrounded as he was by literate, college-trained, older and more experienced friends, Hemingway played to his strengths and masked his spotty background. Only a high-school graduate with no reading command of a foreign language, he was sometimes uncomfortable around his newly found Paris friends. Ezra Pound (37), with his Master's degree from Pennsylvania, knew the Renaissance fore and aft, read French and Italian, knew all of Henry James not to mention British literature. Gertrude Stein (48), a former student of William James, graduated from Harvard Annex (Radcliffe), almost earned her medical degree, and collected modernist painters and their art. The strange learning and arcane knowledge of James Joyce was already legend. Dorman-Smith was educated at Sandhurst; Sylvia Beach, who largely educated herself, was reading years ahead of Hemingway and fluent in French. Among these well-read friends, Hemingway felt, at times, uneasy. He hated discussions of literary theory, and no one ever caught him quoting Plato, Kant or Nietzsche. While beginning his own reading program to offset his liability, Hemingway learned that he could disarm the college-trained by making the playing field less intellectual and more physical. In his enthusiasm for the Paris prize fights, horse races, bike races and in 1923 the Spanish bullfights, Hemingway was able to turn conversations to topics not learned in books. While walking along the streets, he shadow boxed. Writing in the cafés, he fished rivers real and imaginary, drifting his McGinty fly exactly across the sunken log. In the evenings when Left Bank talk took him out of his depth, there was always the war and his wound to rechannel the flow.

By the end of June, there appeared finally at Shakespeare and Company tangible evidence of Hemingway the Paris writer: the summer issue of *The Double Dealer* published his Chicago poem:

> "Ultimately"
> He tried to spit out the truth;
> Dry mouthed at first,
> He drooled and slobbered in the end;
> Truth dribbling his chin.[10]

Within a month, he was writing the editor of *The Double Dealer* about his payment. He was pleased to be published, but publishing for free was not part of Hemingway's agenda. In August, John McClure, the editor, promised that the check was in the September mail. He also said, "Your comment on Pound was interesting. I feel about him much as you do – worried as to whether he will ever write any more first rate stuff." It was, perhaps, a bit presumptuous for a young writer, on the basis of his first published poem, to be worrying about Ezra, but it was a chance for Hemingway to drop Ezra's name to indicate what close friends they were. If you knew a good name, it did you no credit to keep it hidden.[11]

Hemingway's literary prospects were looking up. Harriet Monroe, Chicago editor of *Poetry* magazine, accepted the poems that Thayer turned down for the *Dial*. Pound's name opened Monroe's door, but she accepted the poems on their merit, enhanced by their Paris return address. In his thank-you letter to Monroe, Hemingway apologized for not responding immediately to her acceptance letter. For his biographical blurb, he told her he was "at present in Russia as staff correspondent of the Toronto Star. (passport three weeks over-due now. However, Max Eastman's came yesterday so I might [be able] to get under way shortly. Litvinoff promised me at Genoa there would be no trouble)." Casually dropping names out of the news, Ernest, almost as an afterthought, mentioned that he had "published verse etc in *Double Dealer*." Just as casually he enclosed "some more [poems] you might be able to use."[12]

When the six accepted poems eventually appeared, grouped under the heading "Wanderings," Monroe referred to the author as "a young Chicago poet now abroad, who will soon issue his first book of verse." One good fiction deserved another. Monroe rejected the additional poems Hemingway enclosed, as well as three others he may have sent her later in August. The later ones were rejected for good reason: three of them satirized a prominent Chicago millionaire whose ire Harriet Monroe could ill afford, dependent as she was on Chicago's financial support to publish her magazine.[13]

These satiric poems were begun in late July after a strange conjunction of Paris events. On June 20, Serge Voronoff, a Russian doctor experimenting in Paris with monkey gland transplants, announced that he needed more monkeys for his work. He claimed to be "using different glands of every chimpanzee I receive from Africa. Notably I use the thyroid glands for weak-minded children and the interstitial glands for rejuvenation of the aged. . . . the life of an elderly man can be pushed back twenty or thirty years and his faculties made more vigorous." Voronoff claimed he was "on the eve of being able to transplant any major organ of a chimpanzee into a human being." The café jokes were predictable and blatant. Just what size "gland" did a chimp have?

A month later, a prominent Chicago millionaire arrived in Paris just in time to make a fool of himself on the front page of the *Tribune*:

H. F. McCORMICK,
IN PARIS, CALLS
ON MME. WALSKA

Foils Reporters Who
Would Learn Where
He Is Staying

Mr. Harold F. McCormick . . . spent the afternoon with Mme. Ganna Walska, operatic singer, who is now awaiting a divorce settlement . . . with her third husband. . . . Mr. McCormick made himself virtually incognito in Paris by avoiding the fashionable downtown hotels. . . . He was located at Mme. Walska's home after luncheon, but newspapermen could not get a glimpse of the couple until they came out for their motor ride.[14]

Three pages later the *Tribune* republished two photos of McCormick taken earlier that year: one before his "operation" in which he appears to be a greying, half bald, sedate and tired old man; the second picture taken on his return from the hospital shows a younger face with little or no grey showing. The paper did not specify what sort of operation so rejuvenated the millionaire.

Given the monkey gland jokes abounding and Hemingway's residual dislike for the wealthy in Chicago and Oak Park, we can almost see him sipping his beer while jotting down a few lines in Kipling's voice:

There's a little monkey maiden looking eastward toward the sea,
There's a new monkey soprano a'sobbing in the tree,
And Harold's looking very fit the papers all agree.

L'Envoi
It was quite an operation
But it may have saved the nation,
And what's one amputation
To the tribe?

His second imitation parodied a Stevenson poem; the third, one by Robert Graves. All three poems centered on transplanted glands rejuvenating impotent men; three years later Hemingway's Jake Barnes will stare in the mirror at his war-mutilated genitals, a man of his time.[15]

III

On July 21, Hemingway's twenty-third birthday passed without fanfare in the summer heat of Paris. His parents sent him handkerchiefs which he said he appreciated (all good boys keep their noses blown). Headlines proclaimed that Lenin's brain was paralyzed, his rule finished. Once a month the papers declared the bolshevic revolution moribund. A new Paris-to-London record of one hour and forty-two minutes was set by a British flier in a Handley-Paige, and the St. Louis Browns were in first place in the American League, a game and a half ahead of Babe Ruth and the New York Yankees. Ernest and Hadley, in Paris for only a month, were planning their next adventure.

On August 1, Hemingway met Bill Bird at the German Embassy on Quai d'Orsay where each paid the stiff ten dollar visa fee and got his joint husband/wife passport stamped for German travel until September 10. Ernest first met Bill Bird, an experienced newsman in Paris, at the Anglo-American Press Club and got to know him better while covering the Genoa Conference. The Hemingways, Bill and his wife Sally, Lewis Galantière and his fiancée Dorothy Butler were about to leave on a Black Forest walking trip in Germany. It seemed a pleasant way to escape the gawking tourists flooding Paris, and the German mark had fallen to 605 to the dollar, making the trip inexpensive. For Ernest it was also a chance to find feature material for the *Star*, for he had sent Bone only a few stories since returning from Italy.[16]

One of the stories would describe the plane flight from Paris to Strasbourg, which Bird said he would pass up. A few days earlier, the Hemingways, while dining with friends, learned of cheap tickets available to journalists on the Franco-Romanian Aero Company's flights. For 120 francs, about $10, Ernest bought two one-way tickets that cost less than the slow train. No amount of economic argument could convince Bird, for despite his name, he had better sense than to climb into a wood-and-canvas biplane flown by some aging war-hero. It was early times for commercial air travel when hardly a week passed without news of another flimsy plane falling out of the sky. The Atlantic would not be flown for another six years, but already five flights a day connected London and Paris, less than three hours by air. Two airlines – Daimler and C.M.A. – advertised regularly in the *Tribune*: Daimler emphasized two pilots at the controls; C.M.A. displayed a line drawing of its two-engine Goliath biplane.[17]

Bird would not be budged. Who ever heard of the Franco-Romanian Aero Co.? He refused to go into the air with anyone from Romania at the controls and certainly not to Strasbourg. On July 16, four passengers and their pilot enroute to Strasbourg died in a crash at Saverne; another crash four miles outside of town the next day injured everyone involved. That second accident was a Franco-Romanian flight whose stalled engine forced a crash landing. Ernest argued that the trip was only two and a half hours rather than the ten hours by train. Yes, but the other scheduled airline made the trip in one hour and a half. Sure, but that was with two motors instead of the one powering the F–R Aero flights. While Bill and Ernest were arguing about aircraft safety, twenty bodies were pulled out of the wreckage of two trains near Lourdes.

Ernest and Hadley flew without the Birds to Strasbourg. At three thousand feet, with cotton plugs in her ears and the odor of burning castor oil filling the small cabin, Hadley slept in her fur coat, and Ernest watched the landscape turn into a cubist painting. In his Toronto *Star* feature, he wrote:

> Sometimes we came down quite low and could see bicyclists on the road looking like pennies rolling along a narrow white strip. At other times we would lift up and the whole landscape would contract. . . . We went over great forests, that looked as soft as velvet, passed over Bar le Duc and Nancy, gray red-roofed towns, over St. Mihiel and the front and in an open field I could see the old trenches zigzagging through a field pocked with shell holes. . . . Beyond the old 1918 front we ran into a storm that made the pilot fly close to the ground and we followed a canal that we could see below us through the rain. . . . The plane headed high out of the storm into the bright sunlight and we saw the flat, tree-lined, muddy ribbon of the Rhine off on our right.

Moving through a landscape and taking his reader with him: he practiced it in his journalism and perfected it in his later fiction.[18]

The six hikers gathered in Strasbourg and on August 3, passed through customs and crossed the Kehl bridge into Germany. The best hotel in town served a five-course meal for 120 marks or 15 cents; a stein of beer was less than two cents. Marveling at their new-found wealth, the group was less impressed with the open hostility of many Germans. The Black Forest was full of curt, over-fed Germans on summer holidays who resented what they took to be exploiting foreigners. At Freiburg the music was as mushy as the apple fritter dessert, but the price was right: about twenty cents a day in the hotel. At Triberg-in-Baden, they found a trout stream to fish and a Gasthaus where the bill was about four dollars a week. The mark continued to fall. By August 10, the dollar was worth 833 marks; August 17, 1011 marks; August 22, 1250 marks; August 25, 1972 marks.

For Hemingway's feature, the falling mark was a joke: "A Swiss hotelkeeper can raise prices with the easy grace of a Pullman car poker shark backing a pat full house, but the mark can fall faster than even a Swiss in good training can hoist the cost of living." Hemingway did not yet understand any better than most of the post-war world that Germany's future was his own; as Germany went, so, eventually, would go Europe and the West. Economic chaos ruined shop keepers and day-wage toilers, creating the climate that eventually brought Hitler to power. But in 1922, no one west of the Rhine was feeling too sorry for the Germans who lately had been the military wolf at the door of Europe.[19]

The Birds, Galantière and Dorothy Butler eventually returned to Paris, leaving the Hemingways alone to travel the narrow down-river reaches of the Rhine toward Coblenz. Swift and dark in the channel, the river flowed past vineyards, romantic ruins and gothic castles; at regular stops the boat put in to small havens like Assmanhausen where the lovely tart wine, the color of fine brandy, was pressed from the vines surrounding and covering the hotel veranda. At Coblenz, Chink Dorman-Smith met them at the pier. Almost immediately Ernest's stories for the *Star* became much more knowledgeable, as Chink filled his ear with insider's information.

Then, on August 23 while Ernest and Hadley were still in Germany, the Turks launched a devastating offensive against the Greek front in Asia Minor. More than 200,000 troops of Mustapha Kemal Pasha smashed through the thinly defended Greek line and moved toward Smyrna. By August 27, the Greeks were forced out of their main strongholds by the Turks who apparently intended to reduce as much as possible Greek control of Asia Minor prior to the fall conference in Venice designed to settle their conflicting territorial claims. On August 31, as the Hemingways were departing Coblenz by train for Paris, the Turks captured two key Greek positions on the Berlin–Baghdad railway. By the time Ernest and Hadley reached Paris, the Turks were within sixty miles of Smyrna. Headlines proclaimed: RETREAT NOW ROUT. King Constantine of Greece sat on a tottering throne.[20]

Chapter Five

ON THE ROAD
PARIS, FALL AND EARLY
WINTER, 1922

I

By September 7, news bulletins out of Asia Minor became more urgent. England asked for joint Allied action, but France and Italy declared they would not become involved. British troops were already in Constantinople, and two American destroyers arrived in Smyrna with three others enroute to protect Americans there.

> American blue jackets have taken a large theater on the waterfront to use in case of trouble. Landing parties of fifty from each boat are prepared to hold the waterfront . . . with rifles and machine guns. The situation is critical as hordes of refugees are entering the city.[1]

With Turkish cavalry within twenty miles of Smyrna and armed American sailors patrolling its streets, there was a strong possibility that the local war might expand. The last conflagration, its scars yet unhealed, started with less provocation.

On September 8, the retreating Greek army abandoned Smyrna to the Turks while American ships waited in the harbor to evacuate the last sixty Americans who remained ashore "to see things through." While Hemingway was at the Paris Velodrome watching Eugene Criqui destroy the featherweight champion of Belgium, the Turks entered

Smyrna. By the following day all British patrols of that dying city withdrew, leaving French, Italian and American patrols still ashore. Turkish forces occupied the town in an orderly fashion with little violence observed.

On September 11, Hemingway accompanied Bill Bird to St. Vincent du Jard to interview Georges Clemenceau, the eighty-year-old "Tiger" of France and war-hero, who was making an American tour in November to correct false views of post-war France. Hemingway asked the old warrior if he were going to visit Canada as well. Clemenceau's reply was vitriolic. He said that Canada had neither fully supported the war effort nor used general conscription to raise troops. When Bone read the interview, he wondered if Clemenceau was ignorant or had another purpose in mind. He instructed Hemingway to inform the old man of Canada's war record and to get another interview, for he would not print what Hemingway sent him. He did, however, enclose a check for Hemingway's expenses. By the time he got Bone's letter, the interview was pointless. Clemenceau was looking backwards, still fighting the last war: wrong man, wrong time, wrong conflict. The world was elsewhere.[2]

Meanwhile in Smyrna, occupying Turks celebrated while the world held its breath. A sniper attack on the American Collegiate Institute, where a thousand Armenians huddled, was repulsed by American guards; it appeared to be the work of local brigands, not invading Turks. Many thought that conflict was finished, that Kemal, with his objective achieved, would now be satisfied to enter the Venice Conference on Asia Minor from a position of strength. Then, without warning, Paris woke September 15 to the headlines:

1,000 ARE DEAD AS SMYRNA BURNS

Fire starting . . . near the American Collegiate institute in the heart of the Armenian quarter has rendered 60,000 Armenians and Greeks homeless, left the entire western portion of the town in ruins, and destroyed the beautiful foreign quarter completely. More than 1,000 persons were killed in the fire. . . . As we left the harbor last night, the flames were entirely beyond control . . . The quays were packed with refugees. . . . Foreign destroyers in the harbor kept the searchlights playing on the crowds along the quays all night.

From the relative comfort of his Paris apartment, Hemingway read the story with mixed feelings. The best newsmen in town were already enroute to Constantinople.

Within three days, Hemingway received a telegram from Toronto asking him to cover the affair in Asia Minor, which appeared out of control. Simultaneously, Frank Mason, Paris chief of Hearst's International News Service, approached Hemingway with an offer to be the Hearst man in Constantinople. Perhaps Ernest knew the newsroom gossip that John Bone sometimes rewrote the lead on *Star* feature stories and sold them to American papers under his own name. Certainly he knew that Bone had not printed all the features Hemingway sent back. Or maybe Hemingway thought that he could take the money from both papers honestly, giving each what it wanted. Hearst needed spot news, Toronto needed features.[3]

Somehow he rationalized his decision to work for both the *Star* and I.N.S. and cabled Bone:

EXPENSES CONSTANTINOPLE TWO HUNDRED DOLLARS TRAVEL INCLUSIVE AND NINE DOLLARS PER DAY LIVING STOP WONDERFUL ASSIGNMENT BUT IF WAR HASTE NECESSARY STOP IF NO WAR NEAR EAST ARTICLES ANYWAY

On September 20, as the British rushed units to the Dardanelles and Mustapha Kemal threatened to unseat all military forces of occupation at the Golden Horn, John Bone cabled Hemingway $500 to cover his trip.[4]

At about the same time Ernest's argument with Hadley became serious. As she opposed his planned trips to Russia and Ireland, so she argued against this trip into middle eastern chaos. Hadley did not want her husband reinforcing his already terrorizing dream patterns with more armed violence. Nor did she want to be left for another month, maybe longer, alone in Paris, not when everyone they knew was out of town. Nor did she want her husband risking his life just for the money. But especially she was angered by his arrangement with Mason's I.N.S. It was not right. They both knew it was not right. She married him to support his creative writing, not his journalism, and certainly not unethical journalism. If Hemingway felt guilty about his arrangement with Mason, it was too late; he was committed.[5]

On September 21, the U.S. Congress overrode President Harding's veto of the veteran's bonus while England and France tried to establish a Greco-Turkish cease fire and peace conference. That was the standing British solution: bog down belligerents in another conference. Mustapha Kemal refused to talk; there was nothing to discuss for it was not the Allies' problem. Hemingway spent most of the day trotting his passport through the embassies of Greece, Bulgaria, Yugoslavia and Italy. Three hundred and thirty francs later, he had purchased the required travel visas. The next day he reserved a sleeping compartment on the Simplon–Orient Express to leave on September 25. The round trip ticket used up two hundred of Bone's five hundred dollar advance.[6]

The day before Ernest left, Hadley was not speaking to her husband, had not spoken to him for two days and would not accompany him to the afternoon prize fights at Buffalo stadium. Georges Carpentier, the pride of France and light-heavyweight champion of the world, was defending his title against the West African fighter, Battling Siki, in what most thought to be a match preliminary to a Carpentier challenge to Jack Dempsey, the world heavyweight champion. Two days before the fight Hemingway wired the *Star*:

> Siki confident carp confident spectators confident but of early ending . . . ten oneward on carp offered untaken stop only siki backers in Latin Quarter cafes where battler exsenegal did early training stop siki tough slowthinker but mauling style may puzzle carp

At fight time the odds were steady at 10-to-1 that Carpentier would win.[7]

As sixty thousand spectators, including Hemingway and Lincoln Steffens, watched, Carpentier took the first two rounds, floored Siki in the third, and seemed in total control. Spectators hooted, calling it a frame-up. As the *Tribune* reported:

> But the ebony Tarzan staggered up with his face like a chocolate eclair smeared with catsup. The blow had knocked his mind back thousands of years to the days when his ancestors swung a mean stone sledge from the tree tops. . . . The pride of French Africa cut loose with a wild right packed with dynamite and Carpentier dropped for the count of four.

At that point the fight turned in Siki's favor. For the next three rounds, he punished the champion, opening a cut over his right eye, closing his

73

left eye. Blind and with blood flowing from his mouth and eye, Carpentier lasted until the sixth when he could no longer defend himself. At the last moment the referee tried to give the match to the champion on a foul, but was overruled by both the crowd and the judges, who had seen something they had not anticipated. Traditional powers no longer held sway, not in Asia Minor, not at Buffalo stadium. The power vacuum created by the Great War was filling in unexpected ways. Lincoln Steffens saw the fight as an example of the great powers defeating themselves just as they were botching the various post-war peace conferences. The center was no longer the center, much less holding as once it had.[8]

The next evening Ernest left the apartment in a huff, slamming the door behind him on his equally angry wife. At the station the taxi driver dropped Hemingway's portable typewriter, jamming the carriage of Hadley's birthday gift of a year earlier. It figured somehow. Ahead of him lay the tedious journey to Constantinople: four nights and three days of steady rail clicks broken by passport checks and a few stops. In Milan he read the latest papers to find that Kemal was already stating his demands for peace. In his compartment, Hemingway began writing.

> There is a blue, late-September haze over the fields and since we crossed the Croatian frontier early this morning we have been moving through . . . fields of corn and yellowing tobacco . . . flocks of sheep and herds of cattle . . . beech groves and peat smoke from chimneys.[9]

He did not know if it was peat smoke or not, but it sounded right for Canadian readers. As he watched the fields of stubby corn spreading across Yugoslavia, King Constantine of Greece was abdicating under coup pressure from his entire military establishment. Hemingway arrived saddle-sore in Constantinople to find the Greco-Turkish war essentially over. All that remained was the huff and puff between the British, who refused to give up their control of the Dardanelles, and Kemal, who refused to let Constantinople remain under British control.[10]

There were plenty of stories to write, of course, but no front-line action. Reporters were confined to the Pera section of town and given regular briefings by the British. A censor kept the single telegraph office under erratic control; one could not predict what news might or might not get through. Hemingway did his best, filed his features in the mail and sent eight expensive cables to Bone via Frank Mason in Paris without bothering to write two versions. Bone later paid for the cables when Hemingway filed his expenses; Mason may have paid for them as well. On October 1, Bone wired Hemingway to send his cables via a London address. On the same day Mason wired Hemingway: TRANSMISSION ON SIXTEEN HOURS STUFF ALL NEW HERE STOP CASE URGENT FLASHES DUPLICATE MESSAGE INTERVIEWS LONDON. Did he mean that in case of urgent flashes he would duplicate messages and interviews to the *Star*'s London address? Apparently that was what was happening. In less than a week John Bone, wise to Hemingway's duplicity, wired him: SPOT NEWS CABLES DUPLICATING SERVICES WANT SPECIAL INTERVIEWS COLD. Hemingway may have started sending two versions of his cables, but a month later one of his last news stories appeared in the *Star* under his by-line and in the *Washington Times* under the name John Hadley. Since this was the wire service name he continued to use at the Lausanne Conference a month later, it would appear that Hemingway also sold at least one of his feature stories twice: once to the *Star* and once again through Mason in Paris.[11]

When Hemingway submitted his final expenses to Toronto, he tried to explain the duplications to John Bone. Stranded twelve hours away from the telegraph office at Pera with a "great story," Hemingway said that he sent the story back to Constantinople by an Italian colonel who wired it "Receiver to Pay" to Frank Mason in Paris. Hemingway said he included instructions to forward the wire to Bone's man in London. "Mason's office relayed it promptly but proceeded to steal and re-write as much of it as they could get away with. I . . . placed more confidence in Mason's honesty than it deserved. At any rate I have had it out with Mason. It was a personal matter and a question of ethics . . . I was disgusted with the matter." It seems unlikely Bone would believe Hemingway's weak explanation, for all eight cables from Hemingway filtered through Mason on to the I.N.S. wire service. Even though that service did not play Toronto, John Bone read the better American papers regularly. He could not have missed John Hadley's stories that read like Hemingway's.[12]

From his hotel on the heights of Pera, Hemingway looked out on the Turkish cemetery and down the hill to Galata and the Golden Horn that reminded him more of the Chicago river than anything golden.

> I . . . looked down at the harbor, forested with masts and grimy with smoky funnels and across at the dust-colored hills on the other side [Stambol] where the Turkish town sprawled in square

mud-colored houses, ramshackle tenements with the dirty-white fingers of the minarets rising like gray-white, slim lighthouses out of the muddled houses.

Within a few blocks stood all the European embassies, the Eastern Telegraph office, Café Luxembourg and McGill's bookstore carrying English papers. From McGill's he took the tunnel down the hill to the French post office and the central money exchange. With plenty of journalists swapping stories and a few decent bars, it would have been a good life if there had been any real news to report. For the most part Hemingway's information came from the British briefings and what he picked up at the bar. Kemal wanted all the Greeks out of Thrace; the British wanted to keep their control of the Dardanelles; France wanted access to Mesopotamian oil; and the Greeks wanted to go home. Two days after Hemingway arrived in town, peace talks began in Mundania, from which American and British newsmen were barred.[13]

On Saturday, October 3, Hemingway and the other journalists began hearing stories about the evacuation of 260,000 Smyrna refugees. Three days later, October 6, the *Tribune* said:

> From early morning until late at night, with searchlights from warships playing on the huddled crowd, American and British patrols shepherded the Greeks and Armenians aboard steamers. . . . Dr. Esther Lovejoy of the American Women's hospital was present three days handling maternity cases in the streets and docks. More than 100 such cases occurred during the three days. Many women are going aboard ships expecting babies momentarily.

Hemingway did not see the evacuation, but he either heard or read the detailed stories, remembering them five years later with great clarity. On October 4, Greeks and Turks reached an accord but not peace at Mundania, into which only the *Tribune*'s resourceful reporter, John Clayton, scraped and bribed his way. Ernest could not have cared less. Once again sick, he was rapidly losing interest in all of Asia Minor. By October 6, he was taking quinine from the British pharmacy for a fever which felt like malaria. For the next week he was unable to cover what news briefings were available. With little to report, Hemingway sent back rumors, fears and features on the squalid, beautiful city, where ankle-deep dust swirled underfoot and streets were filled with strange sights.

On October 13, his fever worse, Ernest went scared to the British hospital for treatment. Two days earlier the armistice was signed, giving the Greeks fifteen days to abandon eastern Thrace. On October 16, still running a fever, Hemingway left Pera for Anatolia for his only close encounter of the war – the exodus of Greek refugees. Years later in his fiction, Hemingway's Harry Walden remembers a wild, sex-drenched night before leaving for Anatolia – "a hot Armenian slut, that slung her belly against him so it almost scalded." The fight with Hadley makes us want to believe the fiction true, but after ten days of fever, night sweats and bug bites, Hemingway was probably in no shape for sexual adventures.[14]

Two nights of sleeping in lice-ridden beds in Anatolia left him infested and weary. With his head shaved against the vermin, Hemingway watched wet refugees herded from their homeland. As they struggled past him, he wrote down a long cable, in his own misery catching the misery of that crowded road.

> Chickens dangle by their feet from the carts. Calves nuzzle at the draught cattle whenever a jam halts the stream. An old man marches under a young pig, a scythe and a gun, with a chicken tied to his scythe. A husband spreads a blanket over a woman in labor in one of the carts to keep off the driving rain. She is the only person making a sound. Her little daughter looks at her in horror and begins to cry. And the procession keeps moving.[15]

A few months later he returned to this description in his fiction, freezing the moment of the woman giving birth and the horror on her daughter's face.

Hemingway grew up with an unusual awareness of woman's painful and bloody birthing process. Early, before he understood sex and death, he was marked by birth's pain and its accompanying screams. His mother, Grace, continued bearing children until she was forty-three and he was fifteen; at age eleven, Ernest was present when Grace bore his sister Carol at the summer cottage. His father specialized in obstetrics in his home office: all his early life Ernest lived in the presence of pregnant women who carried the secret and suffered the pain. That woman birthing on the Andrianople road brought it all back to him, the mystery and the pain. Nowhere in his later fiction would babies ease gently into this world. There would be a baby born dead, a Caesarean baby, an unwanted baby, an aborted baby.

Hemingway filed his refugee story and boarded the October 18 train back to Paris, arriving early on the morning of the 21st. Hadley, who had written him almost daily letters but still felt guilty over their angry parting, met at the Paris station a shadow of her husband. Head shaven, eyes fever burned, pants baggy from lost weight, he came bearing gifts from the East – amber and ivory, black coral and silver beads, attar of roses: peace offerings and early birthday gifts.[16]

II

Awaiting him in Paris was a London letter from Frazier Hunt, literary talent scout for the Hearst line of quality magazines. Written on September 21, the letter had arrived just after Hemingway's departure for the Middle East. Hunt said that "My Old Man" was a great story; he was sending it immediately to Ray Long, editor of *Cosmopolitan*, hoping he would buy it. Ernest, he said, should not be discouraged if the story were turned down. "You can write," Hunt said. "You have got lots of freshness and everything they want. . . . I will give you just one hunch. What they can't buy in the States at this time is enough nice love stories with youth and beauty and spring and all that stuff – and humor stories. . . . if you do some more stories and if you can just as easily do a bright and 'sweet' yarn as you can a tragic one, you will find your market will be 50% easier to make." Hunt's praise was welcome even if his suggestions were not. Ernest had tried that popular fiction formula in Chicago, producing the worst sort of sentimental drivel. Youth and beauty would have to muddle along without him somehow.[17]

From his sick bed above the *bal musette*, Ernest wrote to Greg Clark in Toronto, enclosing a copy of "My Old Man," the only story from that first Paris year he showed anyone. "Up in Michigan," begun in Chicago and finished in Paris, he kept out of sight after Gertrude told him it was unpublishable. His race track story, however, was the real thing, an Anderson story but better, less sentimental, tougher. After ten months in Paris, he had taught himself to write as well as Sherwood, but that was not enough and he knew it. Sherwood was last year. Now he wanted to write as well as Joyce. Still weak from his eastern fever, Hemingway caught up on his correspondence, a sure sign of recovery. Some of the letters he got out easily, but it took him a full week to compose the fiction of his expense account for John Bone. To make amends for his wire service duplicity, Hemingway jockeyed the expenses until they totaled 300 francs less than Bone's advance money. Ernest tactfully enclosed a check for the 300 francs, knowing that he could have kept the money as an advance on the salary Bone would eventually pay him for his five-week trip.[18]

Transatlantic mail in those days took two weeks minimum between sender and receiver, or up to five weeks for a cycle of question and response to be completed. Thus Hemingway's expense account, mailed October 27, crossed paths with a John Bone letter mailed from Toronto on November 2. Bone was responding to a Hemingway letter from October 8 in Constantinople, written two days after Bone's reprimand. Earlier Hemingway had suggested to Bone that he might return to Toronto to work on a salaried basis. Depressed, sick and worried in Constantinople, Hemingway had raised once more that possibility. Bone now wanted to know a definite date for the return. In mid-November, when Hemingway read Bone's reply, he and Hadley were forced to think seriously about their future.

Later Ernest would say that they returned when Hadley became pregnant, implying that her biology forced them back to better medical care than Paris offered. But Hadley did not know she was pregnant until February or early March of 1923; long before then, they had already made their decision to return. Bone's November 2 letter, asking for a fixed date, must have relieved Ernest's fears that after his unethical play in Asia Minor, the *Star* might not want him back. During his first days back in Paris, cuddling in bed, Ernest probably told Hadley he asked Bone about a regular Toronto job. On October 26, Hadley went to Sylvia's bookshop to renew her lending library card for a full year. Previously, they renewed in three-month increments. Given Hemingway's attention to small expenses, it would appear they had decided to spend one more year in Paris before they received Bone's query in mid-November. On November 24, Hemingway promised Bone that they would be back in Toronto in the fall of 1923.[19]

That gave him one more year to prove himself a writer of fiction. The next twelve months needed to be better: less journalism and more fiction. He had little to show for their first ten months: a few stories, some poems and the novel still unfinished, never to be finished. There were only two solid stories: "My Old Man" and "Up in Michigan." Add to that his *Double Dealer* poem and the six poems that *Poetry* magazine accepted: not much to say grace over, but a beginning. Sometimes he felt good about his writing, sure that he was getting better. Just as often moody depression made the pages seem futile. Hadley, who was beginning to catch the early warning signs of his moodiness, looked for ways to offset it, but nothing she could say about his writing seemed to help.

There was, however, plenty of promising news waiting for Hemingway when he returned from Constantinople. In July, Bill Bird, his newsman friend, had purchased an ancient Mathieu hand press which he installed at 29 Quai d'Anjou on the Ile Saint Louis, founding the Three Mountains Press, a serious hobby that would take up more of his time than he imagined. When Bird told Hemingway of his venture, Ernest suggested he might ask Pound about potential manuscripts for limited, hand-set editions. By August 1, Ezra agreed to be the general editor for "an inquest into the state of contemporary English prose," and immediately began lining up authors. First he invited Ford Madox Ford to pull together some of his old essays on male–female relationships. When Ford agreed, Pound gathered other writers: his friend William Carlos Williams, an old love B. M. G. Adams, B. C. Windeler, T. S. Eliot, Wyndham Lewis, and young Hemingway. Eliot and Lewis eventually backed out of the scheme, but Ernest was excited to be included in such company.[20]

While Hemingway was in Constantinople, Bird printed the prospectus for his series. Pound, not knowing what Ernest would submit, was forced to put "Blank" after Hemingway's name, certain something publishable would develop. If Ernest returned from Thrace depressed, Pound's prospectus was a bracing antidote. As quickly as possible he mailed the advertisements to friends and relatives. Greg Clark, who got his flyer along with the typescript of "My Old Man," told Ernest, "Send a copy of that book of yours or you're a dead Dago." By early in December, Pound received two letters from Oak Park, both responding to the flyer. Dr. Hemingway wrote:

> I am the father of Ernest M. Hemingway and want to thank you for all you have done to encourage my son. I hereby subscribe for five (5) volumes of the new book "Blank" by Ernest M. H. and will remit upon notice.

Apparently without consulting her husband, Grace Hemingway also wrote to reserve five copies at two dollars each. Like fond parents buying up their child's raffle tickets, Clarence and Grace Hemingway tried to support their son in his precarious profession.[21]

Ernest's problem was how to fill in the "Blank" of the advertisement. Quickly, he wrote a gossipy letter to Harriet Monroe, telling her which literary star was where doing what to whom. But the real purpose of his letter was in the opening lines: "I have been wondering when you were going to use the poems, as the Three Mountains Press here, Ezra Pound editing, is bringing out a book of my stuff shortly and I want to use the poems you have if you will give me permission to republish them." It would, in fact, be another fifteen months before Bill Bird published Hemingway's contribution, the last of the series. It is worth noting, however, that in mid-November Hemingway did not know what his first book would include. Had he been pleased with the quality of his Paris-written short stories, he would not have considered padding the book with poems. If the unfinished novel had been any good, he could have given part of it to Bird. That he took neither of these options says something about the quality of his year's work.[22]

While Ernest was worrying about his Blank-book, Ezra was still trying to get T. S. Eliot out of Lloyd's Bank in London. During the previous spring, Pound began sending pleas to his literary friends and contacts to raise money to underwrite Eliot's literary career. He proposed that thirty patrons guarantee fifty dollars a year for as long as the writer were in financial need. He called the program Bel Esprit, stating firmly it was not charity, rather it "proposes simply to *release more energy for invention and design.*" William Carlos Williams subscribed for twenty-five dollars a year, suggesting Pound get himself crucified on Montmartre and use the proceeds to finance art. He offered to pass the hat among the Paris crowd himself, but added that he had no particular use for Eliot. When *The Waste Land* appeared a bit later, Williams must have regretted promising anything at all, for Eliot with a single poem turned the direction of modern poetry away from the post-Whitman line so dear to Williams.[23]

On November 1, Pound asked Hemingway to bring some St. Louis visitors around to his studio where he would make his Bel Esprit pitch. Moral scruples, he said, could not stand in the way. Hemingway was always slightly amused by Pound's fanatic venture; Tom Eliot, or Major Eliot as Ernest sometimes called him in reference to Pound's hero Major Douglas, seemed to be doing quite well in the bank. Pound's anxiety increased when, a few days later, he received an almost hysterical letter from Eliot's wife, Vivienne: Tom was coming apart once more; "Lady R" was out at "La Prieure" dancing naked with Katherine Mansfield who hated Eliot and poured poison in "Lady R's" ear. A few days later

Pound got a similar letter from Eliot, saying that Vivienne was coming apart. In the midst of the crisis, Eliot's *The Waste Land* appeared, November 4, in the first issue of *The Criterion*, edited by Eliot and underwritten by Lady Rothermere. When Hemingway read the poem, he wrote Pound: "I am glad to read Herr Elliot's [sic] adventure away from impeccability. If [unreadable] Herr Elliot would strangle his sick wife, buggar the brain specialist and rob the bank he might even write a better poem. The above is facetious."[24]

If his wife's problems were not sufficient to keep Eliot preoccupied, on November 16 the Liverpool *Post* made Pound's Bel Esprit an item for public gossip, saying, in part, that the plan arose when Eliot "suffered a severe nervous breakdown which necessitated a three months' leave of absence" from his work at Lloyd's Bank of London. The *Post*'s story came almost completely from Pound's circular, labeled "for private circulation only," which told of the breakdown and its result, *The Waste Land*. Eliot was furious. On December 12, the Liverpool paper printed "Mr. T. S. Eliot's Contradiction," which said: "nor have I received any sum from 'Bel Esprit,' nor have I left the bank. The 'Bel Esprit' scheme in the manifesto referred to by your correspondent is not in existence with my consent or approval." The *Post* apologized for the mistakes Eliot specified, which included everything but his breakdown, the most painful disclosure of the story which his honesty would not allow him to deny.[25]

On November 4, Ernest, his head still close-cropped from Anatolian lice, took Hadley to the Anglo-American Press Association's annual banquet at Hotel de Petrograd on rue de Caumartin. After much drinking and honoring of guests – the American ambassador and the Prefect of the Paris police – the audience was entertained until the early morning hours by an elaborate program of stars from leading Paris theaters. There were dancers, singers, comedians and knockabout artists: "The Ford Sisters and Lester Sheehan did their new shimmy number direct from Broadway, and Revel and Lili put on their burlesque Apache dance which they feature at Zelli's club in Montmartre." The entire program was pieced together by the tireless Harry Pilcer, who was both master of ceremonies and performer, dancing with his new partner, Winnie Richards. There were plenty of old hands in the audience who remembered his routines of years past with the feathery Gaby Delys.[26]

The following Thursday, November 9, was Hadley's thirty-first birthday. With the franc fallen to 15-to-1, its lowest point of the year, they could afford a fine restaurant meal. A good bottle of wine erased the year's low points and brightened the retrospective: Switzerland, Italy, Germany together; the bob-sledding, the walks, different people they'd met and another year before going back. Maybe not even then if Ernest connected with a major publisher, which was his goal all along. Maybe the Bird book would open a door. Anything could happen in another year. So they drank to another in Paris and to the up-coming Christmas vacation at Chamby. Chink, the hero of St. Bernard pass, would be there. Good old Chink.

On the other side of the Atlantic, Republican President Harding watched as the country elected a Democratic majority in the House while Republicans controlled the Senate. In spite of tax cuts to individuals, the economy lagged and federal expenditures ran 10 percent ahead of revenues. Interest rates and the stock market rose while export sales fell, for the high exchange rates were making it impossible to sell American products abroad. But that did not lessen the interest of Standard Oil in the up-coming conference at Lausanne. At stake were the oil reserves of what would become Saudi Arabia, Kuwait, Iraq, Iran – reserves far richer than anyone's dreams. America's heels might be dug into an isolationist trench, but Standard Oil was bigger than a nation's political posturing. In Paris, the Lausanne delegates began arriving, saying their mild, cautious words to reporters before training on to Switzerland. America sent its official observers; Standard Oil sent its unofficial participants. The Greco-Turkish war had cracked Asia Minor wide open, attracting the usual array of international opportunists. With U.S. Marines occupying Russia's Vladivostok and Mussolini now declared the dictator of Italy, the world market was too volatile for Standard Oil to stay home.

All of Hemingway's pressmates – Steffens, Bird, Guy Hickok – were packing their bags for Lausanne, but Ernest was not going with them. The expected wire from the *Star* did not come. Perhaps Bone was punishing him for his double-takes in Asia Minor. Then, almost the day before the conference opened, Frank Mason asked Hemingway to cover Lausanne wire service releases for I.N.S. and Charles Bertelli asked him to do the same for the Universal News Service, both Hearst organizations. The money was tempting. Hadley blinked. He told her she could come along, stay at the hotel, a first-rate hotel, shop a bit, run over to Chamby by train. It would be a paid vacation. But no *Star* double-crossing, she insisted. He was not going to Lausanne for the *Star* and would not be collecting any money from Bone other than whatever features he might sell exclusively to the *Star*. Hadley agreed and then came down with a terrible cold. Ernest delayed a day in Paris, missing the opening of the conference. When Hadley did not improve, he left without her. On November 21, armed with an advance of 250 Swiss francs and two press cards – Frank Mason's and Guglielmo Emmanuel's – he passed through customs once again at Vallorbe.[27]

III

Lausanne was another Genoa with closed-door meetings, secret suppers and bland news releases as the British and French tried again to manipulate the future. Ernest walked down the hill from his hotel to the conference site and up the hill to file his news bulletins. Up and down the hill, early morning to late at night, he sent enough news to collect his pay from the Hearst people. The conference was supposed to reach a fair and diplomatic settlement to the Greco-Turkish conflict, but it quickly became apparent that the "fair" part applied only to England and her Allies. The Turks were given small voice in the matter. By the second day, the Allies rejected all Turkish claims to the conquered territory in Thrace, agreed to give Bulgaria an outlet to the Aegean Sea and declared all further meetings secret. By November 24, a sub-committee was ready to recommend complete disarmament of Turkey. The Turks were furious.[28]

Hemingway, having underestimated both the work involved and the expenses, wired Mason that he needed more money to keep the wire service running. Hemingway knew that Mason's job depended on the wire service staying open: it was a holdup, but Hemingway was making only $60 a week plus $35 expenses, which was less than the *Star*'s standard $75 a week and all expenses covered. Ernest grumbled about the late and early hours, but sent out the regular bulletins under the name of John Hadley. On November 27, headlines announced: CONFERENCE AT LAUSANNE BREAKS DOWN. Lord Curzon's "Open Door" policy shut in his own face. England wanted the Dardanelles and all access to Mesopotamian oil open to England but not particularly open to anyone else. The Turks lost patience: they now controlled Thrace and did not need English gentlemen telling them how to run their country. Mason wired Hemingway that New York was pleased with his efforts; they had scooped other American papers on Curzon's policy statement.[29]

No matter how Lord Curzon tried to bribe Ismet Pasha, the Turks refused to accept British occupation of Constantinople and their control of the Black Sea. Although America was not officially involved with the conference, it was soon obvious her fingers were coming out of the pie sticky. Mason wired Hemingway to find out if there were a Standard Oil man at Lausanne, and if so, to interview him. Soon the world knew that "American interests" (read Standard Oil) wanted the oil lands and the Dardanelles as open to America as to Britain. There was plenty of Asia Minor for both countries to exploit. All agreed to disagree on almost every proposal, banding together only to deny Russia a full vote in the proceedings. England and her so-called Allies were proceeding as if the Great War had not happened, as if the world still turned on an English axis. In India a young man named Gandhi was making local headlines, and at home novelists began to write apologies for the demise of Britain's empire while Conservative financial policy put the nation out of work. At Lausanne, Lord Curzon, still secure in his sense of British supremacy, conducted diplomatic business as if nothing were changed.[30]

As talk broke down in Lausanne, the lights went out in Athens for other failed politicians:

GREEKS EXECUTE SIX OF OLD REGIME

Ex-Premier Gounaris and Chief Aides
Of Constantine Condemned And Shot
For Part In Asia Minor Defeat

[The six] . . . were condemned to death at dawn today and shot before noon. They died silently, refusing to answer when they were asked to express their last wishes.

Later the whole sickening story would come out: broken men huddled in the rain facing rifles they once commanded.[31]

Hemingway read the news stories hurriedly as he ate his late lunch. He remembered Gounaris from Genoa, tried to imagine that dark face against the wall. Going up and down the hill of Lausanne, carrying his cold with him like an old friend, Ernest thought about the firing squad, as interesting an idea as the guillotine: how men act in the face of death. Did they really die so silently in Greece? He did not have time to find out. Secrecy was lifted now from the conference sessions, which only made his job more difficult. No longer could he rely on British press briefings, and the sessions, spread out over the town, were conducted in French which he could barely understand.

Feeling sorry for himself, he took the time to answer Hadley's latest letter which told him her flu was worse; between taking castor oil and vomiting, she was in no condition to make the train trip to Switzerland. Surely he understood that. She simply could not face the tedious customs inspection at Vallorbe. He was, as always, just the man to tell one's medical problems, for his own condition and circumstances were invariably worse. Sure, she had a cold and must feel terrible, but his cold was really terrible – pain, headaches, coughing up green and black stuff out of his chest. Not only that, but Mason was paying him so little that he might give up the job any day. She could, with the joint passport he had mailed back to her, fly to Lausanne on the newly opened route. What he needed most was her warm body in bed with him. Keeping track, as he usually did, of her menstrual periods, he said:

> Anyhow both being laid out with colds we haven't lost so much time on the time of the month because you've probably been too sick. I do so hate for you to miss what is the most comfortable and jolly time for mums. Won't we sleep together though?

Hadley's "comfortable and jolly" time – apparently November 22–28 – was her supposedly infertile period at the beginning of her monthly cycle when they did not need to use a birth control device. During the rest of the month, she apparently was using either a diaphragm or a chemical contraceptive, something to make her feel less comfortable.[32]

Two days later, while Hemingway was writing an old Oak Park friend how wonderful the bob-sledding would be at Les Avants and complaining how lonesome he was without his wife, Hadley was packing up her ski clothes, various medicines and three folders of her husband's fiction for the trip to Lausanne. On December 2 at Gare de Lyon, while she was buying Evian water for the night trip, a thief stole the suitcase with the manuscripts. Hadley arrived in Lausanne the next morning in tears so intense she could not tell Ernest their cause. When finally the jerking subsided enough for her to say the words, he could not believe them. There was just enough time to get someone to cover his wire service duties and then board the train back to Paris.[33]

Part Two

1923

Chapter Six

STARTING OVER
WINTER, 1922–3

I

The Monday night train back to Lausanne was as empty as Hemingway's briefcase. He asked at the station lost and found, but nothing of his was recovered, no folders, nothing. That was it. Ask your wife up for a visit and she loses a year's work. That was it all right. He wanted to talk to a friend but Ezra was in Rapallo, Gertrude still in St. Rémy. Calmer now and relaxed on a bottle of wine, he knew the worst, and there was nothing more they could do to him. Trying to digest his bitterness, he reviewed the loss. The Chicago novel, the one set at the war, was not worth the grieving; untouched for months, it needed rewriting from the start. He'd known that since last summer. The lost poems were expendable, but not the stories and not the Paris sketches.[1]

The loss was great but not total. From the back of a drawer, he recovered "Up in Michigan," the story Gertrude judged unprintable but which he knew was right. Harriet Monroe had his six poems to appear in *Poetry*, and other poems were out in the mail. Both Lincoln Steffens and Greg Clark had copies of "My Old Man." But the long fishing story, the one that he thought might be a novel, was gone. Last spring, while fishing the Alpenstock, he remembered the streams and lake in Michigan, saw himself again on the Black and the Sturgeon with water cold against his thighs and a trout heavy on his line. That started the story going in his head, the young man Nick fishing on his river. But even that story was not completely lost. In June, he had sent the first chapter to Greg Clark in Toronto, and it would be there in the fall when Ernest returned to the *Star*. The loss could have been much worse. As the winter night country went darkly past the window of his dining car, Hemingway took out his notebook to begin again.[2]

"They all made peace," he wrote. "What is peace?" Detached, terse, ironic, letting the words flow, he vented some of his frustration and anger on the Lausanne diplomats: Mustapha Kemal, Chicherin and Lord Curzon, all of whom, they said, liked young boys; on the American ambassador's wife with her flat breasts; on Mussolini's "nigger eyes."

> We all drink cocktails. Is it too early to have a cocktail? How about a drink George? Come on and we'll have a cocktail Admiral. Just time before lunch. Well what if we do? Not too dry.

Nothing led to nothing, business as usual: the war, the lovely muddy deadly dull war was over and now they were losing the future in sub-committee meetings. Who could take politicians seriously again? A few more days of wire service duty and then he could junk it. Mid-month, when Chink arrived, the bob-sled run above Chamby would be hard as iron. They'd get roaring drunk and make jokes about his losses. Sure they would.[3]

Early the next morning, Hadley met him at the Lausanne station, her face frozen in vague fear, eyes still swollen, blotched. He smiled to her down the platform, not letting his hurt show through. (Never let anyone know how deep the hurt.) It was different between them now. He saw it in her face. Whatever else happened between them, he would always have this edge. As they hugged and he kissed away her tears, perhaps Hadley knew it as well.

Two days later, Lincoln Steffens and Bill Bird joined Guy Hickok back in Paris, where, at Hemingway's request, they poked through three days' worth of travelers' debris at Gare de Lyon, but no Hemingway valise. Steffens wrote Hemingway:

> Billy Bord [Bird] . . . suggested advertising, but he said that would cost a couple of hundred francs and would get us no where unless we offered a big reward. We didn't feel that you would spend so much and your letter to Billy Bord, received today, shows that you think only of 150 francs reward. No use, I think and Billy said so. He would have to get somebody that wrote French well

to do the free ad you asked for. More expense.

I'm afraid the stuff is lost. Hem. Guy has still to hear from his letter of enquiry . . . you would better wire instructions: whether you wish to spend what it would evidently cost to induce the thief to take a chance and bring back what you want and he doesn't.[4]

When rewards of hundreds and sometimes thousands of dollars appeared regularly in the English and French papers, 150 francs would get no one's attention. That Hemingway was unwilling to offer more than ten dollars' reward says something about the value he placed on the lost manuscripts. The money was less than one day's wages. Later that month he spent more than 150 francs for a month's ski pass on the railway up to Les Avants. Years afterwards Hemingway would turn the stolen manuscripts into a tragedy whose pain was almost unbearable, but a few days after their loss, he valued them at no more than he paid for eighteen days' rent in Paris. If an ad ever ran in a French Paris paper, no one has yet found it.

Steffens' letter arrived on December 10; the next day Ernest and Hadley took a day off at Mason's expense and went to Chamby. Hadley wrote to Grace Hemingway:

Yesterday, Monday, Ernie and I put on all our adored outing togs and . . . had three long runs on our old bob Theodore, or rather two, then a lovely . . . tea at our own Chalet, seeing the Gangwisches our hosts of last winter then rushed for the train up to Les Avants again and "bobbed" down a last time thru the most glorious rosy sunset in the midst of all those snow-covered mountains swooping down toward the lake.[5]

Of course, Hadley was not about to tell her mother-in-law about losing Ernest's manuscripts, nor would she have let Grace know about any difficulties in the marriage.

After he returned to Lausanne there was little time for self-pity. Although the conference was marking time while the major powers met in emergency session in London, Hemingway still had his morning, noon and night wires to file. The British briefings always had something for the papers. Keeping his anger concealed from Hadley, he took it out on Frank Mason's organization. The day he returned to Lausanne, Ernest sent off a testy letter to Mason's secretary, saying he had been shorted $3.33 in his last pay check and expected to see the sum added to his next check. In his most bitching voice he asked if dividing the week into sixths meant that I.N.S. did not pay for his Sunday work. He did not say he was in Paris the previous Sunday and Monday.[6]

As mid-month and the end of his tour with I.N.S. approached, Hemingway faced more expenses than anticipated. Hotel Beau Séjour, where the journalists stayed, was more expensive lodging than the Hemingways were accustomed to. At twenty-five Swiss francs a day for double pension, their checkout bill approached sixty dollars American – enough money to pay more than three months' rent in Paris. Then there were the nights he took Hadley dancing, trying hard to make her forget the manuscripts. Added to those basic expenses were the meager Christmas presents Hadley sent to Oak Park with small checks for his siblings. Simple addition told Ernest he did not have enough money to cover their extended stay in Switzerland. He could not cash a Guaranty Trust check in Lausanne because the local bank had not yet received confirmation of his signature from Paris.[7]

A little edgy and secretly nerve raw, Ernest sent Frank Mason a long, expensive wire asking him to rush 800 Swiss francs ($150) and Ernest would mail a signed, blank check written on the Guaranty Trust. He would also send in his final set of expenses, including telegraph receipts which he called "unrequired," reminding Mason of some earlier agreement. It was important, he told him, that the money arrive before banks closed on Saturday, December 16. Either Mason misunderstood the request or willfully misread it. On Thursday he wired Ernest:

ERNEST OUR BOOKS SHOW APPROXIMATE 500 SWISS FRANCS WILL BE DUE YOU SATURDAY BUT MUST HAVE YOUR RECEIPTS FOR CONTINENTAL TELEGRAMS AND ACCOUNTING FOR 250 ORIGINALLY ADVANCED YOU BEFORE CAN MAKE FINAL SETTLEMENT. SEND EXPRESS MAIL AND SAY IF WORKED SAT AND SUN NTS.

Furious, Ernest flashed back his now famous wire:

SUGGEST YOU UPSTICK BOOKS ASSWARDS   HEM-INGWAY

In his letter to Mason written the next day, Ernest tried to explain his anger at what he took to be Mason's lack of trust. At fifty dollars a week he claimed to have lost fifteen dollars on the Lausanne assignment which he took only as a favor to Mason. Actually Mason was paying him, by this time, ninety dollars a week and another thirty-five in expenses; Ernest never worked as a favor for anyone. He was not broke, and there were plenty of people who would have loaned him money in a pinch. Frank Mason must have been puzzled by Hemingway's disproportionate response.[8]

That Saturday Ernest shut down his I.N.S. operation, checked out of the Beau Séjour and with Hadley met Chink at the Lausanne station for the short trip down the lake and up to Chamby. In his late-life memoir of that Christmas visit, Dorman-Smith confused one winter with another, mixing his three trips to Chamby. He dates the manuscript loss, which "almost broke Hem's heart," a year late. Yet he remembers quite clearly Hemingway's high spirits that Christmas.

> We . . . stayed for Christmas [meal] at the Hotel in Les Avants. The hotel gave a concert party at which Hem agreed to perform. He sang a bawdy song in some sort of German about a particularly unfortunate family with unlimited domestic troubles. This was ill-received by a stodgy Anglo-American audience. When the curtain fell and there was no applause except from Hadley and myself, Hem reappeared before the curtain to say "I seem to have displeased the more respectable members of the audience." Thereafter we patronised the less hostile Bains d'Alliez and the Montreux beer-hall. Nevertheless it was a good song.

Christmas night at Les Avants so long ago: see Ernest among the proper Englishmen, stroking his new mustache while reeling off his song: remember, as Chink did, how happy he seemed that Christmas after losing his manuscripts. Now that all participants are under the earth, we have only these fragments to tell us how things were. No doubt Hemingway was deeply hurt by his loss, but he was young, resilient and his life went on.[9]

Ernest, Chink and Hadley were a comedy act, playing off of each other's lines as they roistered and drank the old year out. Each day they rode the electric railway winding up through the woods of Chenaux past fields where May narcissus once bloomed and on to Les Avants, there switching to a cable railway to the ski and bob-sled runs on the Col de Sonloup. Chink stayed long enough to be a member of their team riding the bob "Eclaire" to victory in the Prix de Molard. (Around the lip of the silver fluted cup are engraved the names: Horton O'Niel, Eric E. Dorman-Smith, George Blackman O'Niel, Ernest Hemingway. The O'Neil boys, sons of the St. Louis lumberman and sometime poet Dave O'Neil, probably did not mind their names misspelled, but Hadley may have objected when the paper said that Hadley "Hermingway" and the two Barbara "O'Niels," mother and daughter, ran second in the women's race.)[10]

It was a cold, clear Christmas, with powder snow over a deep base, plenty of wood for the evening fire and hot rums all round. Plenty of laughter, plenty of good friends close together. That first and last Christmas at Chamby was as good as the lake in summer, as good as the summer people, almost as good as fishing. No sooner had Chink departed to return to post than Isabel Simmons, the Oak Park girl down the block, arrived for another two weeks of good times. Almost immediately she and Hadley, meeting for the first time, were two girls together with a man both courteous and bawdy, another triad, one of the several that formed, performed and dissolved so quickly in those Paris years. On the day Izzy arrived, the *Tribune* reported from Constantinople:

There was joy in the Sultan's abandoned harem here today. It was payday. The eleven sultanas, queens of the old sultan who had to flee on a British warship to Malta, drew their checks ranging from sixty-five to ninety dollars a month from the nationalist government.

The next day, Izzy, Hadley, young Barbara O'Neil and the lovely Janet Phelan began calling themselves Hemingway's harem. New nicknames sprang up: Izzy became Fatima and Ernest was called the Moslem. He loved it. As a boy growing up with a houseful of sisters, he was once accustomed to their worship and always fond of rooms filled with women. (On January 2, when Izzy arrived, his older sister Marcelline married in Oak Park: one Oak Park girl replaced another.) During courtship, Hadley pointedly enquired if there would always be several women in his life. It was a rhetorical question, for she understood, or thought she did, his need for female presence. That Christmas at Chamby when they were all together by the fire sipping drinks, she had her man, sharing him in high humor.[11]

Years later, when paranoia and depression became his more frequent visitors, Hemingway blurred the joy and deepened the pain of that Christmas when Hadley lost his manuscripts. What old men remember is not what young men taste and touch. Memory is its own country outside of time where old men remake their lives unencumbered with remembering right. Certainly the lost stories hurt, but he was only twenty-three. There were lots of stories left to tell, and there at Chamby he began to work on them.

When Izzy departed on January 16, Hemingway left Hadley alone for at least two days while he went to Paris for reasons not completely clear. On January 23, he wrote Pound that he went "to see what was left and found that Hadley made the job complete." This sounds as if it were his first trip to check on his losses, but all other evidence suggests he checked first on December 3. As he constantly rearranged his life to fit his immediate needs, he may not have wanted to explain to Ezra why he waited seven weeks to speak of his loss. He goes on to tell Pound, "You, naturally, would say, 'Good' etc. But don't say it to me. I ain't yet reached that mood. 3 years on the damn stuff. Some like that Paris 1922 I fancied. Am now working on new stuff." Ezra called it "an act of Gawd," telling Ernest that "no one is *known* to have lost anything by *suppression* of early work." If the structure was sound, the stories would recreate themselves; if not, then well lost.[12]

The "new stuff" was not all exactly new. Evidence shows Hemingway trying to recreate his lost "Paris 1922" manuscript – his six true sentences written the previous summer. He wrote them as best he could remember: the horse falling at Auteuil; Peggy Joyce and her Latin lover; police May Day violence; tired Prufrockian men bussing home in winter rain; the prostitute under the clergyman's umbrella; Senegalese soldiers teasing a cobra in the Jardin des Plantes. They were five-finger exercises, beginning "I have seen," "I have watched," "I have stood": passive observations, a reporter's point of view. Getting them right did not matter so much as the writing of them. When he left them in Paris these sentences had been proof of his sharpened skills. Even if he never used them, he was compelled to get them once more on paper. Like a kid after falling off his bike, he got back on immediately to prove to himself he could do it.[13]

The first attempt fell on its face:

On the first of May at the Porte Maillot in the evening the crowd
were trying to get back into the city through the gate.
     The Police
xxxxxxxxxx / charged the crowd and I saw xxxx from the top of

nineteen
a taxi-cab the scared, white, proud face of the xxxx / year old boy

who [had just shot two policemen] looked like a prep school quarter-back and had just shot two policemen.

Hemingway, as we know, spent May Day sick in bed, nowhere close to the shooting. The news accounts put the incident at the Saint Ouen gate, not Maillot; the killer's age was twenty-five, not nineteen. These differences may indicate that Hemingway was working from half-remembered material.

On the second try, the sentence smoothed out.

I have watched the police charge the crowd with swords as they milled back into Paris through the Porte Maillot on the first of
white beaten up
May and seen the frightened proud look on the / face of the sixteen year old kid who looked like a prep school quarter back and had just shot two policemen.

His changes tell us what he learned that year in and out of Paris. "Trying to get back into the city through the gate" becomes "milled back into Paris through the Porte Maillot." Two vague nouns become specific and the verb change produces more action. The killer became young enough to have been a prep school quarterback. In moving the "I" narrator to the front, he set the pattern for the remaining five sentences, but how unnecessary and intrusive that passive "I," the same self-referential touch he used so often in his feature journalism. It was not yet enough for the event to take place; he had to be part of the scene, inactive but observing. The result splits the reader's experience: part of him observes the event and part observes the narrator observing the event.

The remaining "true sentences" were similarly split in focus, but their precise images show us a young writer who has profited from Pound's edicts: "An Image is that which presents an intellectual and emotional complex in an instant of time . . . use absolutely no word that does not contribute to the presentation." So Hemingway gave us the "beefy red-faced Episcopal clergyman holding an umbrella" over "the one legged street walker who works the Boulevard Madeleine." No judgements, no moral tone, let the reader judge if he wants.[14]

Some of the scenes were first-hand experience – the Auteuil track, the back of the Battignolles bus – and some were not. The two sentences based on real events acquired second hand – the Porte Maillot shooting and the Peggy Joyce scene – were just as convincing as the others.

> I have seen Peggy Joyce at 2 a.m. in a *dancing* in the Rue Caumartin quarreling with the shellacked haired young Chilean who had long pointed finger nails, danced like Rudolph Valentino and shot himself at 3:30 that same morning.

As we saw earlier, Peggy and her lover did not quit dancing until four in the morning and the shot came two hours later. Hemingway may not have remembered it right, but his training in journalism taught him that precise facts make for a convincing story: 3:30 a.m. is just as convincing as 6:00 a.m.

Too much journalism could ruin a writer, he said, repeating Stein's advice. But the effects of reportage on Hemingway's style were both positive and negative. The newspaper game taught him the necessity for exact and believable facts, a lesson reinforced by Pound. It taught him to avoid passive voice, long sentences and polysyllabic words. But it also taught him the reporter's passive role of being witness to the event without participating in it. This point of view produces the unemotional news stories we are accustomed to reading. In Hemingway's early fiction, the reporter's stance produced oddly passive characters to whom things happened but who seldom took action on their own.

II

The first weeks of 1923 were filled with contradictory signs, mixed indicators pointing toward a strange new year. Until mid-January, Izzy, Hadley and Ernest skied with the O'Neil troupe, laughing and joking through cold clear days into starry nights. Early mornings as Ernest worked on his Paris sentences something new appeared: a terse form without a name that extended the emotionally detached sentence into paragraph length. The first jerky, broken off attempt he called "Romance":

> In the moonlight the long alley of trees in the
> Luxembourg gardens were sharp and black. The boy
> and girl stood against the iron fence looking
> hungrily in at the shadows.

Something was beginning, he wasn't sure what and it did not matter what: he was writing and it was going somewhere. The lost manuscripts were not a permanent wound, and the source of his writing, which he always feared to analyze, was not poisoned.[15]

Izzy's departure left Hadley lonely. When Ernest made a quick trip to Paris, she wrote Izzy, "It really is too hard not to have you any more. There isn't anyone around expressing things in a delightful and utterly congenial and feminine way. Even the Moslem when he returns will not be feminine, now can he? You are genuinely missed, Fatima." Perhaps her husband could not be feminine, but Ernest was most interested in female sensibilities. His first mature story, "Up in Michigan," took a young girl's point of view, and Molly Bloom's long, erotic soliloquy at the end of *Ulysses* was, for Ernest, the best part of Joyce's book, the part he came back to time and again in his later fiction. Joyce made her up and she was wonderful. To write, a man must cultivate that feminine side of himself, become both male and female. Up in Michigan, flattened on the boat dock, the girl and her seducer were both himself; they both came out of his imagination and experience. His sisters left their imprint on his fertile memory that continually reimagined the past and helped create his fictions. And always women's hair stimulated his erotic imagination: all those sisters drying hair in the summer sun; the long, flowing, pre-Raphaelite hair of his mother or Gertrude Stein; the short, mannishly-styled female hair so ambiguous in the Twenties. At Chamby, Ernest began letting his hair grow to reach the bobbed length of Hadley's so they could be the same person: man and woman blending to oneness in sexual union, one whole person at last: Plato's egg reunited.[16]

Just how difficult it was to maintain their shared oneness was about to become apparent to the Hemingways. Within Hadley's womb, cells were subdividing into an embryo neither planned nor yet suspected. In another week she would miss her first period without realizing her condition: the daily physical strain of skiing might have kept back her monthly flow. Besides she and Ernest took precautions during her fertile period. A week later in a letter to Pound, Hemingway joked that the "high altitude has made me practically sexless. . . . it has checked the activity of the glands."[17]

Christmas mail arriving late via Paris brought him the January issue of *Poetry* with his six "Wanderings" poems, and a check for $18, his first payment for creative writing. Also arriving from Paris came his mother's Christmas present: *Literature in the Making*, a collection of interviews with popular writers, edited by Joyce Kilmer. In her duty thank-you letter to Grace Hemingway, Hadley assured her mother-in-law that Ernest was enjoying the book: 'I see his nose in it often." Filled with names long since forgotten, this collection nonetheless gave young Hemingway sound advice and confirmed some of his newly formed ideas about writing. Robert Chambers, for example, told him that all fiction was invention but the base of its "construction must rest on real life." Self-conscious imitations of established writers, Chambers said, would spoil a young writer, keeping him from finding his own style. As soon as Hemingway published "My Old Man" he would find himself regretting his Andersonian story; having mastered the style of a master, he found it unusable.[18]

The advice Hemingway found in *Literature in the Making* was, at points, ironically amusing. Arthur Gutterman's sixteen "don'ts" for poets included: "Don't have your book published at your own expense." On his bedside table lay his review copy of Gertrude Stein's *Geography and Plays*, another of her vanity press publications. Next to it was Hadley's reading, the second volume of George Moore's *Héloïse and Abélard*, a medieval romance that she called "a book to set you dreaming. Love is so lovely when it's like that." Those two historic Paris lovers, crossed by fate, time and place, gladly suffer all in the name of love, burning incandescent in a world well lost.[19]

Toward the end of January, Hemingway began looking for a different location to finish the winter out of Paris. With Chink and Izzy gone and only the O'Neils left for fun, he was feeling restless. In his letters to Pound, he enquired about the cost of living in Rapallo, for he claimed to have enough money for six or eight months of steady creative work. He was working on some new stuff, he said without elaboration. Pound urged him to come on down to Italy where in a pension hotel a couple could get by on 500 lire a week, or $25 at the exchange rate. If one did not tease the fascists, the climate was fine; Mike Strater was there painting and eager to go a few rounds for exercise. Nancy Cunard, traveling about Italy, was not yet in Rapallo, where Ezra would be for another fortnight, his wife Dorothy probably longer. Hemingway's immediate reply queried the "fortnight": was Ezra going to be in Rapallo at the end of February when the Hemingways planned to come down? Or "are you, as it appears, going to Calabria with Nancy [Cunard]. Drop this unbecoming delicacy . . . are you going somewhere else where we would be unobjectionable? Or are you running down the road? The conventional spring running down the road? I aims to cramp no mans stride on the Road."[20]

Hemingway could never resist kidding Pound, who himself asked when Eliot died, "Who's left now to share a joke with?" In his January *Dial* "Paris Letter," Ezra, complaining about the paucity of new fiction, said, "I am a little tired of heroes and heroines who work off their Freudian complexes by running down roads." Knowing Ezra as he did, Ernest suspected that the red fox was leaving his wife Dorothy in Rapallo to pursue some horizontal pleasures with Nancy Cunard, that gaunt, pale, lovely inspiration of more than one writer in the Twenties. Pound was, in Oak Park terms, a womanizer; in Paris terms, a poet who appreciated beauty. Dorothy Pound, behind her mask of British decorum, knew of her own mother's lover, William Butler Yeats, tolerated by her father, and she may have expected artists to have several sexual attachments while having one wife. If she did, her expectations were more than met by her husband's philandering. One idea that Hemingway heard from Pound was the connection between sex and writing. Creative genius needed bathing in the seminal fluid; Pound claimed it was necessary to be sexually excited by more than one woman at a time for creative genius to flower. Hemingway, who was half in love with Dorothy Pound as with any other attractive woman within his radius, was sympathetic with Ezra's idea of creative stimulation rising from the crotch to the brain. Pound, however, was a dangerous model to take too seriously if one did not have a wife as tolerant as Dorothy Pound.[21]

On January 29, Hemingway asked Ezra how their meeting in Rapallo or elsewhere in Italy might be coordinated at the end of February. Pound's reply accelerated Hemingway's plans by almost a month; in a fragment Hemingway remembered "a letter from Ezra saying we must come at once, with all the words underlined and half the letters in capitals, because he HAD TO LEAVE ON A CERTAIN DATE" to pursue the dusty past of Sigismundo Malatesta across the Romagna. A year later, Hemingway said, "We started within twelve hours after the letter came as a tribute to Ezra's prose style." It would appear the Hemingways packed quickly and left Chamby by February 7, taking the Simplon–Orient Express to Milan where they spent the night after dining at Campari's, which, Ernest said, was "by far the best restaurant in Europe."[22]

The next morning they boarded a train that carried them past flat, fallow corn fields and leafless vineyards toward Genoa. "The country was dead and brown and very dull and damp." After a station lunch, they took the milkstop *locale* down the coast toward Rapallo, passing through tunnels and into light with quick glimpses of walled gardens where oranges hung on damp trees and further out, if one could focus quickly enough, the blue-grey sea. After several stops, the train pulled into the Rapallo station, pausing barely long enough for Ernest to get their bags out of the carriage. They walked the tunnel beneath the tracks and the white station, coming out at a stand of horse-drawn open cabs and motor taxis. Grey skies and mist hiding the hills above, below them the town of red tiles on mansard roofs looked more French than Italian: it was a steep but short walk down to the row of hotels on the cupped, narrow beach at the heart of Rapallo. Hidden in an amphitheater of hills coming down to the water, the old fishing village was now winter quarters for the carriage trade. There on the beach road, behind tall palm trees dripping in the afternoon light, they found the Hotel Riviera Splendide, dirty white with green wooden shutters and bell-skirted iron work on its small balconies. From their upper story room the Hemingways looked down on the promenade anchored at the far end by a statue of Columbus and directly below them by the war memorial. Less than a year old, the bronze angel held its sword-hand high, bearing an olive wreath of peace. At the angel's feet, fallen bronze soldiers lay strewn. Atop a fifteen-foot-high block of white marble, the bronze memorial loomed over strolling tourists who came there especially to stand in respectful silence beneath the sword and wreath. A generation later God's militant angel of peace would be melted down for fascist cannon.[23]

For all its charm, Rapallo left Ernest uneasy and empty. "The sea," he said, "is weak and dull here and doesn't look as though there was much salt in the water. The tide rises and falls about an inch. When the surf breaks it sounds like someone pouring a bucket of ashes over the side of a scow. The place ain't much." After two months of brisk, sharp air, clear nights and powder snow, Rapallo's humid warmth took some adjustment. When the breeze died, as it did for almost a week of his stay there, the air turned slightly fetid with the ghosts of departed fish. Morning mist shrouding the surrounding hills did not burn off until mid-day, revealing the 2000-foot hills covered with cedars and pines. Sometimes when an afternoon storm cleared the air, thunder came in flat claps echoing off the hills to die on the water.[24]

Mornings at seven, bells from two churches woke anyone still sleeping while swallows twittered shrilly, feeding in the early light. On the concrete bridge across the wide canal, old men with wormed hooks and bobbers dangling from delicate poles fished for eels on the changing tide. Off the piazzas, black-skirted women swept the walks with twig brooms; shutters banged open; vendors filled their open-air market bins with local vegetables and fish wrapped in wet seaweed. From brown and ochre plastered walls, faded by the sea air, hung quaint signs of trade, and every street had its merchant of lace, Rapallo's gift to visitors. If Ernest was bored by Rapallo, it was not for its lack of charm or its food: basil green, garlicky pesto sauce clinging to linguini or stuffed into pasta bathed in a sweet walnut sauce.

Forty years later, Hadley remembered the village quite fondly.

> Rapallo was beautiful, and Mike and Maggie Strater and their baby were there. Nice hotel with a tennis court. Mike and Ernest and I played a lot of tennis and were very congenial . . . . Ezra and Dorothy Pound had a small apartment . . . We went there often, and had tea (of course).[25]

The illustrated tourist guide to Rapallo failed to recommend the Riviera Splendide surrounded as it was by several more elegant hotels. In a story fragment using the hotel as its setting, Hemingway said that the morning rolls and coffee were good but jam cost extra. That Hadley remembered the village as beautiful while Ernest cared for it little at the time says more about the difference between their states of mind than it does about Rapallo itself.[26] When the rain lifted, Ernest was actually quite content and busy in the village, where a ten-minute walk in any direction took him to its limits. Mike Strater, an American painter, managed to get Ernest to sit for two portraits in morning light. Afternoons put the Straters and Hemingways on the tennis court, and evenings they lingered over restaurant meals and brocche filled with wine.

It was Hemingway's luck that, there in Rapallo, Pound introduced him to Edward O'Brien, a visiting Englishman who anthologized the "best" short stories published each year. O'Brien was staying higher up in the mountains at the Albergo Montallegro, close by the monastery and church of the same name. Hemingway went up the mountain to spend an evening with O'Brien, drinking and talking about the need for heroes in an unheroic time. Hemingway argued that simple, courageous men working steadily in dangerous occupations gave one a feeling of admiration, men like those who hunted seals or fished the dangerous northern banks in small boats. Their talk might have been triggered by a visit to the white marble church famed for its miraculous spring whose water insured sea voyages and safe military service. The church interior, rich in gold candlesticks and gilt edging, cast reflected light on silver hearts and military epaulets left by grateful returnees, men who survived shipwreck and battlefield. Such a church, where prayer seemed valid, would have been an appropriate sanctuary for Ernest, a survivor of war wounds, to visit.[27]

When O'Brien asked to see his work, Ernest explained his recent loss, showing O'Brien the surviving copy of "My Old Man." The anthologizer was so impressed with the story that he offered to recommend it to his friend Arthur Vance, editor of *Pictorial Review*, advising Hemingway to submit the story separately. O'Brien's approval could not have come at a better time for Hemingway; combined with his newly published poems, the O'Brien response helped offset the loss of his manuscripts. After the O'Brien encounter, Hemingway began once more to write steadily, working on terse paragraphs and at least one free-association piece showing what he had learned from Gertrude.

On February 18 he wrote Gertrude about "two new things" he'd written. He had thought about the advice she gave him, and was "starting that way at the beginning." Stein's advice was to let things flow, let the words leap on to the paper without passing through any rational censor: free association and automatic writing. Her manuscripts from 1922–23 support her claim that she never revised. As she reportedly told William Carlos Williams in 1924,

> You would not find a painter destroying any of his sketches. A writer's writing is too much of the writer's being; his flesh child. No, no, I never destroy a sentence or a word of what I write. You may, but of course, writing is not your metier, Doctor.[28]

Hemingway's sketch, which he called "Rapallo," was as close as he could get to automatic writing.

> Cats love in the garden. On the green tea table to be exact. The big cat gets on the small cat. Sweeney gets on Mrs. Porter. Ezra gets nowhere except artistically of course. Mike paints better but he stops before he spoils it. He spoils many but he has money. He can afford to spoil them but if he spoils too many it will not

make any difference after. Spoils are not spoiled. That is an old usage. Mike is good. He married Maggie.

Hadley and I are happy sometimes. Her friends call her Hadley. We are happiest in bed. In bed we are well fed. There are no problems in bed. Now I lay me down to sleep in bed. There are no prayers in bed. Beds only need be wide enough. If the beds wide enough we will be bride enough. Sheets are over rated but nice. The big linen ones are damp. Sleeping is good. I used to lie awake all night. That was before. This is after.

You cannot tell about the tide.[29]

Sweeny getting on Mrs. Porter came straight from Eliot's *The Waste Land*:

> But at my back from time to time I hear
> The sound of horns and motor cars, which shall bring
> Sweeney to Mrs. Porter in the spring.
> O the moon shone bright on Mrs. Porter
> And on her daughter
> They wash their feet in soda water.[30]

That year many who mattered to the Paris crowd were quoting Eliot. Less than a month later Nancy Cunard wrote Ezra: "If I stay a week there [Rome] . . . it brings Aunt This and Cousin That . . . a different kind of Sweeney to Mrs. Porter in the Spring."[31]

Cats in the garden. Mike marries Maggie. Hadley in bed. One thing leads to another in the lighthearted world of Stein songs. In Paris Gertrude was writing,

> Racket is a noise. Noise is a poise. Boys with the b spelled like
> a p is poise. Boys is poise.
> And then I read the men. Men say. Leave me and be gay. Men
> say tenderness today. Men say go away.

Hemingway picked up the technique and rhythms from her to try in his own voice, an experiment he continued off and on for the next three years. "We are happiest in bed. In bed we are well fed. There are no problems in bed." No problems he was yet aware of, but the problem was there, growing in Hadley's womb.[32]

III

The Hemingways were supposed to leave with the Pounds on a walking tour through the haunts of Sigismundo Malatesta, a medieval brigand upon whose records Pound based four of his *Cantos*. That was the plan, but somehow it changed in execution. Ezra and Dorothy Pound did leave Rapallo three days after the Hemingways arrived and did not return. Ezra spent the next month tracing Malatesta in the medieval manuscript collection in Rome's Vatican Library. At some point in February or early March, Hadley and Ernest joined the Pounds for at least three days on a trip that ended up at Orbetello, 200 miles south of Rapallo. Hadley remembers a walking trip through hill towns such as those between Siena and Orbetello. "This was a good trip," she said. "Ezra was at his best, knowing a lot about all the places. This was also a rucksack trip, and we always lunched from our sacks on some hillside – native cheese, figs, and wine." But she then remembered the trip including Sirmione, Siena and Pisa – towns so distantly separated it would have taken months to make such a journey by foot. Memory speaks, but needs much fine tuning.[33]

Ernest the tyro and Pound the tutor walked down to the three fingers of land where Orbetello connected sea-surrounded Monte Argentario with the mainland. All the way, Ezra provided Ernest with historic background, while Hemingway imagined how the battles were fought. In 1923, Ernest was probably amused to hear of Ezra's research in dusty libraries, but he had a lesson reinforced in spite of his amusement: even in fiction, historical facts must be right, terrain map-accurate. Five years later, when Ernest began *A Farewell to Arms*, he did so much background reading on the Great War in Italy that everyone was sure he had seen it all.[34]

In this archeological dig, sifting bone fragments from the dust, we must account for all that we find. To use only the bones that fit our preconception of Hemingway may reconstruct a man who looks more like ourselves than like the young writer who hiked into Orbetello. Hemingway was a contemplative man who called the books of others his ammunition and who said that after writing, he most enjoyed reading. It is easy to remember him at the river in Anatolia watching peasants struggle past, but it is more important to remember the solitary hours in rented rooms writing his fiction. Certainly there were Dôme days and Select nights, but there were quieter, more intense days and nights alone with his craft. Everyone remembers him well on the ski slopes of Switzerland, but none picture him reading the seventeen volumes of Turgenev that we know passed through his hands. All dwell on the war wounding's effect on his writing, but few are interested in the impact of Turgenev's *A Sportsman Sketches*, which he checked out three times from Sylvia's library.

To underestimate the young man from Oak Park is to be in mixed company. During those first years in Paris, many sold him short, took the boulevard shadow-boxer for the whole man. They did not understand how compulsively determined he was to master his craft or how quickly he learned from all around him. A few loose remarks across a Dôme table could return in print to haunt a short-seller of Hemingway. The best parts, he insisted, were imagined on the basis of experience. But the experience could be anyone's, for in those early days his mind caught and held the voices almost as accurately as a tape recording. It was an ear attuned to gossip; he once said he was a safe man to tell a secret: it went in one ear and out his mouth. That February in Rapallo he met a gossip virtuoso who gave him a few good lines.

"Rats," said McAlmon. He said it twice, "Rats! Rats!" That's how Joyce remembered the man who typed Molly Bloom's soliloquy for him. Robert McAlmon arrived in Rapallo looking like the experienced traveler he was. One small suitcase was large enough for a change of clothes, a bottle of whiskey and a sheaf of manuscript. Few could leave on a moment's notice like McAlmon: here for supper, gone before breakfast, the itinerant preacher's son was always moving on. There in Rapallo, Robert McAlmon became another part of Hemingway's luck, for he had recently decided to become a Paris publisher, reviving the Contact Press to publish his own work and that of other likely writers. He came to Rapallo for the sea breeze and to talk to Ezra, but the red fox was holed up in the Vatican library, leaving McAlmon to make the chance acquaintance of Hemingway. Both men claimed Paris as their temporary home, but neither had spent enough time there in the previous year to make contact.

Short but lithe as an acrobat, McAlmon was a bitchy man who supported artists with his father-in-law's money and paid more bar tabs than most on the Left Bank. Later Hemingway would say that McAlmon had a mind like an ingrown toenail, but that March of 1923, Ernest said, "He wrote seven or nine new stories while at Rapallo. If I was in the tipster business I would whisper into the shell like ear of a friend, 'go and make a small bet on McAlmon while you can still get a good long price.'" Just how well McAlmon wrote can be judged by the way he caught Hemingway's physical presence with the short, deft, envious strokes of a caricaturist:

> At times he was deliberately hard-boiled, case-hardened and old; at other times he was the hurt, sensitive boy, deliberately young and naive, wanting to be brave, and somehow on the defensive, suspicions lurking in his peering analytic glances at the person with whom he was talking. He approached a café with a small-boy, tough-guy swagger, and before strangers of whom he was uncertain a potential snarl of scorn played on his large-lipped, rather loose mouth.

But that was eleven years later when their friendship had long since festered. Ernest had a way of burning friendships into ashes, intense three-to-five year bursts of correspondence with a friend who then disappears. McAlmon lasted less than three years, but considering his need to gossip about Hemingway, he lasted longer than one might expect.[35]

Tight, thin lips under a sharp nose and blue eyes, McAlmon was attractive to both men and women. Eventually Hemingway realized that even though Robert was married to an English heiress, he was a bisexual who delighted in experiencing whatever action was available on the decadent fringe. Ernest recognized that McAlmon was sexually ambiguous as soon as he read the stories Robert shared with him: stories about transvestite drag queens, male homosexuals and Berlin cocaine parties. But since McAlmon did not wear his sexuality like some gaudy costume, Hemingway did not draw back from this man with the sharp tongue.[36]

Scott Fitzgerald once said that Hemingway would "always give a helping hand to a man on a ledge a little higher up." Perhaps that is why he tolerated McAlmon's cynical and sometimes malicious tongue as long as he did, for Robert McAlmon was wonderfully connected with the literary scene: in New York he was part of the *Contact* and *Little Review* circle. Marsden Hartley, William Carlos Williams, Marianne Moore, Djuna Barnes and Hilda Doolittle all knew McAlmon. One of the *Broom* magazine crowd remembered him as being "wild and daring and hard as nails . . . a coldly intense young man with hard blue eyes." After marrying Winifred Ellerman, daughter of wealthy shipping magnate Sir John Ellerman, McAlmon found himself a husband in name only. Winifred, who now called herself Bryher, wanted a husband to escape from the protective clutches of her parents. The arrangement produced for McAlmon a generous cash flow from the Ellermans, money which kept him independent throughout the Twenties, paying not only his keep and others' bar bills but also supporting needy friends like James Joyce and publishing unknowns like himself.[37]

Hemingway, who harbored an Oak Parker's respect for money and achievement, was attracted to this fellow midwesterner who at twenty-six had already published a book of poetry and a collection of short stories which Joyce had titled *A Hasty Bunch* (1922). In his suitcase McAlmon carried a mostly finished autobiographical novel, *Post-Adolescence* (1923), and was working furiously on more short stories to be published as *A Companion Volume* (1923). During his brief stay in Rapallo, McAlmon was churning out new fiction at a startling rate, which was exactly the impetus Hemingway's competitive nature needed to prod him along. Before Ernest left Rapallo, the terse new form, which he now called "Unwritten Stories," was shaping up, and he finished another satirical poem – "The Lady Poets With Footnotes" – which he sent to Pound on March 10.[38]

One lady poet was a nymphomaniac and wrote for Vanity Fair.[1]
One lady poet's husband was killed in the war.[2]
One lady poet wanted her lover, but was afraid of having a baby.
When she finally got married, she found she couldn't have a baby.[3]
One lady poet slept with Bill Reedy got fatter and fatter and made half a million dollars writing bum plays.[4]
One lady poet never had enough to eat.[5]
One lady poet was big and fat and no fool.[6]

[1] College nymphomaniac. Favourite lyric poet of leading editorial writer N. Y. Tribune.
[2] It sold her stuff.
[3] Favourite of State University male virgins. Wonderful on unrequited love.
[4] Stomach's gone bad from liquor. Expects to do something really good soon.
[5] It showed in her work.
[6] She smoked cigars all right, but her stuff was no good.[39]

Hemingway's footnotes have been taken as a satire on Eliot's footnotes in *The Waste Land* and on Marianne Moore's footnotes in *Observations*. Neither supposition is correct. Neither the October *Criterion* nor the November 1922 *Dial* publication of *The Waste Land* had footnotes, and *Observations* was not published until 1924. The six lady poets were probably Edna St. Vincent Millay, Alice Kilmer, Sara Teasdale, Zoe Akins, Lola Ridge and Amy Lowell – none of whom Hemingway knew personally. In fact, the entire poem with its essentially bad taste came straight from the mouth of Robert McAlmon. Lola Ridge, editorial assistant on *Broom* magazine, and Edna St. Vincent Millay appeared as thinly veiled characters in McAlmon's novel *Post-Adolescence* which Hemingway saw at Rapallo in manuscript. In the letter to Ezra that enclosed the poem, Ernest said, "McAlmon has given us the dirt on everybody. It is all most enjoyable."[40]

IV

Barely a year out of Chicago, Hemingway's public voice was becoming more confident and cocky; his gossipy Lady Poets poem says that the author is an insider, privy to the private lives of at least two well-known women. Of course, he knew no more about Amy Lowell or Edna St. Vincent Millay than McAlmon told him, but to judge only by the poem, a reader might take him to be most current in the literary world. One can see this same public guise being created in another piece he wrote that late winter in Rapallo.

On February 18, he sent Gertrude Stein his review of her newly published *Geography and Plays*, telling her, "You can cut out any or all of it and if you don't like it I'll do another. That's the liberalest offer I know how to make." We do not know if Gertrude made any changes to the review, but it ran two weeks later in the Paris *Tribune*.

Gertrude Stein is a sort of gauge of civilization. If you think Mr. Sinclair Lewis is a great writer and Babbitt a great book you probably won't like Gertrude Stein. If you think Mr. Lewis is doing the best he can employing a *Saturday Evening Post* technique to prove an H. L. Mencken theory with masses of detail and occasional interjected shots of BEAUTY, or if you hold any other theory about Lewis that you have thought up for yourself – and if somebody ever lends you a copy of Geography and Plays, or if you buy one, you will be very happy for a number of hours. You will also be very disturbed. You will also learn something, if you happen to be a writer – or a reader.

Gertrude Stein is probably the most first rate intelligence employed in writing today. If you are tired of Mr. D. H. Lawrence who writes extremely well with the intelligence of a head waiter or Mr. Wells who is believed to be intelligent because of a capacity for sustained marathon thinking or the unbelievably stupid but thoroughly conscientious young men who compile the Dial you ought to read Gertrude Stein.

There is an introduction to the book called "The Work of Gertrude Stein," by Sherwood Anderson. You ought to read that before you start the book and you ought to read her Three Lives. The Melanctha story in Three Lives is one of the three best short stories in English. You can select the other two stories to suit yourself. Sherwood wrote the introduction soon after he won the Dial prize and the new respectability was still on him. It is a little restrained, the introduction. But the next to the last paragraph is a corker.

E. M. Hemingway[41]

A testament of admiration and good will, the review ultimately focuses not on the book but the reviewer, telling the reader precious little about *Geography and Plays*. In fact, on the basis of the review, one cannot with certainty say that Hemingway read the strange collection.[42]

If the review says little about Stein's book, it tells us a great deal about the education of Ernest Hemingway. When he arrived in Paris in December 1921, he carried with him a sheaf of stories written in the "technique of the *Saturday Evening Post*," stories laboring under the burden of his still somewhat sentimental taste in popular literature. During 1920–21 he and Hadley wrote each other almost daily letters, many of which contained remarks on their joint reading. The books they most loved included d'Annunzio's *The Flame*, Lewis' *Main Street*, Anatole France's *The Red Lily* and Kipling's *Brushwood Boy*.[43]

Barely a year later, Hemingway makes fun of the *Saturday Evening Post* school of writing and its indulgent sentimentality. Sinclair Lewis, the hottest young novelist in America, is dismissed as a formula writer, and *Babbitt* no great book. Having met and read Joyce, Pound and Stein, Hemingway had undergone a profound change; his goals and techniques of a year earlier, abandoned. With nothing yet in print, he declares in this review his independence from his earlier models. The authority of his review is really bluster; he has no credentials to support his literary judgements, and his apparent confidence is thinner than he would like to admit. Read it rather like a veiled promise. Putting statements on paper was a ritual from his youth; his high-school notebooks contain promises to himself, made and signed. Once it was on paper, there was no going back. Here, in his first European literary publication, he is once more making a promise and signing it in public.

Without making more of it than it deserves, we should also remember the audience for this review: the Left Bank literary crowd whose allegiance for or against Gertrude Stein was already fixed. By March 1923, most of the Left Bankers knew of Hemingway, had seen him in cafés or heard some gossip about him – another disciple of Stein and Pound. But after a year in and out of Paris, Hemingway had nothing published to show the literary fringe his true skills. This review was his first Paris platform, his initial opportunity to declare himself. Lewis, Lawrence, Wells and the *Dial* are the past. Anderson is, in part, still a viable force, but the future is Gertrude Stein: that's what the review says. Hemingway declares himself in her camp, and in the process draws more attention to himself than to her new book. As Pound's "Mr. Nixon" (read Arnold Bennett) once said: "I never mention a man but with the view of selling my own works. The tip's a good one." When, later that year, Hemingway's first Paris fiction was published, many were prepared in advance to be impressed by this brash young American.[44]

He was learning a simple lesson, a message coming to him from every direction. He saw it on the boulevards and in the lives of the artists. He got the message from Pound, always willing to pass pontifical judgements reflecting well on himself. He got the message from Joyce, whose reputation as genius flowered from his careful watering of the soil and cultivation of the crop. And he got the message from Stein, who could, with a straight face, say, "No, nobody has done anything to develop the English language since Shakespeare, except myself, and Henry James perhaps a little." It was a very simple message: *believe in yourself or no one else will.*[45]

V

Besides a modicum of talent and much hard work, a man needed confidence and timing to succeed. When he was young, Hemingway's timing was like that of an African cat – instinctive, requiring no thought. At Rapallo his confidence was growing and his timing was perfect. He saw just enough of Ezra to receive encouragement without being sucked under in the poet's wake. A little Pound went a long way, and Ezra was, as Ernest said later, right only fifty percent of the time. Perhaps more instructive than Pound was Mike Strater, whose sprained ankle kept him in his hotel room painting during Hemingway's first week in Rapallo. Strater did two portraits of Ernest which gave them time to talk, discussing similarities between writing and painting. Three years later, Hemingway began a story about a writer who took up painting when his fiction would not flow, but the story did not work. Modern painting, despite some correlations, bore little resemblance to narrative fiction, for Picasso and company abandoned nineteenth-century story telling as they emphasized the flatness of canvas and exposed their illusions as fakes. *This is not a pipe* read Magritte's statement beneath his flattened pipe.[46]

Strater did not remember what they talked about – just "painting and writing" – Ernest, sitting by the window in the good light, and Mike on a stool to rest his bum ankle, and the two talking and Ernest walking around to see himself forming on the canvas. The first one with the grey background he said looked too much like H. G. Wells, so Mike painted another with a red background and a tougher face like a boxer. A painter could do that – change the light, alter the line, shift the color of reality until it suited his purpose. So could a writer, Ernest realized: reality was not art and realism was not photography. Once he knew his purpose, all that mattered was telling the story right; if the light needed to fade or the image to shift to make his point, then, like the painter, he changed what he knew and what he heard of reality to meet art's necessity. He came to understand what Ezra told him: fiction and painting were both based on selection. Mike did not put everything into the painting, and what he left out was still invisibly present if he did it right.[47]

Getting it right is not easy, not in painting or writing or reconstructing the past. We know so much about that month in Rapallo: Ezra and

Dorothy left; McAlmon arrived; Strater and O'Brien were there; Hadley missed her first period; the Pounds and Hemingways took a walking tour; tennis was played, portraits painted, art discussed; and Ernest worked on his "unwritten stories." In groups they sat down to mixed seafood platters, fried calamari, rich pesto sauces and tart white wine. What we don't know is the sequence, the timing that changes the story. The portraits came before the tennis, but McAlmon may or may not have been present. We don't know when Hadley's pregnancy made itself certain to her; we don't know when she told Ernest. Multiple scenarios suggest themselves, all of them plausible fictions.

If one wants to paint Hemingway as a reluctant father-to-be whose egotism outweighed his love for Hadley, the data can be arranged to support the view. We know that on February 18 Ernest proposed to John Bone a feature tour of Germany's Ruhr industrial area, which a month earlier France occupied to squeeze out war reparation payments. To paint Hemingway as true bastard, we have only to imagine that he knew Hadley was pregnant when he wrote Bone, and that the solitary Ruhr trip was a way of punishing her for becoming pregnant. To arrange that scene we have only to ignore what is not in the picture: no one – not Strater, McAlmon, O'Brien or the Pounds – no one remembered Hadley being pregnant in Rapallo. Afterwards they realized she must have been, but at the time no one remarked on it. Nor did anyone remember Ernest being noticeably depressed in Rapallo. Later, when Hemingway wrote "Cat in the Rain," a story set in a Rapallo hotel about a dissatisfied American wife and her uninterested husband, we wanted it to be about that February in Rapallo when Hadley was pregnant with a child Ernest did not want.

It's so easy to fall in love with one's own fictions. Hemingway's Rapallo story was not written in Rapallo and to substitute his later story for that February's reality is to use his fiction to create further fictions of our own. Better to examine what he did write in Rapallo. His February and March letters do not mention Hadley's pregnancy, and in his unpublished piece called "Rapallo," he said he and Hadley were "happy sometimes," but "happiest in bed." There were "no problems in bed": not the words of a man whose wife has just declared herself pregnant. Hemingway's writing from February to late March shows only a young man working diligently to perfect his metier, crafting his "unwritten stories" into finely chiseled paragraphs.[48]

Jane Heap, Ezra's strange friend and co-editor of the prestigious *Little Review*, had asked Hemingway to contribute to the spring "Exiles" issue of the magazine. At first he wanted to give her his recreated "Paris 1922," but when the longer paragraphs began to develop, Ernest saw he was on to something. By March 10, he and Hadley were in Milan on their way to Cortina in the Italian Dolomites. In hand were several drafts of his new and curious short fictions. To make Jane Heap's April publication date, he needed to get them in the mail soon. There were six of them now, but they did not hang together. Three were about the war, not his war, the one in France. Two of those came from Chink, who fought at Mons and told good stories. Reading them aloud, he could hear Chink telling the story at Chamby.

> It was a frightfully hot day. We'd jammed an absolutely perfect barricade across the bridge. It was simply priceless. A big old wrought-iron grating from the front of a house. Too heavy to lift and you could shoot through it and they would have to climb over it. It was absolutely topping.

That's how they all went – detached voices speaking, describing tightly focused events, small pieces of modern times.[49]

Only one of the six pieces came from his own experience: the Greek retreat across the Anatolian plain. He got that right, paring away details from his newspaper report until only its hard essence remained. The other five pieces came from friends or out of the newspapers. One of them was Mike Strater's voice telling of a Spanish bullfight where the first two matadors were both gored badly; the last matador, a young kid, had to kill all five bulls. On the fifth bull he kept missing with the sword.

> He tried five times and finally got it through and the crowd was quiet all the time waiting and never razzed him. Then they raised hell when he finally put it through and the bull went down.[50]

That was an early draft. He listened again to his memory, rearranging it ever so slightly, changing a dead word here, a weak word there, until he could see the bull ring that he had never seen. Hearing it, seeing and feeling it, he became the man watching the matador:

> He tried five times and the crowd was quiet because it was a good bull and it looked like him or the bull and then he finally made it. He sat down in the sand and puked and they held a cape over

114

him while the crowd hollered and threw things down into the bull ring.[51]

Much better: the kid puking and the cape were right. Hemingway could hear it and feel it being right.

Most young writers in their first fictions almost instinctively use their own lives as subject matter. Not so with young Hemingway whose earliest fiction has almost no basis in his own life. Because Hemingway so carefully provided his readers with glasses of his own tinting, they have assumed that he wrote only from first-hand experience. That first year, however, his greatest difficulty was learning how to use his own experience in his writing.

From his newspaper work, he had developed great confidence in his ability to create fiction from secondary sources, to write about what he had not experienced. One of his most powerful "unwritten stories" came completely from the newspapers. While he was covering the Lausanne Conference, the *Tribune* headlines screamed:

GREEKS EXECUTE SIX OF OLD REGIME

Ex-Premier Gounaris And Chief Aides
Of Constantine Condemned And Shot
For Part in Asia Minor Defeat

The sickening story told how the six men were taken from prison to Goudi Square outside Athens and lined against a wall. As the firing squad drew to attention, the condemned men refused to make any last statements. Gounaris was said to be so sick with typhoid he had to be carried to his execution. At 11:30 a.m., rifles fired and the men slumped back against the wall.[52]

Hemingway knew no one who witnessed the executions; he had only the news stories as a basis to imagine that morning in Athens, six men backed against their final wall. He worked the material over and over, moving the execution back to early morning, inventing the rain soaking the victims, creating an ironic hospital for the wall's buttress. Finally he got it exactly right.

They shot the six cabinet ministers at half-past six in the morning against the wall of a hospital. There were pools of water in the courtyard. There were wet dead leaves on the paving of the courtyard. It rained hard. All the shutters of the hospital were nailed shut. One of the ministers was sick with typhoid. Two soldiers carried him downstairs and out into the rain. They tried to hold him up against the wall but he sat down in a puddle of water. The other five stood very quietly against the wall. Finally the officer told the soldiers it was no good trying to make him stand up. When they fired the first volley he was sitting down in the water with his head on his knees.[53]

"... *the wall of a hospital ... pools of water ... rained hard ... into the rain ... against the wall ... puddle of water ... quietly against the wall ... sitting down in the water*": repeat the key elements until they create their magic. He invented the rain, and the newspaper provided him the wall, final destination for more than a few in Hemingway's time. He got it right, as if he were there, and he was. He was there in his imagination.

VI

In Cortina, with nothing to distract him but a thick snow pack and fast skiing, Hemingway refined his six pieces and searched for a title to hold them together. As was his habit, he jotted down a page of possibilities, some merely frivolous: "Unwritten Stories Are Better," "Perhaps You Were There At The Time," "That Was Before I Knew You," "Romance Is Dead," "The Good Guys See A Thing Or Two." Second from the last title on the page was:

In Our Time
subtitle
I Am Not Interested In Artists

The April issue of the *Little Review* grouped the stories as "In Our Time," without the subtitle.[54]

He was a writer uninterested, he claimed, in being called an artist. Artists talked about their art, its theory and how it related to the grand scheme of literary flow. Everyone on the Left Bank was an artist, sitting around cafés and never working. He worked all the time. Writers wrote stories, not art, and they did not pontificate about their work. But Gertrude and Ezra talked always about their work, about art, and he admired them. It was a confusing problem: who was Ernest Hemingway? Sometimes he was a reporter for a Canadian newspaper, sometimes a writer of fiction trying to craft a publishable style, but he was no artist. That was fine for Ezra and Gertrude, but the Latin Quarter housed too many poseurs for Ernest to feel easy with that identity. How then did he account for hair down to his collar and his work appearing now in arty little magazines and amateur Left Bank publications? There was no simple answer to his internal conflict, nor did it ever go away. He became eventually what he pretended to be, one of the best writers of his time, all the while working diligently to create a public persona one could not mistake for an artist. If he led, at times, a difficult life, the seeds of his difficulty were planted early.[55]

For three months now, ever since the Lausanne Conference, his only work was his ficiton, but about March 18, when the cable from John Bone caught up with him at Cortina, he became once more the *Star*'s newsman. Bone asked Hemingway to make a month's tour of the French-occupied German Ruhr, sending back two to three feature stories a week for an announced, front-page series in the *Star*. Hemingway's response apparently indicated that the Ruhr was no longer news, but Bone would not accept his answer. On March 20, he wired: NOT TOO LATE FOR GERMAN ARTICLES. Ernest and Hadley looked at the telegram for a long time. Neither wanted him on the road for a month. Hadley's pregnancy, probably unsuspected by Ernest in Rapallo, was now an established fact, and he was loath to leave her. Both of them realized, however, that he could not afford to turn Bone down, not when they were returning to Toronto in September. Ernest compromised: he would take the assignment but not for a month. He would do it quickly, returning to Cortina in a couple of weeks.[56]

By Friday, March 23, Hemingway was back in Paris, where the apartment was musty, light rains were falling and the city various as always. The Minister of the Interior, worried that indecent nude revues might offend summer tourists, banned certain gestures, phrases and words in time to arrest Harry Pilcer on obscenity charges for his music hall performance of "L'Après-Midi d'un Faune." When Pilcer's female dancers were asked in court to produce their costumes, "they fished in their handbags among lip-sticks and handkerchiefs, extracting bits of this and that." It wasn't their scant apparel, said the prosecutor, but their suggestive movements that were obscene. Meanwhile an American poetess, of whom no one had ever heard, insisted in the papers that "The entire American colony has been conspiring to drive me into white slavery." In spite of rain, it was looking a lot like the usual spring madness in Paris.[57]

No one seemed terribly excited about French troops invading the heart of Germany's industrial empire, the Ruhr basin, in the name of war reparations. It was three-month-old news, barely holding the front page, but that did not make it any easier for Hemingway to enter Germany. Neither France nor Germany wanted uncensored stories in the press. For six days he worked his press and political contacts, trying to get a German visa. Guy Hickok, his good friend from the Brooklyn *Eagle*, helped out as he could and served as Hemingway's mail service, receiving Hadley's letters and forwarding them when he knew where Hemingway was staying.[58]

While waiting for officials to act, Hemingway went by rue de Fleurus to show Gertrude his new short form of almost-stories before delivering them to Jane Heap in time to make the "Exiles" issue of the *Little Review*. Both Jane and Gertrude were impressed with his experiment, but he was frustrated. Just when the writing was going well, he had to stop to write Bone's stories. Because he did not know where the fiction came from or how his internal creative process worked, any intrusion that stopped the flow was frightening: the well might not flow when next he opened the valve. His journalism, he later insisted, should not be considered as part of his collected works, for he did not write it to last. Had he realized that his fiction and non-fiction flowed from the same well, he might have worried less. He may have had no time for fiction on his Ruhr assignment, but his feature stories were among the best of his early career.[59]

Waiting for visas, Hemingway eased his frustration by slipping Bone three long, detailed analyses of current French politics as they affected the Ruhr occupation. In that way he was able to count an essentially wasted week as part of the assignment. The stories, written with the aid of Guy Hickok, were more structured than any of his earlier *Star* work, and their style was, at points, not unlike the style of his latest fiction. The first of the series began,

> To write about Germany you must begin by writing about France. There is a magic in the name France. It is a magic like the smell of the sea or the sight of blue hills or of soldiers marching by. It is a very old magic.

He returned to the journalist's point of view, but he was repeating the key words to set up his story. All the stories were filled with interesting, focused and detailed information from a variety of sources, and all made to sound as if it were coming from the insightful mind of Hemingway alone.[60]

Nothing in Paris eased Hadley's absence or made Ernest feel any better about their separation. Pseudo-artists were marching under a rainbow banner to unite Montparnasse with the Free Commune of Montmartre. The best boxers were out of town, and the race tracks were wet most of the week. In Germany, a French reporter was jailed on trumped up charges of technical irregularities with one of his several required visas. The Tuesday before Easter, Sarah Bernhardt's failed kidneys finally put out her lights; her death played the front pages of every Paris paper, burying the government releases on the Ruhr. Two days later, Hemingway finally found the key to the visa deadlock: a letter from the American embassy.

> This is to certify that Mr. Ernest Hemingway is the duly authorized correspondent of the International News Service of New York, and is personally and favorably known to me. He has been directed by his newspaper to proceed to Germany to report on the situation there.

Hemingway used his I.N.S. connection to secure the American embassy's cover letter only because the Canadian embassy might not give such a letter to an American. After being caught by Bone at double duty in Constantinople, Hemingway was not about to jeopardize his Toronto job with Bone by selling Frank Mason *Star* material from Germany. When he found that Bone's cables directing him to Germany were of no interest to the American embassy, Ernest went to Mason for a letter to satisfy American officials. Turning his visa ordeal into a feature story, Hemingway wisely changed the facts, reporting to Toronto readers that his embassy letter read: "Mr. Hemingway, the bearer, was well and favorably known to the embassy and had been directed by his newspaper, the Toronto *Star*, to proceed to Germany."[61]

Letter in hand, Ernest made his way through the throngs of mourners and gawkers lining the boulevards to catch a glimpse of Sarah Bernhardt's slowly passing funeral cortège. At the German embassy across the river, he finally got the necessary visas, and early the next morning, as church bells called the Paris faithful to Good Friday Mass, Ernest boarded the nine-hour train for Strasbourg and the Kehl bridge into Germany. Bone wanted four weeks in the Ruhr; Hemingway gave him ten days, barely scratching the surface of the Ruhr situation. Bone expected eight to ten stories; Hemingway wrote ten, but three were from Paris, and three more written from material gathered on the train between his Kehl crossing and Frankfurt. Unable to converse in German, Hemingway was limited to interviewing English speakers, and the stories sounded less authoritative than the first three from Paris. Of the four stories he actually wrote in the occupied area, only two had any substance, and one of those was date-lined Cologne where Chink Dorman-Smith provided him good material.

While Hemingway was in Germany, French troops fired on a mob at Essen, killing six and wounding thirty-five as Franco-German relations worsened throughout the occupied area of coal mines, coke mills and heavy industry. In Essen, where the local telephone operators refused to work, Paris operators manned the switchboards. The German government was powerless, and in the Tyrol a plot was afoot to put Prince Rupert on the throne of South Germany. Little of this turmoil appeared in Hemingway's feature stories, which focused on how the tense situation affected the lives of specific people. With his limited sources he could do little else. In his letters to Hadley, he tried to sound enthusiastic, but she did not believe him. "I wish," she said, "you'd tell me a few interesting things like whether you're going back thru Paris or how long you think the job will take, etc. You sound awfully keenly interested, are you?" She reminded him to bring from Paris "fishing things" to Cortina for the approaching season.[62]

By April 8, Hemingway was back at Chink's quarters in Cologne, where he obtained a safe conduct pass from his friend to get through the militarized zone and back to Paris. Two nights later he was watching Georges Carpentier, Battling Siki and other notable boxers fight a benefit performance for war veterans at the Cirque de Paris. The next day he boarded the familiar Simplon Express for Milan, crossing the Italian border at Iselle on April 12. His Ruhr stories were in the mail to Bone. Maybe they were not what the *Star* expected, but Bone seemed to like them well enough. As late as April 29, three weeks after Ernest left Germany, Bone was wiring for more articles. By that time Hemingway was back in Cortina where Hadley, as she promised in her letter, put "all four paws around the puppy and [made] him squeak with delight."[63]

Chapter Seven

FORM AND RITUAL
LATE SPRING AND SUMMER,
1923

I

On May 2, four months after Hadley left Paris in tears for Lausanne, she and Ernest crossed the Italian frontier into Switzerland and ten hours later reached home. The world, without them, had continued in familiar ways. Yet another conference was trying to satisfy Turkey's national pride while stealing her birthright of undeveloped oil. Letters to the editor of the *Tribune* continued to debate the silliness of prohibition and the evil of expensive visas. The franc stood officially at 14.85 to the dollar: their musty apartment now cost them only $16.83 a month. Back in the states, President Harding was preparing for a summer tour of the American West to bolster his shaky political base.[1]

They arrived at rue du Cardinal Lemoine with sweat running down their backs. After months at high altitude, neither was prepared for the humid heat sweltering Paris, and Hadley, entering her fourth month of pregnancy, was becoming uncomfortable in clothes too tight. Many of their friends, they discovered, were taking early vacations to the country, escaping the steady 80 degree temperatures. Among the market stalls along rue Mouffetard, they were strangers once more. Ernest had been out of Paris almost nine of the previous sixteen months, during which time he wrote at least ninety-five feature stories for the *Star*, over 20,000 words of copy. Two days after they returned, Bone wired, once more asking Hemingway to make a Russian tour: British ships and sailors were being seized, and England threatened to break already fragile diplomatic relations with the bolshevik government. Because of censorship, no one knew if Lenin had recovered from his reported stroke, or how serious the court charges against Catholic priests were.

It was hot enough in Paris to make the offer attractive, but Ernest knew he could not leave Hadley for another month, nor could he let his own writing go stale for that long. The six sketches he'd given Jane Heap were a start, but he needed at least twelve more to make a book for Ezra's "Inquest" series. He now had three stories finished: the two saved from Hadley's disaster and a new one he called "Out of Season," written after leaving Cortina, but they were not as exciting as his new form. In Rapallo, Robert McAlmon contracted with Hemingway on a handshake to print his two remaining stories and as many poems as Ernest felt good about. They decided to call the small book "Two Stories & Ten Poems." Back in Paris Ernest, eager for a publication that might establish his reputation, gave McAlmon his newly finished "Out of Season," but too late to change the title in the *Little Review* ad. Two books printed in Paris would make the year seem more productive than it actually had been.[2]

On May 11, Ernest wired Bone: RUSSIA UNFEASIBLE FOR ME AT PRESENT UNLESS EMERGENCY STOP LETTER FOLLOWING. With only a handful of vignettes completed, Ernest needed the summer to complete his "Inquest" book. Now if only the creative well, the source of his fiction, would flow. He was always a little nervous when he first reopened that valve. Much later, still not understanding the process, he said:

> Of course you can work anywhere except when it cuts out on you. . . . There is nothing much to do about that except to remember how it has been other times . . . And finally it always comes again. But you need a lot of confidence and a good memory because every time it cuts out it is new and every time it is worse than it ever was before.

That late spring in Paris he was not truly worried, for "it" had never really "cut out" on him, but after a week he had made little progress on his "unwritten stories." After four months on the road, Ernest was not adjusting easily to being home.[3]

One Sunday afternoon, he and Hadley joined the throng of people jamming into Buffalo stadium to watch the comeback of Georges

Carpentier as he knocked out Marcel Nilles, heavyweight champion of France. Ernest winced as Carpentier absorbed five rounds of heavy punishment before taking command of the fight. By the end of the fourth round blood was flowing from Carp's nose and mouth. Nilles went to the canvas in the sixth round, claiming a low blow that the referee disallowed. After that it was Carpentier's fight. Everyone loved the Carp, but it was obvious to most in the stadium that he was not going to regain his once world-class form. "They never come back," Ernest said later. In the other bouts, they saw the Belgian, Piet Hobin, and the Frenchman, Charles Ledoux, successfully defend their European titles in two fifteen-round decisions.[4]

It was a pleasant way to spend Sunday afternoon, and a way to avoid thinking about the writing he was not doing. In the cool mornings he tried to work in the apartment, but it was slow going. Between Hadley's pregnancy and their new puppy, the small rooms closed in on him as he tried to find the center of his "unwritten stories." The first six he gave Jane Heap had no governing scheme, but now it was coming clear to him that violence was the constant of his time and the focus of his sketches. From his brief pre-war stint on the Kansas City *Star*, he remembered a good police-beat story in which cops shot down two of three Italians robbing a cigar company. When ordered by police detectives to stop their horse-drawn wagon, Cap Gargotta and Joe Musso, both armed with revolvers, tried to run over the officers. When the smoke cleared, Cap and Joe were dead and a third Italian wounded. A little fuzzy on details almost four years cold, Hemingway began playing with the idea, subheading one draft "Crime" and another "Crime and Punishment," but using a running title of "Blank" as Bird had advertised the book. After three drafts it was almost right.[5]

For neatness, he reduced the robbers from three to two, and for irony changed them from Italians to Hungarians. As they back their wagon out into the alley, Officer Boyle, a good Irish cop, shot "one off the seat of the wagon and one out of the wagon box." When his partner says, "There's liable to be a hell of a lot of trouble," Boyle tells him, "They're crooks, ain't they? They're wops, ain't they? Who the hell is going to make any trouble?" Officer Boyle "can tell wops a mile off." No need for comment. The reader got it all from the conversation, got the violence and the irony without being told what to think. The racial prejudice against Italians was going to work out with a nice irony because now that he saw the scheme, Hemingway knew he must use his war experience in Italy.[6]

The only problem with his Italian experience was its rather limited view of the war. After three weeks at the front and having seen little action, he was blown up on the Piave river. What he learned that night at the forward observation post was fear, the common denominator among veterans who'd been under fire, their shared heritage along with their inability to speak of it. His fear was no different than that of his shell-shocked acquaintances Krebs Friend and André Masson. Inventing on the basis of his own fear and what he had heard from others, Hemingway began to mold his experience into the new form.

He started with a soldier crouching in a trench as an artillery bombardment begins to blow the line apart. The first draft read:

> Oh Jesus Christ, I prayed, get me out of here. Dear Jesus please get me out. Christ. Please, please please Christ. If you'll only keep me from getting killed I'll do anything you say. I believe in you and if you'll only take care of me I'll tell everyone in the world that you are the only thing that matters. That was during a shelling in the line near Fossalta. The next day my leave came and that night I was drunk in the officer's whore house in Mestre.

With the heart of it on paper, he began to revise with a cold eye to effect. First he tried beginning with the setting: "While we were lying in the sunken road at Fossalta during the bombardment waiting for the attack," but broke off in mid-sentence. On the second try, Hemingway described the terror from a first-person point of view: "While the trench was going to pieces under the bombardment at Fossalta I lay very flat and sweated and prayed Oh Jesus Christ get me out of here." By the third draft, he changed the "I" speaker to "he," more in keeping with his studied detachment. His revised verbs became more descriptive and active: "While the bombardment was knocking the trench to pieces . . ." The terrified, hysterical prayer changed little in the revisions: "Christ please please please christ. If you'll only keep me from getting killed I'll do anything you say. I believe in you and I'll tell every one in the world that you are the only thing that matters." Then came the ironic twist: "The shelling moved further up the line. They went to work on the trench and in the morning the sun came up and the day was hot and muggy and cheerful and quiet. The next night back at Mestre he did not tell the girl he went upstairs with at the Villa Rossa about Jesus. And he never told anybody." Looking over the final draft,

Hemingway changed "They went to work on the trench" to "We went to work on the trench" – a subtle but telling shift in view point. The speaker was now another soldier overhearing the terrified trench conversion and reporting on its ironic aftermath in a detached voice. That was the thing, lots of different voices. Eliot used so many voices in *The Waste Land* that it was hard to say when he was speaking. When Hemingway finished *in our time*, he achieved something of the same effect. He titled the Fossalta trench experience "Religion," which was as close as he came to commentary in draft and which he removed before publication. There would be no road signs directing traffic in his newly discovered country.[7]

On May 9, the chief cashier at the Guaranty Trust, where Hemingway banked, was accidentally shot and killed as police were arresting a war deserter. The next day a Russian delegate to the new Lausanne Peace Conference was assassinated by an old Czarist officer avenging the prison deaths of two relatives. A pair of fourteen-year-old lovers drowned themselves in the Seine, and the Paris–London air connection fell out of the sky, killing all six aboard. Wherever he looked, random, senseless violence was the norm, making his title *in our time* all the more appropriate for his collection of short-takes.

II

Staying in Paris and making the best of it, Hemingway worked on his vignettes all of May. The writing went smoothly as he finished eleven of the brief stories, including a terse account of a young soldier's disappointing affair in Milan with a nurse named Luz. She sends her lover home to the states engaged and then writes that "theirs had been only a boy and girl affair." It was, in fact, the slightly fictional story of his own relationship with Agnes Von Kurowsky, his Milan nurse during the war. He had written Agnes a letter before the December loss of his manuscripts, telling her the wonderful married life he was leading in Europe, implying that this was the life she turned down. Her reply had caught up with him at Chamby: she never doubted he would become famous, she told him, and such an old woman as herself (eight years older than he) would have been only a hindrance to his career. Obviously Ernest did not tell Agnes that Hadley was also eight years older than himself.

The "Luz" vignette, the first one to come out of his own life, was not as tightly focused on a single, tense moment as were his earlier pieces; it followed a story line and was truly "A Very Short Story" as he later retitled it. The best of the "unwritten stories" had little or no narrative structure, leaving out almost everything but the central moment, the epiphanal scene, as we see in his completely imagined description of a wounded soldier on the Italian front. The following drafts and revisions of the opening sentence show us the author at his craft, working the words for the right effect:

> Nick was sitting in the trench twisting a tournequet around his ankle.

>   the church
> Nick was sitting against the wall of / a house where
>   to be
> they had dragged him / clear of what was going
> forward down the street.

> Nick sat against the wall of the church where they had dragged him to be clear of machine gun fire in the street.

This is as close as we will ever get to Hemingway's hand moving across the paper, as near as we can come to the mind of the author. *Trench* becomes *wall*, binding the wounded Nick to his blood brothers, the Greek ministers against their wall. *House* becomes *church*, a touch of irony, not just any wall: the ministers were against a hospital wall, dying where men should be cured; Nick is against a church wall whose Christ was prayed to by the hysterical soldier, the same church that blessed the men going into battle and later buried the dead ones in quick lime with equally quick prayers. The "machine gun fire in the street" gives substance to "what was going forward," the sort of specific detail Ezra asked for. Nick, "sweaty and dirty," looks at the sprawled figure of his wounded mate, Rinaldi, lying "against the wall." Nick, looking "straight ahead brilliantly," tells his friend, "You and me we've made a separate peace." Rinaldi doesn't smile at the topical joke: Russia, after the 1917 revolution, made a separate peace with the Austro-Hungarians which almost defeated the Allies when German troops from the closed Eastern front were moved to the West. Rinaldi, we are told, "was a disappointing audience." Hemingway called the chapter "Humor."[8]

The "Nick" of this experience was probably based on Ernest's Chicago friend, Nick Nerone, a much-decorated and three times wounded Italian officer in the war, but the sentiment of a "separate peace" was not Nick's, the super patriot; that sentiment came from post-war American reaction. Although Ernest never saw Nerone after leaving Chicago, Nick's name became part of Hemingway's most famous character, Nick Adams, whose education in his time would be at the heart of Hemingway's short stories for the next four years. The last name, Adams, first appeared in an unused vignette called "Did You Ever Kill Anyone?":

> We were moving along on the far right. The advance was going like clockwork. We'd shelled the shit out of everything. Adams and I and two men were on the extreme right of C Company. Cra-pung.
> Adams went down like a batter that has been beaned. There was an old boche in a round cap and spectacles standing up out of the shell hole with the rifle in his hands and a foolish look on his face. The men sort of hesitated for me to do the honors.

Unused but unforgotten, this brief passage narrated by an American voice reappears several years later as part of Nick Adams' war trauma in "A Way You'll Never Be."[9]

By the middle of May his "unwritten stories" were going so well, Hemingway felt confident enough to turn over to McAlmon the typescript for *Three Stories & Ten Poems*. Trying to give the haphazard collection more cohesion, he connected some of the poems, retitling them and adding prose pieces to focus them. He left three different versions of one attempt called "Heroes" which was going to introduce the war poems. What appears to be the final version reads:

> Some shit heel correspondent with a green brassard wrote that our top-kick hollered, "Come on you sons of bitches do you want to live forever?" Top-kick my ass, the top-kick was so god-damned scared that he was pissing in his pants if he wasn't praying.

But when he looked it over, he could see his inserts did little to give the collection unity. Finally he took out the prose connectors and returned the poems to their original titles.[10]

With his literary poke cleaned out, he had nothing left but the vignettes for the "Inquest" series. With three months remaining before their return to Toronto, Hemingway felt confident he could finish the series before leaving Paris. His confidence received a jolt when *Pictorial Review* returned his submission, "My Old Man," which Edward O'Brien had promised to support with a letter that apparently never arrived. Hemingway immediately wrote O'Brien, whom he had cultivated at some length in Rapallo, asking for advice. His letter's tone was a little desperate, a little depressed: "Throws me all off and makes it almost impossible to write. Seems to destroy any reason for publishing. . . . And yet I want, like hell, to get published. What do you advise? If anything." O'Brien's reply has disappeared, but when his *Best Short Stories of 1923* appeared the next year, "My Old Man" was included. By that time it had appeared in *Three Stories & Ten Poems*, but neither O'Brien nor Hemingway thought McAlmon would publish that book so quickly. From the evidence it would seem that Hemingway's plaintive letter prompted O'Brien to break his rule of collecting only published stories for his annual. Within two years, "My Old Man" would be published three times between hard covers.[11]

III

He knew the eleven vignettes were good, but he needed more of them to fill out the Bird book, and he had almost exhausted his backlog of subject matter. No problem. He would find the rest of them in Spain. Ever since listening to Mike Strater's description of the bullfight, Ernest hungered to see the spectacle for himself. Gertrude and Alice further whetted his appetite with talk of a primitive fiesta in Pamplona at the Spanish foot of the Pyrenees. He had to get to Spain, but expenses held him back. Hadley was doing her best to cut costs, remaking old clothes to fit her swelling figure and taking hand-outs from friends. No telling what it would cost them to resettle in Toronto. That's when Ernest went to work on McAlmon, whose Ellerman money took the two men to Spain.

Early in June, Hemingway and McAlmon boarded the Sud Express for Madrid, where Bill Bird agreed to meet them later in the week. By the time Bird joined them, he found Ernest needling and baiting McAlmon with what Bill thought unnecessary spleen. Within Ernest lurked a mean, bullying streak that some people brought to the surface without even trying. On the other hand, McAlmon was a well-known provocateur who could be just as pissy as Hemingway. Bill, kind hearted and maybe too sensitive, was caught in the middle of their barbed remarks. Both Hemingway and McAlmon were accustomed to dominating discussions. Two such men together for any length of time were bound to produce sparks. Given McAlmon's bisexual nature, Bill should not have been so surprised by the tension between the two men, but he did not know that Hemingway was a man whom homosexuals found attractive, an embarrassment over which Ernest had no control. (In Italy he was propositioned at least once by an older man and perhaps again by a fellow Red Cross man who took him on an expense-paid trip to the Sicilian village of Taormina.) There is no evidence that Hemingway found homosexual advances attractive, or that he ever encouraged them, but neither did he necessarily rage in the presence of homosexual men. Given the thin, almost dainty young men to whom McAlmon was attracted, it is rather unlikely he made any advances to Hemingway, but he may have approached or teased other homosexuals passing in the Madrid streets. That would have been enough to have triggered Ernest's temper. Whatever the source of their friction, Bird's presence quieted it.[12]

The three men – two amateur publishers and their fledgling author – never forgot those days in Spain, but their memories differed. Forty years later, Bill Bird remembered the bullfighters' pension, recommended by Mike Strater, where they stayed until leaving for Seville's Corpus Christi bullfights. Bird thought Hemingway "was already behaving like a new initiate in a secret society and laying plans to make a trip through Andalusia with a crew of matadors." Ernest, unable to speak a word of Spanish, was bluffing his way along on his limited Italian. He was, Bird said, almost too enthusiastic about the brave bulls and the courage of their killers. Hemingway was equally interested in the courage of the spectators, noting carefully who turned away with a weak stomach when deeply gored horses dragged their entrails after them in the ring.[13]

Twelve years after the trip, his memory jaded by jealousy of Hemingway's literary success, McAlmon said: "There are countless English and Americans who were bullfight enthusiasts many years before that summer of 1924 [sic, 1923] when Hemingway and I both saw our first, but he made it into a literary or artistic experience. . . . Bird also liked bullfights, but neither he nor I were putting ourselves through a 'hardening process' . . . Upon returning from Spain, he substituted shadow-bullfighting for shadow-boxing. The amount of imaginary cape work and sword thrusts he made in those days was formidable." It was partly Hemingway's boyish enthusiasm and his need to be the insider, the expert, that soured McAlmon's memories of the exciting trip. He and Ernest went to Spain seemingly good · friends; they returned nominally friends still but with no joy. McAlmon published the book as he had promised, but the two were never close again.[14]

That summer of 1923 in Spain, Robert McAlmon was relatively wealthy, well known in New York and Paris, a published author, and the good friend of James Joyce. Everyone on the Left Bank knew McAlmon's blue eyes and his thin lips often on the verge of a sneer. Bob McAlmon had been around, knew the scams and the street life. If he was sometimes seen courting a pretty young man, his behavior was not remarkable in Paris. However, when Robert McAlmon wrote his memoirs in 1934, few remembered either his promise or his presence. The Left Bank American colony that once twittered to his gossip had departed, leaving no forwarding address; in New York and Paris his name wouldn't buy a drink. The young man whose hotel bills he'd paid in Spain had become one of the best-known American authors of his time. In 1923, when he and Ernest were both promising young men, it was an even bet as to which writer would make it big. By 1934, the question was decided, and Robert McAlmon must have wondered how his balloon lost its air.

To listen to McAlmon tell it, he was the truly hardened realist, Hemingway the poseur. Going down on the train, a little hung over, McAlmon said he turned away from the nauseating sight of a dead dog on an adjacent flatcar. Hemingway studied the dog, advising a "detached and scientific attitude." He accused McAlmon of pretending to be a realist: "Are you going to go romantic on us?" he asked. Cursing, McAlmon left for the dining car to get a drink. He assures us that he had seen "many dead dogs, cats, and corpses of men borne in on the tide of New York harbor."[15]

Perhaps that is exactly what happened, but McAlmon missed the punch line of his own story. While he was in the bar, Hemingway was making notes which have survived. On that warm day at the wayside station, probably grinning a little at McAlmon's reaction, Ernest took out his notebook and with the diligence of a natural historian wrote:

Death in the sun,
black, – shiny and
tar like, lumpy,
sun glints,

maggots squirm.
Knuckles, big, cracked.
face puffed, black, shiny, tar-like, puffed like a child's balloon

Was the sun-swollen body a dog or a man? Dogs have no knuckles to crack, but Ernest was probably making a quick comparison between the present dog and an imaginary or war-remembered man. Dead meat, no matter whose, bloats and blackens the same in the sun. Taking the notes etched the scene into his memory where it waited to resurface in "A Natural History of the Dead":

> If left long enough in the heat the flesh comes to resemble coal-tar, especially where it has been broken or torn, and it has quite a visible tarlike iridescence. . . . The first thing that you found out about the dead was that, hit badly enough, they died like animals . . . in the hot weather with a half-pint of maggots working where their mouths have been.

Every experience Hemingway probed to its core, harboring it for future use. It simply did not matter whether Robert McAlmon was piqued or not. Hemingway was working at his craft.[16]

Ernest took notes all through that first trip to Spain. He jotted down whatever struck him as odd, different or essential to the sense of place: Valentino hats in Seville; dead bodies piling up in Barcelona from anarchist terror; the late-hour dining in Madrid; the different sugar on the table. But mostly his notes centered on the bullfights, for he knew he was going to use them for his vignettes. He wrote out the names of "the great ones": Chicuelo, Villalta, Maera, Joselito, Belmonte; and he picked out the telling details: the dead white face of the picador; the horse trailing intestines and half-formed dung from his gored side. In his notes, Hemingway tried out good lines:

> Madrid, Pensione Aguilar
> —only popular amusement on which it is impossible to bet
> —an art not an amusement
> In the first place, not going apologize for bull
> fighting. Is a tragedy – not a sport. Have only seen
> 16 – hope to see 300 more before I die. Only thing that
> brings man opposit[e]s of life and death.

Part of these fragments ended up in *The Sun Also Rises*, part in a

Toronto *Star* feature story, and part in his three-part poem "The Soul of Spain With McAlmon and Bird the Publishers," which said: "There is no night life in Spain. They stay up late but they get up late. That is not night life. That is delaying the day."[17]

After Madrid they went to Seville, Ronda, Granada, back to Madrid and eventually home to Paris in the third week of June where Hadley, waiting patiently, entered her sixth month of term. Ernest returned full of childlike enthusiasm for the new country. Not at first, he told her. At first it was too big, too open, the meals heavy with too many courses, and the language barrier made it all surface without really seeing it. But once the bullfights started, none of that mattered. It was like the silent movies with accompanying music and crowd response. You did not need any Spanish to understand the drama down there on the sand, but it had gone by too quickly to digest or understand. He needed to see more fights before writing about them. They simply must go back in July for the San Fermin festival at Pamplona.[18]

IV

Back from Spain, Ernest was relieved to find Hadley, who all her early life was warned of her fragile constitution, happy that pregnancy agreed with her. Her face glowed, her red hair shone in the Paris sun, and she was very much with Ernest. All their friends, who now knew she was pregnant, were kind. On his first Saturday home, they went to the boxing matches at the Velodrome with a crew strange enough to be going to the Quat'z Arts ball. There was Ezra in his usual velvet jacket and wild hair; Jane Heap looking tough with her man's haircut, white shirt and tie, and a cigar; McAlmon looking very McAlmon; and Mike Strater without his wife. Tiny, as Ernest playfully continued to call Hadley, held her own through the five bouts that climaxed with Battling Siki turning the ring once more into a comedy act. The papers had followed his boulevard antics with glee: Siki walking into a café with his pet lion on a leash; Siki, dressed in silks, drinking his way into his next fight. The Velodrome crowd, expecting to be irritated, were not disappointed. In the third round against Morelle, the French heavyweight champion, Siki, grinning throughout, deliberately turned his back to the champ, letting him pound away on his black back and sides. This burlesque performance enraged the hooting crowd. Then in the sixth round, Siki let fly with his usual wild blows, one of which apparently hit Morelle below the belt. When the champion collapsed to the canvas in what looked like agony, the referee awarded him the fight on a foul.[19]

The next afternoon, Ernest and Hadley joined eighty thousand other Auteuil race fans who braved the abnormally cold June weather to watch what the *Tribune* called "one of the longest, most expensive, and most thrilling races in the world's turf calendar" – the Grand Steeple Chase de Paris. The odds-on favorite was Héros XII, and Master Bob was also running: two jumpers Ernest later remembered with great fondness. Carrying their picnic lunch and Côte de Beaune red wine, the Hemingways reached the *pelouse* early to secure a good position on the giant figure-eight course. That day, everyone who mattered in Paris came out in his finery; the crowd cheered when President Millerand arrived and again when General Foch appeared.

At the first double hurdle, Mouzu went down throwing his jockey, leaving six horses in the race. By midpoint, Master Bob and Héros XII were running first and second in a broken field, but approaching the last obstascle the aging L'Yser moved to the lead. The three of them – L'Yser, Master Bob and Héros XII – came into the stretch tightly bunched with the old horse showing enough heart at the last to burst away to a two-length victory. Ernest won 250 francs on the race, betting across the board money on Master Bob who ran second and Héros XII who placed third.[20]

The rest of the month disappeared into afternoon coffees and evening drinks. The Thursday after the Auteuil races, the Hemingways visited at rue de Fleurus, where Gertrude and Ernest talked avidly about the bullfights and going to Pamplona. Ernest performed, unable to talk about veronicas without demonstrating his new-found knowledge. It was no sport, he kept saying, it was a tragedy where the bull's death was fated from the start. He joked about buying a bull calf in Toronto to practice his torero moves. Alice, while talking with Hadley and pouring the tea, watched, listened and kept her own counsel. Already wary of the way Ernest could make Gertrude's face light up, she was not enthusiastic about the Hemingways' trip to Navarre; she and Gertrude discovered Pamplona, and Alice was not one to share gratuitously with handsome young men. Alice B. Toklas was very small, but she was a survivor who outlasted almost all the Left Bankers. And very much in the room was Hadley, radiant in her pregnancy, reminding the lesbian couple of their own biology. It was an evening of bulls and babies, uncommon talk for the rue de Fleurus.[21]

Everyone knew about the Hemingway baby. Ezra knew, giving Hadley strange advice about how motherhood would soften her brain. Gertrude and Alice knew but kept their opinions at home. In Oak Park, Isabel Simmons knew, and in Chicago, Bill Horne was told by letter. Everyone knew except the grandparents, Clarence and Grace Hemingway, who were not told until three weeks before Hadley delivered. Isabel, living only a few doors down from the Hemingways, knew how to keep a secret. No one knows why Ernest did not tell his parents sooner about their grandchild-to-be, but it does seem curious that he kept the news from them so long. Perhaps he did not want his parents interfering in his life with advice and suggestions. Certainly Dr. Hemingway would have offered to deliver the baby in the Oak Park hospital, and Grace might have offered to be in Toronto with Hadley before the delivery. Ernest wanted none of that. Grace and Clarence did not see their first grandchild until 1927, when Hadley brought the boy to Oak Park. It was almost as if Ernest did not want anything from his Oak Park past to interact with the new persona he had fashioned for himself. Later some blamed it all on his alleged hatred for his mother, but that does not answer the question. Ernest Hemingway did not hate his father, yet after leaving Chicago in 1921, he saw the Doctor only twice more before he buried him in 1928; one of those encounters was unavoidable and the other accidental. Perhaps it was not only his parents but also his entire early life in Oak Park that he wanted forever buried. Ernie Hemingway, the Oak Park boy with dirty nails whom no one remembered as particularly promising, died and was buried at sea when Hadley and Ernest first crossed to France. The new Ernest Hemingway – courageous war veteran, experimental writer, veteran newsman, skilled sportsman and European traveler – was his own creation, a persona whose early roots would not bear close examination.[22]

V

Bullfights were one thing but the feast of San Fermin in the town of Pamplona was not merely a week of bullfights. It was days and nights that ran together without stopping, drinking without stopping; Ernest got key elements down quickly in fragments for later use:

the Riau Riau, fifes, drums, reed pipes, blue shirts, red neckerchiefs, circling, lifting, floating dance, all day all night, leather wine bottles over shoulder, flat basque caps or wide straw hats, faces like smoked buck skin, flat backs, flat hips, dancing, dancing, giants slowly turning, solemnly dancing, beautiful children, hair, few dogs, no cats, old men in blue shirts and dark blue caps, big, hard muscled, work slowed bodies, club men.[23]

Pamplona was fireworks, cannon shots, band music on the plaza and crowded, noisy cafés. It was strange, heavy food and brandy still tasting of the Spanish earth. It was late night meals never beginning before ten and early morning music pounding in the street beneath their window. It was rabbit and trout on the menu, wonderful trout with a slice of country ham inside and outside crispy brown, and rich olive oil in everything. From the balcony of their rented room, Ernest and Hadley watched the dancers in the street below them. There seemed no point sleeping; sleep was dead. No one slept during San Fermin.[24]

They had arrived by bus to find their reserved hotel room occupied and prices outrageous. With luck and belligerence, they got a room in a private house that cost them only two months' Paris rent for the six days of the fiesta. In spite of the long train ride and bumpy bus roads, Hadley seemed to thrive on the chaos. Early each morning the two of them rose to watch local heroes race insanely ahead of charging bulls, channeled by wooden barricades through the cobblestone streets to the Plaza de Toros for the afternoon spectacle. From the top of the arena, Ernest noted carefully the morning details: the way the mountains framed the brown, pink and blue buildings of the town, the crowd moving "like a busy street seen from a high window." The cannon fired and the crowd began to run, shouting, men racing down the barricaded street, and then a space between them and the bulls, massed together, heads tossing, clattering into the arena.[25]

They drank hot, creamy *café con leche* with their breakfast rolls and lunched on the south side of the plaza at the Iruna café, watching their reflections in the silvered mirrors. Under the arcade they waited their turn to grab a sidewalk table where they could sip a brandy, filled exactly to the etched line of the glass, and wait for the late afternoon's bullfights to begin. Some days they walked through the old town out on to what remained of the original French fort's walls, or shopped for a Basque boina in the market below the plaza. Ernest feasted on the primitive faces caught up in the chaos, the "faces of Velasquez's drinkers,

Goya and Greco faces." Parading through the town, carried by fifty men, came the mitered statue of San Fermin wreathed by rising clouds of incense, the festival's religious center around which flowed the more ancient ritual of the bulls.[26]

The first three days of the bullfights were splendid, hot, dusty afternoons in the Plaza de Toros where Ernest and Hadley watched the "tragedy" unfold. He warned her about the bulls goring the horses, and when the time came Hadley simply turned her attention to the embroidery work she was sewing for the baby moving in her womb. In the ring, horse and bull blood soaked into the sand while her stitching went on. She turned away when the bull and the matador began their dance, but for Hemingway, it was like watching the war from a ringside seat; that week five of the eight matadors were tossed or gored. Fantastic, mean, prehistoric, the bull, he said, "is death right up until he is absolutely dead himself and is stupid and brave as the people of any country and altogether wonderful and horrifying."[27]

On the morning of July 10, as Ernest and Hadley were rising to watch the bulls run through the barricaded streets, their breath caught and held as the earth moved beneath them. The hotel rocked gently bringing loose items crashing to the floor as a twelve-second earthquake woke the town to terror. The drunks in the plaza did not feel a thing, but more sober citizens ran into the cobblestone streets immediately. The quake was followed by torrential rains that drenched the province of Navarre, cancelling the *corrida*. That afternoon near Zaragoza, a tornado smashed through the countryside, followed by an intense seven-hour storm. The next morning, Wednesday, another quake of three seconds rocked Pamplona, and once more the rains kept bulls in their pens and the matadors in their hotel rooms, moody with waiting. Hadley, soaked in the downpour, was sniffling before the week was out.[28]

Although the last two scheduled bullfights (July 10–11) were washed out, the festival continued until July 18. It was, therefore, a small matter to reschedule the fights. Thursday, July 12 began in rain that slackened by noon and cleared by 5:30 when the *corrida* began. The sandy arena was soggy, the matadors' capes damp and heavy, but Maera, Gitanillo and young Algabeno gave brilliant performances under difficult conditions. However, it was the Friday finale that most impressed Hemingway. On his first bull Maera sprained his wrist so badly he could not continue. Olmas came in to fight the second bull, but was hooked almost immediately and taken from the ring. Algabeno came into the ring to

1 Sylvia Beach in the doorway of her bookstore, Shakespeare and Company. (Princeton University Library)

2 Ezra Pound inside Shakespeare and Company, where there were ''photographs on the wall of famous writers both living and dead. The photographs all looked like snapshots'' (*A Moveable Feast*). (Princeton University Library)

3 (left), Edward Eric "Chink" Dorman-Smith, on leave from his Rhine military duties, posing on the tennis court that Hemingway, Ford and Pound rented in Paris. (Princeton University Library)

4 (below), Hemingway and Robert McAlmon in Spain, 1923: "Hemingway wanted much to see a bullfight, and after a week of talking about it, we headed towards Spain" (*Being Geniuses Together*). (John F. Kennedy Library)

5 (left), ''If George Antheil asks you to write a Jazz Opera with him say, 'Yes George' and let it go at that. He asks all his friends. It is his way of paying a delicate compliment'' (Hemingway MS 376a). (John F. Kennedy Library)

6 (below), Bill Bird, American newsman and Paris printer, who hand-set the type and published the 1924 edition of Hemingway's *in our time*. (Princeton University Library)

7 (above), Ford Madox Ford, James Joyce, Ezra Pound and John
Quinn, November 1923, in Paris founding the *transatlantic review*.
(Humanities Research Center, University of Texas)

8 (below), ''I walked past the sad tables of the Rotonde to the Select.
There were a few people inside at the bar, and outside, alone, sat
Harvey Stone'' (*The Sun Also Rises*). (Roger-Viollet, Paris)

9 (above), ". . . the rue Mouffetard, that wonderful narrow crowded
market street which led into the Place Contrescarpe" (*A Moveable
Feast*). Living in their first apartment on rue Cardinale Lemoine the
Hemingways shopped on this street. (Roger-Viollet, Paris)

10 (below), ". . . at Auteuil it was beautiful to watch each day they
raced when you could be there and see the honest races with the
great horses, and you got to know the course as well as any place you
had ever known" (*A Moveable Feast*). (Roger-Viollet, Paris)

11 (right), "Battered to a pitiful pulp after one of the cruelest beatings a boxer ever took, Georges Carpentier, France's greatest athletic idol, was hammered into a has-been by Battling Siki, young Senegalese slugger, in the sixth round . . . at Buffalo Stadium" (Paris *Tribune*, September 25, 1922). Hemingway was in the crowd the afternoon that Carpentier lost his French title. (Roger-Viollet, Paris)

12 (below), Café du Dôme "which has been the rendezvous of American Bohemians in Paris for the past thirty years is now as up-to-date, modern, shiny and completely equipped as the bath room in the home of an American 'Babbitt'" (Paris *Tribune*, 1924). (Roger-Viollet, Paris)

13   The old order and the new: at the 1922 Lausanne Conference,
Hemingway with his arm around the shoulders of Lincoln Steffens.
(John F. Kennedy Library)

14 Hadley Hemingway, winter 1925, at Schruns, Austria, with her heavy wooden skis. (John F. Kennedy Library)

15 John Hadley Nicanor Hemingway, called Bumby, born in Toronto and raised in Europe speaking Breton French. (John F. Kennedy Library)

16 Hadley Hemingway (c.1925), her hair close-cropped and dressed in her no longer new fur-collared coat. (John F. Kennedy Library)

17   Pauline Pfeiffer modeling Paris fashions for her *Vogue* editor, Main Bocher, the skirt still creased. (Princeton University Library)

18 (right), In January 1926 at Gaschurn, Austria, Ernest took this picture of his wife, Hadley, and his wife-to-be, Pauline Pfeiffer. As he said later, ''The husband has two attractive girls around . . . and if he has bad luck he gets to love them both'' (*A Moveable Feast*). (John F. Kennedy Library)

19 (below), Riviera Splendide Hotel in Rapallo where the Hemingways stayed. Directly across the broad street is the public beach. (Tourist Authority, Rapallo, Italy)

20 (left), "Their room was on the second floor facing the sea. It also faced the public garden and the war monument . . . the war monument was made of bronze and glistened in the rain" ("Cat in the Rain"). This Rapallo monument was melted down in World War Two for the munitions industry. The hotel behind it is the Riviera Splendide. (Tourist Authority, Rapallo, Italy)

21 (below), Panorama of Rapallo, much as it was in 1923. Riviera Splendide is the small hotel facing the sea to the left of the Savoia. (Tourist Authority, Rapallo, Italy)

22   "There were so many people running ahead of the bulls that the mass
thickened and slowed up going through the gate into the ring,
and as the bulls passed, galloping together, heavy, muddy-sided,
horns swinging, one shot ahead, caught a man in the running crowd
in the back and lifted him in the air" (*The Sun Also Rises*). The
conclusion of the Pamplona *encierro*. (National Archives)

23 (above), "`. . . you could see the plateau of Pamplona rising out of the plain, and the walls of the city, and the great brown cathedral, and the broken skyline of the other churches. In back of the plateau were the mountains . . .`" (*The Sun Also Rises*). (Roger-Viollet, Paris)

24 (below), Hemingway, Duff Twysden, Hadley, Don Stewart and Pat Guthrie at a sidewalk cafe in Pamplona during the 1925 San Fermin festival. (John F. Kennedy Library)

kill the remaining five Villar bulls. It was an extraordinary afternoon in which life seemed to imitate Hemingway's art. His bullfight vignette based on Mike Strater's experience described just such an afternoon in which a young matador killed the last five bulls on the program.[29]

VI

Bone weary, they returned to Paris where a record heat wave was driving many people out of town and literally killing some of those who remained. To Ernest's discomfort, his pregnant wife was sniffling from what developed into a terrible summer cold. As he was ready to write, Hadley was sick, and Paris, stifling in 96 degree heat, began three days of Bastille Day celebration. It was too hot for army troops to parade the boulevards but not too hot for the booming cannon shots to start the day. That night a huge bonfire at the Bastille Column lighted up the night sky just before the fireworks from the Pont Neuf sparkled in the dark. Streets were jammed with feverish bodies dancing, moving, singing, stopping traffic. Street dances sprang up throughout the Quarter, and where the Dôme faced the Rotonde, Americans jammed the Montparnasse street.[30]

Neither of the Hemingways found the Bastille Day madness exhilarating. After five days of continuous, primitive chaos in Pamplona, they could not respond to the French celebration that now appeared by comparison a little self-conscious. In their apartment that day no air moved, and heat sat down with them, a tangible presence fraying nerves and melting butter in its dish. Hadley felt too sick to go out, and Ernest could not write in the heavy air. That evening a slight breeze came up the Seine, giving the city some relief, but neither man nor wife slept well on rue du Cardinal Lemoine where sheets turned sweat-damp in the night and street music came in the open windows.

The week passed in much the same way: Hadley got no better and he could not write. By night he could not sleep, and by day Hadley's face whitened steadily, worrying him almost enough to take her to a doctor. He did the housework and tried to write, but the heat and visitors kept him from it. "I can't write," he complained. "Our wax puppy is losing his fur. Hadley has a cold in her head and snuffs or blows. . . . A day no sooner starts than it is over. We have only a month more and a quarter of it is gone already. I waste each day away in little things that don't matter." In his head he tried to write the Pamplona sketches for the "Inquest" book, but something always interrupted the flow. Feeling sorry for himself, he wrote, "I wish Hadley would get well because she is so miserable. She may go on like this until the first of August. I wouldn't wonder."[31]

The *Tribune* review of Pound's *Indiscretions*, the first volume in Ezra's inquest into the state of letters, reminded Ernest that he needed to finish what he had started in Chamby. By July 17, the heat wave lifted as rains cooled Paris, and galley proofs arrived for *Three Stories & Ten Poems*. Seeing his stories in print for the first time was just the kick needed to move Ernest out of his doldrums and into a productive cycle, which began, as it would so often, with letters and then eased into the fiction. For two days, while correcting proofs, he composed a long letter to Bill Horne in which he reviewed his past eighteen European months in great detail, reliving them as he typed the words. Such letters were a warm-up exercise for him, but for his old Red Cross buddy he particularly enjoyed summarizing his adventures: Genoa, Lausanne, Thrace, the Ruhr; skiing, fishing, bullfights, boxing matches. Because Hadley was pregnant, he said, they were coming home for his son's first year. They were certain it was a boy. Hadley, he said, "hasn't been sick a minute or even nauseated all the time. She's never felt better and looks wonderfully." As he typed those words on his Corona, Hadley sat across the table, white-faced and miserable.[32]

Gradually the weather cooled, Hadley improved and the words began to take shape. During the last ten days of July, he wrote five bullfight vignettes, almost enough to complete his experiment. There was the gored horse with his guts hanging out and the blood pumping between his legs: "They whack-whacked the white horse on the legs and he kneed himself up." Nine years later, nostalgic about his apprenticeship, he told us how he forced himself to study death in the afternoon sun, not turning his head away when the bull's horns went into the horse. He said,

> I found the greatest difficulty, aside from knowing truly what you really felt, rather than what you were supposed to feel, and had been taught to feel, was to put down what really happened in action; what the actual things were which produced the emotion that you experienced.

With the white horse he kept his eyes fixed on the action with the intensity of a natural historian, registering exactly what parts produced the jolt. And with Villalta the same, watching him in the ring for the essential detail:

> the bull charged and Villalta charged and just for a moment they became one. Villalta became one with the bull and then it was over. Villalta standing straight and the red hilt of the sword sticking out dully between the bull's shoulders. Villalta, his hand up at the crowd and the bull roaring blood, looking straight at Villalta and his legs caving.

That was the way it was, and he got down on paper the hard line of it forever so that years later when Villalta was as dead as that afternoon bull, it was still there, fresh always, happening now. Sentence fragments and present participles kept it alive – *standing, sticking, roaring, looking, caving* – not letting the blood stop or the bull die. No matter the years in between, the reader would have it happening in his own present time. That was what Hemingway was after.[33]

But it was not the only thing. The "whack-whacked" white horse came from observation, as did Villalta, but the one that began "I heard the drums coming down the street" is told by a matador trying to get the drunken Luis back to the hotel to be in shape to fight bulls the next day. No matter what Hemingway saw in Pamplona and no matter what he said in letters about hanging out with bullfighters, he spoke little Spanish that summer. Maera commenting from the hotel balcony on Luis drunk in the street was an act of Hemingway's imagination. Compare Villalta with his bull with Luis in the street and find no difference; they are equally believable. "Oh leave me alone," says Luis. "You're not my father."[34]

Here Hemingway was not remembering detail that once produced an emotion, for the drama took place only in his head. In the final vignette he describes the death of the bullfighter Maera, who, when it was written, was as alive as a bullfighter slowly dying from tuberculosis can be. But there on the paper Hemingway created a hospital room in which the gored Maera listened to others telling him he would not die. After numerous starts, Hemingway wrote:

> It was very hot in the room and a little light came in through the shutters. The doctor sat on a chair in the corner. Maera lay with the sheet pulled up to his chin. There was a big hump under the sheet where he was bandaged.

He broke it off and tried again. The doctor tells Maera he will not die, but the matador does not listen. His last words to the narrator are: "I'm going to die. Tell Luis I'm going to die."[35]

When Hemingway showed his experiments to Pound, Ezra was enthusiastic about most of the vignettes, but did not care for Maera's death. He sent Hemingway back to his typewriter, not to revise, but to create an altogether different death for Maera. Kill him once, kill him twice – the imagination can murder and create as it pleases. This time Hemingway kept it all in the arena: Maera down in the sand, the bull bumping him, and then driving his horn all the way through, and Maera "felt it go into the sand." Totally detached, Hemingway sees the doctor washing his hands, Maera on the cot, and hears the shouting in the grandstand above.

> Maera felt everything getting larger and larger and then smaller and smaller. Then it got larger and larger and larger and then smaller and smaller. Then everything commenced to run faster and faster as when they speed up a cinematograph film. Then he was dead.

Maybe that is the way one dies, but it was not as convincing as the horn going through into the sand. Hemingway saw the horn and could imagine how it felt. About dying, it was anyone's guess. If not his best piece, it was still a valuable experiment in shifting the point of view from detached observer into Maera's head and then back again to the narrator who could say, "Then he was dead."[36]

Looking over the vignettes, Ezra questioned their arrangement: was there any controlling logic to the experiences? Nothing indicates that Hemingway wrote with a larger plan in mind, but now he was forced to arrange a sequence. Ezra also felt there needed to be more frozen moments for the book to feel right. They discussed possibilities while Dorothy poured more tea. Ernest told him about the hanging of an Italian gangster in Chicago. He remembered it from the papers. He could do the hanging and maybe another one about the King of Greece. His friend Shorty Wornall, a newsreel camera man, told him about the deposed king in his rose garden wanting to go to America. With less than three weeks left in Paris, Ernest sat down to finish the book.[37]

VII

As Hemingway worked on the Greek king, President Harding of America felt a stomach twinge from crabs eaten in Seattle. Next thing he knew it was ptomaine poisoning, but not serious his doctor said. Two days later it was acute, and then pneumonia, with Harding "fighting for his life." Then he was dead. All the newspapers said so in banner headlines, which shrank the next day, unable to compete with news of short skirts at Deauville. As Harding faded from attention, Ernest caught the Greek king clipping his roses and left him there suspended in literary time forever.[38]

The day after reading of Harding's death, he wrote Ezra that the book was ready except for the hanging which was about to begin. Now he saw how it all fit together. Ezra was right. Take out the ironic titles: too cute. Call them Chapter 1, Chapter 2, right up to 18. "The bulls," he said, "start, then reappear and then finish off. The war starts clear and noble just like it did, Mons etc., gets close and blurred and finished with the feller who goes home and gets clap. The refugees leave Thrace, due to the Greek ministers, who are shot. The whole thing closes with the talk with the King of Greece and his Queen in their garden (just written). . . . America appears in the cops shooting the guys who robbed the cigar store. It has form all right. . . . I will commence the hanging."[39]

In the upstairs rooms above the dirty Paris street, he hanged Sam Cardinella "at six o'clock in the morning in the corridor of the county jail." He could see it all with the clarity of a victim: tiers of cells, condemned men watching, Sam carried in between two priests, full of fear, unable to walk. "Be a man, my son," said one priest. When they came at him with the black cap, his sphincter let go. He could see disgust on the faces of the guards. They were Hemingway's guards, his priests, his Sam on the scaffold, strapped tight into his chair on top of the drop, "which was very heavy, built of oak and steel and swung on ball bearings." That's when he saw the priest skipping back before the drop fell and Sam . . . no need to take it further. He left Sam there, the drop beginning to fall away beneath him.[40]

While Ernest was creating his death, the remains of Sam Cardinella lay two years molding in a Chicago grave, his name fading from local memory. Nothing about his criminal life was significant, not even the leaving of it. Only the random intersection of his death and Ernest's presence in Chicago created the vignette, eventually translated into most of the world's languages, making Sam Cardinella a name better known that Warren G. Harding.[41]

The same day that Hemingway began the Cardinella hanging, he received from McAlmon the page proofs for *Three Stories & Ten Poems*, the book that he expected to follow, not precede *in our time*. McAlmon was an impatient man: if it did not happen quickly, he quickly lost interest. His Ellerman money greased the press wheels of Maurice Darantier, the same Dijon printer who printed Joyce's *Ulysses*. Later Ernest would complain that his "Inquest" book should have been first because Bird had copy in hand before Ernest gave McAlmon the stories and poems. This is not accurate. McAlmon had only to hire a professional printer to publish his volume. Bill Bird, on the other hand, first worked all day at his news desk, and then had to hand-set his own type in the evenings and at weekends.[42]

Ernest proudly took the page proofs of his first book to both Bill Bird and Gertrude Stein for advice on typeface and layout. In his letter back to McAlmon, he enclosed a new cover design that Bird suggested and Stein approved, asking for a type less squatty and darker than that used in the proofs. The result was plain, bold and professional.

On August 13, in what must have been a record for the Dijon print shop, the first copies of the slim, greyish-blue book appeared in Sylvia Beach's bookshop. Ernest and Hadley looked at it long in the window before going inside where Sylvia handed him his four author's copies charged to McAlmon's account. Ernest opened the cover to the dedication page: This Book Is For Hadley. It was the only substantial result they had to show for their twenty months abroad, and both were quite proud of it. Before leaving Sylvia's, the Hemingways began saying their good-byes all round, for they had only three more days in Paris. Sylvia gave them both hugs, a gentle one for Hadley now entering her eighth month. As a farewell present, Sylvia gave them copies of Mina Loy's *Lunar Baedecker* and William Carlos Williams' *Spring and All*, both part of the "Inquest" series that would eventually include *in our time*. She also loaned the Hemingways $100 to get them through until Ernest's first Toronto check.[43]

They packed their clothes and a few books, crated their small paintings by Masson, Kumae and Dorothy Pound, threw out the trash and gave their mongrel dog to Bill Bird for safe keeping. A year, they told him, and they would be back. Ernest claimed to have already leased a large studio apartment for October of 1924. As they made their rounds of

Soft cover of Hemingway's first book published by Robert McAlmon in 1923. (John F. Kennedy Library) farewells and had their last drinks at the Dôme, boat loads of late summer tourists streamed into Paris from French ports, eager to spend cheap francs, now at eighteen to the dollar. The Turks and the Greeks were finally at fitful peace, accepting the last of the Lausanne proposals, the burning of Smyrna and the refugees of Thrace apparently having served their historic purpose. In the *Tribune*, letters to the editor continued to complain about visa costs, prohibition, rude Germans, the presidential hopes of Henry Ford and the shocking sight of black men dancing with white women. Harding buried and Coolidge laconic, Americans abroad were uninvolved in Europe.

Their last weekend in Paris was hot, humid, and the town was filled with noisy Americans and Frenchmen from the provinces come to Paris for the long Assumption Day weekend. On Thursday, August 16, as they were closing up their last bags for the morrow's train trip to Cherbourg, the morning paper announced that their ship's Friday departure was delayed. The Cunard liner *Andania*, scheduled to sail August 17, would not depart for Canada until August 26. Having eaten and drunk their farewells with Guy and Mary Hickok, Gertrude and Alice, the Pounds and the Birds, the nine-day reprieve was a little awkward and more than inconvenient. Everything was packed, and new renters scheduled to move into their tiny apartment which Hadley, at least, was happy to abandon.

How the Hemingways spent their extra days in Paris is not recorded. All eighteen vignettes were finished and now in Pound's editorial hands. The Paris tracks were closed, the horses running summer races in Deauville and other fashionable resorts. They could not see "Birth of a Nation," whose Paris showing was stopped by authorities opposed to the film's racial bias. The night before they left Paris, a violent Atlantic storm swept the French coast, crippling channel traffic and breaking ships loose from their moorings. With all omens against their departure, they took the Sunday morning train to Cherbourg where afternoon storms made their boarding unpleasant. Their entire voyage was even more unpleasant as the Atlantic heaved under summer storms. Departing in heavy weather, Ernest, Hadley and their unborn son left unnoticed among the other cheap fares.[44]

Chapter Eight

RETURN TO TORONTO
FALL AND WINTER, 1923

I

They went to Toronto to have a baby, planning to stay a year, maybe two. They only lasted four months. Four months was a long time in Toronto. No sooner had they landed than Ernest was explaining to Ezra what a mistake they had made returning, but that was only an estimate made before he knew the full consequences of his decision. Four days later, he began working under Harry Hindmarsh, the assistant managing editor of the *Daily Star* who was married to the owner's daughter. Hemingway's pay was right ($125 a week) but the editor was not. Ernest returned as the featured pet of John Bone, now managing editor and no longer his direct superior. Hindmarsh, who disliked prima donna reporters and distrusted any of John Bone's boys, was determined to break Hemingway to his command by sending him out on cub reporter stories, keeping him at work early and late, and not giving Hemingway his share of by-lines. At one time or another, Hindmarsh treated most of his by-lined reporters in similar fashion to establish his authority. With Hemingway, Hindmarsh made a serious mistake. Within a month they were enemies, and within three months Ernest, without telling Hindmarsh, booked return passage to France.[1]

Of course Hemingway was a prima donna, but for that first month back in Toronto he played the Hindmarsh game as well as he could. His days and nights filled up with trivia, leaving no time for writing, not even letters. On Monday, September 10, he reported for work and found himself that night bedded down in a Pullman sleeper enroute to Kingston to cover Red Ryan's escape from the Kingston penitentiary. No sooner did Ernest return than Hindmarsh put him to work researching and investigating a sometime geologist, Alfred Coyne, who specialized in mineral con-games: one year it was oil; this year it was coal in northern Ontario.[2]

Thursday through Sunday, Hemingway worked on the Coyne story, reading through a pile of background material and interviewing the Toronto officers of British Coal Mines, Limited, who claimed from their offices without a title on the door that Alfred Coyne was no longer associated with their venture and no amount of *Star* publicity could sell their stock, for it was already fully subscribed in Ottawa. Then, in soft voices, came the hard sell: coal samples, drilling logs, geological surveys. With his sharp eye for telling detail, Ernest conveyed his distrust without editorializing:

> Another man in a brown suit, a hawk face, his hair parted on the side and a little inclined to hang dankly forward at the parting, commenced talking. He had a very charming voice. He started right out speaking very slowly and convincingly and smiling quizzically.

The story closed with Hemingway's note to Hindmarsh, suggesting that the paper should follow up the story, noting the possibility that the whole operation was crooked.[3]

Hemingway filed the story Friday evening, but by Sunday Hindmarsh had yet to read it. On Sunday, Hemingway wrote a cover memo to Hindmarsh which he pointedly dated "12:30 Sunday night."

> Enclosed is the British Colonial Coal Mines Ltd. up to date. I have written it out in detail with the atmosphere and verbatim conversations in case we get proof they are crooks and you decide to do an exposure.

The next morning, Hemingway found the following note in his work file:

> Mr. Hemmingway:
> I am attaching clippings on Sudbury coal from yesterday's paper and previous issues, also a memo from Mr. Bone which has been

standing over for some little time. I think you had better make arrangements to go up to Sudbury field and get the necessary article. I think you had better make some arrangements for taking a camera with you before you go, however. Please see me about it.

H.C.H.

The son of a bitch, Ernest must have thought, could not even spell his name right.[4]

Wednesday night Ernest was once again sleeping in a Pullman car bound for Sudbury, where he tramped across broken terrain following mining engineers and company spokesmen who showed him black outcroppings that looked like coal. He stooped over core barrels examining what the drillers brought of the ground: "I saw several long rods. It was very black, and hard looking, streaked with quartz, shining iron pyrites, and slate." There was no way for him to know if it was commercial coal or not. Thomas Watson, mining engineer, said no. The company men said yes. The article Ernest filed on his return did not settle the Sudbury coal question, but it raised nagging doubts for the reader. It was a straightforward and first-class piece of investigative reporting that should have earned him a few days' rest, but all Ernest got was an evening off at the race track. With nothing more than the form chart and his pregnant wife to guide him, Hemingway put ten dollars on "My Dear" in the first race and "Baby Mine" in the third. Both horses, he wrote Ezra, came home first at odds that paid him $225. "This," he said, "making altogether about forty dollars more than I make in two weeks of eighteen hour a day toil, it has destroyed whatever pleasure I got from dragging down the pay envelope. Thus are we buggared by destiny, as Hamlet remarked."[5]

When he returned from Sudbury, Ernest found a letter from his father, who was overjoyed at the news of Hadley's pregnancy and was boxing up Ernest's belongings, as requested, to ship to Toronto. Hadley's furniture arrived from St. Louis a few days after they signed a year's lease on a fourth-floor, walk-up apartment on Bathurst Street. Next to their bed, a door opened on to a balcony looking out over a wooded ravine, pleasant enough in the early fall, but when the arctic wind howled they had to stuff blankets around the door and window and huddle next to the electric grate for warmth.

Working at the *Star* was far more time consuming and annoying than either of them had anticipated, but they were there for the year.

Although he spoke at times of killing Hindmarsh, Ernest was willing to live up to his commitment. Hadley, however, was worried. She wrote Grace Hemingway, "Ernest is *distracted* by the job which is run on the most crazy uneconomical principles – so many trips, no sleep and countless assignments." That Saturday, September 29, Ernest was once more out of town on assignment, leaving Hadley in her ninth month to face the move on her own. She managed to hire and borrow enough helping hands to move their old clothes, furniture and new cat up four flights of stairs.[6]

Five days later Hemingway was enroute to New York City to cover Lloyd George's arrival and to accompany him on his special train into Canada. A running feature of Lloyd George's magnitude produced multiple stories and side-bars, requiring at least two reporters to hustle the material. Hindmarsh, at the last moment, sent Ernest by himself to cover the story. It was a six-day circus: dock-side report and interview, speeches, evening at the theater, and the trip back to Toronto. It was early mornings and late nights. It was eight stories or more filed in four days. While in New York, Hemingway bought a copy of the *Little Review*'s so called "Spring" issue to see in print, finally, his poem, "They All Made Peace," and his six vignettes of "In Our Time." There, back to back with his sketches, was Gertrude Stein's "A Valentine To Sherwood Anderson," which began:

I knew too that through them I knew too that he was through, I knew too that he threw them, I knew too that they were through, I knew too I knew too, I knew I knew them.

She was as enigmatic as ever, but it sounded to Ernest a lot like Paris, and afternoons at rue de Fleurus flooded back into his mind that did not want to think about Lloyd George.[7]

Losing sleep, patience and enthusiasm for his work, Ernest deeply resented being sent out of town, for Hadley now tired easily in her ninth month. Although the baby was not expected until the end of October, he did not want her to be alone. Once again they were seeing each other in letters. She told him that the apartment was shaping up. She was lugging the groceries in small bundles up the four flights of stairs, trying to be careful of her condition. She was also answering the letters from Oak Park, thanking the Doctor for packing, shipping and paying for the trunk full of Ernest's old life and some stored wedding presents; thanking him also for the check he sent to buy things for the baby. "Remember," she told Ernest, "were we wiz be This Time Next Year – We wiz gonna *be* there too." On Monday, October 8, not expecting him to return for two more days, she ended her letter: "Articles grand. Love my Bubby and will smooch with him so joyously come Wedens tag morgen."[8]

At Tuesday evening supper, while she was listening to Harriet Connable play the piano, Hadley's contractions began. Before midnight she checked into Wellesley Hospital where her labor pains became more intense. Hadley may not have expected the baby for another two weeks, but it was coming now. They gave her nitrous oxide gas, dulling the pain and dissolving the world. At 2:00 a.m. Wednesday morning she delivered a healthy seven-pound baby boy – John Hadley Nicanor Hemingway. At the same time, Ernest was in the press car of the Lloyd George train, trading jokes with the boys. That morning, he was awakened ten miles outside of Toronto by the news of his baby. The terse message said nothing of Hadley's condition, leaving him ten rail miles plus a cab ride to worry about her. Giving his copy to someone else to deliver to the *Star*, Ernest went straight from the station to the hospital. There "he quite broke down from fatigue and strain," Hadley told Izzy Simmons, "and was so sweet as you and I know he can be."[9]

When Ernest got to the office, Hindmarsh bawled him out for not filing his copy before visiting Hadley. And that was the end of Toronto: Ernest and Hindmarsh facing each other, both furious, saying things that could not be taken back. As a consequence, he wrote to Ezra, his position on the *Star* was shaky, for he told Hindmarsh that he "would never forgive him of course and that all work done by me from now on would be with the most utter contempt and hatred for him and all his bunch of masturbating mouthed associates." Within five days, Ernest was transferred to the *Toronto Star Weekly* staff, but he was never completely free from Hindmarsh's presence. Hadley saw it in his eyes. Up until the birth of John Hadley, they both were determined to stick the year, but by mid-October Hadley wrote Izzy, "I think we are going to leave here as soon as I am safely strong again. It is too horrible to describe or linger over and it will kill or scar my Tiny if we stay too long. He is almost crazy and our hearts are heavy heavy just when we ought to be so happy. . . . I haven't the faintest idea but what I'd come out an old, care-ridden THING from another big move – And staying is Hell."[10]

Others remembered it differently. Gordon Sinclair, a cub reporter on the *Daily Star*, thought that the break came over a promotional stunt that Hemingway refused to participate in. The *Star* had bought an elephant and a white peacock for the Toronto zoo. As Sinclair remembered it:

> They assigned Hemingway to do [a] . . . welcome to the peacock. He felt it beneath him, because it was for promotion. And he quit. When he quit, he pinned a long list of grievances to the noticeboard close to Hindmarsh's office. . . . It included the complaint that Hindmarsh treated him like dirt, overworked him, and lied to him. The very first sentence was . . .: "I Ernest Hemingway will not now or ever write about any goddamn peacock."

Morley Callaghan, another reporter at the time, does not remember the list at all. Others swear by it. Despite what people remembered, Hemingway's relationship with the *Star* ended that Wednesday morning when Ernest was not at the hospital when Hadley needed him. He wrote for almost three more months with only one by-line from Hindmarsh. Three months put Hadley back on her feet and gave Ernest time enough to force the break with his editor.[11]

II

For the *Star Weekly* he wrote features about trout fishing in Switzerland and Germany, about bullfights in Pamplona, about Paris gargoyles, hunting in France, Italian Christmas, Swiss skiing and European nightlife. At the end of his "Pamplona in July" feature, Hemingway wrote:

> That was just three months ago. It seems in a different century now, working in an office. It is a very long way from the sunbaked town of Pamplona, where the men race through the streets in the mornings ahead of the bulls to the morning ride to work on a Bay-Caledonia car. But it is only fourteen days by water to Spain."

If John Bone was paying attention, he must have sensed that Hemingway's heart was not in Toronto.[12]

Although Toronto could not, in Hemingway's view, have been a worse experience, his Paris luck continued unabated. No sooner had he sent out birth telegrams to the world – SEVEN POUND BOY THREE

HOURS ALL JAKE – than literary news from his Paris contacts began to arrive. From Ezra came a gossipy letter addressed to "Col. Hemingway Tomato Star, Tomato Can" which agreed that Hemingway made a mistake in returning. "I hope," Ezra told him, "you won't do it again, there was once a troubadour who said that if he 'ever went to Syria again, he prayed God wd keep him there, fer bein sech a damn fool.'" Strater, Pound added, was in New York reconciled with his wife; McAlmon had returned from London; Bird was in Venice but had a "noble plan" for the typography of *in our time*. The book would be published, not soon but certainly.[13]

What Bird had in mind for Hemingway's new form was typography that would "put a real kick into the design of the book." Given the title and the subject matter, he wanted to frame each page "in a border of newspaper print," using bullfight journals for the matador vignettes and something from Athens for the Greek king in his garden. But he would not be able to begin setting type until October. All of which was comforting news, but it could not match the letter from Edward O'Brien that reached him late in October.[14]

Hemingway shrewdly had sent O'Brien a copy of *Three Stories & Ten Poems* which, of course, established that "My Old Man" was a 1923 story. O'Brien now said that all three stories were "damn fine" and that he wanted to dedicate to Ernest Hemingway his 1923 collection of "best short stories," which would include the Paris race track story. Neither Hadley nor Ernest could believe the letter. Twenty months in Paris and not a single acceptance; now, stuck in Toronto where no one except Greg Clark gave a damn about Ernest's fiction, and O'Brien reprints "My Old Man" and puts his name up in dedication lights. At the end of his letter, O'Brien asked, "have you got enough stories for a Boni & Liveright book?" That last question knifed deeply into the quick of Ernest. No, there were no new stories. No new anything. He was not writing in Toronto.[15]

In his reply to O'Brien, Hemingway said that his elation could not have been greater if he "had been given 1 million dollars, the V[ictoria] C[ross]" and "been elected to the Academie [Française] to replace Anatole France." Yes, O'Brien could dedicate the book to him, and in the future he would write his stories with only O'Brien and God in mind. Speaking of which, he wondered how many stories one needed for a book? In Toronto he stayed too tired from newspaper work to write fiction. "In the morning," he said, "a story starts in your head on the street car and [you] have to choke it off because it was coming so perfectly and easily and clear and right and you know that if you let it go on it will be finished and gone and you'd never be able to write it. I'm all constipated up with stuff to write, that I've got to write before it goes bad in me."[16]

Immediately Hemingway relayed the O'Brien news to Sylvia Beach, asking her not to say anything about it for fear it might not happen. Of course, he knew how Sylvia loved to gossip; telling her was as good as leaving a message at the Dôme. On November 11, he sent Edmund Wilson a copy of *Three Stories & Ten Poems*, which Wilson said he liked and would put into the *Dial*'s "Briefer Mentions." Hemingway asked him to wait until *in our time* got published "sometime next month" to do a joint review. Initiating the correspondence with Wilson, who was quickly becoming the best critic of the period, was a studied and ambitious move. If Hemingway learned nothing else in Paris, he learned that a young writer needed to cultivate influential reviewers. That was the game. In response to Hemingway's young-writer-without-New-York-connections letter, Wilson offered to help find a publisher, for which Hemingway was grateful. He told Wilson about O'Brien's dedicating the collection to him: "As the book isn't out yet that is confidential." Then Ernest confided to Wilson that after Hadley lost his manuscripts, he had eaten "a very fine lunch at Gertrude Stein's and talked there all afternoon and read a lot of her new stuff." It would have been true, if only Gertrude and Alice had been in Paris that day, but they had not yet come back from St. Rémy. The point, which Wilson could not miss, was that Ernest and Gertrude were close friends. As Hemingway was obviously learning, writing well was only half the game; making sure that influential people knew you were writing well was the other half. Before another year was out his game would be impeccable, the two halves complementing each other perfectly.[17]

It was becoming almost funny at the Hemingway apartment: they were stuck in Toronto where he could not write while the critical notice he so badly needed was beginning to appear. Early in November, Gertrude Stein sent him a copy of her review of *Three Stories & Ten Poems* which would appear later that month in Dawson Johnson's "Notes on New Books" in the Paris *Tribune*. The review was Gertrude first and last, the sort to be dreaded from anyone but her:

Three stories and ten poems is very pleasantly said. So far so good, further than that, and as far as that, I may say of Ernest Hemingway that as he sticks to poetry and intelligence it is both poetry and intelligent. Rosevelt [sic] is genuinely felt as young as Hemingway and as old as Rosevelt. I should say that Hemingway should stick to poetry and intelligence and eschew the hotter emotions and the more turgid vision. Intelligence and a great deal of it is a good thing to use when you have it, it's all for the best.

Ernest knew she would not like the sexuality of "Up in Michigan," for she said so the first time she read it. Still she might have mentioned the stories. Stick to poetry, she said. He told her he had stories to write, but that he would "try not to be turgid." What was "turgid" about "My Old Man"? You never knew what Gertrude meant by any word for she sometimes gave them private meanings. Maybe it was not a great review, but it was his very first, and anything from Gertrude was nice to have.[18]

If only he had some new stories, but he did not. In September, Bill Bird told him that Ford Madox Ford was getting up a new literary magazine. "McAlmon," he said, "was going to contribute and so is everyone else." In October, Ernest promised Ezra he would try to submit something to the publication, possibly a piece called "Oh Canada" now beginning to take shape. Wishful thinking. "Oh Canada" never got past the first few pages. On December 3, Ezra demanded to know

WHHHHHHHHere's your copy? Wot's the use your pore old grandpa Ford sittin in a dammap cottage sweating 'is nek off to perduce a revoo where the Young can exPRESS 'emselves IF you aren't goin ter com across wif de PUNCH! I think, meself, you'd better come bak here and direk the policy of the damn thing.

By the time Hemingway received Pound's query, he had given up on writing anything in Toronto.[19]

III

On November 6, the *Tribune* announced that Ford Madox Ford's new literary periodical's first edition would include H. G. Wells, Joseph Conrad, James Joyce, e. e. cummings, Ezra Pound, T. S. Eliot and Robert McAlmon. On that same day Ernest wrote Sylvia Beach, asking her to help find him a Paris apartment: the Hemingways were returning

to Paris, probably in January. "It is," he told her, "impossible for me
to do any writing of my own. The paper wants all day and all night.
Much longer and I would never be able to write anymore." The
following day in a thank-you-for-the-baby-gift-money note to his father,
he said, "We made a mistake to come back here. But the only way to
do with mistakes is to pay for them and get out of them as soon as
possible." Two days later he began a letter to Gertrude Stein, confirming
a return to Paris in the new year. "The paper," he told her, "is full of
the Hitler and Ludendorf fiasco. It sounds very funny." Two days later
Hitler's attempted coup in Bavaria failed. He was only another bad
German joke in a year full of sour humor, a year that ended with the
mark at two billion to the dollar if anyone was interested.[20]

Early in December, Ernest got Bill Bird's November letter telling him
that the Hemingway's dog, the Waxen Puppy, was so incurably sick
that the vet had to "dispose" of him. So that was it: first he lost his
fur and now Waxen Puppy was dead. They should never have had a
dog in Paris or a cat in Toronto where the Humane Society "disposed"
of cats by the bagful. But now they had a cat and a baby boy; the cat
was less trouble. "I suppose," Ernest said about his son, "he will yell
his head off for the next two or three years. It seems his only form of
entertainment. No one gets as much pleasure out of it as he does."
Bird's good news was the half promise that *in our time* would be at the
bindery in "another ten days if nothing happens." Something happened,
for Bird's next letter contained only proof sheets and the promise that
a woodcut was being made based on Strater's portrait of Ernest. When
the woodcut arrived, he could pull the last form, but the cover remained
to be printed. The Bird house, he told Ernest, was now filled with
music no bird ever sang. Ezra had commandeered it as a rehearsal hall
for the violinist, Olga Rudge, and the young American self-proclaimed
genius, George Antheil, who were preparing for a December concert
of Antheil and Pound compositions. Pound's own neighbors had
complained about their discords, forcing them to impose on Bird.[21]

Ezra was, Bird said, exacting and inconsiderate of non-artists such as
himself who was merely tolerated in his own house, and not even
tolerated during rehearsals. "Ezra is there waving his arms and crying
No, No, No, and turning the pages. He says my presence would make
them nervous." Ernest had to smile. He could still hear Ezra trying
gamely to master the bassoon while Dorothy tried not to wince. Now
Ezra was giving concerts with the squatty little Antheil, who was
freeloading off of Sylvia Beach and anyone else who would put up cash

to forward his career. Pound told the *Tribune* reporter that George Antheil "interests me more than any other modern composer, and in spite of his extreme youth, I consider he is already Stravinsky's most formidable opponent . . . I have been specializing in men of genius and I am more interested in Antheil than I have been in any man since the death of Gaudier Brzeska."[22]

The only kind words of the *Tribune*'s reviewer were for the violinist, Olga Rudge (who would eventually as Pound's mistress bear his first child).

> We admire this young artist for having enough courage to sacrifice on the altars of Mr. Antheil's conceited art, personal honors which otherwise might have been hers. Both her enterprise and her playing merit commendation. . . . the tone produced by Miss Rudge and Mr. Antheil in that lat[t]er's compositions, frequently imposed a severe strain on the naked tympanum . . . the ear drank hence a copious draught of sound, which, in the memory of some listeners was classified as "music" pure and absolute, in that of others as degenerate noise and crash.[23]

About that same time, Ernest's sister, Carol, was pleading with him to come home for Christmas, a request he could hardly ignore. His father and mother between them had sent $150 in baby-gift money, paying all of Hadley's hospital bill. On December 8, Hadley wrote Grace Hemingway that the Christmas trip was too expensive since Ernest was quitting the *Star* on the first of January. They had, she said, already cancelled a trip to visit her sister Fonnie in St. Louis. They would need all the money they could save to live in Paris without Ernest's pay check. But more than the money was the problem of breast-feeding the baby: "the least little worry or fatigue on my part so often pretty nearly ends the supply and we feel that I *must* be able to nurse him on the ocean voyage."[24]

Hadley did not tell her in-laws about the year's lease they were breaking or the furniture that friends were walking piecemeal down the four flights of stairs, hoping the landlord would not notice. Jimmy Cowan, a reporter at the *Star*, later remembered being "married in the apartment about the day before he [Hemingway] left and there was nothing there but the grand piano. . . . Young John was tied to the piano leg during the wedding ceremony." Bumby, as they called him, was not yet three months old, too young to be tied to the piano, but it was a good story. All the *Star* men had good stories about Ernest and Hadley, stories filled with factual errors and exaggerations from too much retelling. But the essence was rightly remembered:

Greg	I fell head over heels for Hadley. She was gorgeous on the piano. Do you remember the way she could play?
Jimmy	Gorgeous red hair too.
Greg	And freckles. But she made no attempt to cosmeticize.
Mary	He [Ernest] took pride in his acting.
Greg	The man was on stage whenever it was a public occasion.
Morley	When you were with him for five minutes . . . this sense of eagerness came out of him . . . that this [whatever they were doing] was the most wonderful thing in the world.
Greg	Hemingway would come to my house and he had this cape from his Italian uniform . . . you remember the cape with the Italian marks on it. He'd use the cape which was part of his Italian uniform for showing the movements of the bullfight. Remember those demonstrations.

Forty years after Hemingway departed Toronto, they still remembered the look of him, the sense of his presence, the way his eyes focused intently on a speaker. And they remembered Hadley's piano. No matter where they were or how small the space, Ernest always found her a piano to borrow or rent.[25]

By December 9, the family was tentatively booked on the Cunard liner *Antonia* scheduled to depart New York on January 19. At $290 for the three of them, it was the least expensive passage Ernest could find. He tried to book the *Homeric* but the only space available cost $500, an impossibility, he told Ezra. Three days later, Hadley wrote Izzy Simmons that it looked doubtful that they would meet in Oak Park at Christmas. "Perhaps," she said, "Tiny will run down there alone . . . and I shall be darn jealous." Even though Dr. Hemingway offered to buy the train tickets in order to see his grandchild, his first son's family did not come home for Christmas, not that year nor any other.[26]

Ernest went home alone, taking the night train out of Toronto to arrive in Chicago on December 24. The visit lasted less than a day. With everyone on his best behavior, there was hardly enough time to start an argument. The Doctor was more emotional than Ernest remembered him, and his mother cried sentimental tears to find him so mature and caring, "a thoroughbred" she called him. Ernest was even nice to his sister Marcelline and her new husband, Sterling Sanford. Late that night he gave her a copy of *Three Stories & Ten Poems*, telling her not to show it to their parents for fear of offending them. He might have guessed that she would be equally offended, but maybe in the Christmas spirit he thought, mistakenly, that Marcelline was changed. Maybe with all of the food, presents, pictures on the lawn and much hugging by relatives, he thought that Oak Park was not so narrow-minded as it once seemed. It was his last Christmas at home, the last time but one they would gather as a family. (Five years later he would return in early December to bury his father, suicide victim of depression.) Late that night of Christmas Eve, Ernest was back at the Chicago station holding a sack of presents for Hadley and baby John. His father shook his hand long and hard at the Pullman steps.[27]

When he arrived at their apartment on Christmas morning, Ernest found his stocking decorated, hung and stuffed by Hadley for their first family Christmas. He handed out the presents: a jar of the Doctor's quince jelly; a copy of Clement Wood's *The Mountain* from Grace; a dress and a toy duck for the baby. And nothing for each other until they got to Paris. The next day Ernest began composing letters to John Bone, trying to explain how Harry Hindmarsh had made the job unbearable: Hindmarsh's fits of temper, outraged dignity, wounded vanity and inferiority complex. But the letter sounded wrong, too wordy, too many explanations. Finally he simply said it straight:

> I regret very much the necessity of tendering my resignation from the local staff of the Star. This resignation to take effect January 1st, 1924 if convenient to you.
> Please believe there is no rudeness implied through the brevity of this memorandum.

Maybe "local staff" left some hope of feature work from Europe, but it was a clean break. Toronto was finished. They paid the January rent as if all were in order, and on the morning of January 10, boarded the train for New York. Hadley's furniture had been shipped to Paris and their tickets paid for. With $1000 cash on hand and only Hadley's quarterly dividends to support them, they both knew that this was the beginning of a different life, one filled with economic risk and uncertainty. The only sure thing was Ernest's fiction. The week before they left, Bill Bird's December letter arrived saying that the woodcut portrait of Hemingway was finally finished and that as soon as the press was cleared he would pull the last sheets for *in our time*.[28]

Part Three

1924

Chapter Nine

TRANSATLANTIC PASSAGE
WINTER, 1924

I

As if they specialized in rough weather, the Hemingways recrossed the winter Atlantic in windy rain and high seas that stretched the *Antonia*'s trip to twelve unpleasant, heaving days. On January 30, two days late, they docked in foggy Cherbourg and took the boat train to Paris under drizzling rain, a reprise of their first coming with obvious differences. Two years earlier every glimpse from the window was new, and Paris an adventure waiting their discovery. Now, with the baby sleeping in Hadley's lap, the passing wet country was a good deal less charming, the smoking manure piles no cause for comment. This time in his suitcase Ernest had no manuscripts, but in his head, where they could not be lost, he carried seven stories ready to write. Two years made a difference; two years made two books, small but books. Before, no one knew who he was; now, he was connected. They were returning on short rations and long hopes. The next morning's *Tribune* noted, without special comment, their arrival among ninety-nine other *Antonia* passengers.[1]

In Paris, they were expected to move temporarily into the Pounds' studio until Ezra and Dorothy returned from wintering in Rapallo, but it did not happen. "The concierge," Ernest told Ezra, "recognized me as yr. beau frere but due to an utter manque of the key, entrance was not effected." In truth, the Pounds' studio was Ernest's idea, not Hadley's. She never liked its darkness, nor did she particularly enjoy the British teas she associated with the place. Ernest gave up the idea. Nothing, it seemed, was going as planned. Hadley, sick with an intestinal virus, was having difficulty nursing the baby, whose crying became more and more annoying. To add to their problems, prices in Paris had risen as the franc fell in value. With 32,000 permanent American residents and twice that many British, the city offered no cheap accommodations. The Hemingways took a hotel while Ernest scoured the district for space to rent. On February 4, he woke to the headline MR. WOODROW WILSON IS DEAD. With the idealism that he once epitomized already decomposed, the ex-President's death was almost an afterthought, an oblique comment on the times whose deliberations were framed by profit and loss. The same front page announced the tip of the Harding administration scandals: the Naval oil reserves at Teapot Dome were being privately drained. In cold, wet Paris, the Teapot Dome was far away and vaguely amusing. It was only money.[2]

On February 8, after much shopping, Ernest leased a second-floor apartment at 113 rue Notre-Dame-des-Champs, a stone's throw from Ezra's studio and directly behind Montparnasse. A month's rent was 650 francs, almost three times their Cardinal Lemoine rent, but the space was better, the location closer to their friends, and with the franc fluctuating at twenty-one to the dollar, the real cost was about $30 monthly. The apartment had no electricity, and the lumberyard buzz saw in the courtyard below whined steadily during working hours, but their old *femme de ménage*, Marie Rohrbach, returned to help with the baby. As February rain mixed with snow, Hadley, sick and physically worn out, watched her furniture move once more into new quarters. "We have the whole second story," she told mother-in-law Grace, "tiny kitchen, small dining room, toilet, small bedroom, medium size sitting room with stove, dining room where John Hadley sleeps and the linen and his and our bath things are kept and a very comfortable bedroom. . . . you're conscious all the time from 7 a.m. to 5 p.m. of a very gentle buzzing noise. They make door and window frames and picture frames. The yard is full of dogs and workmen[,] and rammed right up against the funny front door covered with tarpaulin is the baby's buggy."[3]

Despite the lumberyard's noise, the new apartment was an improvement over their first Paris home. Here they were only a few minutes walk from the Notre-Dame-des-Champs Metro station, the Luxembourg Gardens, Sylvia's bookshop and Gertrude's place on rue de Fleurus. The neighborhood was less working class, less down at the heels. At one end of the street stood the Clinique d'Accouchement, for which both Ernest and Hadley hoped they would have no use. (In his 1924 day book, mostly blank, Ernest was keeping careful track of Hadley's monthly periods.) Nearby, on the Boulevard Montparnasse, in good weather and bad, their American friends gathered to drink and talk at the Select, the Rotonde and the Dôme where one could gossip, leave messages, borrow money, repay debts and keep generally abreast of local news.

The Left Bank was changing in ways that had not been apparent four months earlier. Of course, the American summer tourists were an unavoidable feature of Paris before the Hemingways returned to Toronto, but Ernest and Hadley now found Paris Americanized year round with an American Chamber of Commerce, two American movie theaters, more American painters than French, and American students nominally attending the Sorbonne but hanging out in Montparnasse. Eight American banks offered Paris service "for the convenience of American clientele," as the ad read. There were the American Y.M. and Y.W.C.A., American Art Association, Women's Club, University Women's Club and American Legion. The Paris branch of the Daughters of the American Revolution met regularly. Ernest's French, never particularly fluent, had little reason to improve, for throughout the heart of Paris, English was thriving as shop owners competed for American dollars and English pounds.

Soon after their return, the Hemingways joined the American crowd celebrating the reopening of Café du Dôme whose dingy walls and scarred billiard tables had disappeared forever. In its place rose a Dôme resplendent with red and gold awnings, plenty of mirrors, bright lights and signs in English. As the *Tribune* said:

> The famous café which has been the rendezvous of American Bohemians in Paris for the past thirty years is now as up-to-date, modern, shiny and completely equipped as the bath room in the home of an American "Babbitt." . . . Patron Chambon has chosen red as the basic color of his scheme: red flowers, red woodwork, red benches and last and most apparent, red wall-paper with a wriggling design that needs only a little imagination to look like snakes. Green palms here and there make the red more red and the total effect is multiplied many times over by plate glass mirrors which take up all the space not occupied by red.

On that same day, a French theater owner in Amiens was carried to his grave to the tune of "Yes, We Have No Bananas."[4]

As the city around him rapidly transformed itself, Ernest tried to settle into his new quarters and write. Between Bumby's demands and the ripping sawmill, he found it difficult to begin; for five months he had written no new fiction, and now the pump needed priming. He wrote Ezra, "Don't know when or where able to write. The town seems, when you can distinguish faces through the rain and snow, to be full of an enormous number of shits. I however am quite happy eating oysters and drinking the wine of the country." He also spent those first days back re-establishing contact with old friends like Gertrude Stein and Sylvia Beach, taking Hadley and the baby around to show them off. At Shakespeare and Company he was pleased to find *Three Stories & Ten Poems* still on the shelf at fifteen francs, but he must also have been disappointed at its slow sales. Since the Hemingways' August departure, Sylvia had sold only seven copies and given one free to Jane Heap. During the next eight months, she sold only twelve more. The previous winter, Ernest told his sister Marcelline that *Three Stories & Ten Poems* was sold completely out, a claim he would repeat two years later, but not to any of the Paris crowd who frequented Sylvia's shop.[5]

At rue de Fleurus, Alice Toklas was less than ecstatic about the Hemingway baby, but Gertrude spoke to Bumby in her deep, velvet voice and was pleased when Ernest asked them to stand at the christening as the boy's godmothers. She was also pleased that he remained enthusiastic about her long novel, *The Making of Americans*, which he had read, in part, the previous summer. Early in February, when Ernest began helping Ford Madox Ford with his new periodical, *transatlantic review*, Ford professed to be looking for American writers. Ernest told Gertrude that he might be able to get Ford to serialize the novel and actually pay her by the page, for Hemingway had signed on as an unpaid assistant editor of the periodical. By February 17, Hemingway convinced Ford to accept *The Making of Americans*; he wrote Gertrude, "He is going to publish the 1st installment in the April No. . . . He wondered if you would accept 30 francs a page." Ford probably did not understand the length of the manuscript to which he had committed himself, but Hemingway certainly did. Advising Stein to treat Ford "high wide and handsome," he added that no matter how successful the *transatlantic* became, it could never afford to publish the 9000 pages the novel required.[6]

Despite the bitter February weather, Ernest quickly re-entered Left

Bank life: the cafés, Sylvia's bookstore, Bird's print shop and the sporting arenas. The racing season at Auteuil opened in weather so cold that he was not even tempted, but on February 19, Ernest was in a $4.00 balcony seat at the Cirque de Paris to watch Ledoux challenge Mascart for the featherweight championship of Europe. At thirty-one, Ledoux was given small chance against the younger champion, but Ernest always loved the underdog in the ring. He lost money on Luis Firpo when helping hands pushed the groggy Jack Dempsey back into the ring to chop the Argentinian down. Then Hemingway said, "All I gave him [Firpo] was a chance. Someday I will learn not to bet on those I think have a chance but on those I think will win." But he almost never did, betting against Jack Dempsey at every chance.[7]

That Tuesday night at the Cirque, he cheered himself hoarse as the aging Ledoux in twenty bloody rounds stripped Mascart of his championship by a unanimous decision.

> Fighting in a ring slippery with his own blood, out-boxed, out-generaled, unmercifully beaten, but never mastered, Edouard Mascart lost his title . . . to Charles Ledoux . . . After the twelfth round the contours of his [Mascart's] face were lost in a bloody, swollen blur, his eyes were almost closed, and every few seconds he was forced to clear his mouth and throat of blood. Ledoux was covered by blood, too, but it was not his own.

It was the sort of fight Hemingway most admired, one where both men went at each other without fear, giving no quarter. Even better, the old pro came back to retake the title.[8]

Early the next morning, before the baby made writing impossible, he was working on his third story since returning to Paris. In Toronto he began writing it in his head on the morning bus ride to work, letting it develop slowly but not wanting it to finish. Now he was able to start it right up, and he was glad to see how nicely it came out on paper, so smooth and clear that he was living there in the story. It was about Nick Adams when he was a boy on the lake in Michigan, not Walloon Lake but an imaginary lake. He could imagine lakes very well. He could imagine Nick, the young kid, there in the tent on the lake in the dark, afraid to go to sleep alone, waiting for his father to return from night fishing. As he wrote later that year, "Nick in the stories was never himself. He made him up." Now he was making it up so clearly that it was real: night sounds, the oars on the water, and Nick's fear of dying.[9]

That was how the story started, telling the vague first fear in Nick's mind of dying, but when it was finished, he saw that he'd told too much. The fear was in the story without telling the reader about Nick firing three shots to call back his father and Uncle George. So he cut the opening pages and let it begin: "At the lake shore there was another row boat drawn up. The two Indians stood waiting." Just like that. No explaining. He was learning something from the way Joyce began his stories. Now he understood how to do it, and the story told itself. There was Nick standing beside his father, the doctor, in the Indian shanty with the pregnant squaw screaming in pain, and the baby would not come out. No medical bag, no anesthetic, no scalpel, nothing but a jack-knife to make the Caesarean section and tapered gut fishing leaders to sew her up. "Nick held the basin for his father. It all took a long time." But he did not let Nick look. It was there for the reader to see but he did not show it: "his father put something into the basin. Nick didn't look at it." It was all there in the blank spaces around the words waiting for the reader to feel it.[10]

Then the baby began to cry. Not that baby. His baby, John Hadley, that baby began to cry, and he left Nick there holding the basin until he could get to a warm café to finish the story. The streets were misty and cold, with frost on the black drains. At a back table close to the stove and undisturbed, he sipped a creamed coffee trying to get the story moving again, remembering all his own fears rushing to the Toronto hospital, not knowing if Hadley were alive. Now he was back in the shanty where he left Doctor Adams and Nick with the basin and the Indian father in the upper bunk with his leg cut by an axe so he could not move, lying there, listening to the screams that the doctor said were not important.

"Ought to have a look at the proud father. They're usually the worst sufferers in these little affairs," the doctor said. "I must say he took it all pretty quietly."

He pulled back the blanket from the Indian's head. His hand came away wet. He mounted on the edge of the lower bunk with the lamp in one hand and looked in. The Indian lay with his face toward the wall. His throat had been cut from ear to ear. The blood had flowed down into a pool where his body sagged the bunk. His head rested on his left arm. The open razor lay, edge up, in the blankets.

And Nick saw it all: bloody birth and bloody death; jack-knife or cut-throat razor, it was all the same, the coming and the going. The sun was coming up now on the lake, and Nick had to ask his father the question on his mind all night long. "Is dying hard, Daddy?" he asked. So at the end he brought it all back to Nick: "In the early morning on the lake sitting in the stern of the boat with his father rowing, he felt quite sure that he would never die."

They all went exactly like that, one story after another, exploding out of his head perfectly on to paper needing little revision. It was like a mystical experience, an emotional rush that took him outside himself almost as if someone else were writing the stories. In less than three Paris months, Hemingway wrote eight of the best stories he would ever write, stories so spare and tense they outlasted his prime and later foolishness, outlasted the generation for which they were written, their publisher and their critics. "I am writing some damn good stories," he told Ezra. "I wish you were here to tell me so, so I would believe it or else what is the matter with them." Because he knew that Joyce sometimes labored an entire day getting one sentence right, Hemingway was troubled by the ease with which these stories wrote themselves. Later he would create his own legend of slow composition and tedious revision, but it was mostly protective camouflage. In five difficult years of completely dedicated writing, he had learned finally what not to do, how not to write. Five years of rejections, false starts, clichéd plots, five years of reading, listening, studying led finally to these ninety days when it all came together: style, form, subject matter – they were all his own now. No one could touch him. He had become the writer he set out to be.[11]

II

The day after Hemingway started "Indian Camp," The American Women's Club of Paris banned the February issue of the *transatlantic review* from its library, canceling their subscription. The directress "refused to say why the club had taken this action, but when pressed stated that she thought the reason would be clear to any one who read the magazine." The American ladies brought across the waters the prevalent home mood to suppress and censor frank literary treatment of the human condition.[12]

Incited by fundamentalist preachers and reactionary politicians, the American middle class enjoyed the so-called "roaring Twenties" a good deal less than they might have. What America saw on its movie screens, imagined going on in the rumble seats of cars parked on dark lanes, what it heard about the dance floors of speakeasies, brought out deeply seated fears and reactions. Listening to their children only reinforced parents' worst suspicions. Whenever sales needed a boost, newspapers were always ready to feed those fears with stories of daughters sold into white slavery, the evil effects of jazz, the horrors of cocaine, the dissolute lives of movie stars and the shocking behavior of Americans in Paris.

Because shocking behavior was ultimately more interesting than moral lectures, we now remember thigh-high skirts, hip-pocket flasks, jazzy music and Charleston dancers kicking higher than momma would allow. It was Libby Holman "Moaning Low," and Bessie Smith, who sang about needing "a little sugar in my bowl, need a little hot dog for my roll." It was bootleg scotch and bathtub gin; it was learning to kiss in the silent movies with the Sheik of Araby. And the cool singer said, "In olden days a glimpse of stocking was looked on as something shocking. Now, heaven knows, anything goes." But that was only the frosting; the cake itself was deeply conservative.

Those were the days when Billy Sunday and Aimee Semple McPherson led Bible thumpers down the fundamentalist trail that Americans periodically seem compelled to travel. We remember the Scopes Monkey Trial in Tennessee, but forget that the school teacher lost, that the law forbidding Darwin's presence in the classroom was upheld. We forget about the Anti-Saloon League and the Clean Books Bill. We forget that the *Little Review* lost its case in the first *Ulysses* trial and that the meanest sort of reactionary spirit resulted in a resurgent Ku Klux Klan. American voters filled their presidency with conservative men determined to keep America isolated from the world, pretending that an inflated dollar was good for business. We all remember Lindbergh's daring 1927 flight across the Atlantic, but forget that he later admired Hitler's well-oiled military machine.

For Hemingway, who grew up protected by the stalwart arms of Oak Park's moralists, America's attempts to preserve its collective virtue were nothing new. These were, however, his times whether he chose them or not, times hardly propitious for his new fiction. The seduction scene from his "Up in Michigan," no matter how convincing, would never appear on the magazine racks of America.

"You mustn't do it, Jim. You mustn't."
"I got to. I'm going to. You know we got to."
"No we haven't, Jim. We ain't got to. Oh, it isn't right. Oh, it's so big and it hurts so. You can't. Oh, Jim. Jim. Oh."

Nor were the popular magazines ready for the violence of "Indian Camp"; primitive Caesarean operations and bloody suicides without benefit of redeeming religious experience would not appeal to middle-class America. Even Ernest was a little surprised and, of course, pleased when Ford Madox Ford accepted "Indian Camp" for the *transatlantic review*.

By early February, when Hemingway joined Ford's small staff, the first two issues of the magazine were already published and the March issue at the binder's. Little in those first issues particularly interested Ernest: Ezra giving advice on music when he should be writing poetry; Ford serializing his own novel and padding out the second issue under the pseudonym Daniel Chaucer; and some old ghost called Luke Ionides whose "Memories" began "I first knew Whistler in 1885." It all sounded to Ernest safely respectable and dull. The presence of e. e. cummings and William Carlos Williams could not dispel the musty odor rising from the pages. When he opened the March issue, it was all he could do to read past the first page which began: "Once upon a time there was an old farm, and it was Christmas Eve and the sky was overcast which foretold much snow and a biting north wind." Nor was he impressed with the art supplement's line drawings by Cedric Morris, one of the more visible Left Bank homosexuals.[13]

It seemed to Hemingway that Ford, who made his reputation as the editor of *The English Review* before the Great War, was looking backward. In a letter to Pound, Ernest explained the problem: "Ford ought to be encouraged, but Jesus Christ. It is like some guy in search of a good money maker digging up Jim Jeffries at the present time as a possible heavy weight contender. The thing to do with Ford is kill him. . . . I am fond of Ford. This ain't personal. It's literary. You see Ford's running the whole damn thing as compromise. In other words anything Ford will take and publish can be took and published in Century[,] Harpers etc. . . . Goddam it he hasn't any advertisers to offend or any subscribers to discontinue why not shoot the moon."[14]

Ernest's reaction against Ford was as much personal as it was literary. He told Pound that Ford "is so goddam involved in being the dregs of an English country gentleman that you get no good out of him." Ernest had seen enough pompous behavior in Oak Park to last him a lifetime. None of which was quite fair to Ford, but there was something about the man that brought out the worst in Hemingway. Partly it was Ford's age (fifty-one, only two years younger than Ernest's father); partly it was his refusal to break with the nineteenth-century, pre-war tradition of his own literary past, particularly his association with Henry James and Joseph Conrad; partly it was his unfortunate appearance.[15]

Robert McAlmon, whom Ford called, in print, one of the worst writers he met in Paris, remembered the older writer most unkindly:

> He was stout and blond, with a walruslike mustache. He wheezed and talked in an adenoids-clogged voice, often in a secretive manner, so that I had difficulty understanding him, and did not necessarily believe him when I did. . . . On one occasion Ford assured me that he was a genius . . . [and] that his works had more readers than those of H. G. Wells, but that his readers were willing to get his books from the library.

What McAlmon chose not to remember, though he knew it quite well, was Ford's war experience in which a gas attack left his voice raspy and his lungs continually gasping for air. Harold Loeb's memory of Ford, while less biased, was also unflattering:

> Ford moved ponderously, with his feet at right angles to each other. His hair was white, his teeth imperfect. His head resembled Humpty-Dumpty's except for the walrus mustasche and the rosy complexion of a retired officer of the Indian Army. . . . he spoke with a slight, sibilant hesitation, as if he suffered from asthma. I was not favorably impressed. Yet after he sat down and we had talked a while, I felt drawn to him. Something of his spirit, courage, and generosity came through.

Yet this same irritatingly British gentleman wrote *The Good Soldier*, one of the finest French novels written in English; Ford, like Pound, took Flaubert for his true Penelope. He was also the man who simply changed his last name when his first wife would not divorce him; the man who kept a succession of young and lovely mistresses.[16]

In 1924, with his own marriage still vital, Hemingway could not yet approve of Ford's unconventional relationships, but the real rub was Ford's attitude of superiority. To hear him tell it, he was the only writer producing crafted prose, which was like waving a red cape in front of Hemingway. When Ernest asked Ford to critique his new stories, Ford gave him little help. "He has never recovered," Hemingway wrote Pound, "from the mirricale, or however you spell it, mirricle maybe, of his having been a soldier. Down with gentlemen. They're hell on themselves in literature." The two were curiously well matched: neither was able to tell the unvarnished truth about his war experience. Ford, however, was actually at the front line during the Battle of the Somme, had lived through bombardment, suffered shell-shock, lost his memory for thirty-six hours and returned from the war a mental basket case. Hemingway's war wounding was more physically serious than Ford's chipped teeth, but Ernest's three weeks at the front forced him into retailing the war stories of others embellished by his imagination. If Ford's continual refurbishing of reality grated on Hemingway, it was not unlike his own creative fictions.[17]

And if Ford was sometimes imperious, so could Ernest be in little ways. Once, in joking, Hadley said that, like the Kipling tale, Ernest was the man who would like to be king and that he would have made a good one. She might have said the same about Ford, who expected the rising young literary Turks to pay him some deference, if not homage, as the living incarnation of the James–Flaubert tradition. Like a petulant son, Ernest seldom had a kind word for the "Master," as Ford liked to be called, and like a too-patient father, Ford never punished him for it outright. It was a curious editorial relationship in which Ford tried desperately to keep some continuity between the pre-war gentlemen of literature whom he sorely missed and the post-war brood of iconoclasts so eager to abandon their heritage.[18]

III

The bitter cold and intermittent snows of that first February back in Paris barely slowed Hemingway's recharged life. In the mornings, his new stories were springing alive on the page; between Bumby's crying and the buzz saw's grind, he found himself, more and more, writing in the cafés and leaving Hadley alone until Marie arrived. During the afternoons he read incoming *transatlantic* manuscripts while sitting in the brief sun on Quai d'Anjou outside Bill Bird's Three Mountains Press, which Bill generously shared with Ford. As Bird remembered it,

> At the rear, accessible by a flimsy flight of stairs, was a sort of gallery running the whole width of the shop, say 15 feet, and perhaps 6 ft. deep. There Ford, a hefty 6-footer, installed a desk, an editorial chair and a chair for callers, and there he edited the review.

In his tennis shoes and patched jacket, Ernest made his comments for Ford's use and sometimes, he claimed, practiced rewriting the stories. With his hair growing longer by the week, his clothes shabbier, Hemingway was rapidly becoming the epitome of the Left Bank writer: one saw him now inside the Closerie des Lilas, writing at a back table, or explaining something quite excitedly at the Dôme.[19]

As a member of Ford's editorial board, Hemingway was charged with scouting up new writers, the first of whom was Gertrude Stein, hardly new and already well known to Ford. When Stein's *The Making of Americans* was accepted for serialization, Ernest and Alice jointly retyped enough of the already typed and bound manuscript at rue de Fleurus to stay ahead of the *transatlantic*'s schedule. When not involved with his own work or Ford's, Hemingway found Paris even more various and exciting than on his first visit. No sooner had he returned, than his friend, the painter André Masson, asked to borrow back "Le Coup de Dès" for a gallery exhibition. In 1922–23, Hemingway had accompanied Gertrude Stein as a casual visitor to Masson's studio on rue Blomet, where he watched both Masson and Joan Miró paint. Sometimes Ernest served as a boxing coach when the two painters worked out. Miró, he said, "takes a good stance . . . but forgets there's an opponent in front of him." Like so many young Frenchmen, Masson was a war veteran, surviving two and half years (1915–17) of combat before being seriously wounded in the chest. Although his physical injuries healed, he came out of the war depressed, never completely adjusting. "It took me," Masson said, "months to get back my ego, assuming that term's fullest meaning. That ego had been pillaged. Forever."[20]

In the Masson–Miró studio, where the adjoining factory rattled the walls patched with biscuit tins, Hemingway got a close view of the future, for both painters were experimenting with synthetic cubism bordering on the surrealism for which both would become famous. Masson was painting fantastic forest landscapes, still lifes, card players, and a few portraits. Ernest and Hadley bought four of his small paintings. Three were forestscapes, one dark, a little ominous; another, pale greens and browns of sensuous, curving bare trees back-lit by a swirling sun. Years later one of Hemingway's characters, looking at an African landscape, would say, "The trees are like André's pictures. . . . Look at that green. It's Masson." The fourth painting was "The Throw of the Dice," shallow and flat, crowded with men's faces, only one of whom watches the three die (5, 5, 1) tumble almost off the bottom of the canvas. One could see that Masson was learning from Picasso and Braque, but there was also something of Cézanne in his early work. Both André and Ernest admired Cézanne's "House of the Hanged Man" in the Louvre, as well as the wonderful portrait of Madame Cézanne hanging at Gertrude's.[21]

When the Hemingways returned to Paris in 1924, Ernest found Masson experimenting with automatic drawing not unlike Stein's automatic writing. Without money coming in from the *Star*, he could not afford to buy any paintings that year, but something of Masson's new-found freedom may have helped Ernest release his stories that seemed to be writing themselves. Both Hemingways were proud to be among the early supporters of Masson and prouder still to be part of the young artist's first one-man show. On February 24, the day before Masson's exhibit opened, heavy snow fell all across Paris, continuing late into the night. Monday afternoon, in the cold and snow, Ernest and Hadley took the Metro to the St. Augustin stop, and made the short, cold walk down rue d'Astorg to the Galerie Simon. They were pleased to see their painting among the fifty-three Massons, but had to laugh at the program: "Le Coup de Dès . . . . . Appartient à M. Hemmingway." Any day now someone would get his name spelled right.[22]

Hemingway was never a major collector of art, but he bought some extraordinary paintings, finally owning five Massons, an enormous Miró, a stunning Paul Klee, some Fernand Léger sketches and two oils by Juan Gris – paintings now worth at least two million dollars. He may not have been ready for Modernism when he first arrived in Paris, but he learned quickly, buying well with Hadley's money. He not only bought art, he also admired the lives of the artists, their apparent freedom and their ability to deal directly with reality. He admired their life styles, their colorful, paint-spattered clothes. He drank with them in the cafés where they joked with models who earlier that day stood naked, posing in chilled studios. Painters, he saw, remained the local heroes of bohemian life, and from his close observations, Hemingway adopted some of their public behavior for his own persona. At Café du Dôme, where, despite the new gaudiness, local painters collected out of habit, Hemingway took his place as one who understood their art and could speak of it easily. Under the now bright lights, the conversations continued much as one poet remembered them:

> Stell auf den Tisch die Blühenden Stilleben
> Die letzte Tube Zinkweis bring herbei.
> Und lasst uns wieder von Cezanneen reden,
> Wie einst im Januar, Februar, Marz, April und Mai.

> [Put the blue still-life on the table,
> Bring over the last tube of zinc white.
> And let's discuss once more Cézanne
> As we did in January, February, March, April and May.]

And with them was Hemingway, sometimes alone, sometimes with Hadley, but with them.[23]

IV

In spite of freezing, wet weather, Paris was better than either of the Hemingways dared hope in Toronto. Quickly slipping back into the flow of Left Bank life, Hadley and Ernest could have been happier only if Bumby cried less or if their apartment retained heat better. (Their friends were appalled to find them without either gas or electricity, but they were happy in what some called their hovel.) Their "carpenter's loft," as Archibald MacLeish later named it, was so inexpensive that they had money to indulge lightly in café life, attend boxing matches and enjoy an occasional meal in a reasonable restaurant.

During the day, with Bumby in the care of Marie, Hadley could leave Ernest writing at the dining room table while she slipped out, up the street, through the baker's back door and out the front into Montparnasse. There, in the chilly basement of a musical instrument shop, she practiced regularly on a badly tuned upright piano. It was her art always and a part of her identity that no baby or husband could take from her. There in the damp cellar by candle light, she kept that part of herself intact. In Paris, the women were different from those she knew in St. Louis. In Paris, many women did not marry, did not bear children and did not give up their lives to men. Hadley saw them in the cafés, women shining like polished brass. She was not that kind of woman. She needed Ernest, relied on his confidence and lived on his ambition, needed him close to her in bed. But she was not going to be merely wife and mother.[24]

Marie, who tended the baby boy and cooked the mid-day meal, gave Hadley almost as much freedom as Ernest enjoyed. Only the nursing of Bumby kept Hadley close to home, for her ample breasts remained his only food source. Ernest insisted. His father was an obstetrician, he told her. (Dr. Hemingway also experimented with puréed baby food long before it became an American staple.) At night, when he wanted to be in the café, Hadley was frequently left behind to nurse Bumby. But sitters could be arranged and she was with him at the fights and at the six-day bike races. She was with him sometimes in the cafés, sometimes in the studios. Always, she promised, his career was foremost, but that did not mean that she should disappear. In Paris, where women led their own lives, Hadley Hemingway was learning to be herself.[25]

She was also learning more about Ernest and the way he created characters in his fiction. During that bitterly cold February, he finished a story about a married couple trapped by the rain in a Rapallo hotel room very like the room they had shared in the Riviera Splendide a year earlier. She remembered the story's first broken draft when it was going to be about the hotel owner's fascist son who "looked insultingly at the guests as they passed in and out." In that story the wife could not sleep and did not like the food, but that was not her, not Hadley. The new version was different. The fascist son was gone, leaving only the husband reading on the bed and the wife who wanted to rescue a wet kitten outside in the rain. She wanted the kitten, wanted to let her bobbed hair grow out, wanted "to eat at a table with my own silver and I want candles. And I want it to be spring and I want to brush my hair out in front of a mirror and I want a kitty and I want some new clothes." "Oh, shut up," her husband tells her, "and get something to read."[26]

Hadley read the typescript sitting at the table with her own silver in the cabinet beside her. Her hair remained bobbed, but she had her candles and her mirror. And she still sometimes wanted new clothes when all the women dressed better than she could. It was about parts of them all right, but not only in Rapallo. Some of it was then, but some was now in the February rain and snow of Paris. He called it "Cat in the Rain," just as he sometimes called her "Cat" or "Kitty." It was not a nice story, but it was a great story.

That March, when the chestnut trees blossomed, she wrote her own "Kitty Love Story" about a local black kitty she watched in courtship with a neighboring tom cat. "Oh Kitty," she wrote, "he will smell so sweet and look so silky fluffy and treat you so rough and wonderful." Once pregnant and looking for a nesting spot, the black kitty does not "understand why the lady with the red bobbed hair that shone gold in the sun would say scat and close the window when she stumbled along the roof toward her." After delivering, the mother cat has no interest in the prowling tom father. Her life has changed. The narrator tells someone,

> We are not the only ones that breathe in suffocatingly the scent of the chestnut candles thru the open window as we lie pressed together in our bed. The black cat, now shapeless and baggy draws it in thru her small neat nostrils, as she steps heavily over the roof in the shining dark of spring night, remembering with her whole doleful body the new love of only a few weeks ago – and wonders why she is called out almost never now.

She wrote it down quickly, making changes, crossing out as she went: a poor kitty trapped by her biology, once a mother no longer the same. She signed the page Hadley Richardson. Ernest was not the only member of the family gaining confidence in Paris, nor was he the only one who felt, sometimes, trapped.[27]

V

Early March mornings, before the buzz saw began, they woke to the odor of fresh bread baking somewhere up the street. Days warmed slowly and chestnut trees began to bud along Notre-Dame-des-Champs. At sidewalk cafés people one knew reappeared at familiar tables, sipping and talking. Sparrows worked steadily beneath the tables and in the gutters. The O'Neils returned to the Quarter, the Straters left for New

York, and every day fresh Americans arrived, eager to spend cheap francs.

On Sunday afternoon, March 16, John Hadley Nicanor Hemingway, with his bullfighter's middle name, was baptized at the font of a small Episcopal chapel where earlier that morning Giorgio Joyce, James' son, sang in the choir. That afternoon, Ernest and Hadley, in their best clothes, dressed the baby in his father's baptismal gown to meet his godparents at the chapel of St. Luke's in the Garden, less than two blocks from their carpenter's loft. Chink Dorman-Smith was in Paris a week early to visit with the Hemingways before the ceremony. At the chapel he stood solemn and stiff, his mustache trimmed and only his eyes laughing. Gertrude Stein and Alice B. Toklas arrived, looking most twosome and ready to be joint godmothers. After the brief ceremony all three signed the baptismal certificate. It was a strange triad of godparents to renounce the devil and all his works: Chink, an Irish Catholic professional military man; Gertrude and Alice, devout Jewish lesbians. On that breezy, warm March day with the ceremonial salt still on Bumby's lips, they walked back to the Hemingway apartment for wine and Jordan almonds. The ritual was completed.[28]

Two months later, Ernest wrote to quell his parents' doubts. "Don't worry about J.H.N.'s spiritual welfare," he told them. "He is a member in good standing of the Church of England and has both god mothers and god fathers who are sworn to instruct him in religious things as he grows up. He will probably be found occupying a much higher place in the heavenly grandstand than any of his congregational relatives."[29]

Chapter Ten

TWO-HEARTED PARIS

SPRING, 1924

I

With the rising spring, Ernest faced a real money problem, one that had been festering since the previous fall: part of Hadley's trust fund had disappeared. On the advice of George Breaker, husband of Hadley's St. Louis friend Helen, Hadley had cashed in $19,000 worth of almost bankrupt railway bonds for $10,802, which she left in George's hands for reinvestment. Something secure, Ernest suggested, nothing speculative. Buy something solid with a steady income. George bought Manila railway bonds with the Philippines enraged at American occupation and Democratic presidential candidates advocating pulling out. Ernest was furious: Philippine rails and Missouri marble. If that was Breaker's idea of safe investments, they needed a new adviser.

Late in March, they wrote Hadley's St. Louis bank, the Mercantile Trust, instructing it to take over the whole matter but without insulting the Breakers and without causing them pain. That was Hadley speaking. Ernest was not so worried about the Breakers' feelings, not when Hadley's trusts produced their only income. By May 11, the bonds Breaker said he purchased were yet to be delivered to the Mercantile. Ernest wrote for Hadley to wire: IF UNABLE DELIVER BONDS PLEASE DEPOSIT MY ACCOUNT AT MERCANTILE SEVEN THOUSAND FOUR HUNDRED DOLLARS AND FIFTY SEVEN CENTS DUE ME AND ADVISE ME OF DEPOSIT BY CABLE. The "fifty seven cents" was absolutely Ernest, who, when moved to it, could be as strict an accountant as his father. Nine days later, in reply to Breaker's assurance that all was well, not to worry, Ernest drafted another cable: WOULD PREFER IMMEDIATE DEPOSIT ALL FUNDS MERCANTILE STOP WORRIED SICK UNABLE UNDERSTAND PURCHASE QUESTIONABLE BONDS MATTER SUCH THIS STOP BREVITY DUE CABLE COSTS MONTHS RENT LOVE HADLEY.[1]

The loss of annual income from the original rail bonds was $760, a sizable amount of money but not all of Hadley's income. In various trusts she still had $40,000 producing at least $2000 a year, enough for them to live in Paris. Ernest complained to everyone that they were destitute, but he did not sell any of their paintings as Gertrude Stein was forced to do during the 1930s, nor did he look for work. Later he would tell great inventions about their Paris poverty: trapping pigeons in the Luxembourg Gardens for supper; working as a sparring partner for professional boxers. Yet on April 9, he bought $200 worth of Spanish pesetas for their Pamplona trip which he never considered cancelling. The money came from Hadley's account in St. Louis which showed a balance of $1140.[2]

Harold Loeb, who met Hemingway that spring at one of Ford's tea parties, said Ernest denied himself decent clothes but not much else. Certainly not the plump oysters in season nor the chilled Pouilly-Fuissé to accompany them. Kitty Cannell, writer and Loeb's sometime lover, said Ernest was self-indulgent in his poverty. She saw him, once, on the street in the sweat shirt and ragged pants he made his costume, and he was complaining "in the half-joking, half-sneering way he sometimes adopted: 'Some of you rich guys ought to buy the old man a pair of pants so he wouldn't have to freeze his ass in this weather.'" Loeb, Kitty said, went home and brought back to Ernest a pair of new flannel slacks. It wasn't true. Several sizes larger than Loeb, Ernest could never have fit into his trousers. But Kitty never did like Ernest, particularly did not like the way he left Hadley alone while he was free on the boulevards, nor the way he kept her so poorly dressed. Separated but undivorced, Kitty wanted all women to be as free as herself. Hadley accepted her handouts of used clothing and sharp advice, remaining always Ernest's essentially compliant wife. He needed her that way and she knew it, just as she knew their money worries, while not desperate, were real enough.[3]

But it was another Paris spring and not even money worries could depress Ernest for long. It was good to be on the streets early in the morning when shopkeepers swept their swatch of sidewalk and waiters began putting out café chairs and tables. April sunlight drenched grey, tan and pink brick buildings, glittering off slate roofs and chimney pots. In the Luxembourg Gardens the bone white statue of Flaubert was wet with dew and black in its hollows, and the uncircumcised Pan continued piping atop a full wine skin. If one started early, before tourists filled the streets, the walk to Ford's office, on the Ile St. Louis was the best part of the day. Pruned trees of winter burst open apple green, and down cobblestoned streets of the Sorbonne district, buildings leaned together with bulging walls. Stray cats poked in gutters for scraps, and the drunks, dull eyed and disinterested, backed up to sun-warmed walls. Walking along, Ernest always had time to poke in the bookstalls in rue de Seine or along the quais, time to observe the gallic noses of old men deep in their morning news, time to watch quiet barges coming up river, decks festooned with drying laundry.

That spring the New York Yankees discovered Lou Gehrig, and the public discovered that Harry Sinclair, the oil man tapping Teapot Dome, personally paid off the Republican 1920 presidential campaign deficit. While Paris prepared for the summer olympics, America prepared for a fall election: silent Cal Coolidge running against maybe Bill McAdoo. In the Quarter the Mi-Carême festival opened in rain but none of the café drinkers seemed daunted in their celebration. At Missolonghi in Greece, preparations were being made to honor the centenary of Byron's death; in Boston, Sacco and Vanzetti waited in their death cells for news of their latest judicial appeal. In the Luxembourg Gardens, children in sailor suits watched small masted ships breeze across the octagonal pool, and old men played boules along the gravel walks.

At the Dôme, Quarterites argued about the sexual identity of Fano Messan, a young sculptor who was convincing as a woman at parties and equally convincing as a man in the cafés. Or, with a Messan exhibit soon to open, was the question simply another publicity stunt? With George Antheil starting rumors of being kidnapped in North Africa in an effort to get his name in the paper, it was enough to make a writer wonder if he were in the wrong business. In the *Tribune* Ernest read that many men of superior capacity as writers were insane. Nothing that he saw or heard that spring in Paris made him doubt the statement.[4]

Sitting on the sun-warmed stone quai in front of Three Mountains Press, Ernest read through the Sunday paper a day late: Ford's *Tribune* column pumped up Joyce's balloon in time for the *transatlantic* April issue featuring Joyce's "Work in Progress." That was the game all right.

But there in the *Review* after Joyce's piece from *Finnegan's Wake* and Tristan Tzara's four-part Dadaist fragments came the sentence: "At the lake shore there was another row boat drawn up." There he was, finally, in print: his first paying short story; 150 francs, less than ten dollars, but in print. Following "Indian Camp" came Marjorie Reed's in-house review of *in our time*, which Bird had finally gotten back from the binders. "Minute narratives that eliminate every useless word," she called them, "the sort of detached circumstances that always penetrate deep into the consciousness." It was a fair start in the literary game he was learning that spring.[5]

At the Shakespeare and Company bookstore, his thin book with the collage cover was in the window beside *Antic Hay* and *Swann's Way*. Only thirty pages long, *in our time* was priced at thirty francs, less than two American dollars, which would also buy the Huxley book, a decent mid-day meal, or cover six small bets at Auteuil. Sylvia sold her first copy of Hemingway's book on April 3, but sales were slow: five copies the first month, eight the next. By the end of the year she'd sold only twenty-four copies. During the same period Bill Bird's own book on French wine sold sixty copies at her shop. A month after Hemingway's book was published, he wrote Edward O'Brien that "In Our Time sold out fast but of course the profits on it went to offset the losses on the others Bill published." Only 170 perfect copies survived printing and binding, but if they "sold out fast," it was not at Sylvia's shop.[6]

II

Hemingway made no money from *Three Stories & Ten Poems* or from *in our time*, for no royalties were involved. MacAlmon published the first book on a handshake and no promise of payment. Later Ernest would say that it made him angry to see his drunken publisher vomiting what should have been Hemingway's royalties, but that was spite speaking. With limited distribution and slow sales, *Three & Ten* probably did not break even on publishing costs. Bill Bird's Inquest series may have paid Ford Madox Ford as much as $250 for his *Men and Women*, but nothing was promised Hemingway, nor did he expect any royalties. Bird, he knew, was barely meeting his printing expenses. The money, he told himself, would come eventually. Down deep there was a part of him that firmly believed in Horatio Alger's formula for success, hard work and a bit of luck.[7]

Hard cover collage for Hemingway's *in our time* published by Bill Bird in 1924. (John F. Kennedy Library)

Later, when he got the national reviews and big sales, some in Paris, who did not know him well, thought Hemingway sold out the avant-garde for commercial success. Ernest laughed off the criticism. From his Oak Park beginnings, his eye was always on commercial sales. His style and subject matter may have been permanently altered by reading Joyce, Pound and Stein, but he never intended, like his models, to scratch out a living among the literary poor while others took their talent to the bank. The trick was to make the sales without compromising his writing. It was a good trick and he learned to do it in Paris through trial and error. All the while, looking for access to the New York publishing world, he cultivated the friendship of anyone who might help and publicized himself at every chance. That was the game. All the writers played it, some better than others, but no one better than Ford.

As much as he disliked Ford's pompous monologues and British demeanor, Hemingway learned from the older gamesman. At every turn, Ford promoted himself. In his weekly column in the Paris *Tribune*, he managed to keep his own work continually in the public eye. In the *transatlantic*, he serialized his own novel, wrote well of it under the pseudonym Daniel Chaucer, and in his editor's column reminded readers of his connections with the literary past. The name of Henry James was much on his lips: the old Master from whom Ford, the Master apparent, listened and learned. Literary controversies, Hemingway saw, were a crucial part of the game, creating free publicity.

When Ford asked him to write an editorial column for the May *transatlantic*, Hemingway did his best to create a literary uproar, insulting two well-known Left Bankers – Tristan Tzara, co-founder of the Dadaist movement, and Djuna Barnes, the attractive lesbian author of *A Book* (Boni & Liveright). Writing more like a gossip columnist than a literary man, Hemingway announced:

> Dada is dead although Tzara still cuddles its emaciated little corpse to his breast and croons a Rumanian folk-song . . . while he tries to get the dead little lips to take sustenance from his monocle.
> . . . Djuna Barnes, who according to her publishers is that legendary personality that has dominated the intellectual night-life of Europe for a century is in town. I have never met her, nor read her books, but she looks very nice.

Both Tzara and Barnes had appeared with Hemingway in the April issue of the *transatlantic*. In attacking these two writers, Hemingway was also attacking Ford who spoke well of Tzara and had picked the Barnes story for publication.[8]

Reasonable explanations cannot account fully for Hemingway's dislike of Ford, for reason had little to do with it. Nathan Asch, young and poor in 1924 Paris, remembered how grateful he was to Ford for first publishing him in the review but remembered "that Ford was not easy to be with," and that Ford failed in his attempt to mix the pre-war generation with the new age rising out of the trenches. "I prefer," Asch said, "the image of the young bulls against the old bulls, one that is personified by young Hemingway then in Paris, who could not function unless he fought and destroyed older men."[9]

Ernest wrote that he preferred watching the boxer Criqui, whose work gave him "a certain ecstasy which is not given me by reading the works of my contemporaries." Any reader of his column put it down knowing that Hemingway was knowledgeable about boxing, horse racing and bullfighting, was friends with Gertrude Stein, Ezra Pound, George Antheil and Robert MacAlmon, and was a man who knew his way about the Paris literary world. Most of his three-page column reflected as much on Ernest as on his various subjects.

Critics, against whom he would rail life-long, he already loathed for reasons not altogether clear. Perhaps it was their feeding habits, battening on books they themselves could not write. In his column, called "And To The United States," Hemingway moaned, "For every writer produced in America there are produced eleven critics. Now that the *Dial* prize has gone to a critic [Van Wyck Brooks] the ratio may be expected to increase to 1/55 or over. As I have always regarded critics as the eunuchs of literature . . . But there is no use in finishing that sentence." He left the sentence dangling as a commentary on his opening paragraph attacking Lewis Gay.

An American citizen, not yet thirty-five years old, of French-German-Jewish parentage, writing in the Paris Sunday Literary Supplement of the World's Greatest Newspaper under the name of Lewis Gay says:

"Remember that less than twenty years ago the reading matter to be found in the home of the average American of means – the American who sent his boys to college – was composed almost entirely of the New England Poets, the *Christian*

Register and the *Youth's Companion* . . ."

As Mr. Gay is frequently denunciatory, rarely unpersonal, and always insistent on the lack of a cultural background of almost everyone of whom he writes, the above selection from his article will have a certain biographical significance in the critical study of American Criticism which should be written to carry to its end the present phenomenon on American letters.[10]

Lewis Gay was the pen name used by Lewis Galantière, the same man so helpful to the Hemingways when they first arrived in Paris. About May 2, Ernest wrote Ezra:

Galantiere in the Chi Tribune Sunday mag. sets out to prove that the mantle of Abe Lincoln, Wm. Dean Howells, Hamlin Garland, Sherwood Anderson and yourself is descending upon me. The article takes up some space. In the same week, unknowing he was preparing this blurb, I prove in a squib for Ford that Galantiere is a little Jewish boy and a fool.[11]

Maybe it was the Jewishness that irritated Hemingway. Certainly in writing Pound he knew the reference would tickle Ezra's growing anti-Semitism. More likely it was Galantière's superior attitude toward young writers in his literary column "Reviews and Reflections." Not that Hemingway's anti-Semitic remark was atypical of himself and his times. In the same letter he refers to David O'Neil "kiking everybody with big promises."

Three weeks later, Dorothy Butler, Galantière's fiancée, wrote Hadley a letter seething with anger: she had forbidden her husband-to-be from visiting the Hemingways who pointedly disliked her and made fun of him in print. After their Black Forest walking trip, Hadley apparently warned Lewis that Dorothy was selfish and that he should not marry her. When Lewis told Dorothy of Hadley's remarks, social niceties between the two women temporarily disappeared.[12]

Answering for Hadley, Ernest wrote Dorothy,

. . . Even while I kissed you, I never liked you but was willing to make the effort to like you for the sake of seeing Lewis occasionally. I made this effort successfully numberless times. Finally it could no longer be made. That was quite a relief. . . .

As for Hadley's telling Lewis you were selfish . . . I believe my own language on that occasion was that you were a selfish bitch . . .[13]

For all his boyish charm and raw enthusiasm for life, Ernest also had a hair-trigger temper and the mean habit of picking on those weaker, smaller or more vulnerable than himself. Often his temper was beyond his control, an irrational response for which he just as often apologized the next day. But his need to attack others with words may have come out of his own divided self, for he was never easy in those early years with his literary identity. Always he reached out for the active, physical life, refusing to let the sedentary and contemplative role of writer control who he was. Sometimes he reached too hard. Sometimes he reacted too violently against others in whose mirror he saw his own reflection. Lewis Galantière was letting his wife-to-be dictate his life in the same way Ernest felt his father was dominated by Grace Hemingway's selfishness. Whenever he saw a woman dominating a relationship, his hackles rose. As he wrote Ezra, "Mrs. Ford, i.e. Stella [Bowen], confided to Hadley twice in same evening that she had 'you know I caught Ford too late to train him.' I don't know whether this means house-break him or what."[14]

III

Despite his one-sided antagonism toward Ford, or perhaps because of it, Hemingway's spring was incredibly productive. Through March and April, stories continued to flow. In late March, soon after Bumby's baptism, Ernest began writing "The Doctor and the Doctor's Wife," in which Nick Adams' father backs down from a physical confrontation with Dick Boulton, a half-breed Indian. Dick, who has come to saw logs to work off his bill with Doctor Adams, jokes about the beached logs actually belonging to the company whose mark they bear. The doctor finally orders Dick off his land:

"Now, Doc—"
"Take your stuff and get out."
"Listen, Doc."
"If you call me Doc once again, I'll knock your eye teeth down your throat."

"Oh, no, you won't, Doc."

Dick Boulton looked at the doctor. Dick was a big man. He knew how big a man he was. He liked to get into fights. He was happy. Eddy and Billy Tabeshaw leaned on their cant-hooks and looked at the doctor. The doctor chewed the beard on his lower lip and looked at Dick Boulton. Then he turned away and walked up the hill to the cottage.[15]

The doctor, angry and unmanned, retreats to his bedroom where he pumps yellow shotgun shells through the chamber of his weapon. His wife, ironically a Christian Scientist and the least likely wife for a doctor, quotes to him "he who ruleth his spirit is greater than he that taketh a city." Doctor Henry Adams is not soothed.[16]

Just as he was drawn magnetically to the primitive violence of the bull and boxing rings, Hemingway's fiction from the Paris years frequently confronts a man with violent possibilities that he could clearly imagine, projecting himself into their conflict. He admired boxers capable of taking a beating and still performing well; bullfighters who risked the sharp horns passing close to their groins: men whose bravery was documented at every performance. His fictional Doctor Adams failed the test, his capacity for violence too diluted by civilizing forces. Partly the story was biographical: Dr. Hemingway in 1911 hired Dick Boulton to saw up some drift logs on their beach at Walloon Lake; Grace Hemingway, while no Christian Scientist, was deeply committed to religious mysticism. In 1921, shortly before his wedding, Ernest wrote Bill Smith a cryptic letter that his father was the yellowest man he knew – a terrible admission for a son.[17]

But it was more than a story about his father: he, Ernest, became the doctor, felt the shame, knew the anger. The relationships were classic: vulnerable father, less than supportive wife, observant son and an outside threat. The code violated was that of Theodore Roosevelt: be self-reliant. If Ernest wrote well about such failures, it was because he was raised to their contemplation by a society which no longer required the violence once needed to pacify its western frontier, but which continued to admire inordinately the self-reliant frontiersman who defended his own domain, enforcing justice when necessary. It was a difficult model to follow, one that demanded physical challenges of the sort seldom found in middle-class urban settings. But in Hemingway's imagination, Indians or their equivalents were always there, threatening, waiting to be confronted.

"The Doctor and the Doctor's Wife," begun in late March as an eleven-page manuscript, was a classic Hemingway story: nothing happened on the surface where violence was deferred but beneath the surface the doctor studied in anguish his public failure to which his wife was witness. The hand-written, revised draft Hemingway dated on April 7, 1924. That same evening in rue Magellan, Dr. Walton Hubbard gave a lecture to the faithful and the curious on Christian Science.[18]

During the following three weeks, while working afternoons on Ford's review, Hemingway finished the first drafts of three more stories: "Cross Country Snow," "Soldier's Home" and "Mr. and Mrs. Smith." Nothing deterred him, not Bumby's crying, not the buzz saw in the lumberyard, not even intrusive friends bothering him at his back table in the Closerie des Lilas. The stories were almost writing themselves, some in fragments ("Cross Country Snow"), some full blown ("Soldier's Home"). "I always write well in the spring," he said years later. That Paris spring of 1924 he wrote better than well, better than a man could hope to write. Between March 17 and May 2, he suspended all correspondence, working only on the stories. He worked steadily through a freak Palm Sunday snow, through the tolling bells of Good Friday and the pomp of Easter. And when he was done, he had created a disturbing portrait of marriage in his time.[19]

"Cross Country Snow" was an important part of what developed into his "marriage tales": stories focused on conflicts between husband and wife. In this story Nick (Mike in first draft) and George, skiing cross country in Switzerland, stop for wine and strudel in an isolated village inn. Served by a pregnant, unmarried waitress, the two young men talk about skiing across the spine of Europe – Oberland, Valais, Engadine – both knowing it will be impossible. That night George must board a night train to return to college; Nick must return to his wife Helen. George asks him, "Is Helen going to have a baby?" "Late next summer," Nick replies. "Are you glad?" George asks. Nick says, "Yes. Now." Once attuned to Hemingway's subtle surfaces, we can hear the pause between those two words: "Yes," period. "Now," period. In that silence between the words lies the implication that once Nick was not glad about his approaching fatherhood. Without saying it, both men realize that this is the end of something, for whatever future snows may fall, they will never again ski this freely. Babies change everything. No matter how much they want to ski together in the future, Nick knows "There isn't any good in promising."[20]

Later, those fallaciously constructing his biography straight from his fiction, would use this story to show how trapped Hemingway felt during the winter of 1922–23 when Hadley became pregnant. But that December of 1922, when Hemingway was skiing with George O'Neil, Hadley was not yet pregnant. Not until late February or early March were the Hemingways sure of the baby, by which time Switzerland was far behind them. This story, written seven months after Bumby's birth, reflects, perhaps, those trapped feelings that a parent can truly know only after the fact. Writing in the Paris spring with Hadley's trust money diminished, Ernest's thoughts turned to skiing in the same way that they once turned to fishing on Walloon Lake. The "summer people" at the lake were disbanded by marriage, and now he and Hadley might not have the funds to gather the men for skiing that coming winter. Maybe that triggered the story. Or maybe it was watching the way babies changed the lives of Mike Strater (returned to the states) and Lincoln Steffens (no longer the companion he once was). But the story was not unvarnished biography, not even close except for the skiing. Later that summer he wrote,

> The only writing that was any good was what you made up, what you imagined. That made everything come true. . . . Of course he'd never seen an Indian woman having a baby. That was what made it good. Nobody knew that. He'd seen a woman have a baby on the road to Karagatch and tried to help her. That was the way it was.[21]

The more he said it, the less anyone believed him.

Of course, there was enough of his life in the fiction to keep the controversy alive. "You have to invent from something," he told Carlos Baker. "Everyone," he said, "writes about living people. But you have to invent away from them." In "Soldier's Home" he did just that, beginning with his own experience coming back from the war and combining it with stories he'd heard from other vets. He called his soldier Harold Krebs, using part of Krebs Friend, a badly shell-shocked vet he first knew in Chicago who had turned up in Paris married to a wealthy older woman. Hemingway gave to his fictional Harold Krebs bits and pieces of other men's wars. Harold, we're told, fought with the Marines at Belleau Wood, Soissons, the Champagne, St. Mihiel and in the Argonne – all major American battles from late in the war, and none of which Hemingway experienced. The resulting story illustrated the gulf between patriotic parents who still believed the war propaganda and their returning sons who learned fear in the trenches, an experience the young vet cannot explain to his parents. "His town had heard too many atrocity stories to be thrilled by actualities. Krebs found that to be listened to at all he had to lie, and after he had done this twice he, too, had a reaction against the war and against talking about it."[22]

More than the other stories from that spring, "Soldier's Home" revealed how adroit Hemingway had become with Gertrude Stein's style which he was reading in galley proofs at the *transatlantic*. As Krebs contemplates young girls walking past his house, Hemingway uses a variation on Stein's repetitions to observe Krebs' thoughts and to increase tension:

> . . . He would have liked to have a girl but he did not want to have to spend a long time getting her. He did not want to get into the intrigue and the politics. He did not want to have to do any courting. He did not want to tell any more lies. It wasn't worth it.
>
> He did not want any consequences. He did not want any consequences ever again. He wanted to live along without consequences.[23]

The girls are on Krebs' mind and on the surface of the fiction, but the tension is more than sexual. There is something wrong with Krebs that we're never told directly because of the skewed point of view (objective but much in the head of Krebs). He has come back from the war unfit to re-enter a family world. What is left unsaid becomes as important as the words we hear.

Krebs' father does not understand why his son sits around the house when other boys are married and hard at work. Krebs cannot explain, nor can he listen to his mother's homilies. "God has some work for everyone to do," she tells him. "There can be no idle hands in His Kingdom." Flatly, Krebs replies, "I'm not in His Kingdom." When pressed, he says that he does not love his mother, does not love anyone. "It wasn't any good. He couldn't tell her, he couldn't make her see it." Trying to make amends, he kneels down with his mother, allowing her to pray for him. The mother's Christian piety, untouched by the horrors of the western front, is similar to Grace Hemingway's religious positivism that her son found so irrelevant after being blown up at Fossalta. That first spring back from Italy, Ernest was told by his mother:

I do hope . . . that you are just growing every day in strength of character, and purpose to make your life count for the best things. I know you won't disappoint me or the grandparents in Heaven who are watching you and counting on you in this wonderful day of opportunity.

Hemingway's home life contributed to this story but not on a one-to-one ratio, nor did he write the story in 1919, nor was Krebs' war experience anything like his three weeks as a Red Cross man on the Italian front. "Soldier's Home" is, far beneath its surface, about Hemingway's anticipation of his parents' inability to accept his fiction. That spring of 1924 he was writing stories that he knew his parents could not read without being deeply hurt. They read, with some pride, all of his Toronto journalism, subscribing to the *Star* for that sole purpose. Like all parents, they wanted to tell neighbors about their son's achievements, brag a little around the block. He was not ashamed of the stories, but the previous Christmas he asked Marcelline not to show *Three Stories & Ten Poems* to their parents, knowing they would not approve. When "Indian Camp" appeared in the *transatlantic*, he did not send a copy home. Deep within him he needed their approval and support, but a part of him continually raised barricades to prevent the possibility. It was not light baggage that he carried out of pre-war Oak Park into the world.[24]

IV

As April's end approached and the weather warmed, tables appeared in front of the Closerie des Lilas and the faint odor from its lilac bush hung on the morning air. From an open table he could see sunlight falling across the bronze statue of Marshall Ney, his sword forever cocked above his head, his body thrust forward on his right foot, urging invisible troops to their Napoleonic duty. Up the street to his left, fountain water played smoothly over bronze horses, reared and prancing in the spray at Place de l'Observatoire. Ten years later and a world away, he would remember it clearly: *water sheen rippling on the bronze of horse's manes, bronze breasts and shoulders, green under thin-flowing water*. More than the Dôme or the Rotonde a few blocks up Montparnasse, this was Hemingway's café, a place where he could linger over a *café crème* or a vermouth cassis to write, talk or gossip.[25]

Sometime toward the end of April, Hemingway sat at his favorite Lilas table, reading through a short, satiric piece he was calling "Mr. and Mrs. Smith," which began:

> Mr. and Mrs. Smith tried very hard to have a baby. They tried as often as Mrs. Smith could stand it. They tried in Boston after they were married and they tried coming over on the boat. They did not try very often on the boat because Mrs. Smith was quite sick.

On their wedding night, they "were both very disappointed but finally Cornelia went to sleep." Mrs. Smith, forty years old, does not conceive in Boston nor in Paris, but her twenty-five-year-old husband, Hubert, writes long poems, a fatherhood of diminished sorts. In Paris they sit "around the Café du Dôme, avoiding the Rotonde across the street because it is always so full of foreigners," and finally rent a chateau in Touraine. Mrs. Smith brings over from Boston an old girl friend for company while her husband makes out his check to a Boston vanity press to publish his verse. By the end of the summer Mrs. Smith and her girl friend are sleeping "together in the big medieval bed. They had many a good cry together." Hubie, as she calls her husband, stays up nights writing more long poems. "They were all quite happy."[26]

Lightly and quickly written, "Mr. and Mrs. Smith" was invented from Left Bank gossip about the career of Chard Powers Smith, a twenty-nine-year-old Yale B.A. and Harvard lawyer-turned-poet. Smith epitomized much about Left Bank intellectuals that Hemingway both despised and resented: Ivy League education, a substantial income allowing him to rent a chateau, literary pretensions, nice clothes and a genteel background. Those who knew Smith found the story malicious, but satire was frequently Hemingway's initial response to pretense. Beyond the malice, which was not deep or particularly personal, Hemingway's story, while adding another chapter to his "marriage group," drew on more sources than Chard Powers Smith for his characterization.[27]

David O'Neil, St. Louis lumberman-turned-poet with whom Hemingway had skied and sledded in 1922, contributed his part to Ernest's first portrait of the artist. On March 17, Hemingway wrote Ezra that the O'Neils were back in Paris. "Have not and don't give a damn about seeing them," he said. As much as anything Hemingway resented O'Neil's money, having grown up in slight awe of the monied gentry, an awe that turned to resentment in Paris. It was a defense mechanism, for as soon as he had the money he lived as well or better than David O'Neil or Chard Powers Smith. He satirized the rich when he was not wealthy, but only because they had what he wanted. That was his secret, which he did not admit even to himself. That Paris spring when Hadley's income was in jeopardy, he particularly resented anyone, like Smith and O'Neil, whose incomes were substantial and secure.[28]

Whatever Hemingway knew about Chard Smith and his wife, Olive, was limited to a brief acquaintance in 1922. Since returning to Paris, he had not seen them, for they were living in Naples. As the story began to form in his head, Ernest could not know that Mrs. Smith, pregnant, was entering a Naples hospital, where on March 11, 1924, she died in childbirth. Nor did Hemingway read Chard Smith's account of his wife's death:

"Good-night, ladies, good-night, good-night," she whispered, her eyes laughing wide and blue in the pale face, framed by the swirl of golden hair whose ends the nurse had braided and tied in pink bows. Suddenly the small, straight mouth trembled. Savagery and scorn moved across her face together, and melted to tenderness. She was able to lift her arms, and to draw down the head of one of us upon her breast. The pressure of her hands was impalpable. Her lips moved, and there was a far-off sound. "You are my heart." Then she closed her eyes.

It was a strange mixture of pre-war sentimentality and Eliot's *Waste Land* where poor Lil, ravaged by five childbirths and a planned miscarriage, is the topic of the pub drinkers' conversation. As they depart, they call out, "Good Night, ladies, good night, sweet ladies, good night, good night." Then came sentiment, a dying fall into death from some popular melodrama, some movie closure, but it did not stop there. Smith added two more sentences so ironic, terse and understated they could have been written by Hemingway: "The doctor was reassuring – 'people don't die that way.' But he was wrong."[29]

Even less obvious contributors to the composite Mr. and Mrs. Smith were Ernest and Hadley themselves. Like Hubie Smith, Ernest married an older woman, who was told by her doctor she could not bear children. Like the Smiths, the Hemingways were living off a trust fund, and Ernest (24) and his fictional poet (25) were about the same age. As the Smiths fled Paris to a country chateau, so did the Hemingways leave

Paris soon after their first arrival for a chalet in Chamby. And like the fictional Smiths, the Hemingways were continually forming triads: with Chink, with Isabel Simmons, and later with Pauline Pfeiffer. The bisexual ménage in this early, slight fiction reappeared thirty years later in Hemingway's *Garden of Eden*. Now in the Paris spring, he was making satiric fun of an unconventional relationship that was actually darkly attractive. Paris was beginning to have its effect upon him, and, like the Left Bank painters he knew, Hemingway placed no great value on his models. In time they would all disappear, leaving only his art.

V

At Arles, he sat in the café, trying to imagine how the square looked when Van Gogh walked across it to fields beyond the village and began to paint. There were days when he wanted to be a painter. In the late spring on the Rhône delta being a painter would have been fine with the light exploding in the early mist and the sun fine in the afternoon. It was warm at Arles and he was happy to be alone there, the first time alone in a long, long time. No wife, no baby, no cat. No one knew him in Arles. Two tables away sat a working man, maybe a farmer, early in the day and drunk, his head falling forward. The drunk looked exactly like Anatole France.[30]

It was a cheap trip, 250 francs he told Ezra, maybe a bit more actually but cheap: Nîmes, Arles, Avignon, Le Baux, St. Rémy. Hadley told him to go after he moped around the apartment talking about the bullfights in Nîmes and how long it was until Pamplona and how they probably could not afford Spain anyway and he might not see another bullfight until God knew when. Hadley was beginning to understand or at least recognize the erratic cycles of elation and depression that could change Ernest before her eyes into someone she barely knew. After two months on a continuous creative binge that produced seven new stories, he was sky high, emotionally tense, ready to explode. So she sent him to Provence on his pilgrimage; better a run down country roads than an explosion in the living room.[31]

Along the way he made notes to himself, looking for a subject. At Gertrude's well-loved St. Rémy, he walked the half mile to see the Roman cenotaph and arch of Augustus with bas-relief warriors lording it over prisoners chained to a tree. Back at the café he began something called "Exercise (stone)":

The line of the stone is softened by the rain.

The line of the stone of the Escorial is hardened by the sun.

The weather of Burgos can not help the cathedral. The weather of Cologne formed the Cathedral of Burgos and the University of Bonn.

The carvings in the Roman arch on the plateau above San Remy are worn away by the wind. The wind is cold and dry and comes down the valley of the Rhone. It is full of particles of dust and dries the head and makes it hard to breathe and has blown the dust against the stone of the arch and worn away its carving.

The streets of La Corina are made of slabs of stone; they are washed clean by the rain and there are no sidewalks nor gutters.

In Madrid the stone is hard and new and white. There is no smoke to discolor it.

This is enough about stone.[32]

It was the sort of exercise Gertrude advocated, leading nowhere. That, too, had its place, for the act of writing was as important sometimes as the thing written.

In Avignon, sitting in the bistro, he wrote, "The most beautiful things in France are the trees in spring, the women and the horses. The ugliest are the modern furniture, the suburban architecture and the men's clothing." A seemingly useless note, but one could not be sure. Joyce kept notes of all kinds never knowing where they would lead. It was a way of seeing. Still the terrain did not move him. It was someone else's landscape. Gertrude liked it at St. Rémy. He tried to imagine her sitting in a field with Alice, on Gertrude's command, chasing the cow about and then Gertrude jotting down her spontaneous response. And then Alice and the cow again. That was like Van Gogh taking his easel and oils into the fields all right, but it was no way for him to write. Nature, certainly, but not sitting in a field. It was much funnier to imagine Alice chasing the cow. Was that at St. Rémy? He couldn't remember where. Maybe St. Rémy. It was a good place to chase a cow.[33]

Ernest was not chasing anything, merely looking, and mostly he looked at the people. He observed them closely in the gardens of

Avignon where once a pope was held in mild captivity. He watched them climb the Tour Magne in Nîmes. "I have not seen one good looking girl in either Nimes or Avignon," he said to himself on paper. But in Arles he saw her before she saw him, saw her standing in the shade watching the passing men watch her. He jotted it down quickly:

> There is a girl selling stockings under a canvas shelter in the square. The plane trees give only a small blotch of shade with sun so high. The girl is letting her bobbed hair grow out. It is very hot under the canvas and she tosses her hair back. She is always posing for the men who pass along the street.

He watched her for a long time but said nothing. Her hair was not much longer than his own. He could imagine exactly how her hair felt.

In his notes he put down two ideas: a story about a man who always wanted to have his hair long, and another about a girl who always wanted to cut hers short, finally did and how she felt. With his own hair now grown out enough to attract attention, grown almost as long as Hadley's bobbed red hair, he saw that it was the same story. Throughout those Oak Park years there was always hair: his several sisters' hair, his mother's hair as long as Gertrude's. He remembered when Marcelline bobbed her hair and how his father looked at her across the table without saying a word. Remembered his mother drying her hair in the afternoon sun at Windermere with only a slight breeze coming off the lake, long hair fanned out on the hillside blanket.[34]

He looked at the girl in the square a long time before writing,

> She was one of the few young and good looking women who had never yielded through six years of the fashion to the impulse to cut off her hair. She knew that sometime sooner or later short hair would be out of fashion. But it seemed such a long time in coming. Six years had passed and it was still a fashion.

The story did not go any further. He was not ready to write anything about hair. No one would understand it. He didn't understand it, but he knew it. Knowing was better than understanding.

As much as he wanted to speak to the girl, he did not, just as he never picked up the lovely whores who worked the *dancings* or the night clubs. Some men did. Men he knew, married men like himself, picked up a casual afternoon in bed. Then there was Ezra feeling up any woman within reach. He thought about Ezra and Olga Rudge and stared hard at the girl but did not move from his café chair. He often wanted a woman who was not Hadley, a woman bending over oranges at the greengrocers', a whore passing in the street, someone else's wife. He loved Hadley, but now that she was a mother, it was different. He could not write about that or about the hair, not yet.

He left her there selling her stockings and kept his ideas to himself. "I have been down in Provence," he wrote Pound, "and discovered it ain't no place for a writer," adding a note: "I made a pilgrimage to Van Gogh's whorehouse in Arles and other shrines." It was true in a way, for he had been to the whorehouse in his mind.[35]

VI

He returned to a Paris lovely in flowers, warm and quiet for a May Day. With taxi drivers on strike, streets were unusually calm. Workers of all stripes, including communists, banded together to celebrate their Labor Day without violence. In the streets, flower women sold lily-of-the-valley as they always did on the first of May.[36]

At the apartment, Hadley showed him the April 28th *Tribune* with the juicy scandal in which his one-time friend, Kenley Smith, was standing knee deep. At Arles, he had read the French wire service story in a Marseilles paper, but missed many of the details. In Detroit, Wanda Stopa, the assistant district attorney of Chicago, committed suicide after failing in her attempt to shoot Kenley's wife, Doodles, in Palos Park, the Chicago suburb where Sherwood Anderson sometimes lived. Kenley's jealous mistress came through the front door of the bungalow firing a little wild. She hit and killed the grounds keeper, who was inexplicably in the house, and Doodles went out the bathroom window. Unable to track down the speedy Doodles, Miss Stopa fled to Detroit, checked into a hotel, put on a white gown, scattered her bed with rose petals, and then, in a hot bath, took poison. When the police found her, Wanda Stopa was three hours dead. Before the end of May, first his parents and then Howell Jenkins sent him the Chicago version of Kenley's scandal.[37]

Neither Ernest nor Hadley could help laughing. Doodles going out the window pursued by Kenley's mistress was too blackly funny to hold it back. It could not have happened to nicer people, they both agreed. Once Ernest's closest friends were Bill and Katy Smith, Kenley's younger siblings. Once Ernest had lived in Kenley's apartment, where Doodles kept flirting with another man and Ernest told Kenley and . . . water long flushed down a drain far away. But bitterness remained. He missed Bill Smith terribly at times, particularly in summer when they used to fish the pine barrens and the lake. He missed Katy, Hadley's close friend and his own almost too close friend. The break with Kenley and ugly words had ruined all that, blood ties proving stronger than the high spirits binding summer people together.

Better news was Ford's brief absence, a flying trip to England that gave Ernest a whole week at the *transatlantic* when forced politeness was unnecessary. As he looked over the up-coming June issue, Hemingway saw little to excite a reader except the continued serilization of Stein's *Making of Americans* and young Nathan Asch's "The Voice of the Office," which Hemingway had helped Asch revise. The down-side of the office news was Ford's financial problem. Never much of a business man, he had foolishly invested a sizable part of his savings in the magazine, naively thinking he could make a profit on its modest circulation (5000). Half-way through the first year, he realized his mistake and tried to regroup. Returning from England about May 7, no more solvent than when he left, Ford began drafting letters to potential investors, trying to sell 1150 new shares in the floundering magazine. It did not work. Gertrude Stein, Natalie Barney and Romaine Brooks bought a few shares, but not enough to save the *review*. Ford, who was no fool, looked for ways to keep the magazine afloat without bearing its financial liability himself. "It seems," Hemingway wrote Ezra, "O'Neil, David, that son of a bitch, is going to get together a syndicate of big business men to run the Mag. Like hell he will."[38]

Little that happened that May gave Ernest much joy. The day that Ford returned from England, Hemingway wrote one of his infrequent letters home:

> My publisher told me that 5 copies of the first/limited edition of In Our Time were returned from some one named Hemingway in Oak Park. He was glad to get them back as they are already worth much more than the sale price. . . . I wonder what was the matter, whether the pictures were too accurate and the attitude toward life not sufficiently distorted to please who ever bought the books or what? . . . a work of art that is really good never lacks for defenders, nor for people who hate it and want to destroy it. Well it doesn't make any difference. . . .

But the books coming back did make a difference, or he would not have said it.[39]

Years later, Marcelline would tell how shocked her parents were by *in our time* and what a scene it caused in their Oak Park living room. Perhaps it did, but she was not there at the time, and when she wrote her white-wash of Oak Park, the principals involved were dead, their tongues stopped. If five books returned to Paris, the Doctor and the Doctor's wife between them ordered ten copies when "Blank" by Ernest Hemingway was announced in the Inquest prospectus. It would seem that five copies remained in Oak Park, but Ernest did not know that, nor would such knowledge have soothed his hurt. Like all children, he never understood his parents, whose intolerance was not so strong as he imagined. He never realized how much pride his father took in all of his writing, or if he did realize, it did not seem to matter. It was Grace Hemingway whose approval was most important to Ernest.[40]

His parents' apparent rejection of his work, combined with rejected stories coming back in the mail, could have pushed Ernest into a black depression. On May 20, he sent George Breaker another wire over Hadley's name, demanding immediate deposit of the errant trust funds, but nothing came of it. Four days later he wrote his scathing letter to Dorothy Butler. When Ford, in a desperate effort to raise money, sailed for America around May 21, he left Hemingway to finish the already laid-out July issue and to put together the entire August issue. Then about June 4, Ernest received from the *American Mercury* a rejection of one of his new short stories. George Nathan meant to be encouraging: "We cannot agree upon this story for *The American Mercury*. But we shall be glad to read anything that you care to submit to us." Sure they would read it. Anyone could read it. He read lots of miserable stories for Ford and sent them back to authors with more encouragement than Nathan gave. What he needed was a sale in America, someone to believe in his new-found techniques. So he put another story into the return mail to the *Mercury*. Let them keep on reading.[41]

If Ford had been a better judge of temperament or, perhaps, less harassed with financial problems, he might not have left the *transatlantic* in the hands of Hemingway. His timing was all wrong, but he thought that it was only the August issue at risk. The July number was all but put to bed, its contents fixed, mostly proofed and ready to print. Ford Madox Ford still had a lot to learn about Ernest Hemingway. Ford handed his all-but-finished editorial section, "Chronique," to Ernest to finish. It began: "We are journeying Westwards, leaving the helm of the review in the hands of Mr. Ernest Hemingway whose tastes march more with our own than those of most other men." It ended with an apology for not previously running more essays and a list of the essays in the present volume, which he called a "relatively serious number." But he ran out of time. Meaning to comment on each of the essayists, he handed the column over to Ernest with the direciton, "Mr. etc . . . Hemingway continue . . .," meaning, of course, for Ernest to wrap up the paragraph. Hemingway ran the column without changing a word, including Ford's instructions to him, "Hemingway continue . . .," making the paragraph appear insincere at best.[42]

Hemingway then added an unnecessary "Chronique" introduction to Ring Lardner's satiric skit satirizing Dadaist writers. In two paragraphs Hemingway managed to insult, without cause, the French sensation, Jean Cocteau, the Dadaist Tristan Tzara, and Gilbert Seldes, editor of the *Dial*, the most influential literary magazine in America. Cocteau, he said, "has a very good minor talent and a certain amount of intelligence," was "amusing in French and often instructive," but unable to read or write English, Cocteau had translated *Romeo and Juliet* into French. The editor wonders "what school book edition of Shakespeare" Cocteau used. "With this example, however, we expect a translation of Marlowe by Mr. Tzara who is also ignorant of English."

Not having done enough damage, Ernest then batted the *Dial* editor about the ring with short, satirical chops: Gilbert Seldes repeated the "mots of Mr. Tristan Tzara with a childish enthusiasm and wonder at how splendid they are and how splendid it is that he has heard them and understood them in French and the wonder of it all that he is hearing them in French but for the wonder of it all he might be, say, Professor of Slumming or something in, say, Columbia University." The only funny remark the editor ever heard from Mr. Tzara "was something about what you could tell about a girl from the way she peeled a banana," an old joke which Ernest said he first heard from Sliding Billy Watson in Kansas City.[43]

In that same July issue of the *transatlantic*, two Cocteau texts appeared, and Gilbert Seldes' new, important book, *The Seven Lively Arts*, was favorably reviewed by Lewis Galantière. Tzara's work had appeared in the April issue. In two paragraphs Hemingway not only made public fun of three influential literary figures, he also made Ford look like a fool, implying that no editor would take the three writers seriously, much less print them in his magazine. It was also a back-handed slap at Galantière, whose review praised Seldes.[44]

Judging only from his editorial comments, one might conclude that Hemingway was trying to sabotage the *transatlantic* for no obvious reason. That was not true. As he continually told Pound, he wanted the periodical to be better than it was, to print truly experimental work of the sort no commercial magazine would dare print. But that attitude did not explain his rather childish behavior whenever Ford gave him a public opportunity. His insulting editorials and "Letters" were more calcualted to anger Ford than to delight the readers, who must, at points, have wondered what it all meant. It was as if Hemingway wanted Ford to throw him off the magazine.

VII

Immediately upon returning from Provence, Hemingway wrote Edward O'Brien once more, sending out luck lines. He had sent to O'Brien's London address copies of *in our time*, *Three Stories & Ten Poems* and the April *transatlantic* carrying his "Work in Progress" ("Indian Camp"), but there was no reply. This letter Hemingway sent to Rapallo.

> I have ten stories done now and think it might be a good idea to have a literary agent or something peddle them around. Also there is this Harper's Contest. At any rate I ought to get them moving. . . . What I would like to do would be bring out a good fat book in N.Y. with some good publisher who would tout it and have In Our Time [*in our time*] in it and the other stories, My Old Man and about 15 or 20 others. How many would it take? . . . I'm enclosing a couple which I think might sell and one (Mr. and Mrs. Smith), which I'm sure wouldn't, but for you to read and keep it as a souvenir . . . Would it be too much to ask you to send the other two to an agent or to somebody you think might take them direct? And what about this Harper's Short Story Contest?[45]

Oddly repetitious, the letter alternated between pleas for help and statements of poverty, saying nothing about the *American Mercury*'s rejection.

The question about how many stories to make a book was a little forced, for Ernest knew how many it took. He counted pages at Sylvia's bookshop and studied carefully Joyce's *Dubliners* as his model. *Dubliners* was not merely a collection of unrelated stories, but a new form like Anderson's *Winesburg, Ohio* – a set of stories bound together by location, themes and characters. Looking over his ten stories, Hemingway saw that setting was not a possible unifier; already they were too geographically divided. In fact, there was no real unity, for he had not written them to be a whole. But he also saw how Joyce had used his massive story, "The Dead," to weld the *Dubliners*' themes together, placing it last to anchor the collection. Ernest needed such a story to end his book, a story bringing together everything he had learned.[46]

In mid-May, Hemingway pinned to the wall in front of his writing table a detailed, blue-tinted map of the northern Michigan peninsula. Whenever he looked up, the names were there: Horton Bay, Lake Charlevoix, Walloon Lake, Petoskey, Boyne City – the setting of every summer from his birth until the war. There was the Charlevoix "point" where summer people bottom-fished for trout, and there was where the creek came into the lake. He could see the sun turning silver the chop on the water, smell the pine smoke again. If ever he had a true home, the cottage on Walloon Lake was it, the one place to which he could return, always pristine in memory's keep.[47]

To the east in the pine barrens ran the Black and Pigeon rivers; further north, on the upper peninsula close to Little Two-Hearted Lake, was the Fox where he and high-school friends caught big trout that summer of 1919 after the war. Some of that summer he had used in the *Star* on a series of trout fishing stories, but this was a fiction, not journalism, a story he tried out in Paris the first time, but it broke his line. He tried it once more with three men on the river, but gave it up; it wasn't right because it wasn't enough fiction, too much the straight story about fishing the Fox. This time he took what he knew about the Fox to a river he had not fished. He did not need the other two men, only the river and his invention, Nick Adams. Nick was there in four of the stories, and he would be there in this last one, holding the book together. Nick was like his son, only older, more like a twin brother. He knew everything about Nick, the way he felt in the boat with his father rowing back from the Indian camp, the way he set up the picnic on the point to break up with Marge. Sometimes he could not tell the difference between himself and Nick, except Nick seemed to have experiences in a different way than his own. Like with Marge. He and Marge never broke up on the point at the lake, but with Nick she did.

202

And like the war where Nick really got it bad. His own was bad enough and sometimes he could not sleep with remembering it and when he did sleep the nightmares came: Germans chasing him across a field, Germans he had not come close to seeing. He thought he was brave, but he never truly found out at the war. There had been no time to find out. The mortar shell in the night had come too soon. Nick knew all about mortars.[48]

The story started in Seney after the war with the town all burned out and gone. Nick got off the train and Ernest got off with him, watching him at the bridge study the clear water where trout held steady in the current, almost invisible against the gravel bottom. Nick watched as "they changed their positions by quick angles, only to hold steady in the fast water again. Nick watched them a long time." Ernest watched with him. Study the trout holding steady under pressure. Well, Jesus Christ, he had all the pressures he needed just then: Bumby demanding attention; Hadley needing attention; George Breaker unable to explain where the money went; his folks sending the books back; stories in the mail and no response; bloody Ford and his bloody review. He could handle pressures better now, but not too many. It was like juggling balls. Maybe he could handle four, but toss a fifth up and they all came down. He came down with them, sometimes. Not this time. This time he had Nick and the river, and each day he fished it a little until the story grew like it should. It was so good that it scared him a little. He did not know how it would end; neither did Nick. But they were there each day together, and he called it "Big Two-Hearted River."

VIII

In mid-May, the Paris weather warmed quickly. They called it a heat wave, but it was only a touch of early summer, nothing to keep a man from his work. All around him Montparnasse was preparing in a self-conscious way for the tourist trade: Isha, the gorgeous black model, street dancing in front of the Rotonde with an American artist in an Indian bonnet; foul-mouthed Flossie Martin telling everyone at the Dôme about her movie role in "Chamber of Horrors." The summer Olympic competition was doubling the usual tourist invasion, but the games remained an amateur's delight. The American rugby team from southern California crushed the Romanians 37–0 and the French 17–3 to become Olympic champions. Only three matches were played, and no one, except some rabid Frenchmen and a few expatriates, was particularly excited about the outcome. Sometimes in the evenings Ernest would go over to the Cirque de Paris where the French amateurs were trying out for the boxing team.

Whenever he could – early in the morning at the table or after lunch on the quai – he was with Nick moving toward the river in the summer heat of upper Michigan. Always one to sweat easily, he knew exactly how the pack fit against Nick's back and how the salt sweat ran down beneath his arms. He could see the black hoppers there in the burned-over land and feel Nick's tension easing the closer he got to the river. He worked the story slowly, steadily, not wanting to rush it. It was all the fishing he would get that spring.

As temperatures rose, the streets absorbed heat, radiating it back long into the night. Along Montparnasse, street vendors sold lemonade, ice cream and fresh strawberries to the young men from Harvard in their straw hats and white flannel trousers. Ernest and Hadley were part of it, drinking sometimes at the Dôme, sometimes at the Dingo, going to parties and laughing together down the street. Everyone agreed they were a lovely couple. Periodically when Hadley's check arrived, they ate well and inexpensively at the Nègre de Toulouse, so local then it was not yet listed in the tourist guides. At night they slept above the lumberyard with open windows, waiting for the breeze that sometimes brought rain.

At the river Nick made his camp, carefully preparing the ground beneath his tent, pulling taut the rope and hanging his pack from a nail pounded into the pine tree. It was a good camp. Ernest looked it over, sentence by sentence, to be certain it was all there, even the cheesecloth to keep out mosquitoes. He could hear the river, but he did not go to it yet. There was no hurry, he told himself. But he was wrong. Ford left quickly for America to raise money, and Nick barely got his supper cooked before Ernest ran out of writing time. He left Nick there in his home that he'd made by the river, his fishing line still dry, and there Nick waited patiently for Ernest to return.

Chapter Eleven

THE LITERARY GAME
SUMMER, 1924

I

When Ford left for American gold fields to raise magazine money, Nick Adams was sleeping there in his camp by Big Two-Hearted River, where Ernest left him while he put the August *transatlantic* issue together. After all his complaints and surly remarks, this was Hemingway's chance to show what a literary magazine should be. From his experience on the *Co-operative Commonwealth* in Chicago, where he wrote much of the copy, edited the rest and got the issues through the print shop and into the world, he was not intimidated by the job in hand, but neither was he happy. His real writing, which was going so well, was interrupted, and because it was a process that he did not completely understand, he feared and resented such intrusions. Were there a choice, he would finish the story and let the *review* wait. But there was no choice.

The first question was what to leave out of the next *transatlantic*. The answer was easy: leave out Ford and all of his doppelgangers. If any readers were waiting for the eighth installment of Ford's novel, *Some Do Not*, they were going to be disappointed. Hemingway left out not only Ford, but also Daniel Chaucer, the pseudonym under which Ford published rambling essays, and Luke Ionides, the old duff whose memoirs Ford insisted on carrying. That was the easy part. Now the empty space must be filled with something interesting.

From Hemingway's new friend, John Dos Passos, came a story, "July," but that was solicited by Ford, as was the Nathan Asch story,

"Marc Kranz." From McAlmon's wife Bryher, Ernest took three undistinguished poems to open the issue, followed by the slightly insane poems from the barely sane Baroness Elsa Von Freytag Loringhofen, whose work Ford personally vetoed earlier when Hemingway tried to print it. From Guy Hickok, Ernest's close friend and foreign correspondent for the *Brooklyn Eagle*, came a funny, insider travel piece on Premier Herriot's American tour, preceded by yet another installment of Gertrude Stein's massive *The Making of Americans*. The issue also contained an appreciation of McAlmon's prose by his friend William Carlos Williams, a piece that Ford probably would not have printed.

On June 8, Hemingway wrote to Dorothy Richardson in England for a contribution. At Hadley's insistence, he first read and enjoyed her novels in Chicago. When *in our time* appeared in March, he sent her copies of it and *Three Stories & Ten Poems*, which she said by note that she liked. Thanking her for this encouragement, he asked her to send a story for his August issue, any story at all,

> because I would like to get Ford out one real number of his magazine. The time is quite short as I have just now had to take over and must have the copy in by the 20th of this month. Any length up to 4,000 words and I could use a much shorter story just as well.[1]

By return mail, she sent him "The Garden," an interior monologue from the mind of a small girl. On the page it appeared quite regular: punctuation and capitals all in place; paragraphs indented. But it was filled with childlike impressions from a mind either too young to understand completely its experience or one slightly disturbed. Only three pages long, "The Garden" was the most distinguished piece in an issue not exactly bubbling with experimental work.

Ernest may have realized his failure to produce a "real number," but he never said so. In his efforts to find fresh material, he discovered the difficulty of the job. One easy solution that he did not take was publishing his own work. He had at hand several new stories which, in retrospect, would have made the August issue a collector's item. His apparent restraint may have been the desire to sell them to a magazine with better pay rates, or they may have been out in the mails. Eventually he published "The Doctor and the Doctor's Wife" and "Cross Country Snow" in the last two issues of the *transatlantic* after they had been turned down by at least two American periodicals.

When Ford returned, it was too late to change the issue. With ironic restraint, he merely added to his "Chronique" a half page which said, in part,

> During our absence . . . this Review has been ably edited by Mr. Ernest Hemingway, the admirable Young American prose writer. Except for the London Musical Chronique . . . the present number is entirely of Mr. Hemingway's getting together . . . [providing] an unusually large sample of the work of that Young America . . . with its next number the Review will re-assume its international aspect, the final installments of Mr. Chaucer and Mr. Ionides . . . and, should any large body of readers so demand, some more of *Some Do Not*. Other works of English and French writers will also be again allowed to creep in.[2]

Although he had every reason to do so, Ford did not throw Hemingway out of the literary house on Quai d'Anjou, a failure which Ernest saw only as a weakness in the older man. Ford never understood Hemingway's animosity, and Ernest never understood the walrus-like Ford of the wheezing voice. The man could never tell the truth, Ernest said. Perhaps he saw something of himself in Ford, something he did not like but could not control any more than could Ford.[3]

II

There was more to Hemingway's month than merely editing the *transatlantic*, for Paris was throbbing with the excitement of another summer. During the first ten days of June, eleven liners docked in Cherbourg with American tourists who were packed into Paris-bound trains like rich refugees. They arrived, groggy from too much ocean drinking, to find the Left Bank behaving with its usual summer self-consciousness, putting on a street show for the Cincinnati and Chicago gawkers. The costumes of painters were daubed with fresh color; artists' models sported new and longer cigarette holders, and young prostitutes shopped in Bon Marché to outfit their summer season.

With the tourists came American Olympic performers, straggling in to Paris in a disorganized way, for there was no central focus to the summer games. The American rugby team departed before the polo and rifle teams arrived. On June 16, half of the American team sailed from

Hampton Roads on the new battleship *West Virginia*, which promptly ran aground; in New York the remainder of the U.S. Olympians boarded the *America* for the trip across.

Paris, of course, had other summer attractions to offer and the price was right, for the dollar was worth nineteen francs. Sergei Diaghilev's Ballet Russe de Monte Carlo opened a new season with costumes by Juan Gris. Theaters sent new works on to the boards: Jean Cocteau's *Romeo and Juliet* played at the Cigale, while the Grand Guignol scared everyone with a graphic version of the Russian monk Rasputin's melodramatic death. It was proving to be another gala Paris summer of Right Bank night clubs, bare-breasted show girls, quick divorces and slow taxis. In mid-June, one of the Grand Guignol actors, in the heat of action, nearly strangled an actress to death on stage. Or was it merely another stage trick? Whatever it was, it sold out the house.

Just as the madness was getting under way, Ernest received his copy of Edward O'Brien's *Best Short Stories of 1923*. Hurriedly he turned to the dedication page, and there, as O'Brien had promised, was his name. He felt like crying. The book was dedicated to "Ernest Hemenway." Would they never learn how to spell his goddamn name! Early in June, Eugene Jolas, the *Tribune*'s literary man about town, gave him a nice plug:

> We met in one day Miss Gertrude Stein, Mr. Ernest Hemingway, and Mr. Ogden Donald Stewart [sic], recently. Mr. Hemingway explained to us his esthetic theories, although he is the least theoretical of writers. His Three Stories (of which "My Old Man" has just been republished in O'Brien's Best Short Stories of 1923) have a dynamic directness and go straight to life, without being "literary" at all. Watching him engage in a friendly boxing match, as we did, gives a definite index as to his method. He told us he had never read Zola.[4]

But when the *Tribune* reviewed the book, there was no mention of Ernest or "My Old Man."

Hemingway's working days on the *review* were shortened by an influx of friends and visitors regrouping in Paris. McAlmon reappeared from the south of France, and John Dos Passos was in town. Then Bryher and H.D. trained in from Territet, depressing McAlmon no end. At supper, nothing was more silent than a silent McAlmon. Nancy Cunard appeared, stark, beautiful and bespangled with ivory bracelets.

Ezra and Dorothy arrived early in June to meet with Pound's old friend, William Carlos Williams, who, with his wife, had been touring Italy and France since the previous January. The Hemingways missed Williams his first time through Paris, but not the second. Pound brought them over to the Hemingways' apartment, and Williams, a doctor, examined Bumby, whose pallor bothered him. At eight months, the baby was still nursing and not yet on solid food. Dr. Williams told Ernest and Hadley it was time to wean the child and also to have him circumcised. That night they all went to the fights at the Cirque de Paris, where Ernest was happy to see Floss Williams pounding the shoulders of the man in front of her and yelling at the boxers, "Kill the bastard!" The next morning Williams returned with his surgical instruments to remove the baby's foreskin. Bumby screamed; blood flowed, and Ernest blanched.[5]

All that June it went like that, one interruption after another. Each time he came back to Nick there on the river, each time moving the story forward little by little. He could feel the coldness of the water now on his bad knee and see the fly line floating with the current, carrying the grasshopper into the swirls. When the first trout hit Nick's line in upper Michigan, Ernest felt the heavy tug in his Paris apartment. It was almost as good as fishing. Hell, it was fishing. If he made it all up exactly right, first remembering the real rivers and then putting them aside and creating his own river, then it was both fishing and writing. Whatever it was, it was good and the story moved along until he had to leave Nick completely alone. There was not enough time to finish. Quickly he jotted down some notes on how the story might end.

He thinks   gets uncomfortable, restless, tries to stop thinking, more uncomfortable and restless, the thinking goes on, speeds up, can't shake it – comes home to camp – hot before storm – storm – in morning creek flooded, hikes to the railroad.[6]

Maybe that was how it would end. He did not know. Nick's mind working and him trying to shut it off as it speeds up: that might get it right about Nick whose mind was not right, but Ernest did not want to say that. He wanted the reader to feel it without being told. He was living in the story, and the best part was not knowing how it would end.

By June 20, with the August *transatlantic* ready for the printers, Ernest was eager to get down to Pamplona for the San Fermin festival.

With Bumby, now weaned, spending the next month with Marie, their faithful *femme de ménage*, Ernest and Hadley were alone together for the first time since his birth. Hadley wrote not long afterwards that Marie

> put my heart at ease about his care in her hands when she told me in an excited whisper that she had stop[ped] the old Brittany grandfather clock in her hall at night because she was afraid J[ohn] H[adley] might wake in the night and be frightened by the ticking! What more could a mother ask than to have her child in such hands.[7]

While Ernest finished up his work and safeguarded his manuscripts, Hadley tried to assemble something like a set of decent clothes for the holiday. As usual she was clothes-poor, but her friend, Dossie Johnston, helped out, lending Hadley clothes and sewing frantically at the last moment to finish a home-made copy of a designer scarf.

Hadley, dressed in borrowed clothes, almost reached her seat on the Sud Express before the argument erupted between Ernest and a tall grey-blond man occupying the window-seat in their compartment.

"There are no tickets to these seats," the Frenchman said, "therefore I have my chocie to sit near the window."

"How do you know there are no tickets," Ernest demanded, pulling two blue ones from his pocket. "What do you call these that were sold to me five days ago?"

"That's just what I say," the older man replied, pulling his cap down lower over his eyes, "exactly what I said before. There *are* no tickets. What you have there makes no difference to me. The company has not put any duplicates here, so it's just as I say, there *are* no tickets."

Leaving Hadley in the compartment, Ernest went to find a railroad official. Hadley turned her back on the man to show her disdain. Red-faced and blowing, Ernest returned with a conductor who settled the matter: yes, the Hemingways reserved the window seats, and yes, the older gentleman must move. The Frenchman reluctantly agreed to do so, but only if Hemingway apologized for being disagreeable.

"Disagreeable!" Ernest screamed, and it continued until the man from Bordeaux discovered that the Hemingways were Americans, not British. The British he could not abide. Americans, well, that was different. He loved Americans, had spent twelve years in Chicago. If Ernest was from Chicago, they were practically brothers; the unpleasantness forgotten, the two old soldiers were ready to spend the evening discussing the war. Then Hadley realized that Dossie had not found them to say good-bye. She rushed out on to the platform, but no Dossie. As the train began to move out, Ernest hung from the window yelling at Dossie whom they finally saw looking sad and lost amidst the steam and rush of bodies.[8]

And that it how they left Paris, rushed and ragged, for their second trip to Pamplona. There would be two more summers with the San Fermin bulls before they could no longer go there together, but this would be the best one, the one before the fall.

Traveling south through the night toward the Basque coast, Ernest read once again the latest rejection of "Cat in the Rain," arriving via Lincoln Steffens, who had tried to sell it for him. Mr. Van Doren at *Century* magazine said "that from the literary point of view it was most suggestive of an ability which he is sure we will want in the magazine. He thinks the sketch you sent is a little slight. He asks you to urge Hemingway to send us other stories from time to time." A slight sketch? Well, to hell with you Mr. Van Doren. A little slight, from time to time, went a long way. Any day now someone would figure out what he was doing.[9]

They slept cuddled together in the compartment and woke in the early morning when the Express dropped them off at the coast to catch the connecting train to Pamplona. This year their reservations were on the plaza at Hotel La Perla where, after lunch, there was time to nap in their cool, high-ceilinged room, darkened by heavy, wooden shutters. In the late afternoon they strolled down the Plaza de la Constitución and out into the bright sun, glaring white off the baked mud in front of the grey stuccoed Plaza de Toros. They had the town almost to themselves, for it was another ten days before the San Fermin madness began. They meandered past the old French star fort, the remaining walls of which, now part of the town, were still visible at spots. The dusty road led them down to the green river where dark-haired women spread washed linens to dry. Like the children they watched, Ernest and Hadley crossed the river on stepping stones.[10]

The next morning, Ernest stood in line at the House of the Sisters of Mercy to reserve seats for all of the San Fermin bullfights. This day, June 27, was the first chance for ticket holders from the previous year to renew or change their seats. After a good deal of sign-language, he was able not only to get his two tickets of 1923 renewed, but also to secure five new ones, most of them ring-side seats, costing about ten dollars each and covering the three regular bullfights, the two extraordinary ones and the Prueba, where local bulls would be ring-tested for fierceness of breeding. With tickets in hand for himself, Hadley, Chink, McAlmon, George O'Neil, Dos Passos and his girl friend Crystal Ross, Ernest and Hadley had no reason to stay longer in Pamplona. They took the train south to Madrid to attend several bullfights before returning for the San Fermin festival. Living was easy, cheap and sensuous – late afternoons at the bull ring, late suppers in modest cafés, good wine and Spanish brandy, and strong black coffee the next morning to start the day.[11]

III

Afterwards no one could remember Pamplona right. After a week of madness without real sleep, how could anyone remember anything right? Each day began the same at 5:00 a.m.: the brass band sounding off right outside their window on the plaza, followed by flute-and-drum Riau Riau dancers and giant, papier-mâché figures bobbing gracefully along behind them. Who could remember which day it was that Saint Fermin's procession caught them by surprise? Who saw the bull gore the fallen runner? "Oh my God, did you see the horn slip into him!" It was a boy from Sanguesa who caught the horn in the small of his back and felt it slide into his right lung. Whatever one missed, someone else saw, making it part of the jumbled short-term memories of the group.[12]

No time to shave or shower. Slip quickly into the daily costume – rope-soled alpargatas, trousers, dark coat, scarf and black boina – and try to find a steaming *café con leche* before the *encierro* begins. The waiter's half drunk. No, he's half sober, looking as if he's not been to bed at all. "Pronto! Pronto!" Everything is *pronto* – musicians, morning crowd, and especially the bulls pounding up the barricaded, cobblestoned streets toward the bull ring. Ahead of them are the runners with enough head start to outrun the horns that bob along behind them, but not for all the mile run. Sooner or later the bulls close the distance, forcing the runners to either leap the barricade or flatten against it. Ahead new runners enter the game. At the arena the crowd waits, restless; the first runners arrive and scatter. Finally the bulls enter, heads tossing, frothy and wild. To see them from the safety of an arena seat is to know, for the first time, what raw power is about. To be on the ground level, buttocks tight against the wooden wall, hoping the bulls will pass without hooking, is to know fear forever. They pass, following the steers through the gate and into the holding pens.[13]

Then the amateurs, armed with old blankets and bits of rag, drop into the sandy ring, waiting for the entrance of the young bulls with their padded horns to complete the morning fun. Even Don Stewart, half blind, is there in the ring, wondering why and not having time enough to find an answer better than Ernest's saying he must try it. It is madness, but who can deny Ernest his passion? Up in the air goes Stewart, his glasses flying to the spectators' glee. "Come on, you stupid son of a bitch," he yells at the bull he can almost see. A mistake. The bull sees him for an instant and cracks two of Stewart's ribs with another toss. Later Don can only say that it seemed important to prove himself to Hemingway; bravery, that trench-dead word, became important because Ernest, out of his vitality, made it so. He had a way of doing that, infecting those about him with his enthusiasm, taking them out of themselves, men older than he but caught up in his passion.[14]

Men, like Dorman-Smith, are in the ring with nothing to prove, knowing that bravery is a matter of circumstance and an ability to turn off one's mind, but he's in the ring nonetheless, hooting the steer and a little crazy with adrenalin flow. The steer with leather pads on his horns knows the bull ring very well and seems to enjoy chasing the men up over the *barrera*, sometimes tossing one into the air like a rag doll. The men almost stumble over the bloody heap of sandy entrails left by yesterday's dying horse.

"My God, what's Hemingway doing? Stop him!"

[He is] . . . holding a proper matador's cape . . . about to receive a lesson in how bulls are fought. . . . Hemingway is facing the steer. The steer charges. The veronica is all right as far as it goes, but the steer is out for the man, not the cape. He isn't a fighting bull whose first experience will also be his last. He knows all about it. Bump!! Hemingway swings under the impact of the horn on his ribs, and slides forward on to the steer's head. He grips the horns as the steer dashes on, pushing him over the sand. We rush to the rescue, and the steer, his head released, turns to some less strenuous fun.[15]

Later that month the story reached Oak Park as a Chicago

Tribune front-page headline: BULL GORES 2 YANKS ACTING AS TOREADORS. The following story made it sound as if Ernest had actually been gored. Clarence Hemingway, anxious about his son's condition, contacted the Chicago paper immediately. His fears were relieved by the cablegram reply:

> Part of the initiation of young manhood in Pamplona consists of being thrown by the bandaged bull. Mr. Stewart and Mr. Hemingway participated the first day successfully and on the second day Mr. Stewart was thrown. It occurred when he said he could leap on the bull's back and blow smoke in the bull's eyes and then beat him down. The chief toreador presented Mr. Stewart with a scarlet cloak, which he could not refuse, and during the hand shaking, the bull rushed for Mr. Stewart, lifted him on his horns and tossed him over, and then threw him into the air and tried to horn him. Mr. Hemingway rushed to rescue Mr. Stewart and was also gored, but was saved from death on account of the horn bandages.[16]

Grace Hemingway, summering as usual at Walloon Lake, soon got the story from her husband by mail. In his letter the Doctor referred, in passing, to the two Chicago joy-killers, Leopold and Loeb, whose murder trial was almost over. The Doctor said, "Glad our boy is in Spain instead of the County Jail with the celebrated little Jews he so despised."[17]

With each retelling, the story changed slightly, enlarging here, sharpening there. Dos Passos, keeping to himself and Crystal Ross, thought the risking silly. McAlmon who, not many years later, would dress himself up in a bullfighter's "suit of lights," said:

> Hemingway had been talking a great deal about courage, and how a man needs to test himself to prove to himself that he can take it. I am doubtful. If one takes it too much one may begin to get nervy, or shellshocked, or plainly fed up. Hemingway, however, had persuaded himself that he must prove himself.[18]

None of them, not even Hadley, understood how important the bull ring was to Hemingway. In the fiesta's aftermath, he wrote Pound in all seriousness: "I appeared in the bull ring on 5 different mornings – was cogida 3 times – accomplished 4 veronicas in good form and one natural with the muleta, the last morning, received contusions and abrasions in the pecho [chest] and other places . . . was offered a job as Picador by Algabeno after hanging onto the bull's horns for about 6 minutes and finally getting his nose down on the sand." If he retold it less than right, blame it on his deep need to test himself, and on his childlike admiration for courageous bullfighters whom he seriously tried to imitate. With his bum right knee, Ernest was even more heavy-footed than the young boy who once tried so hard to be an Oak Park football hero, but part of him never grew up or older, never relinquished his boy's dream of heroic action. In the bull ring, civilization and its charades fell away, leaving only a man and his skills, fortified by courage and honed by his personal sense of honor. Honor and courage were words so corrupted by the war years he could not use them straight out but, spoken or not, they were there in the afternoon sun. If, in the morning *encierro*, Ernest needed to test his inner self, he came to that need via his boyhood dreams of courageous action, dreams spawned by Civil War veterans, Teddy Roosevelt's Rough Riders and the frontiersman's long shadow. They were American dreams of enormous vitality, strong enough to power all of his post-1920s fiction.[19]

It was not easy to explain about the bulls to friends because many of them, who did not want to know about dying, got to feeling sorry for the gored horses. Even Chink did not enjoy the horse with his entrails hanging down between his legs after a solid gutting by the bull, but Chink, a professional soldier, understood perfectly the rest of it. He said:

> The Spanish bull is a magnificent, deadly savage. . . . From the instant he charges out of the shaded corral into the sunlit and hostile arena to face his slayers, to the time when, blood gushing from his mouth with each defiant bellow, he yields to his fate and sinks on reluctant knees before his victor, he is arrogant, fierce, fatal, doomed to die, but destined to die fighting. It is no small thing to die with one's banner nailed to the masthead.[20]

Of course Chink would see it all in military terms: two armed forces dedicated to killing each other. And he got it right about "doomed to die" – soldiers, bulls, anyone – all doomed to die and better to go out fighting.

That night at Fossalta when the observation post exploded like a blast furnace and he felt himself disappear in the roar that would not stop,

Ernest was sure he was dead. Caught without warning by the trench mortar shell, he had no chance to nail his banner to the masthead. No courage was required of a passive victim; all he got were residual scars and a nagging fear of death. Not in the explosion. The fear came later when he found he was not dead, merely bleeding and his right leg useless. When he saw what was left of the others in the post and found their bloody parts splattered across his chest, he knew real fear for the first time. There is never a good time for that lesson, but at eighteen he learned that he was not immortal and many times at night he could taste the lesson still in his mouth. So he came back to that night of his first wound again and again, the way one replays a lost football game in his mind before sleep, trying to catch the pass suspended high in memory.

There in Pamplona he brought to the bulls his early training as a naturalist, his reporter's eye for detail and a finer perception forged in the mortar's fire. He saw the art of it clearly, the bending skills, graceful moves and precise wrist work of the matador; the dying bulls were transformed by the artist out of time into beauty itself. From a *barrera* seat he could see it up close: the shadow crossing the matador's face after a close pass of the bull; the blood streaming crimson in the afternoon light; the sword slipping into the killing spot between the shoulders so easily when done right; the bone whiteness of the killer's drained face afterwards. It was the artistry of death, the final ballet. Ernest needed the bulls then to study his own death. One could not face a mortar shell bravely or any other way. It simply happened. But in the bull ring nothing happened simply: there one's whole life was visible in the afternoon's artful death. He studied the moves so closely he knew them by heart. Already a story was forming in his head, but he did not let it go on too far.

IV

The week ran its course of music, street dancing, night drinking, and afternoons at the Plaza de Toros. McAlmon claimed everyone slept until noon, but Chink said they were up at dawn for the *encierro*. Don Stewart took his bull tossing and cracked ribs back to Paris, and Crystal Ross disappeared somewhere when the week was over. There were jokes that no one remembered afterwards and imagined slights too long remembered. Having them all there in Pamplona was, for Hemingway, another version of Walloon Lake and his summer people at a heightened intensity, jamming everything into a single week.

Later he said the fiesta was not the place to bring a wife. "It's a man's fiesta," he claimed, "and women at it make trouble." The trouble began when Ernest booked a double room for Dos Passos and Crystal Ross, assuming a sexual intimacy which two years earlier he would not have assumed, and two years before that not even considered. Paris was changing him in ways that he did not see in the mirror; slowly his turn-of-the-century values from Oak Park were eroding. Behavior that once shocked him had, through its daily presence, become almost normal and acceptable for others, if not yet for himself. There was real trouble all right, but not with Dos Passos and Crystal. That was only an afternoon's embarrassment covered up with bluster. Hemingway's real trouble was forming like a cyst beneath his healthy surface.[21]

None of the Pamplona gang took special notice of Ernest's embarrassment about the double room, for, among strange and noisy distractions, they had little time for small details. The music seemed to go on endlessly: brass bands of cornets and trumpets in military march; shrill flute and drum corps; delicate woodwinds of haunting strain. In the July heat, sweat ran freely in the open air where one seemed always rushing somewhere else. Each day was the same but with enough variations that disorder became normal. On July 8, Don Antonio Canero, on horseback and armed with a long lance, fought and killed two young bulls. That same night the first of several *zezenzusko* effigies was publicly burned, exorcising whatever winter bad luck might hang yet in the summer air. Three nights later in the plaza there was a humorous parody of the Battle of Castillejos accompanied by much music and some bawdry, little of which the Paris gang understood, but they loved the ending: 350 meters of fire crackers went off in a long, sustained string of noise.[22]

In the streets, Spaniards wore necklaces of garlic and drank cheap local wines from goat-skin botas, some shaped like ships, some like animals. In the streets a brotherhood of drinkers moved instinctively to the primitive music. Don Stewart's solo dancing and comic charades were in a language the locals understood immediately. In the melee, the Paris group lost each other, wandered with strangers, drank from friendly botas, the red wine staining their shirts. Then, without effort, they found each other on the plaza as if it were planned. In the streets there were tents covering displays of wares, crafts, jewelry and food.

At the city's edge a livestock fair continued through the week: cattle, goats, rabbits and fighting cocks.[23]

Each morning the bulls ran through the streets; each afternoon at 5:30 they began dying bravely in the ring; and each night the meals lasted longer. In the cafés one could always get an egg tortilla, or from the shops some bread and sausage, but the evening meal was layered in the simple richness of the region: quail basted in olive oil, garlic and herbs; crisp lamb chops so tiny the bones had not set. With each course came pitchers of wine, tart rosé and rich, red riojas tasting of the Spanish earth. After late suppers, the gang rejoined the crowd on the plaza to watch the evening's fireworks display. In the dust of the early afternoons, one could watch Señor Oroquieta and his strong-armed son build the evening's wonder out of boards, wire lines and Japanese fireworks. One night he launched illuminated balloons that lifted into the darkness to explode in brilliant showers of colored lights that drifted down on the crowd, singeing an arm here, burning a shirt there. No one complained, for these too were marks of passage. On the last night of the bullfights, Señor Oroquieta outdid himself in the plaza with an enormous volcano that exploded in a fountain of colored sparks and rockets. Then at midnight, the trumpet and cornet bands of the Spanish Cavalry and Artillery paraded once more, signaling the end of the *feria*.[24]

San Fermin was ended, and not a moment too soon, for nerves were frayed to the breaking point and stomachs acidic from too much wine. McAlmon with Bill and Sally Bird, who came south at the last moment, left early to establish a base camp higher up in the Pyrenees at the small village of Burguete. They were soon joined by the rest of the gang – Ernest and Hadley, Chink, Dos Passos and George O'Neil – stretching the small inn's capacity to house and feed so many. For five days they relaxed in what then seemed almost unnatural country peace. Packing picnic lunches, they took long hikes to the Irati river to fish for mountain trout and to visit the metal-roofed monastery at Roncesvalles. That night Chink discussed the tactics of Roland who died bravely in that high pass into France. Goatherds wandered in the mountains, their bells tinkling through the woods, and sometimes the clouds came down to engulf them in swirling mist.[25]

In and among them was Ernest, less happy than he might have been and showing his growing depression like a rash. Partly it was the letdown that followed the week of unnaturally sustained emotional highs, but the main cause was Hadley. Her monthly period, which should have begun by Ernest's calculation on July 13, did not flow.

Hemingway checked his day book, re-adding the numbers. Ever since Bumby's conception, he suspected that Hadley had miscounted the days between periods, leaving her most fertile at the very time they thought it safe to abandon contraceptives. So now he also counted the days, noting carefully when her period should begin and when it actually did begin. In May, when he expected her to begin on the 20th, she started to flow on the 16th. In his calendar, he counted up thirty days (a strange mistake for a doctor's son) and marked June 16 as the expected beginning of her next period. True to her twenty-eight-day cycle, Hadley began her June period on the 13th. In his day book Hemingway then marked July 13 as "Cat due." By July 16, when her period had not appeared, Hemingway became despondent, certain Hadley was once again pregnant.[26]

The more Hemingway moped, the worse Hadley felt. How could they ever enjoy life, he wanted to know, if she were going to be pregnant all the time. Finally Sally Bird, angry and protective of Hadley, told Ernest, "Stop acting like a damn fool and a crybaby. You're responsible too. Either you do something about not having it, or you have it." Ernest retreated into oppressive silence. They all knew that abortions were available in Paris, but a boy raised in Oak Park did not easily accept that solution. All that day and into the next, he continued to be grim company, and there were tears in Hadley's eyes. On July 17, the Birds departed for Paris while McAlmon, Dos Passos, Chink and George O'Neil set out on an arduous cross-mountain hike to Andorra. Ernest went the first five kilometers with them but returned to be with Hadley, who, everyone was convinced, must be pregnant. There on the mountain path he waited as the men began to disappear among the pines. Chink stopped to wave across the distance.[27]

That evening in Burguete, to their enormous relief and Ernest's chagrin for being such a bastard about it, her period began, seven days late but not without reason. After she nursed Bumby for eight months, his weaning alone was enough to disrupt her cycle, but with the added physical stress of Pamplona, her biological clock was seriously disrupted. No longer feeling guilty, she looked at Ernest in a new light. He had made her feel like a worthless drag on his life. It was not a nice revelation, nor did the space between them immediately close.

Alone in Burguete and barely speaking to Hadley, Ernest wrote a depressed letter to Pound, complaining about his lack of money and his inability to write. The money, he claimed, was all loaned out to his hiking buddies. In his day book, he kept careful track of each peseta spent, each loaned out and each gone to pay another's bar tab. "We haven't enough pesetas now," he told Ezra, "to pay our hotel bill and don't know how we'll get away from here." It was not true, but he needed to say it. He was bitched, he said, ruined. He would never write again. Could not finish the story on the river, the one going so well in Paris. Had it with him there and talked it through on the Irati, but it was now busted. Redundantly, he claimed "Now we haven't got any money anymore I am going to have to quit writing and I never will have a book published. I feel cheerful as hell. These god damn bastards." What "god damn bastards," Pound might have wondered, the hikers with the unpaid debts or the literary bastards whom Ernest claimed, "the more meazly and shitty the guy, i.e. Joyce, the greater the success in his art."[28]

But the money wasn't the problem. They had enough money to stay at Burguete until July 25. He made sure of that, totaling up costs and making projections in his day book. To be certain, he had borrowed three hundred francs from McAlmon before he left. So he bitched about the money because that was the easiest way of letting off his anger without naming the real problem. Hemingway did not mention the scare of Hadley's late period or his own behavior as he whipped himself deeper into his depression.[29]

His mood swings were not something he could control. Sometimes they came and passed like a summer thunderstorm, an outburst of anger welling up inside him. Afterwards those in its path were stunned as if struck by lightning. Sometimes it was more gradual, a blackass mood growing inside him that he was unable to shake. He had seen these mood shifts in his father, but he did not yet recognize how much he was his father's son. With the departure of the summer men and the scare of Hadley's pregnancy, Ernest's mood dipped down briefly and then bobbed up to another high. Soon after he wrote Ezra, he unpacked the story of Nick on the river and began to work on it.

Frequently, as Nick said in the story, he wrote well when Hadley's period flowed. He got that idea from boxers who claimed that in training for a fight they kept away from women. Sperm was creative energy to be harbored for a man's true work. In another part of his mind, with the trout heavy in his bag, Nick was waiting patiently for Ernest to return. This time he let Nick think about things out loud, his mind jumping erratically from past to present, and he gave Nick all that he knew of Paris and Pamplona, including the events of the last three weeks. Having fished the Irati for trout and having spent evenings talking literary shop with Mac and Dos, Hemingway tried to get his theory of writing into the story. Maybe that would give it the weight required to hold down the collection. So Nick said to himself, "Nick in the stories was never himself. He [Nick] made him up." There was the twist: Nick Adams was a writer who wrote the earlier stories about the character called Nick Adams. It was not exactly what Joyce did with Stephen in *Portrait* or Gabriel Conroy in "The Dead," but it was something like it, and the device put another filter between Ernest himself and his character. These were Nick's theories on writing, which made it easier to talk about them.[30]

Nick thought about the importance of country, of getting the terrain as right as Cézanne got it in his good paintings. Nick "felt almost holy about it. It was deadly serious. You could do it if you could fight it out. If you'd lived right with your eyes." Nick thought about the wonderful Cézannes at Gertrude's and the others he'd seen at Bernheim's gallery and at the Luxembourg. "He knew just how Cézanne would paint this stretch of river." Nick "stepped down into the stream. The water was cold and actual. He waded across the stream, moving in the picture." That was the way country should be: seeing it clearly the first time and then making it come alive with the words so that there was no difference between the thing itself and the remembered experience. Nick and Ernest felt good about saying it out loud. Now Nick had a story in his head to write. He could feel it growing but he was not thinking about it. It was there all right. "He wanted to get back to camp and get to work." The story was going to be about the old gang at Walloon Lake, the summer people Nick lost when he married Helen. Ernest knew that story by heart.

V

On July 27, the Hemingways boarded the Paris train at San Sebastián alone, all the other revelers long since departed. Tired and tanned, they were ready to get back to the sawmill life. Hadley missed Bumby a good deal, and Ernest, apparently out of his depression, was eager once more to write. For an entire month they had put Paris away, giving it as little thought as possible. They avoided the less than earth-shaking presidential nomination by the Democrats of John W. Davis on the 103rd ballot, and they missed, by design, the entire summer Olympics.

Quite likely they had, in response to the *Tribune*'s plea for summer housing, sublet their apartment, for they left the day that the major contingent of American athletes arrived in Paris and returned the day after the games closed. They did not see Abrahams of England beat the American world champ, Charley Paddock, in the 100 meters, or see Eric Liddell, the Scottish preacher, set a world record at 400 meters. However, when the medals were added up, America, as befitted her new-found power, won the track and field events, as well as the overall games.

Ernest and Hadley arrived in Paris to find the divorce season at its height: twelve American women uncoupled in two days. Paris was, in fact, crawling with Americans. During a single July week, liners brought twelve thousand tourists from the states; despite the extraordinary Paris heat, none of them seemed eager to leave. As the Hemingways entered Gare d'Austerlitz on the Sud Express, across town six hundred American advertising men were arriving, followed soon after by smaller delegations of American lawyers, boy scouts, war veterans and Norton-Harjes ambulance drivers. Each group first laid an obligatory wreath on the Unknown Soldier's grave and then set out to find less solemn entertainment. At the Dôme and Rotonde, chairs were filled with straw-hatted escapees from Prohibition. Sweating profusely as he always did, Ernest bundled their bags up the stairs to the stifling apartment. It was Sunday evening, too late to check his mail at Sylvia's bookshop or at the Guaranty Bank and too late to buy groceries.

As they ate a light supper in the café, Ernest became interested in the Sunday *Tribune*. In his "Rambles Through Literary Paris," Eugene Jolas announced that Harold Stearns, professional expatriate, deliberate drinker and sometime race track tipster, was writing an exposé of the Left Bank American colony. Jolas approved of the idea, for "the pseudo-heretical seekers after cheap fame, the insincere types who would hide their vacuity underneath a hedonistic cloak" were turning Montparnasse into a Greenwich Village annex. Ernest bristled. He, too, disapproved of most of the Left Bankers who pretended to be artists or writers, but he resented anyone other than himself saying so, for he was a dues-paid resident of the Quarter. Still it was a good book to write. Maybe Stearns could do it. Certainly he knew about the vacuous life, since he was one of its more permanent monuments. Certainly somebody should write that book.[31]

Then, at the bottom of the page, Ernest's eye lit on the name Ford Madox Ford. Seems Jolas happened to drop in at the Quai d'Anjou office to chat with Fordie: more clichés about the magazine's mission to bridge generations and oceans. Old Ford returned from New York all right, but no mention of his money problems. Not the sort of thing a gentleman speaks of, you understand. Never know what the newspaper chaps will have you saying next. Spoke to one in New York and the next day was quoted as saying "Americans in Paris were more interested in bars than art." Course, he would never say such a thing. Not by much he wouldn't, and would never remember it right anyway.

According to Ford,

> the writings of the young Americans today are "over-sexed" . . .
> the American . . . expresses in his work a certain erotomania which
> "is the direct product of repressive legislation in the United States."
> He thinks it will disappear when the repression has ceased. . . .
> He regards Mr. Ernest Hemingway as the most representative of
> the young American novelists writing today.

Ernest read the line again. Then he read it to Hadley. How the hell could he be a representative novelist if he did not have a novel written? That goddamn Ford would say anything to anyone. He should keep his foul mouth off Ernest, who did not need any more bad luck. The next morning when he collected his mail, he found another story returned from New York. He wondered what the record was for rejections.

When he entered Bill Bird's print shop, Ford seemed pleased to see him despite the August issue of the *review*. He was, however, despondent about the future of the magazine. The New York trip had not turned up new capital; the dying John Quinn, who had put up $4000 at the *review*'s founding, was too weak to be interested. Ford could not continue supporting the magazine out of pocket. If nothing could be done, the magazine would fold, but in case it continued, would Hemingway be so kind as to write a Pamplona Letter for the September issue.

Hemingway had money problems of his own, having borrowed three hundred francs from Bob McAlmon and another hundred from Gertrude by mail, but he did not want to see the magazine go under. Given the growing stack of New York rejections, the *transatlantic* remained his best chance for publication, and he also felt obligated to the continued serialization of Gertrude's *The Making of Americans*. When Ford threatened to suspend operations, Ernest acted as Gertrude's spokesman, holding on to her manuscript until the waters calmed.[32]

Just when the *transatlantic*'s small boat seemed to be sinking beneath the waves of its logo, Hemingway brought his old Chicago acquaintance, Krebs Friend, together with Ford. Krebs, newly married to an older wealthy woman, wanted to be part of the literary scene; he and his wife agreed to advance Ford $200 a month for the next six months. In return they became members of the governing board. Ernest wrote to Gertrude in Provence: "Now Ford's attitude is that he is selling Krebs an excellent business proposition and that Krebs is consequently a business man and the foe of all artists of which he – Ford – is the only living example and in duty bound as a representative of the dying race to grind he – Krebs, the natural Foe – into the ground." Whatever the truth in this matter, the magazine continued to appear through the fall and into the winter. Krebs Friend became the new president of the Transatlantic Review Company: he and his wife actually wrote "Letters" of no particular merit which appeared in the periodical.[33]

Ernest agreed, grudgingly, to write a "Pamplona Letter" for the September issue, but it was, from his point of view, yet another interruption to his fiction. With "Big Two-Hearted River" finished, he was taking Nick back to the lake where the summer people were diving off a floating dock into the green bay. It was a hot day and Nick wanted to be alone, but could not stay away from Kate. Ernest wanted to be alone with Nick but he took the time to write the piece for Ford. It was an adolescent letter, so bitchy that he thought Ford might not print it. "Can you see how much I do not want to write about it?" he asked.

> . . . when I write journalism I like to be well paid for it . . . when you destroy the valuable things you have by writing about them you want to get big money for it. . . . The less publicity it has the better.
>
> Practically all the people that deserved to be at Pamplona were there this year. . . . For the rest of it . . . the consciousness of what happened is plenty. It is only when you can no longer believe in your own exploits that you write your memoirs.[34]

Ford printed the embarrassing letter, but followed it with a reprimand for Ernest in French from his Conrad essay in the *Journal Littéraire*. To salt his subtle rebuke, Ford printed in the same September issue

Tristan Tzara's measured response, also in French, to Hemingway's insulting comments about him.

No sooner had Hemingway slapped together his Pamplona Letter than the *Tribune* front page announced:

JOSEPH CONRAD, FAMOUS WRITER, IS DEAD AT 67

Ford immediately canceled the "Art Supplement" to run a hastily gathered collection of Conrad memorials. With most French writers out of Paris in early August and with no time to receive English input, Ford was forced to go to regular contributors who happened to be in Paris that day: Bob McAlmon, Ethel Mayne and Ernest Hemingway. Neither McAlmon nor Mayne felt particularly indebted to Conrad. He was, for them, a revered member of that pre-war generation of writers who could not cope with the "extreme savagedom" of the Great War. McAlmon, quite incorrectly, insisted that Conrad did not learn English until he was forty. Ethel Mayne turned a series of politely balanced phrases that reflected more on her command of rhetoric than on Conrad's contribution to literature.[35]

Not so Hemingway.

Conrad remained an important influence on Hemingway's sense of what fiction should be: a testing of values. Take a representative man away from his supporting society, set him down in a foreign country and see if his values hold up. Ernest loved the high points in Conrad when the action moved so smoothly up the scale of emotions. He loved the stories the man told. Now he was dead. That's what they did – wrote well and then died. Ford bursting with sentiment made Ernest a little sick. Why couldn't they simply let Conrad be dead with a little dignity instead of writing memorials that Conrad could never read. So he gave Ford a gut-level response that ended up insulting critics at large, André Germain in passing, and George Antheil and T. S. Eliot in particular. With Conrad dead, he said, it would become fashionable in literary politics to disparage him. In that world, a single mistake called one's credentials to question. "I remember," he wrote, "how I was made to feel how easily one might be dropped from the party, and the short period of Coventry that followed my remarking when speaking of George Antheil that I preferred my Stravinsky straight." Most, he thought, would call Conrad a bad writer and Eliot a good one. As for Ernest:

If I knew that by grinding Mr. Eliot into a fine dry powder and sprinkling that powder over Mr. Conrad's grave Mr. Conrad would shortly appear, looking very annoyed at the forced return and commence writing I would leave for London tomorrow morning with a sausage grinder. One should not be funny over the death of a great man, but you cannot couple T. S. Eliot and Joseph Conrad in a sentence seriously . . . and not laugh.[36]

Ford spluttered when he saw Ernest's typed copy. What was the Master to do with this twenty-five-year-old, talented writer who wore his authorship on his sleeve and was quicker to take insult, real or imagined, than a stage Spaniard? Ford ran Hemingway's testament without cutting a single word, not even adding the bit of punctuation sorely needed.

VI

In mid-August when the galleys arrived for the Conrad Supplement, Hemingway had second thoughts about his George Antheil comment, or maybe he only wanted to needle the diminutive musician. For whatever reason, Ernest sent him the proof sheet with the offer to cut his comment if Antheil did not like it because, he said, he did not want to print anything that would irritate George. "Figured that any publicity was publicity. . . . You probably don't give a damn. But you might." If George wanted to come by that evening, he would be home to discuss it.[37]

George did not want to discuss the comment with Ernest. "Preferred his Stravinsky straight" did he. Ernest certainly knew how to hurt a person; Igor Stravinsky, modernist composer of *The Rite of Spring*, was George Antheil's one-time idol and current nemesis. Because of his fierce competition with Stravinsky, Antheil pushed his dissonant music to almost unbearable lengths. As the *Tribune* reviewer said in July, "Mr. Antheil . . . refuses to recognize the piano as a musical instrument." Ezra Pound was one of the few critics who praised Antheil's music and actually became part of his act. Pound's musical compositions which Olga Rudge performed on violin went in tandem with several of Antheil's performances in which Ezra was on stage turning pages. At first Ernest was amused at Pound's late development as a composer, but he may have resented Antheil's becoming the center of Ezra's attention and the darling of the *transatlantic*'s "Music Supplements" – Ezra's invention and Antheil's forum for his theories. Whatever his feelings on the matter, Ernest did not need Antheil lecturing him on counterpoint, and he was always suspicious of anyone who referred to himself as a genius.[38]

Hemingway left the galley and his note for Antheil at Sylvia's bookshop, knowing that her upstairs tenant would receive it there. That was another thing: George took money from women. Ernest had seen him more than once leaving I.O.U.s in Sylvia's cash box when she, herself, was living close to the edge. George took money from Sylvia in small but regular sums and took money from his American patroness, Mrs. Bok, in periodic but larger sums. Ernest lived on Hadley's money. That was different, he told himself, because they were married. Ernest left the note on Friday morning but did not hear from George who was supposed to be at Sylvia's for Sunday supper with the Hemingways and the Birds. Supper was served but Antheil was not there to share it. Ernest thought it might have been his note but found it in the office apparently unread.[39]

Antheil, using Olga Rudge's temporarily vacant apartment to work on his music, had forgotten what day it was or that he had promised to come to supper. Monday, when he got Ernest's message, he sent back a blue pneumatique message: Hemingway could say whatever he pleased. Neither London nor Vienna understood his music, so why should he expect Paris to see beyond his early debt to Stravinsky? Maybe he sent that message. At least he told Sylvia he sent it. That Monday afternoon, while she was talking with customers in the front of the shop, George sat in the back room typing her a letter on her machine. He wrote:

> I don't like Hemingway because he is a fake artist. . . . [He] has just sent me an absolutely imbecile thing in which he has dragged me in by the ears to illustrate a point . . . in a pointless and imbecile article about Conrad, who is dead enough as it is. . . . Dumb people must have something to talk about and appear smart. Hemingway is among the dumbest.

Telling Sylvia was as good as telling Hemingway but not having to say it to his face. Sorry to have missed the supper, he did not want Sylvia to think that Hemingway's comments kept him away. "I like Bill Bird," he said, "who is yet, I hope, a friend of mine." That Bill and Ernest were telling stories about him was unimportant. All that mattered was the offense he had given Sylvia, whom he rightly called "one of the very best friends I ever had."[40]

The next day Antheil, apparently regretting the tenor of his attack on Hemingway, wrote a qualifying note to Sylvia, asking her to forgive his "bonehead letter about Hem." It was, he said, dumb to be paranoid about what Ernest might have said at supper. "Automatique boneheadness, like Hem's, is better than boneheadness which is a gift, like mine." If Ernest was told about Antheil's comments, he did not bother to react to this typically bitchy Left Bank interplay. For all of Montparnasse's self-inflated image of eccentric artists encouraging each other within a bohemian community, the Quarter was, in reality, a hotbed of gossip, back-stabbing and egotism. The Quarter's finer moments, with much retelling, have taken on a nostalgic glow that diminishes but does not erase the dark rumors, snide remarks and insulting behavior always flourishing along the boulevard. A weekly broadside was needed to keep track of who was not speaking to whom, and who was doing what with whose best friend.[41]

The Quarter was no longer an inexpensive haven for struggling artists; American tourists and permanent expatriates were pricing it out of the artist's reach. The Dôme, the Dingo, the Select were now part of the show for Rotarians from Peoria. One had not seen Paris without a glimpse of a real artist or writer in some public place. Ezra Pound, James Joyce, Sylvia Beach, Augustus John, Pablo Picasso and other rare birds were being sighted and noted by hardware salesmen who had never read Ezra or seen a Picasso. If not the famous, then the outrageous would serve equally well. Bob McAlmon, not the most famous author on the drinking circuit, managed to vomit decorously and otherwise in front of the best Left Bank bars. If McAlmon paled, one could usually find the shabby, sad-faced Harold Stearns holding down his now legendary bar stool at the Select, the saucers to be paid piling up before him. "Occasionally, a startled onlooker paid for the whole collection . . . so that he could talk about it later."[42]

On any given night in the Quarter, Flossie Martin might make a good-natured but foul-mouthed assault on any passing male. "The Dowager of the Dôme, Duchess of Montparnasse and Queen Bee of Drinkers," as McAlmon called her, would impose her "Rubenesque mass of white flesh and orange hair" on total strangers. "Give us a kiss. Tweetie-tweetie. . . . I'm going to take this sweetie home and lose my virginity. . . . Merde, this child's too serious. . . . You sweet thing. I'm scaring the [shit] out of you ain't I, pet." A year later, Hemingway described Flossie as "the girl who can always be depended upon to shout obscenities and whose complexion, appetite and ability to get blind drunk night after night . . . although she is getting to weigh well over two hundred pounds make her the heroine of the quarter." Fifteen minutes in close proximity to Flossie made for an evening of entertaining stories back in Topeka.[43]

On August 5, young Sam Chapin, returning drunk from a Left Bank night, took out his cut-throat razor and did just that while leaning out the window of his Champs-Elysées hotel. Before the week was out, the *Tribune*'s front-page story read:

TERROR SWEEPS LATIN QUARTER AT REFORM BID

Montparnasse Sector Called Big "Sink of Iniquity"

Things seem to have been brought to a head by the epidemic of suicides, which have broken out since spring. A well-known New York lawyer, who came over to open up a business here, got into the vortex. After drinking and drugging for weeks, he took an overdose and died. Last week it was a young New Yorker of twenty-three in a Champs-Elysées hotel after all his friends had failed to sober him during the course of his existence in the drinking spots around Montparnasse and Raspail.

Despite the apparent Bohemian idleness, which is all an average visitor to the quarter sees, there is plenty of hard work being done around the quieter spots near the two big boulevards.[44]

Ernest read the story and grinned. Hard work was going on all right. Pascin was working hard, screwing his models, and Ezra was working hard on Olga Rudge. Hard work was easy to find in the Quarter if you knew the right people. Because he thought about suicide with some frequency, Ernest knew that hard workers were as liable to cut their throats as the next man. "Is dying hard, Daddy?" Nick asked his father after the Indian cut his own throat. Now this Chapin kid was hanging out of his hotel window, blood clotting on the stone facing. Bulls died hard in the ring, blood pumping out of their heaving mouths: hard dying but not hard to do when the matador slipped his sword neatly into the killing spot.

Ernest slipped his pencil back into the groove and continued the story about Nick at the lake. As soon as he got it started, he knew he would never print it, but he wrote it anyway. Being with the gang at Pamplona and Burguete took him right back to the good times at Walloon and he got to missing them all – Bill Smith, Carl Edgar, and Katy with her green eyes and her small, hard breasts that seemed to burn right through her bathing suit. In the story Nick was stretched out on the boat dock, the sun warming him nicely and Katy's toes pressing against his back. Ernest could feel them there, moving, sending a clear message. Nick also understood the message. That night when the guys were sleeping, he let Nick have Katy in the wood lot under the hemlock tree. "He touched one of her small breasts with his lips gently. It came alive between his lips, his tongue pressing against it."[45]

On paper he could give Nick any woman Nick wanted, but there was a good deal of himself in the wanting. If Ernest ever had Kate up in Michigan, no evidence remains. What matters most is that he wrote about her in the Paris heat of 1924, wrote a story that he could show no one, certainly not Hadley. It was his private erotica, truly unpublishable. With an imagination so vivid that readers could not tell the difference between his fact and his fiction, he often thought about women he saw passing, thought about their bodies and how they would be in bed. In the Quarter sex hung almost as richly in the summer air as the morning bread baking down the street. Certainly he loved Hadley, but there were so many women flirting with him in the Dôme, rubbing against him in the dark. Wherever he looked, Ernest saw desirable women. Fornication among those he knew appeared as casual as a shared drink. Ezra was deeply into Olga Rudge, playing scales on her violin; Nancy Cunard, bony but beautiful, was always with a new man. Paris, with its comely whores and lovely lesbians, with its long summer nights and loose, inflaming talk, was slowly but surely changing him. In the Michigan wood lot under the hemlock, Nick and Kate ate the snack Nick prepared: fried chicken and cherry pie, a post-coital American picnic dreamed in Paris above a sawmill's wood lot on the street of Our Lady of the Fields with Hadley in the next room.

VII

With the horses out of town, the heat oppressive and American tourists sitting at all the Dôme tables, August in Paris played itself out in a minor key. Eugene Jolas' literary column declared the August number of the *transatlantic* "one of the best edited issues of this interesting magazine. . . . for which Ernest Hemingway, the young romancer, is responsible." Young romancer? "Any publicity was publicity," was what he told George Antheil. Well, he would be the "young romancer" just to see Ford choke on the Jolas statement about his editing. As the month waned, George Breaker continued to stall on delivering Hadley's Philippine railroad bonds. Then Bumby finally started cutting teeth, and no one got any sleep but Bumby. It was that kind of month.[46]

In mid-August, he wrote Gertrude in Provence that he had finished "two long short stories, one of them not much good and finished the long one I worked on before I went to Spain where I'm trying to do the country like Cézanne." He called the "Summer People" story of Nick with Kate "not much good," but he knew better. Nick came out of it rounder and deeper than before; he could see him now clearly, could feel the sandy road beneath his feet. But he called it "not much good" because he wanted no one to see the story. Even if he changed the names, Hadley would know it was Kate, who would also see it somewhere. Words were dangerous on paper. He put the story away but did not destroy it. Someday, maybe, it would be safe to print it.[47]

August passed slowly. Ezra was around but busy planning another Antheil concert and anxious about Bill Bird's publication of his *Sixteen Cantos*. Once in a while there was tennis with Harold Loeb, Hadley and whoever else was around. They rented weekly time on a small court near the Santé prison, and sometimes Ford would get up an afternoon of mixed doubles. Ernest's game, never very sophisticated, depended more on strength than agility. Hadley described it later: "He couldn't run very fast because of his injured knee. Some of his shots were quite awkward because of his blind eye and every time he missed a shot he would sizzle. His racket would slash to the ground and everyone would stand still and cower – until he recovered with a laugh." "He was a lousy tennis player," Loeb said, "and hated to miss a shot. But he was so exuberant you never had a lackadaisical game." With Ernest nothing was ever lackadaisical. As Henry Strater said, "He liked to win everything."[48]

Through August he worked on the *review* and on his own fiction which, with most people out of town, only Bumby interrupted. McAlmon was in England with Bryher, strangely enough. Joyce was in St. Malo, staring out to sea. On good days Ernest stopped by Shakespeare and Company to pass the time, read the new literary magazines and show off his son whose Breton French delighted Sylvia. When Hadley's dividend checks arrived, they paid off pressing debts and splurged a bit. Ernest put down sixty francs to reserve another copy of Joyce's *Ulysses*; in August alone Sylvia sold 143 copies of the banned book and her fourth edition was quickly selling out to the summer traffic from the states. Adrienne Monnier's new magazine – *Commerce* – would soon publish *Ulysses* in French translation. Ernest subscribed for his copy of her first issue.[49]

By the end of the month, Bumby had cut four teeth, and Ernest was saying that within two weeks his book of stories would be finished. Dos Passos, who was returning soon to New York, promised to show the manuscript to his several publishing contacts. But it was a slim collection: only twelve stories, several of them brief, and one, "Up in Michigan," unprintable. Ernest elected to start the manuscript with the very story guaranteed to offend most readers. Looking for a way to lengthen the manuscript, he decided to interlock the stories with the eighteen vignettes from *in our time*. Starting with a vignette, placing another between each story and calling the closing one an "Envoi" beefed up the book nicely, but used only thirteen of the terse statements. At some point before mid-September he decided to split "Big Two-Hearted River" into two parts and to upgrade the vignettes about the nurse in Milan and the bolshevik on the Italian train to stories, calling them "A Very Short Story" and "The Revolutionist."[50]

August ended with torrential rains drenching the city, driving tourists away from sidewalk cafés and off the streets. Gutters ran full, flushing used Metro tickets, lost handkerchiefs, cigarette butts and other detritus of burnt out summer days into the vast sewer system beneath the city. Advertisements for third-class passage home at less than one hundred dollars said that summer was over. Looking out over the sawmill yard, Ernest was pleased with himself and rightly so. In five months, he had written ten new stories, all but finishing his first solid book. That's what he'd promised himself in Toronto, and it was done. He had his luck lines out and baited with copies of *in our time*. At least four different friends offered to help place his manuscript in New York. As he watched the rain falling general and hard across the city, the light diminished and street lamps came on early.

Chapter Twelve

IN THEIR TIME
FALL AND EARLY WINTER,
1924

I

Arranging and rearranging the sequence of stories, he was now calling his new book *In Our Time*, to be confused forever with his eighteen vignettes of *in our time*. He included all of his earlier fiction, discovering "a certain unity," for the collection. "The first 5 are in Michigan," he explained to O'Brien, "starting with Up in Michigan, which you know and in between each one comes bang! the In Our Time," by which he meant the short sketches from *in our time*. Without explaining the unity of the second half, he said that "Big Two-Hearted River" "finishes up the Michigan scene the book starts with." The taut vignettes he now called chapter headings, claiming that was what he first wrote them to be. "You get the close up very quietly but absolutely solid and the real thing but very close, and then through it all between every story comes the rhythm of the in our time chapters."[1]

A month later Hemingway wrote Edmund Wilson that a chapter of *in our time* came between each story because

> that is the way they were meant to go – to give the picture of the whole between examining it in detail. Like looking with your eyes at something, say a passing coast line, and then looking at it with

15X binoculars. Or rather, maybe, looking at it and then going in and living in it – and then coming out and looking at it again.

The collection had, he said, "a pretty good unity," which, strangely enough, it did, but not the sort he described to Wilson. The vignettes were not "a picture of the whole," nor were they anything like looking through binoculars at a passing coast line.[2]

The unity grew out of recurring and frequently violent images – babies, water, night, wounds, blood, death – and recurring conflict between men and women, married and unmarried, in love and out. It was a collection of fears and uncertainties done with a cool, ironic detachment, the only remaining way to face the questions of his time. *How should a man behave to be called a man? What is the proper relationship between man and woman? How can a man deal with his fears? What must he do to be brave? Where is home?* Unity grew not at any rational level but from deep within young Hemingway. The vignettes, if anything, set the major key for the collection and, rising as they did like small, dense islands in the stream of the stories, they provided counterpoint to those fictions. In the "chapter heading" on one side of "Three-Day Blow" the British were shooting Germans as they climbed over the iron grating jammed across the bridge. On the other side of the story, the six Greek cabinet ministers were being shot against the hospital wall in the rain. In between, Bill tells Nick,

"Once a man's married he's absolutely bitched. . . . He hasn't got anything more. Nothing. Not a damn thing. He's done for. You've seen the guys that get married . . . You can tell them . . . They get this sort of fat married look. They're done for."

Two pieces of violence framing a story centered on a failed relationship: there was unity all right, aperiodic and almost Chaucerian. And there at the end when Nick stepped into the water painted by Cézanne, the reader came full circle, realizing that Nick was the writer telling all the stories. It was a loop, an ending so different that the reader would be forced back to the beginning to read again in a different light.[3]

About the same time that Ernest wrote O'Brien, asking for suggestions for getting his book published, another story came back in the mail from George Jean Nathan:

. . . Nor does this story fit into the general plan that we have for *The American Mercury*. But please do not be discouraged. Don't hesitate to send me whatever you write.

By return mail, Hemingway sent Nathan several stories, which were also promptly rejected:

Mencken and I cannot agree on the enclosed pieces of work . . . But we shall continue to read with the utmost sympathy anything you send in to us.

By the middle of November, two stories Hemingway submitted to the *Harper's Magazine* short story contest – "Soldier's Home" and "Cross Country Snow" – both came back in the mail rejected for publication. Daunted and a little depressed, he could not help but wonder what was wrong. Was the problem with his fiction or the New York readers? Why couldn't Mencken or *Harper's* see that his stories worked? Maybe they were not as wonderful as he and Ezra thought them. Around the first of October, John Dos Passos arrived in New York with a copy of *Ulysses* under one arm and Hemingway's pieced together and newly typed manuscript under the other. Almost immediately he called on Don Stewart at the Yale Club to plan a strategy for getting Doran, the publisher, to look at *In Our Time*. Without a single American publication to recommend him, Hemingway needed all the help he could get. His first substantial book was now out of his hands, his future depending upon faces a sea away.[4]

Then, as if personally rubbing salt in Hemingway's wounded professional vanity, the *Tribune* began carrying a weekly column by H. L. Mencken, who "could not agree" with Nathan on Ernest's fiction. One of Mencken's first columns derided the myth that young writers could not find sympathetic publishers.

. . . the superstition survives . . . that publishers are inhospitable to newcomers . . . that it is impossible to get a hearing without influence. What could be more idiotic? There is not a publisher in America . . . who does not maintain a complex and costly machine for detecting talent through eight thicknesses of oak planking. . . . The post office, for a few cents, provides all the introduction necessary.

If a young writer continually got rejections, Mencken said, then he probably deserved them, and personal contacts would be no help. But if the talent was there, the editors would certainly spot it. Four rejections in six weeks and the great sage from Baltimore tells him that the magazines can spot talent. Well, to hell with Mencken and his *American Mercury*. They had their chance. Never again did Hemingway submit anything to the *Mercury*, and he never forgave or forgot Mencken's rejections.[5]

II

For a few lovely weeks, as Paris edged into fall, nights were cool and days pleasant. With summer tourists departed, only hard-core Americans were left to man the tables at the Dôme and the Select. No matter how irritating Hemingway found his work at the *transatlantic*, he could always lose himself along the quais, browsing among the bookstalls or watching the fishermen bent over their long poles. Visitors passed through the city, exchanging New York for Paris gossip at about the same 1 : 18 rate as the franc.

The Hemingway apartment was becoming a significant address, a literary connection for informed visitors. With only small press and little magazine publications to his credit, Ernest had become in two years a recognized figure in the Quarter. Now that Ford and Stella Bowen were living down the street between the Hemingways and the Pounds, rue Notre-Dame-des-Champs was a most literary street, quickly accessible to any of the café crowd from Montparnasse. Jane Heap of the *Little Review* was dining at the Hemingways', for example, the evening that Gertrude Stein's gift of Provençal apples arrived from St. Rémy. With not much more than a year's total residence on the Left Bank, the Hemingways already belonged to those who arrived before the transformation of the Quarter. When Ernest and Hadley, that first Christmas of 1921, sat down at the Dôme, six thousand Americans called Paris home. In September 1924, the city's permanent American population was thirty thousand and rising. The change was frantic, fast, and as obvious as the Negro jazz bands now playing in most of the clubs and the newspaper ads for Camel cigarettes.[6]

That September an American bought the old Dingo Bar, hired a Chinese cook, put in an American menu (hamburgers, yes, and chicken-fried steaks with mashed potatoes) and English-speaking waiters. Back in the states, Jack Dempsey, showing no great enthusiasm for defending his heavyweight championship, had a nose job to enhance his movie career, and aging Jack Johnson turned up on the Negro preaching circuit, saving souls. Rum-runners still practiced mayhem, regularly making the front page with bloody shoot-outs in the streets of New York, Detroit and Chicago. It was the year that Scott Fitzgerald wrote a novel about Jay Gatsby, a young gangster slumming as a Long Island millionaire. In Paris, the English papers printed a steady flow of letters debating the next war, the yellow peril, the uselessness of the League of Nations and the futility of Defense Day. On September 12, all American military and Red Cross officers from the Great War were asked by the War Department to register with their nearest military attaché as an experiment in mobilization and as a patriotic gesture. Letters to the Editor ran three to one in favor of the exercise being a farce. Two days afterwards, Ernest playfully asked Gertrude, "Did you register for Defense Day?" "Neither did we," he told her. Six years earlier a different young man, a young Hemingway who had not yet seen what artillery shells could do to the human body, eagerly volunteered to drive Red Cross ambulances in Italy. Now on any afternoon he could watch the war's effects on the nerves of Krebs Friend, and any night he might find himself alone in the no-man's-land of terrific dreams. At the Paris branch of the American Legion they might still remember the trench songs from six years back, but no one was singing them at the Dôme.[7]

The post-war Americans, thick on the Left Bank boulevards and many of them too young to have been in the trenches, did not care what others before them had said, done or written. Men did not think it rude to ignore the advice of their fathers, nor did young women place much value on songs or sayings their mothers once knew. As Sisley Huddleston complained, the hurdy-gurdy organs of the Quarter had vanished along with the fiacre. A show of petticoat, a flutter of lace was nothing special to this generation for whom sex was a topic of open conversation. The decorous waltz of Edwardian days disappeared in the war winds, replaced by jazz bands and the tango. "The roles," Huddleston lamented, "are reversed."

> Modesty, in the smart set, is no more . . . there is a confusion of sexes; and notorious public balls are organized where men dance with partners who, in spite of their attire, and their paint and powder, and their finicking manners, are of the masculine gender;

while there are bars reserved for women who seek the intimate company of women.

This generation, which later would be called "Lost," thoroughly enjoyed irritating their staid, sober, conservative elders whose eyes still turned moist to a martial air as they continued to elect conservative Republicans throughout the Twenties.[8]

In mid-September, a representative American elder wandering past the Dôme made the mistake of taking too seriously remarks overheard in passing. His letter appeared in the paper soon afterwards.

> Sir: Couldn't you . . . help get a law passed requiring that muzzles be placed on all our young American intellectual aristocrats before they are turned loose in the iniquitous regions of Montparnasse and the Café du Dôme where they sit on the terrace from noon till midnight, soaking up various forms of alcoholic beverage and categorically condemning America and all things American with the ignorant assurance of youth?
> . . . Among other things I heard them refer to our President as a "cheap politician and an intellectual nonentity" and to the Statue of Liberty as a "monument to our Illustrious Dead."

As an unreformed Southerner, Mr. Adair recommended a tar and feather party for "this scum which has boiled over from our great melting pot."[9]

For the next six weeks letters from Dôme-ites like Dorothy Butler poured into the *Tribune*, filled with witty advice for Mr. Adair, including several things he might do with his tar and feathers. Mr. Adair quite wisely did not reply, which prompted the legendary diabolist, Aleister Crowley, to write:

> To the Editor:
> There was an old man named Adair
> Who said "How I wish that I were
> Back safely at home –
> This Café du Dôme . . ."
> But then he dissolved into air.

The majority of these responses mentioned "freedom of speech," guaranteed by the Constitution even if they were in France, which

238

allowed one to say whatever he pleased when and wherever he pleased to say it.[10]

III

The American voices of the Dôme spoke in the same accents that so befuddled Ford Madox Ford in his daily editorial work at the *transatlantic*. Try as he might, Ford was unable to please his new board of directors, Mr. and Mrs. Krebs Friend, any better than he could soften Hemingway's sarcasm. With something approaching relief, Ford watched through the fall as the *review*'s seams came uncaulked and she took on more and more water.

In his November "Chronique," Ford's British good manners began to wear as thin as the *review*'s finances. Among other problems, he was being continually harassed by Hemingway about the magazine's treatment of Gertrude Stein and the serialization of her *Making of Americans*. In September, in order to cut costs Ford reduced her serial to smaller type and single spacing. After Ernest pounded on his desk, Ford returned Gertrude's novel to a double-spaced format in October. But nothing pleased Ernest. Where, he wanted to know, was Gertrude's payment for the last two issues. That wasn't Ford's business any longer, but Hemingway insisted that he do something immediately. Gertrude got her money, and Ford got in his final dig.

First, he announced the end of his own serial. "If our sub-editors permit it," he wrote, "the end of the first part of *Some Do Not* will appear in this number after which we do not propose to continue the publication." Lengthy, running novels were a mistake which the *review* would not repeat, for "every educated reader should be able to judge from a page or two the nature of a book or the caliber of a writer. . . . Thus we ask readers to take notice that the appearance of the first chapters of a novel in these pages is no indication at all that its publication will be preserved to the bitter end."

As he wrote those words, he suspected that his magazine would not last into the new year anyway. It was time to be as blunt as a proper Englishman could be, so he took another mild swipe at Hemingway by apologizing for Ernest's insulting references to T. S. Eliot in the Conrad Supplement. Explaining that his editorial policy was never to cut solicited material, he claimed to have "hesitated a long time over the ethics of the matter. . . . We had invited that writer to write, we had indicated no limits to his blood thirstiness: our hands fell powerless to our sides. We were besides convinced that Mr. Eliot would not mind. He does not."[11]

Nor did Ford mind when his faithful and patient assistant, Marjorie Reed, took a few playful shots at the Left Bank literati in her parodic "Paris Fashions" letter. Tongue in cheek, she professed to admire every strange mode from artist Cedric Morris' "flame colored shirt" to Robert McAlmon's "cap of mercury carried out in brown felt." Black velvet, made "fashionable by Mr. Pound, the musician and chess player," was appearing now as business dress in the Quarter. Unable to resist comment on Ernest's increasingly bohemian appearance, she said, "While the discussion goes on some smart dressers are following the lead of Mr. Hemingway, the young American writer and mateodor [sic], who favors the beret for general use in literary circles and bull rings although he has several other hats."[12]

Hemingway was amused: any publicity was publicity, and the same issue carried "The Doctor and the Doctor's Wife." Despite rejections arriving regularly from the states, Ernest was, in fact, having a banner fall in Paris. In November, two of his poems – "The Soul of Spain" and "The Earnest Liberal's Lament" – appeared in *Der Querschnitt*, a Berlin house organ put out to display modernist painters carried by the Flechtheim Galleries in Germany and Paris. Edited by Hans von Wedderkop, the magazine was open, irreverent and international in a way that the *transatlantic* never quite achieved. Nothing was sacred. Sometimes a quarterly, sometimes an annual, but that year (1924) a monthly, *Der Querschnitt* printed nude drawings, satires, caricatures and photographs of the physical life: boxers, skiers and other athletes. With its curious German taste, it published frontal photos of nude males in large groups doing physical things: skiers in a snowball fight; runners splashing down a mountain stream. Although it made fun of Hitler, the magazine also fostered the spirit of what would become the Nazi Youth Corps and encouraged the anti-Semitism that led to the Holocaust. Wedderkop "hates Kikes worse than we do," Hemingway told Bill Smith. This was both true and ironic: Alfred Flechtheim, owner and publisher of the magazine, was a Jew, and Hemingway knew it. But so were Gertrude Stein and Harold Loeb Jews, which did not seem to bother Ernest, at least not that year.

Hemingway's contact with Wedderkop came by way of Pound, who often contributed to the magazine. On October 9, at Wedderkop's invitation, the Hemingways dined with the German editor at Ezra's apartment. Ernest was impressed with his opposition to pretense in the arts. His editorial program, according to Ernest, was

> To hell with all Literary Criticism. Publish the stuff the guys write instead of stuff about them. To hell with Literary snobbery and Vanity Fairism. Give 'em all the dope. Not all the dope that's fit to print. He has swell boxing pictures and pictures of all the swell broads in Europe. He's too good a guy to last.

It was the program Ernest had urged on the slightly deaf ears of Ford for the *transatlantic*.[13]

Wedderkop's autumn issue carried the Pound, Antheil, Olga Rudge musical program from the previous July in Paris, as well as a somewhat rambling Pound essay, "Law and the Merchant of Venice." There were two William Carlos Williams poems, a Jack Dempsey essay on his fight with Tommy Gibbons, a notice of Frank Harris' book on Oscar Wilde, and Hemingway's poem, beginning as half parody and half imitation of Gertrude Stein,

> In the rain in the rain in the rain in the rain in Spain.
> Does it rain in Spain?
> Oh yes my dear on the contrary and there are no bull fights.
> The dancers dance in long white pants
> It isn't right to yence your aunts

and continuing as a satiric comment on current fads:

> Democracy is the shit.
> Relativity is the shit.
> Dictators are the shit.
> Menken [sic] is the shit.
> Waldo Frank is the shit.
> The Broom is the shit.
> Dada is the shit.
> Dempsey is the shit.
> This is not a complete list.

It was just the sort of poem one might expect of a young Left Bank American in the year 1924, not a poem to send home to Oak Park.

"Home," he wrote, "is where the heart is, home is where the fart is. Come let us fart in the home."[14]

As more than one survivor remembered and as his letters confirm, Hemingway's language was plain, blunt and sometimes vulgar. Kitty Cannell heard him unthinkingly use "kike" with such casualness and scorn that she warned her Jewish lover, Harold Loeb, to be careful with Hemingway. Loeb, who enjoyed Hemingway's friendship immensely and thought him a natural man, paid no attention to the warning. That fall, the New York publishers Boni & Liveright accepted Loeb's novel *Doodab*; he was ecstatic, telling everyone including Ernest about his good fortune. When his publishers made Leon Fleischman their European scout, taking the job away from Harold Stearns, Loeb wanted Hemingway to submit his *In Our Time* manuscript; it would be fine, he thought, for the two of them to be published by the same firm. Maybe Loeb's good manners and Ivy League schooling had taken the edge off his natural sensors, for he failed, inexplicably, to see how competitive Ernest was. On the tennis courts, Harold beat him so regularly that he must have thought Ernest could always lose with grace. Loeb could not have been more wrong.

Loeb took Ernest and Kitty around to Fleischman's apartment one October evening to make introductions. Ernest seemed a bit surly and grew more silent as the visit jerked along uncomfortably amidst cocktails and expensive snacks. Maybe it was Fleischman's velvet smoking jacket, or maybe it was his somewhat condescending manner: he offered to recommend *In Our Time* to Boni & Liveright without even reading it. That offer would have been enough to trigger the dark side of Ernest, for it confirmed his belief that merit had little to do with New York publishing. It was who one knew that mattered. Whatever the cause, Ernest left Fleischman's in a terrible mood. On the street, Kitty said what a nice evening it had been.

Ernest exploded: "Double god damned kikes!"

As he strode away, Kitty said to Loeb, "Well, Baby there's your future friend."

"Nonsense," he replied. "He used the word as I might say mick or dago. It doesn't mean a thing."

"You always find excuses for him," Kitty replied.

"Top dogs should not patronize," Loeb told her. "Patronize your superiors if you like, but not some poor bloke who has come to you with his life's work. The way Leon spoke, you would think the publisher was doing the writer a favor."[15]

Despite his explosion, Ernest sent Fleischman a copy of the *In Our Time* manuscript. With New York rejections piling up, he saw no harm in flooding the market place. Like the Alger hero he admired as a child, Ernest needed only a little luck to enhance his hard work. His faith was confirmed when he opened the October *Dial* to Edmund Wilson's review of *Three Stories & Ten Poems* and *in our time*. Hemingway's first American notice of any value could not have come at a better time, offsetting the depressing effects of rejection letters. Wilson wrote:

> Indeed, Miss Stein, Mr. Anderson and Mr. Hemingway may now be said to form a school by themselves. The characteristic of this school is a naivete of language, often passing into the colloquialism of the character dealt with, which serves actually to convey profound emotions and complex states of mind.

Wilson went on to say that Hemingway was "strikingly original" and that with the *in our time* vignettes he had "almost invented a form of his own." The bullfight sketches reminded Wilson of Goya's lithographs. "His little book," Wilson said, "has more artistic dignity than any other that has been written by an American about the period of the war." Almost immediately Hemingway wrote Wilson, thanking him for his "cool and clear minded and decent and impersonal and sympathetic" review. Wilson was, he said, "the only man writing criticism who or whom I can read when the book being criticized is one I've read."[16]

Outside in the street, the quieter noises of evening were beginning to rub the edge off the afternoon's racket. The sawmill shut down for the day, and footsteps of working men returning home clacked on the cobblestones. In his upstairs rented rooms, Ernest Hemingway put the stamp on his letter to Wilson. Almost without knowing it, he had turned a corner. At twenty-five years old, his six-year apprenticeship was almost completed. In six years a man could learn to be a writer for his time, if he was lucky, dedicated and driven, if the very act of writing was his passion.

IV

October ended and November began in rain that lasted through the month. All Souls' Day arose dreary, wet and grey. Most of literary Paris continued to mourn the death of Anatole France; the surrealists, however, fresh from their latest manifesto, published a broadside called *The Rotten Corpse*, which declared Anatole's departure a healthy clearing away of the old and oppressive literary order. Hemingway, who arrived in Paris thinking France's *The Red Lily* a great novel, took no special notice of his passing. Nor did he take much interest in the presidential election back home. Half jokingly he told Gertrude Stein: "Being a capitalist I pray for the election of Honest Cal and down with the radicals. We have a Manila R.R. bond and Coolidge's is the only platform that advocates hanging on to the Philippines." The November 5 headline read: COOLIDGE WINS BY BIG MAJORITY. A side-bar to the main story pointed out that all but one candidate backed nationally by the Ku Klux Klan had been elected.[17]

November, with all its chilly rain, was a continuation of Hemingway's manic literary life. The same mail that brought him *Harper's* rejection of "Cross Country Snow" also brought the newest *Querschnitt* with the second part of his "The Soul of Spain" and his outrageous "The Lady Poets With Footnotes." Simultaneously, "The Doctor and the Doctor's Wife" appeared in the *transatlantic*. While he and Ford put to bed what was now obviously the last issue of the magazine, he continued to write well, sometimes in the evenings at home, sometimes at his back table at the Closerie des Lilas.

By Armistice Day, November 11, Ford had given up on the *transatlantic*, and he used his December "Editorial" as a retrospective commentary on the year's work. Last week, he said, a "band bearing ropes" started out to lynch him for printing "Regular Poems" in the last issue, but nothing came of it. Which was to the "Band's" benefit, for were he dead their names would not appear on the cover of the December issue. "When we are gathered to Anatole France," he wrote, "the happy band who are now the crew of this periodical shall issue a pamphlet called *A Rotten Corpse* and so dance upon our remains. This is proper. In the meantime to celebrate the season of the birth of our redeemer we issue what we will as irritatingly as possible style a Children's Number." Youth would have its way: the last issue of the *transatlantic* was almost completely young Americans in Paris: Don Stewart, Nathan Asch, Ivan Beede, Bob McAlmon, Evan Shipman, Jean Rhys, and Hemingway's recently rejected "Cross Country Snow." When he lost financial control of the magazine, Ford's authority as sole editor was seriously undermined. In this last issue he quit trying to balance the literary equation and gave in completely to the young hotheads.[18]

But the month was not a complete loss for Ford. Having spent a good bit of time coaching young Jean Rhys in the finer points of creative writing, Ford apparently was equally successful in coaxing her out of her underwear. Hemingway had to be amazed. How could this old walrus with his wheezing voice, this up-ended hogshead of a man, how could he have an undivorced wife in England fighting with an ex-mistress Violet Hunt, while in Paris he lived with Stella Bowen and bedded down young Jean! Hemingway's apprenticeship was nearly over, but he could see that there was still much to learn about the literary game.

Though still learning, Ernest recognized a gift horse when he saw one. In mid-month, Eugene Jolas published an "Open Letter to Ernest Hemingway" in his weekly *Tribune* column "Rambles Through Literary Paris."

Dear Hemingway. We discussed you the other day with some American writers and we expressed to them our conviction that you have one of the most genuinely epic talents of any youngster writing in English today. In fact, we said that, in our opinion, you were destined to create a new literature on the American continent. We have never hesitated in expressing this view, in spite of some contradictions from men who disagreed with us. When we met you for the first time at Dave O'Neil's hospitable home here, we felt an aura of masculine strength about you that we like to connect with our dreams of America. . . . You have the root of the matter in you. . . . You have created in stark, acid accents the medium which is symptomatic of a great deal of modern hopelessness. . . . To be brief, we like most of your stories. . . . Now, we have just picked up *Der Querschnitt* and noticed two of your poems in them. . . . We ain't able to follow you there. . . . We simply give up. . . . We believe you're on the wrong tack. . . . If you don't watch out, Dr. Sumner will give you a raft of free publicity and then what's going to happen to you. . . . Please give us another "My Old Man" and let it go at that.[19] (ellipses in original)

Ernest, of course, would have welcomed an attack from John Sumner, the secretary of the New York Society for the Suppression of Vice. Trying hard to keep his caustic tongue in check, Hemingway answered

Jolas with an open letter of his own, which the journalist published in his column a week later.

> Thanks for your open letter of last Sunday. The two poems in the *Querschnitt* were not intended to be serious and were written three years ago and a year and a half ago respectively. So if my writing is going bad it must have been going bad for some time.
>
> Unfortunately for passport purposes working for a Canadian newspaper does not make me a Canadian. I have always been told I was born in or near Chicago. I have a son who was born in Canada. Perhaps he is the Hemingway you were thinking of when you referred to talented youngsters.
>
> If you would like to read some new stories in manuscript to ease your mind as to my present mental and spiritual state come around some Sunday afternoon soon. There is a long bullfight story you might like.
>
> With best regards to your column and yourself.
>
> Ernest Hemingway[20]

The story to which Hemingway referred was "The Undefeated," a long, detailed account of the final bullfight, goring and death of Manuel Garcia in the Madrid bullring. The story was a short course in tauromachy: the ugly greed of the promoter, the taste and smell of the bull ring at night, and ending with Manuel's brave but fatal effort in which he and the bull kill each other. Using all he had learned in three trips to Spain and drawing on his vignette sketches from 1923, Hemingway needed the room of a long story for the reader to understand the major aspects of the bullfight. Nothing could be left out. The result was more traditional in form that his earlier stories, but not without experimentation. The first rule of the short story is never change point of view: use one narrator only or the reader will become confused. In this story Hemingway, without making an issue of it, neatly shifted the narrative line from one character to another, much as a movie camera will shift within a scene. It was a bold experiment, one from which he learned a good deal.[21]

"The Undefeated" was, in several ways, more accessible to not-yet-modernist readers than most of the *In Our Time* stories. In structure it was closer to "My Old Man," keeping the reader clearly focused on the narrative line. But "The Undefeated" is a curious story, describing a bullfighter past his prime who, dying on the infirmary table after his goring, remains undefeated. Rather than retire, as advised by an old friend, he chose to go back into the ring. Running in counterpoint to Manuel's bravery are the responses of the promoter, who sees bullfighters as a commodity to be used up for his own profit, and the critic, who refuses to stay until the end of the fight because he can get the results in the morning paper. In the Madrid bull ring the cycle comes round: the older man on his way out coupled with the young hopefuls on their way up, oblivious to their fate embodied in Manuel. As the crowd hoots him, throwing cushions into the ring, Manuel practices his art to the best of his ability. Whether bullfighter, boxer, painter or writer – the artist could not count on the public, the promoter or the press; the artist had only his art form and his integrity to sustain him. It was almost a parable, and a strange one to come from a twenty-five-year-old writer just finishing his apprenticeship. Come, he might have said, let us sit upon the ground and tell sad stories about the deaths of writers. Conrad gone in August, Anatole France in October. That's what happened all right. On the river Nick said it for him: "They died and that was the hell of it. They worked all their lives and then got old and died." Taking on that knowledge was also part of his apprenticeship. [22]

But no matter how sharply honed his new skills had become, Ernest was not yet confident enough to ignore Gertrude Stein's advice. When she returned to Paris toward the end of October, he was quick to show her his new stories, particularly "Big Two-Hearted River," a canvas far larger than any he'd previously painted. She liked it fine as long as Nick stuck to the river, but once he started thinking too much, the story lost its drive. "Remarks," she told him, "are not literature." As a result, Ernest hacked off all of Nick's meditations, and picked up his pencil once more to write another ending. [23]

It was still a story about writing, but he did not have to tell the reader directly: fishing was an art form, so was writing. One art is any art, is all the arts. The care that Nick took with his camp on the river was the care Ernest took with the words to describe Nick's camp. He went back to ideas he wrote down months before:

> open shallows, shadows of trees, the deep pool under cedars, where line always caught,
> the strange country under big bolled cedars, in the swamp,
> out in the open, the breeze, the stream above the dam,
> the Dam, pool, trout, minnows, dead stretches, the wonderful open reaches

With Paris rain noisy in the gutters, he sat down once more with Nick at the river. He was writing and Nick was fishing. Or was it the other way around? This time he finished the story quickly. No thinking about Art or Paris, just Nick facing the swamp and not being able to handle it then. "There were plenty of days coming," Nick told himself, "when he could fish the swamp."[24]

A few days later he wrote Bob McAlmon that he had "decided that all that mental conversation in the long fishing story is the shit and have cut it all out. The last nine pages." It would be humorous, he said, if Doran accepted the book on the basis of Nick's interior monologue. Thus his daring experiment disappeared, leaving the collection thematically linked but without the artifice of Nick the writer telling the stories.[25]

V

By mid-November Hadley's dividend checks arrived, replenishing their bank account and allowing Ernest to repay McAlmon's July loan. Life was looking considerably up on rue Notre-Dame-des-Champs. Despite continuing rains that threatened to flood the Seine, Hemingway's spirits were buoyant. His writing seemed to improve every week, and he thought the stories would never stop, they came so easily. If he could avoid getting his usual infected throat which Paris winters seemed to spawn, it might be a productive season for him. Afternoons and evenings settled down to winter's pace, the street lamps coming on early against the dark. At Sylvia's there was always a warm stove, literary magazines to catch up on, and conversation. With the *review* dead, he saw little of Ford and liked it like that. McAlmon was on the Berlin road and the Pounds in Italy, but Ernest could always find an empty chair at Gertrude's in the late afternoons. Alice was becoming less cordial, but he was as Oak Park polite as ever, never failing to mention how sweet her cookies, how fine her cakes.[26]

November was also marked by one of Hemingway's customary but usually unremembered kindnesses. After having savaged Lewis Galantière in the *transatlantic*, referred to Dorothy Butler as "foecal matter," and having written but perhaps not mailed his insulting note to Dorothy, Ernest was honestly supportive of the Galantières when Dorothy's mother died unexpectedly that month. Dorothy wrote, thanking him:

I was touched with your sweetness and sympathy. You know I appreciate it from the bottom of my heart. And the books are going to help me thru the trip. You and Hadley, I feel sure, are sad about my darling mother. I can't believe it. We'll come to see you if we may, when I get back.[27]

Although never again close friends with Lewis and Dorothy, Hemingway was always capable of such contradictory behavior: volatile explosions followed by charming remorse and recompense.

Some nights above the sawmill were longer than others with Bumby still cutting teeth, but Hemingway did not mind those "white nights," as he called them, so long as there were books to read. Early that winter while his small son fretted with his teething ring, Ernest was in the Arctic with the explorers, Fridtjof Nansen and Vilhjalmur Stefansson, where nights and days were truly white. Part of him never let loose of his boyhood ambition to explore that survival country north of Hudson's Bay. All fall and early winter the papers told of bold American Navy pilots who, while circling the globe for the first time by air, survived crashes, forced Arctic landings, dense fogs and mechanical failures without loss of life. While Hemingway read safely in his room, the explorer Amundsen on his stout ship *Maude* gave up his attempt to drift across the North Pole with the ice pack. Despite the war's disillusioning effect, the age of heroic action was not yet dead.[28]

At the Cirque de Paris good fights were coming up quite regularly now: Mascart went twenty rounds to take the European featherweight title back from Ledoux on points; Vinez trimmed Paul Fritsch for France's lightweight title, and Kid Francis took the bantamweight title away from Montreuil. With money in the bank, Ernest was there regularly in the old hall watching the heads bob and blood run. Guy Hickok still slipped him free press passes whenever he could, getting Ernest close to the ring. Sometimes when Harold Loeb could get loose from Kitty Cannell for an evening, he went with Ernest to the fights and to a café for a late drink after. He enjoyed Ernest's post-fight analysis and his memory for precise details. Everything Hemingway saw, he absorbed for later use: nothing was done merely for pleasure. He sparred at the gym, watched the good fighters in the ring and read about the fight game. Recently he had read fight stories by Ring Lardner and Charles Van Loan where there was always an angle, a fix of some sort, that made the fiction work. He would later use it all in his fiction.[29]

When "The Doctor and the Doctor's Wife" came out in the November *transatlantic*, Ernest sent a typescript of it to McAlmon for his *Contact Collection of Contemporary Writers*. Mac had asked for a new story, but Ernest's two new ones were twice the length needed. Hemingway called the fiction "the best short story I ever wrote," but after McAlmon saw it in the *transatlantic* he sent it back, saying that everyone else was contributing unpublished material. "How about the Smith story ['Mr. and Mrs. Smith']," he asked, "or O'Neil ['Cross Country Snow'] or Krebs ['Soldier's Home']." When McAlmon's letter caught up with Hemingway about mid-January, Ernest rethought the request. If he were going to be in the same book with Joyce, he wanted to publish something so damn good that reviewers would have to make comparisons with the Irish prince of modernism. Some time in January he sent McAlmon "Soldier's Home," replete with Joycean interior monologues.[30]

Early in November, Ernest got to missing Ezra and wondering what the red fox was up to in Italy. No one had heard from him since his going down, but the first week in December up popped ol' Ez in the *Tribune* complaining about the high costs of passports and their limited two-year life span. The whole affair was, of course, merely another government plot to create a slush fund for "malevolent office holders." That sounded like Ezra all right. Not even reclused in Rapallo could he keep his tongue in check. When Hemingway told Edmund Wilson, "Intelligence is so damn rare and the people who have it often have such a bad time with it that they get bitter and propagandistic and then it's not much use," he very likely had Ezra in mind. How could a man so talented waste so much of his time on phonies like Antheil and on pointless paranoias like the government's charge for passports? How could a man who claimed to specialize in genius foist off the maudlin poetry of the village opium addict, Cheever Dunning? Good Christ, such shit as

"Kiss me," said the poppy flaunting at my side,
"Other flowers have failed, I have never lied."

For a first-rate mind, Ezra had some inexplicable lapses, and for a brilliant poet, he always managed to sound like a crackpot in the *Tribune*. As Ernest sat before his fire reading the paper, he was quite sure that he would never get bitter or propagandistic.[31]

Toward the end of November, Hemingway complained that after finishing "The Undefeated" he was "having a period of not being able to do anything worth a shit." But it did not worry him, not this time.

250

No black days and blacker nights this time. Soon he would be high in the Austrian alps at the little town of Schruns where Bertram Hartman, a friend and painter, assured him the living was far cheaper than Switzerland and there were far fewer tourists. Due to Hadley's dividend checks, which were far less than before the Breaker fiasco but still enough to live on, their bank account was once again healthy. On December 17, after $250 worth of withdrawals earlier in the month, the account still totaled $1280, enough money to get them through until the following summer. But there was plenty to do in Paris before leaving. The apartment required subletting; Marie needed a bit of consideration; and he had to set up a way for forwarding mail, particularly mail from the states. He did not want to miss any publisher's letter. As he busied himself with details, the past appeared in the mail: a letter from Bill Smith, his once close friend from whom he had not heard in over two years.[32]

In March of 1922, in reaction to Hemingway's attack on his older brother Kenley and his wife Doodles, Bill broke with Ernest, saying that Ernest was no longer the person he once admired at Walloon; it was like the difference between vinegar and champagne. In the interim the Doodles shooting-suicide scandal opened Bill's eyes to what Ernest tried to tell him about his brother's marriage in 1921. Now Bill was writing to apologize, and Ernest could not have been happier as he spent the evening writing a long reply, telling Smith about Paris, Pamplona, new friends, journalistic travels and European boxers. And, of course, he told Bill about his writing:

> I know how damn good all our old stuff was Bird because everything, almost everything worth a damn I've written has been about that country. It was the whole damn business inside me and when I think about any country or doing anything it's always that old stuff, the Bay, the farm, rainstein [rainbow trout] fishing . . . the whole damn thing.[33]

"Our old stuff" meant the "Cross Roads" sketches that Bill and Ernest wrote jointly in 1921, sketches on their way to becoming the terse paragraphs of *in our time*. In 1921, nothing came of the exercises, but they were the beginning of the Hemingway style and at the heart of his early subject matter. The lake, always his real home, was never far below the surface of his mind. He missed it terribly when summer approached, and having Bill back was like getting a piece of Walloon through the mail.[34]

Bill had to come over for the Pamplona festival. It would be old times again, another good gang of men, another gathering of summer people. There were so few good men left in the world, and those there were ruined themselves, he said, by marrying "foecal matter." Galantière, once a good guy, ended up married to Dorothy Butler, a "copper-plated bitch," and "he ain't a good guy any more." Dos Passos was almost ruined by Crystal Ross. It could happen to anyone, but not to Ernest, you understand. He and Hadley "had and have a damn good time" because she understood boxing and fishing, and drank without remorse. Hash, he said, "hasn't lost any looks and gets better all the time." He thought Doran would publish his new book. "We're dickering now," he wrote with false certainty, having heard nothing from New York since the manuscript left. "Boni and Liveright want it if they [Doran] don't come through but I'm all for keeping out of the manuals of the Semites as long as possible." Back in St. Louis, Bill must have thought it a strange letter, filled with names that meant nothing to him. Why was Ernest going on that way about the effects of marriage? Some of it did not sound like the friend Bill once knew, but that crack about the "Semites" was just like old Ernie at the lake. Smith remembered when the Jews bought the old fishing point and the way they'd planned to harass them with rotten fish down their chimney.[35]

Hemingway poured his last three years into the Smith letter, glossing over some things, embroidering others as he always did. At points the letter got away from him, at points he was talking to himself. He told Bill about his writing, but said nothing about the story "Summer People." Whatever he may have intended to do with that sexually explicit story, Smith's letter made it doubly unpublishable – a small price to get Bill back and maybe Kate back with him. Everything was changing so fast that he wanted to hold on to some vestige of those summer days swimming off the dock and Kate looking incredible in her black bathing suit. Kate was enough to make a man "uncomfortable," his father's euphemism. Maybe she was still that way. Women changed quickly, and there were a lot of good-looking women on the boulevard now. But it was not Kate's looks so much as the way she looked at you, and the almost careless way she carried her body, not like it was a treasure to be guarded, but it was just there. He could still get "uncomfortable" thinking about Kate. Once they were close, too close almost. He loved her there in Chicago, wanted her at the same time he wanted Hadley. Looking back from Paris, he remembered being in love with both women at the same time, and the way Hadley understood. Kate was her bridesmaid at the wedding. The idea of the two women made him even more "uncomfortable."[36]

As December days disappeared into rain and chill, Hemingway wrote Christmas letters and worked on the review of Sherwood Anderson's new book, *A Story Teller's Story*, which he was writing for Dawson Johnston's book column in the *Tribune*. He started out:

> This is the Life and Times of Sherwood Anderson and a great part of it runs along in a mildly kidding way as though Sherwood were afraid people would think he took himself and his life too seriously. But there is no joking about the way he writes about horses and women and bartenders and Judge Turner and the elder Berners and the half allegorical figure of the poor devil of a magazine writer who comes in at the end of the book. . . . He is a very great writer and if he has at times in other books been unsuccessful it has been for two reasons. His talent and his development of it has [sic] all been toward the short story or tale and not toward that highly artificial form, the novel. The second reason is that he has been what the French say of all honest politicians, *mal entoure*.

As with many of his literary evaluations, what Hemingway wrote said as much or more about his own writing than it did about the book at hand. That the novel was a "highly artificial form" was his own current defense for not writing a novel, and for not taking Loeb's *Doodab* or Dos Passos' novels as his competition. In fact he did not understand how one could write a story that he could not hold completely in his head; encouraged by Gertrude, he absolutely distrusted detailed planning. The story needed to tell itself, like Nick on the river where he, Ernest, got to live in the story each day. That was a long story, about as long as he could write. Everyone told him novels needed planning, but then he'd know how it worked out before writing it. Where was the joy in that?

He called Anderson's book "highly successful . . . because it is written in his own particular form, a series of short tales jointed up sometimes and sometimes quite disconnected." In praising Sherwood's devotion to the short story, he was speaking also of his own manuscript which was sometimes "jointed up," sometimes "disconnected." Not satisfied with his generalizations, Hemingway went on to make some murky remarks about New York intellectuals, i.e. *Dial* magazine, whose early praise of Sherwood resulted in "a poor book called *Many Marriages.*" That was behind Sherwood now, and his new book everyone should read.[37]

While Ernest finished his book review, Hadley mailed their Christmas package to Oak Park: a large, framed portrait of Bumby. More and more Hadley's polite St. Louis rhetoric was the link between Ernest and his parents. Whatever he needed her to do, she did. Behind her were burned bridges; Ernest was her future and her religion. What he wanted, she wanted: boxing matches, bullfights, skiing, fishing. On the Irati she caught trout; in the mountains she was with him on the slopes. In Paris they attended concerts as well as boxing matches. When Bertram Hartman suggested Christmas in Austria for its depressed economy, excellent exchange rate and mountain slopes, she was as eager as Ernest for the high country and the chance for exercise, for she still had not lost all the weight gained during pregnancy. At thirty-three with full breasts and wide hips, Hadley Hemingway was an ample, attractive woman whose hair was burning chestnut in the sun, but she did not turn men's heads in Paris, not that year when thin bodies and flat chests were in vogue. If Ernest looked at other women on the boulevard, it was nothing new. If women looked back, Hadley was not surprised. Ernest was accustomed to much attention from women, young and old. Hadley did not worry about the women on the boulevard or in the cafés, for she had talents they did not know of. In Schruns, clothes would not matter, and in their night bed, holding Ernest in her arms against his dark dreams, her amplitude was among her assets.

As Christmas approached and the dark came early, Ernest and Hadley made rounds of cheer and farewells. Gertrude and Alice sent them off with a small package for Goddy, as they called their godson Bumby, and loaned unlikely books for Austrian nights: *Viva Mexico* and *My Dear Cornelia.* At Shakespeare and Company, they checked out more books – Turgenev, Trollope and Wilkie Collins. In vain they looked for the winter issue of the *Little Review* which would carry Ernest's satiric story about the American poet which he was now calling "Mr. and Mrs. Elliot." Ernest Walsh and Ethel Moorhead, who were committed to editing a new review to replace the *transatlantic*, gave them a lovely bottle of Graves and another of Chablis to ease the long train trip across Switzerland. Only the thin-lipped grimace of Bob McAlmon, feeling persecuted for reasons no one could understand, and the faint, familiar rasp in Ernest's throat took the edge off their departure. With their apartment sublet until the end of March, Ernest splurged on a taxi to Gare de l'Est. Tickets and seat reservations in hand, they watched amazed as dense fog transformed their familiar Quarter into a strange, unrecognizable place. Street lamps were mere halos in the dark, casting tiny circles of pale light. When they arrived at the end of Boulevard de Strasbourg, the station clock was invisible in the mist. Leaving late and proceeding at a crawl, their train for Basle slowly moved through the fog-bound suburbs and finally out of Paris.

Part Four

1925

WAITING IN SCHRUNS
WINTER, 1925

I

Swiss Customs officers woke them at Basle the next morning, and came
through the train again at Buchs, where they changed money and trains,
crossing the border into Austria. At Bludenz they changed once more
for the spur line electric tram up the Montafon valley, clicking through
small villages, fields of belled cows, leaf-bare orchards and dark woods.
There was no snow at Schruns except high in the mountains above
them, but they were happy to be there. At Hotel Taube rooms were
large, comfortable, heated and cheap. Everything included – full pension,
heat, milk and a full-time nursemaid for Bumby – came to 2,065,000
kronen per week or $29.50 American. Even with their bar bill and ski
lessons, the Hemingways were spending only $180 a month, less than
Paris cost them. The village with its sawmill, inns and local market was
quaint and peaceful; villagers greeted you on the street with "Gruss
Gott."[1]

The painter, Bertram Hartman, and his wife Gusta were at the Taube
for Christmas; Dossie Johnston, Josephine Bennett, Alma Lloyd and
Harold Loeb were coming in the new year, if Kitty would let Harold
leave her alone in Paris. "Tell Kitty you will be pure here," Ernest
wrote him, "because there is only one beautiful girl in the village and
she eats garlic for breakfast." No sooner had the Hemingways moved
into the Taube, than Ernest came down with another bout of infected
throat which put him to bed for most of the week. "It's quiet here,"

he wrote Ernest Walsh, "and there's no gossip," which he, in fact, missed. The only gossiper he'd seen before leaving was McAlmon who was "very bitter about everybody," including Ernest. "It would be so much more pleasant," he told Walsh, "if the average writer's brain did not become a sort of ingrowing toe nail around the age of thirty." From their balcony on Christmas Eve they watched new snow drifting into the town center where it melted the next day.[2]

His throat still raw, Hemingway fiddled with several starts on new fiction. One he titled "The Bull Ring," beginning with the trip into Italy to visit Ezra at Rapallo a year earlier, but it never got beyond the second paragraph. Then he began a real bullfight story about a young, frail bullfighter with "very small hands" and eyelashes long "like a girl's." In the bull ring his cape skills are pleasing but he is unable to control his fear at the killing point. At Pamplona he thoroughly disgraces himself, unable to kill the bull. Unmanned by fear, the young bullfighter suffers from "a lack of passion," as the story was eventually called. In the bull ring he failed miserably; in the bedroom he failed completely, unable to satisfy the girl. As the story began to circle the question of the bullfighter's sexuality, Hemingway put it away for another day. It was, after all, another unpublishable story if he let homosexuality into it. Der Querschnitt would print it, but nobody in the states would touch it.[3]

"A Lack of Passion" was a strange story for Hemingway to be writing in Schruns or anywhere else. As a companion piece to "The Undefeated," it was another version of the artist/bullfighter, this one a different kind of failure. Both men, called Manuel, undergo professional embarrassment in the bull ring, but the young fighter does not care, having no professional pride: it is merely a business, one that he does not enjoy. Maybe the story bubbled up from reading McAlmon's tales of Berlin transvestites and Paris homosexuals. Strange though it was, "A Lack of Passion" was not unlike a number of stories Hemingway would write over the next ten years, stories exploring the dual sexual nature of men and women. It was a theme that held a dark fascination for him. In Paris he memorized conversations overheard in cafés, watched the way that men like McAlmon and Cedric Morris dressed and moved, and studied the famous lesbians of the Quarter. It was the age of sexual liberation when show girls went naked on the stage, when hot jazz and moaning blues pointed to the same conclusion. Although he did not have the book at hand, Ernest still remembered the clinical details from

Havelock Ellis' study of various aberrations and fetishes, *The Psychology of Sex*.

While Bumby played with the village children in the *Kinderhaus* behind the Taube, Hadley knitted local wool into scarves, practiced her piano technique and chatted with Gusta Hartman, German by birth and not a witty conversationalist in English. Bertram, her husband, painted village scenes, two of which Hadley took back to Paris as her own. While they all waited for snow to make the lower slopes skiable, Ernest continued working on stories.

Each day the mail came up the electric tram line to the village, and each day nothing from New York. Ernest and Hadley took hikes along the stream, ate well and drank the local wines. At night they and the Hartmans bowled German style in the hotel, or played bridge close to the fire. Snow fell in the high mountains, turning them brilliant in the sun. Everyone was sure it would soon fall in the valley. From bright days, Bumby's cheeks glowed apple-red, Hadley's freckles popped out in profusion, and Ernest, for the first time in his life, began to let his beard grow as many of the villagers did. Always there was something to interest him, some detail to note, for he did not bore easily and this was all new country. Much later he remembered it clearly: the smoky air of the *Weinstube* where they all sang mountain songs; the women spinning lamb's wool sticky with natural fats; the Christmas play he reviewed for the local paper. Actually they put on two plays to amuse the winter visitors and the townspeople as well: Hans Sachs' *The Hot Iron* and Bernard Shaw's *How He Deceived Her Husband*. In his review Ernest wrote, "E. Bertle in the role of a Shavianly enraged husband was thoroughly Shavian and enraged."[4]

While Hartman painted, Gusta talked and Ernest listened. She didn't know any better, never having been around a writer. The story he wrote started with Gusta growing up on the Bodensee, less than fifty kilometers to the north, and how she ran away from home to live in Munich. She was an assistant to a fashionable photographer when she met Bertram at a pension. They had an affair and then married. Now she was hooking rugs to Bertram's designs, but sales were slow. Ernest thought she charged too much. At least that's what he wrote down in his blue notebook. Gusta, tiny and dark, looked Jewish to him. The story broke off after six pages and was never finished. Sometimes his writing was peristaltic action. At Schruns he tried to keep the juices from the fall flowing, but little came of it except the exercise.[5]

The patterns, however, were becoming ominous. Over and over again, his stories described the negative impact of wives upon husbands. His fictional Gusta was a drag on her painter husband; the Doctor's wife, deep into her Christian Science, merely provoked her already humiliated husband; Mrs. Smith went to bed with her dear friend while her poet husband stayed up writing long poems; Nick was forced to give up skiing when Helen got pregnant. The same pattern was there in his other life, the one he lived when he was not writing. Kenley's wife Doodles was a "copper-plated bitch." Crystal Ross almost ruined Dos Passos. Dorothy Butler was the end of Lewis Galantière. Lincoln Steffens' new, young and Jewish wife ruined the old newsman. Kitty Cannell, for all her good looks, long legs and blond hair, kept Loeb tied to her as if they were married. Wives inevitably changed the men until they were no longer the good guys he once knew. The stories were, of course, fiction, but the theme was one much on his mind, for reasons not immediately obvious. Outwardly he and Hadley appeared to be happier than ever, but underneath, if his writing and his biting commentary on the wives of others are any indication, all was not well.

In the new year snow fell in the Montafon valley, but in the warm weather quickly disappeared, leaving the skiers disappointed. They continued to take daily hikes to build up stamina for the high country. If they wanted to ski, they would have to climb up to the snow. Dossie Johnston, Jo Bennett and Alma Lloyd arrived from Paris bearing gossip, gifts and fresh magazines. When a fat letter arrived from Don Stewart inclosing a check, Ernest's mouth went dry. Certain that it was advance money on his book from Doran, his heart dropped when he realized the signature was Don's. Ernest had moaned so much about being broke that Stewart sent them a Christmas check, saying that he did not want them starving to death in some place called Schruns. Stewart also inclosed the rejection letter from Doran: everyone loved the book but there was too much sex in it; if it were a novel, the shock would be all right. Maybe Ernest would write a novel and then they could do the stories as a second volume. Don was taking the manuscript to Mencken, asking him to recommend it to young Alfred Knopf's publishing house. If that failed he would take it to Liveright. Ernest felt sick. Mencken! Christ, Mencken wouldn't take his stories for the *Mercury*. Fat chance with Mencken. And Loeb writes to say he can't come to Schruns after all. Has to go to New York because Liveright, who was publishing *Doodab*, wanted to make radical changes to his manuscript. Loeb wanted to be there to approve the surgery. This was the publisher who was likely to get *In Our Time*. Happy goddamn New Year.[6]

It cheered him up some when Hans Wedderkop accepted "The Undefeated" for *Der Querschnitt*. Early in December, Ernest sent out two copies, one to Wedderkop and one to a magazine in the states, figuring it unlikely both would accept. If both did, that was fine too. A sale in German was not a sale in English so there was nothing devious about selling the story twice. When "The Undefeated" came back from the states, he put two copies back in the mail on 21 January: one to the *Dial* and the other to *Saturday Evening Post*. After Wilson's great review in the *Dial*, Hemingway thought maybe they would finally take a story. The *Post* was a long shot, but why the hell not. In his cover letter to the editor, Lorimer, he said he tried to write the story "the way it actually is, as Charles E. Van Loan used to write fight stories." He assured Lorimer that he had traveled all over Spain with "a caudrilla of bull fighters," which only stretched the truth to twice its size. "The story may seem technical," he said, "but all the technicalities, while not obviously explained, are made clear."[7]

Earlier in the month when Ernest Walsh and Ethel Moorhead told him that their new review, *This Quarter*, was definitely going to be published, he sent them the best and longest story he had: "Big Two-Hearted River." He might have saved it to fish American waters, but Moorhead promised to pay on acceptance and Hemingway's nagging worries about money led him to go for the quick payment. Fairly certain they would take the story, he double baited his hook to make them feel good about the story and their payment policy. "The best work," he said, "can never get into the purely commercially run magazines anyway . . . but [the author] will only give away stuff that has no value." This story, he implied, was too well-written for commercial magazines like *Saturday Evening Post*.[8]

About that same time, with Hadley's good friend, Alma, sitting across the table from him at evening meals, Hemingway did a ten-page sketch about a character named Alma Lloyd, a fat girl who came to Paris to study music and have an affair. After a year's study and still a virgin, Alma thrashes in her night bed listening to sounds of love coming through thin walls, a situation he had used before and one that obviously appealed to him. But imagining Alma in her feverish bed while she was downstairs chatting with Hadley was a new form of literary voyeurism for Ernest. It was not difficult to imagine how other women he knew behaved in bed.[9]

The story broke off, unfinished and unpublishable. He could not have it both ways. Joyce put down exactly what he wanted to say, but Joyce was banned in the only countries speaking English. Bloom's masturbation was possible in print, but not in America. There was the rub: Hemingway fully intended to make money selling his fiction to the great American market. Being a young, experimental writer in Paris had a limited half-life; he had no intention of growing old and unpublished like Gertrude, living off patrons like Joyce, or going into exile with Pound at Rapallo. He labeled the notebook "Private."

For the first half of January, Ernest, Hadley and Dossie waited for valley snows which fell but did not accumulate. Beneath the high snow line, mountains looming above them were bleak and brown with beech wood forests. Village life, simple and basic, was soothing after rainy Paris. A pebbly greenish-white stream rushed through the village and down the valley, and on a rise in the center of town stood the Catholic church, its bell tower a green onion-dome. At night the city and country folk drank local pilsner beer and bowled squat duck pins with hard, grapefruit-sized balls that stretched the fingers. At night, walking back to the Taube in frosty air, Ernest and Hadley locked arms and hummed softly to themselves. Above them the mountains, black and silent, seemed close enough to touch, their snow fields eerie white in the moonlight. To look at the couple strolling in the dark, no one would have guessed that Ernest was writing about unhappy marriages.[10]

II

As members of Walter Lent's ski school, Ernest and Hadley began making exhausting day trips up the valley to the high snows above Partenen where they would strap seal skins to their heavy skis for the stiff climb up the slope. The seal skin, with its nap pointing down hill, would grip the snow when the ski began to slip backwards. In those days when there were no mechanical lifts in the valley, alpine skiing was a demanding sport. There was no way to ski down the Montafon slopes without first climbing up. Tall and lean, Herr Lent was a demanding teacher and a good companion who enjoyed life fully, Ernest's kind of man. At day's end they would stop at the Tschofen where the wood of the walls was "silky with years of polishing," where the beer and stews were substantial.[11]

In mid-January, Ernest and Hadley took a three-day trip back down

the valley to the main line and then to Zurs on the Flexenpass where
they skied down into Lech, but the snow was too soft, too deep and
too dangerous for the novices. Dossie was with them, struggling to
keep up. "On skis," Ernest said, "Dossie makes up in endurance what
she lacks in coordination. But she falls more than if it were the other
way." In Lech they stayed at the Hotel Krone beside the silt-white
waters of a glacial river. Their hosts, the Pfefferkorns, were happy to
have the Americans beside their evening fire, but the skiing was
disappointing to everyone. The danger of avalanches kept them off the
slopes, and after four days they returned to Schruns.[12]

Twice in February, the skiers packed themselves and heavy rucksacks
up the steep cut-back trail at the head of the valley into Madlener Haus,
an Alpine Club station kept open in late winter for skiers, serving simple
meals and sleeping sixteen in dormitory beds. From there, under Lent's
guidance, they could climb up to Wiesbadener-Hut, 500 meters higher
up the slope, and then ski back down across the Silvretta-Stausée. The
snow fields were broad and lovely, with fine powder over a solid base.
No need to worry about trails or rocks, merely let the skis flow in
great snaking turns through the feathery powder. Ernest's beard
flourished and his tan deepened. Paris seemed far away, almost forgotten.
At night, after playing poker beside the stove, he and Hadley dropped
into their sleeping sacks like rocks. Outside, snow piled half as high as
the roof and the slopes were radiant in moonlight. There were no bad
dreams at that rare altitude.

They went up the mountain and they came down. Each time they
came down, Bumby's Breton French was more interlarded with Plat-
Deutsch. Soon even his parents would not be able to understand him.
Whenever they came down, there was mail but nothing from New
York. Magazines arrived from Paris: L'Auto to stay abreast of the
sporting world, bullfight magazines from Spain, and whatever Gertrude
sent. McAlmon's study of boyhood in the Midwest farm belt, Village,
came in the mail; Ernest was hungry enough to read it immediately. It
was good but no threat. Knowing that he could do better, he felt at
ease telling McAlmon, "Village is absolutely first rate and damned good
reading. We've all read it down here and everybody thinks it's a
knockout."[13]

Ernest Walsh wrote, asking for a biographical sketch to include with
"Big Two-Hearted River" in the first issue of This Quarter. Ernest's
response was puzzling.

... as near as I can figure out am 27 years old. 6 feet tall, weight 182 lbs. . . . Very fond of eating and drinking. Lives in France for that reason among others. Believes Gertrude Stein to be a great writer. Tried to keep Transatlantic Review alive to publish her Making of Americans. Failed. Friend of Ezra Pound. Believes Pound greatest living poet. This is not friendship. Would like to make bet on subject.

Hemingway was, in fact, twenty-six years old, which he well knew, but there was something about biographical questions that brought out the worst in him almost always. The next day he wrote Walsh, asking him to "suppress" his first letter, for it "was a lot of crap." No sense, he said, in hurting Ford's feelings. He might have added, no sense in dropping the names of Ezra and Gertrude, his surrogate parents. Then, as if giving truthful information, he said that being less than rich, his family lived on one hundred dollars a month. Joyce was poor. Pound was poor. Sylvia was poor. Ernest would be poorer than any of them before he quit telling the tale, poorer and slower. "I write slowly," he told Walsh, "and with a great deal of difficulty and my head has to be clear to do it. While I write the stuff I have to live it in my head." Well, sometimes he wrote slowly, just as sometimes he almost told the truth about his writing. Sometimes the stories came out so fast it scared him, but in Paris, James Joyce was the model for the artist as painstaker, reworking paragraphs until every word was exactly correct and in its proper place. Hemingway seldom wrote this way, but he did not want the world to know how easily the *In Our Time* stories flowed.[14]

The story he did for Jane Heap came off his pen in one afternoon at Schruns. He got her letter that morning asking him to contribute something to the *Little Review's* "Banal Issue," an idea she got from a 1924 farce – The Banal Ball – advertised by Pascin, Braque, Masson, Picasso and others to celebrate the utter banality of 1924.

We promise you the most banal surprises, the most traditional attractions, the usual cottillion, the old "post d'amour," vulgar clowns, trite gatherings, and the sentimental Pierrot. . . . We banally invite you to put on the most banal travesties avoiding any pursuit of art, originality, or any psychological complication. . . . Your travesties should be taken from life."[15]

Hemingway immediately ripped off "Banal Story" which Hadley typed up for him. He told Jane Heap, "Now don't go and switch numbers

on me and put it in A Great White Hopes number. Label it banal."
And banal it was, taken right out of the newspapers, *Forum* magazine
and *Toro y Toros*, the bullfight magazine to which Hemingway subscribed.
Using a parodic version of the Anderson voice, the nameless narrator
briefly considers current events and *The Forum*'s fiction contest. "Think
of these things in 1925," the narrator muses. "Was there a risqué page
in Puritan history? Were there two sides to Pocahontas? Did she have
a fourth dimension?" Then without warning or transition, the reader is
taken in the final paragraph to Spain where Manuel Garcia Maera dies
of pneumonia. "Bull-fighters were very relieved he was dead, because
he did always in the bull-ring the things they could only do sometimes."
Throughout the slight sketch the "he," whose thoughts we overhear,
farts at appropriate points, as if punctuating his ideas. Knowing the
difficulty with civic censors, Hemingway told Heap, "If the word farts
or fart isn't allowed by postoffice leave it out and let it go blank."
Outside grey rain was falling steadily across Schruns as it had since
breakfast. It was a banal day all round.[16]

III

When he was not on the slopes, Ernest spent his days reading Paris
papers and new magazines, keeping up with the literary and sporting
worlds. When Mascart put Danny Frush away in the second round,
Ernest crowed about it two days later in Schruns. In a small, separate
room, he set up a writing table to work on his fiction or answer letters
undisturbed. During the three-month vacation, he was at the Taube
sixty days and wrote thirty-three letters that survived. Because he seldom
wrote letters when his fiction was going well, it appears that the three
months were a dry spell. All he had to show for the period was the
two-page "Banal Story" and another short essay for *The Quarter*. It
was a dry spell he could blame on the skiing, but it was going to extend
another three months, the longest hiatus since he returned from the
war. After finishing "The Undefeated" at the end of November 1924,
Hemingway wrote only one significant story during the next seven and
a half months.[17]

He tried, but for the first time the stories simply were not there, and
it scared him. Early at Schruns he started an untitled story told by a
boxer trying to analyze the effect he had on women. It began: "Boxing

is funny that way. Everywhere you go on a boat or on a train some nice woman always tries to reform you and get you to quit fighting." Without a plot, the monologue continues for several pages in which the boxer says the worst situation occurs when a fighter marries a woman who does not understand his profession. Attracted to him by his fame and money, the first thing she wants to do is turn him into a respectable citizen. But when the money runs out, the woman runs out with it. Count on that.

Hemingway did not know where it was going when he started it, but the basic themes were familiar: the artist's relationship with his art, women and money encapsulating the decline of the artist. Despite his artistic acceptance in literary magazines, Hemingway's obsession with failed artists reflects his concern with his own artistic demise. That winter in Schruns and the following spring, when the stories would not flow, he was particularly sensitive to this theme. They could not live indefinitely on Hadley's fixed income, and there was no word from his friends in New York who were hawking his manuscript.[18]

Not too surprisingly, the concerns of his aborted fictions found their way into Hemingway's extensive Schruns correspondence with Bill Smith. In two months he wrote Bill at least ten letters, one over eight typed pages. Their central concerns were sports and writing, which were not separate categories to Hemingway: in his privately developed metaphysics, bullfighter, boxer, painter and writer were brothers in art. What he said about the matador in the bull ring applied to the writer as well, sometimes metaphorically, sometimes directly. Both were skilled professionals whose best moves were not understood by the masses; in practicing their art, they could not fake anything or it would show.

Hemingway also had advice about the professional writing market which Bill's sister, Kate, was bombarding with manuscripts. Kate was trying to write popular fiction much as Ernest had back in his Chicago days. Hemingway pointed out that popular writers were "geniuses at turning out the crap and it's their artistic fulfillment." They were "born 2nd raters. They ain't underdeveloped 1st raters." Kate was better than that and would never be happy writing second-rate fiction. What she needed, of course, was technique. She had plenty of "the stuff – the ecstasy – or whatever you bludy choose to call it," but without technique, there was no art. Anyone who wanted to work hard enough and long enough could develop the technique. "Now I've worked bludy hard," he told Bill, "Christ how bludy hard – and the stuff *begins*. Just begins to come through." But he did not tell Bill that "the stuff" was not coming through just then.[19]

Instead he encouraged Bill to get away from the states and find a job in Paris. Over their two-month correspondence, Hemingway suggested that Bill become : (1) a bartender, (2) an editor for *This Quarter*, or (3) private secretary to Dawson Johnston at the American Library. That Bill knew nothing about tending bar, editing a literary magazine or speaking French did not dampen Ernest's enthusiasm. Bill could pick up bar-tending in a week. As for French literature at the library, Bill could learn that in half an hour. "The great thing I have found in libraries," Ernest told him, "is that nobody has read the books. You learn the names of them." To Ernest Walsh and Ethel Moorhead, Ernest began writing increasingly pestering letters about hiring his friend to do the Paris work for *This Quarter*.[20]

Encouraged by his old friend's efforts to find him work, Bill began unburdening his private problems to Ernest. The last three years had been a series of disappointments for Smith: he never found his proper profession nor the wife that he needed. His beloved Aunt Charles, who raised him, and his older brother Merrill had both died, and Bill had spent months in a sanitarium for diagnosed tuberculosis. The confidence he once had did not shine through his letters. From Hemingway's responses it is obvious that some of Bill's problems were sexual. Ernest, always ready to give advice, told Bill that "mental philandering" was worse for a man than actually "yencing" or fucking the woman. Pursuit without fulfillment left the woman constantly in "need to crescendo or else bust. A yencing acquaintanceship terminating or continuing more or less normal on account there being frequent crescendoes with normalization afterwards. Wit[h] the mental friendships with over sexed underbalanced women a male is in danger." For a man faithful to his wife, Ernest had given a good deal of thought to the philandering issue.[21]

A month later, in an effort to appear as casual about sex as Ernest, Bill wrote that his St. Louis landlady might be ready to climb into his bed, but he was not sure about it. Hemingway's response was detailed:

> As to yencing the landwoman, I aint seen her. If she's married and wants it they ain't no harm. If not [you] some one else will. That aint serious yencing but should be good. Now serious yencing should be devoid of consequences and entanglements.

Entanglements are what ruin yencing. You ought to yence. Yencing is a great conditioner. Makes a man see clearer, good for the corps. If you get a chance to yence without entanglements and feel like yencing, yence. . . . The screeder [writer] aint promiscuous on account of loving one person and not wishing to spoil anything in any way. But was I not married or was I married and not in love, I'd yence when yencing offered without entanglements. . . .

It was a prophetic and revealing letter, based more on observation than practice, for as he assured Bill, he and Hadley went better together all the time. "As a matter of fact," he said, "we're the only married people I know that do."[22]

IV

The only word from New York was another rejection. On February 6, *Vanity Fair* returned his terse sketch of the war nurse who jilts her American lover, which he now called "A Very Short Story." The editor told Hemingway, "We have been trying for a long time to think of some way of using material like this, but have never been able to use material of this sort . . . clever and amusing as it undoubtedly is." Ernest looked again at the magazine. He was sure this sketch was within their format. Maybe the young man catching "gonorrhea from a sales girl in a loop department store while riding in a taxicab through Lincoln Park" was not "amusing" enough for *Vanity Fair*. Because they were printing occasional bare breasts, albeit in misty, artistic photos, he thought they might be ready for a good dose of the clap. Wrong again.[23]

Trying not to think about his book, now four months in New York, trying not to think about his stories that would not write, Ernest and the ski team packed into Madlener Haus during the second week of February for serious skiing. When they came back down there were letters from Smith and Walsh, but none from New York. Walsh needed a picture of Ezra, patron saint of literary magazines, to whom he was dedicating the first issue of *This Quarter*. Ernest sent him advice on a New York clipping service, Paris lawyers, French rules of the printing road, copyright phrasing, and where he might get Ezra's photo. Walsh, slowly dying from tuberculosis, was living in the Pyrenees with his older mistress Ethel Moorhead, whose inherited money was paying for

Walsh's keep and backing the new magazine. Hemingway, thinking *This Quarter* could be what *transatlantic* should have been, did all he could to help. Besides, the thousand franc check for "Big Two-Hearted River" was his largest fiction payment to date.

On February 18, Ernest and Hadley hiked back up the mountain to Madlener Haus. While they were skiing the Silvretta glacier, Max Perkins, a young editor at Scribner's publishing house in New York, was writing Ernest the first of many letters. Having read and been deeply impressed by *in our time*, Perkins said, "I am venturing to write to you to ask whether you have anything that you would allow us to consider as publishers." But not another small book of vignettes, he added, for there was no commercial way they could publish it. "It occurred to me," he said, "that you might very well be writing something which would not have these practical objections. In any case, whatever you are writing, we should be most interested to consider." The letter, misaddressed, never reached Hemingway.[24]

On February 26, having gotten the correct address from John Peale Bishop, Perkins wrote again, saying he had heard that Hemingway "would be likely to have material for a book before long. I hope this is so and that we may see it. We would certainly read it with promptness and sympathetic interest if you gave us the chance." The letter arrived in Paris about March 10 where it remained until Ernest and Hadley arrived three days later. By that time Perkins' offer was irrelevant, for while Hemingway was at the Madlener Haus, two telegrams arrived from New York: one from Don Stewart, the other from Harold Loeb, both saying the same thing – Liveright was going to make Ernest an offer on *In Our Time*.[25]

Hemingway wrote Loeb that when the two cables arrived at the ski hut, "I couldn't realize it at first and then couldn't believe it and when I did I got very excited and couldn't sleep. . . . Will it be fall publication along with yours? What will I have to cut? How much dough will I get?" As with so much of Hemingway's life, this delivery of cables on the ski slopes has an epic quality about it. See the hearty guide slogging upwards across twenty-one kilometers of snow field to bring the news from Schruns to Ernest. No sooner does the climber enter Madlener Haus, than one begins to wonder who sent him up there only one day before Ernest was due to come down. What motivation could have enticed such a climb? Or was it part of a good story that improved with telling? On March 2, Ernest gave Fleischman a different version: "Returning here [Schruns] last week I found two cables from New York of February 22 and 23rd, one from Loeb and one from Stewart, stating Liveright had accepted In Our Time." Early in his career, Hemingway began revising and editing what would become his longest and most well-known work: the legend of his own life, where there was never a clear line between fiction and reality.[26]

The prospect of a Liveright contract came about the same time Ernest learned that his sublet tenants jumped their Paris contract a month early, leaving the Hemingways with two rents to pay after March 8 if they stayed in Schruns. From Hadley's bank came worse news: George Breaker's $2500 check to her account had been thrice returned for insufficient funds. Offsetting the bad news was the much-delayed appearance of the "Exiles" number of the Little Review with both his poem, "They All Made Peace," and his story with the title now changed to "Mr. and Mrs. Elliot," presumably to avoid a libel suit with Chard Powers Smith. On March 5, the telegram finally arrived from Liveright, accepting In Our Time and offering $200 advance against royalties. By return wire, Ernest cabled: DELIGHTED ACCEPT. Three days later, Ernest Walsh asked Hemingway to contribute an essay for the issue of This Quarter honoring Ezra, which Hemingway agreed to do.[27]

Without any of Ezra's poetry at hand, Ernest wrote a poorly organized, heavily padded essay which began in good humor but only until he saw an opening for another shot at T. S. Eliot:

> Eliot is, after all, a minor poet. Fine poetry is written by minor poets. . . . All of Eliot's poems are perfect and there are very few of them. He has a fine talent and he is very careful with it and is doing very well thank you.

Minor poets, he went on to say, were minor because they had "nothing of major importance to say." Ezra, of course, was a major poet, a judgement the reader had to accept on faith, for Hemingway gave no good reason for his conclusion.[28]

Why Hemingway found Eliot such an amusing target to attack publicly and without provocation has never been completely explained. The two men apparently never met. Ernest's jokes about "Major Elliot," as he liked to call the poet, began in Pound's Bel Esprit period but continued for years afterwards. Eliot was a poet and essayist, not a fictionalist. There was no direct competition, certainly not from Eliot's side: all he knew of Hemingway was what he read in the transatlantic. Maybe Hemingway's penchant was nothing more than a manifestation of his defensive nature, so overly sensitive to criticism that he frequently found cause for a literary feud where none was intended. Being a high-school kid out of the war with nothing more than journalism for credentials, he was never completely at ease with Left Bank Ivy-Leaguers, and liked nothing better than getting one of them into a boxing match where his weight was his advantage. Those same college graduates put Eliot into an untouchable category of his own, the genius of his age. No matter how much friends admired Ernest's work, they never spoke of him in the same breath with Joyce or Eliot, already proven masters. In those days, no one but Hemingway was calling Eliot a minor poet.

Thomas Sterns Eliot was the darling of the literary Twenties, and his poem *The Waste Land* the most influential work of that decade and more than one to follow. In his own mind, Hemingway created a competitive relationship with all post-war writers, the men of his generation, the ones he wanted to out-distance. Any young American writer who received public acclaim was likely to raise Ernest's hackles. In the February *Tribune*, Eugene Jolas wrote:

> There are few American creative writers whose work is being followed in France with more interest than T. S. Elliot [sic]. Without taking recourse to the facile methods of the small fry of present day letters . . . this Bostonian rebel is quietly pursuing his work.[29]

That essay alone might have triggered Hemingway's response, although evidence shows he needed no outside impetus to attack Eliot. Whatever the cause, Ernest's remarks about Eliot in his "Homage to Ezra" applied perhaps more accurately to his own work. All of Hemingway's published stories were "perfect" and there were "very few of them." The biting sketches of *in our time* were more likely to be called the work of a "minor poet" than was *The Waste Land*. Hemingway's less than logical "Homage" ended on the unlikely note that Ezra "was no masochist and that is one more reason why he is not a minor poet." Lack of masochism meant nothing to the general reader, but to an insider like Hemingway, Eliot's unfortunate marriage and tedious bank job looked like self-inflicted pain. Hemingway's homage to his literary father ended up being more of a complaint to Ezra about his favored elder son, Tom Eliot.[30]

As soon as he had "Homage" into the mail, Hemingway began

packing to return to Paris. The Liveright contract would arrive about March 16, and he wanted to be there to meet it. The signs were improving: on March 8, Eugene Jolas picked up from the New York *Evening Post* Ford's article partly in praise of Hemingway, saying,

> The best writer in America at this moment (though at this moment he happens to be in Paris) the most conscientious, the most master of his craft, the most consummate, is my young friend Ernest Hemingway . . . Hemingway, with immense labor and excruciating thought and knowledge, turns out a short paragraph . . . That would damn Mr. Hemingway if it were not for his youthful bloodlust which is an admirable derivative. . . . Mr. Hemingway writes like an Angel; like an Archangel; but his talk – his matter – is that of a bayonet instructor. He never gets very far from the spirit of Berlud!

Ernest did not know who the hell Berlud was, but it was Ford speaking all right, and good publicity. He was glad he took the Ford remark out of his biography for Walsh.

The Hemingways put up their skis and said their Schruns good-byes, promising to return the next winter. The train trip down the valley and into the main line for Basle and Paris seemed longer than coming up. On March 13, they passed through Swiss customs, arriving in Paris early the next morning. Across the grey city, a light snow was falling that turned to rain before they reached rue Notre-Dame-des-Champs. Only the cat was there to greet them.

Chapter Fourteen

PARIS DOLDRUMS
SPRING, 1925

I

Each return to Paris was a new beginning. For three months in Schruns he had been away from the gossip mill, the Dôme gang, the word on the street. New faces in old places were the talk of tipplers, and returning out of date, Hemingway felt a little strange in his own Quarter. The red-headed man with the pock-marked face, the one frequently at the Dôme, was Sinclair Lewis, trying to fit in with the regulars. His table was a center of attention for peripherals trying to impress the man from Main Street. As always, Lewis took notes. He may even have noted Cheever Dunning, who was getting good press in a slow season. Jolas and the *Tribune* were taking Cheever seriously. Ernest shook his head. He could not take the ferret-faced poet as anything other than one of Ezra's mistakes. But then Ezra was an expatriate. That was the new word he heard in the Quarter. Already angry letters appeared in the *Tribune*:

> Men fresh from America . . . go too far when they speak of Americans living in Europe as "expatriates." The word can be twisted by a "hundred per-cent American" to mean anything, but obviously it means one who has changed his allegiance. . . . France harbors few Yankees who are other than Americans. The type of

American that is drawn to France is not of the class that violates laws at home.[1]

It was going to be the year of the expatriate if the gossip level meant anything.

Some things remained stable, of course, like Harold Stearns. Harold remained very stable at the Select, his pile of *soucoupes* about as high as when Ernest left. One needed islands of stability like Harold in the ever-changing stream of the Quarter to maintain some semblance of continuity from one season to the next. Rumors said that Harold was working on a book, an exposé of various Left Bank types. Everyone was sure he would be part of it.

Everyone was somewhere, but the continuing rotten weather kept most Quarterites indoors. Ezra, apparently gone to Rapallo for good, still maintained his studio down the street. Ford and Stella Bowen were mildewing in the country, due back any time. Dunning was starving to death on his opium diet not far away, and Cedric Morris, the painter, was living close by with his lover Lett Haines. But the early spring weather kept most people Ernest and Hadley knew at a distance. In March, the Queen of England could have lived next door and gone unnoticed in the steady rain and grey cold of what some called spring. Ernest knew better. This was not spring. In spring golden leaves budded on the plane and chestnut trees, and chairs from the sidewalk cafés almost blocked the walk. In spring the tourists rode the *bateaux-mouches* beneath the bridges of the Seine. In spring palefaced children appeared in the Luxembourg Gardens. Whatever weather this was, Ernest knew it was not spring. The mid-Lent festival, Mi-Carême, tried to dispel the gloom, but its confetti wilted under a chilled drizzle.

It was just as well, for Ernest had work to do. When the Liveright contract arrived, the cover letter said that "Up in Michigan" would have to be replaced, for it would only cause censorship problems. Did Ernest have another story he could fit in? He had a good one, "The Undefeated," which would have fit in between the bullfight vignettes, but that wasn't Ernest's plan. Nick and upper Michigan were the only structural elements holding the book together, the rest was thematic. If he took out the seduction of Liz Coates, he would be giving up one of the Michigan stories as well as one of the stories about men and women together. "The Undefeated" would replace none of those elements . He needed a Michigan story with Nick in it, a story as good as he could write. That took some thought.[2]

Loeb, who arrived in Cherbourg the same day Ernest arrived in Paris, dropped by with the latest gossip from New York, including the story of how he and Don Stewart kept pressure on Liveright to accept Hemingway's book. Ernest was grateful. Without friends like Loeb, where would he be? But Loeb's tale of the cuts made to his *Doodab* did not make Ernest feel better about Liveright's cutting his own manuscript. Harold brought with him a piece for *This Quarter*, which Ernest took to the printer the next day. Then, in the rain, he went round to Man Ray's studio to find a photo of Ezra for the magazine. Kiki, the most famous model of Montparnasse and Ray's live-in lover, was there looking less exotic than she might for a public appearance, but more dressed than she sometimes was in the studio. Visitors reported her strolling through the room oblivious and nude, but not in cold weather. In the evening at the Dôme, she could be seen at her table, stroking a pet white mouse chained to her wrist, "her olive pallor . . . heightened by a heavy coat of powder, her delicately hollowed cheeks . . . faintly rouged; a domino area of violet powder surrounds her penciled eyes, and her lips . . . the hue of black cherries."[3]

Man Ray wanted one hundred francs for his picture of Ezra, a bit over five dollars for a great photograph. If Ethel Moorhead could afford Walsh his romantic dying and a class magazine to boot, she could afford the photo. She could also afford to pay an assistant in Paris to do the work that Ernest was doing for free. In his letter he was quite explicit about the details of making plates, pulling proofs, harassing printers and running the production of a magazine. "You have to keep absolutely on the printer's tail," he told the editors, "not just in general – because a general publication date means nothing to them – but in detail. You have to get it in, get it set, get it corrected and recorrected! And then be on top to see at the last minute they don't make some adjustments of their own." He would be glad to read the final proofs for them. He would also be glad if they would give Bill Smith, who was arriving in April, a job. That was a good deal of his point, one that he brought up all too often in letters to the odd couple in Pau.[4]

As Hemingway began to search for a story to replace "Up in Michigan," the morning mail brought fresh news from that far country. An unexpected letter from his father told how Clarence had recently and quite by chance read "The Doctor and the Doctor's Wife." Impressed with Ernest's accurate details, Dr. Hemingway got out "the Old Bear Lake book and showed Carol and Leicester the photo of Nic Boulton and Billy Tabeshaw on the beach sawing the big old *beech* log. That

was when you were 12 years old and Carol was born that summer."
He did not need to tell his son who remembered it all quite clearly.
That summer he turned twelve and the next year his father turned
strange, gave up the Agassiz Club, quit taking the young boys to the
woods, gave away the stuffed specimens. That was the year the Doctor
took his first rest cure, alone in New Orleans, trying to get his nerves
under control. That was all a long time ago, and the Doctor's son did
not want to think about it.[5]

"Wish, dear boy," his father wrote, "you would send me some of
your work often." Ernest could not believe his father read the story
and missed the point of the fictional doctor's cowardly behavior. Or
did he see the point and not want to talk about it? What did he mean
calling it an "article"? It had never occurred to Ernest that the
transatlantic would make its way to Oak Park any more than he thought
the people at Horton Bay would ever read their names in his fiction.
"I've written a number of stories about the Michigan country," he told
his dad. "The country is always true – what happens in the story is
fiction." He was, he said, sure no one at home wanted to read his stuff
when the copies of *in our time* were returned to Paris. Then he added,

> You see I'm trying in all my stories to get the feeling of actual
> life – not to just depict life – or criticize it – but to actually make
> it alive. So that when you have read something by me you actually
> experience the thing. You can't do this without putting in the bad
> and the ugly as well as what is beautiful. Because if it is all
> beautiful you can't believe in it. Things aren't that way. It is only
> by showing both sides – 3 dimensions and if possible 4 that you
> can write the way I want to. So when you see anything of mine
> that you don't like remember that I'm sincere in doing it and that
> I'm working toward something.[6]

If he thought about it at all, Dr. Hemingway must have wondered what
his son was talking about. They had sent five books back, but kept
five. And there wasn't anything that ugly in the story. He could not
know that his son was preparing him for the shock of *In Our Time*.
And Ernest could not know that his father was less easily shocked and
more supportive than he supposed.

Turning from his letter home to his problem at hand, Hemingway
culled through manuscript fragments, looking for something he might
develop as a replacement for "Up in Michigan." He re-read the opening

lines of a Nick Adams story started in December: "Nick stood up. He was all right. He looked up the track at the lights of the caboose going out of sight around the curve." Nick on the road, away from home, riding freights in the Michigan night. But then what was going to happen to him? Ernest knew a story about a boxer long past his prime and punchy as hell. If he could bring Nick together with the boxer, the story would work. It would be educational for Nick, walking along the track through the tamarack swamp and then this really beat up boxer and his nigger companion. That was the word Hemingway used – nigger – the word of current choice among most people he knew and some he'd only heard about. Huck Finn used the same word forty years earlier and for the same reason: it was the word most in use by the society that raised him. It was also the word loud in the mouths of the Ku Klux Klanners who were spreading racial hate throughout the American Midwest and deep into the South. In 1921, Hemingway objected to Hadley's use of "nig" in her courtship letters, but that had nothing to do with his art which demanded he be true to his ear, to the sounds of his time. But the times were changing. When Ernest sent the story to Liveright, every use of "nigger" was turned to "negro," uncapitalized.[7]

It was a good story and Hemingway knew it, working it steadily through the last days of March. Ad Francis, the punchy boxer, was a scary article. "I'm crazy," he tells Nick. "Listen, you ever been crazy?" When Bugs, the Negro companion, arrives, Ad tells him that Nick has never been crazy. Bugs replies, "He's got a lot coming to him." That was it. A lot coming to him. Ernest had seen the way Krebs Friend acted at times, seen the crazy look in street faces, seen his own father behave strangely, changing moods so quickly it left Ernest empty and helpless. Ad Francis was like that, only worse. His face "was misshapen. His nose sunken, his eyes were slits, he had queer-shaped lips. . . . the man's face was queerly formed and mutilated. It was like putty in color. Dead looking in the fire light." That was the way it ended – the boxer who stayed too long in the ring until his brains were scrambled and one ear beaten off, leaving only a stub.[8]

When Ad got into an argument with Nick over his knife and started to take Nick apart, Bugs gently tapped Ad out with his blackjack. First Ad was friendly and talking, then turned mean so fast it was like two people there. Nick did not understand it. "What made him crazy?" he asked Bugs. There was no easy answer: too many beatings made him simple. Then his sister who managed him, not really his sister because they were married but some said his sister, she up and left, and "he just went crazy." She still sent enough money for Ad and Bugs to live on, but she was gone. Nick listened intently. It was a good lesson to learn. Before Ad regained consciousness, Nick took the sandwich Bugs made and moved out into the dark toward Mancelona.

When Hemingway finished the story, he knew it was good. No thinking, no conclusions, just Nick, the experience and walking away in the dark. The reader could figure it out. Maybe Liveright would like the hint of incest better than Liz Coates getting yenced on the boat dock up in Michigan. Dark things happened on that peninsula in Hemingway's imagination. Here was another story of a bitched marriage, this time driving the boxer/artist crazy. Years earlier before he knew Hadley, Ernest made some rough notes on an old Italian count who gave his formula for living beyond one hundred: "Don't marry. Don't live a family life. Don't eat or drink too much, don't fall in love – and – don't marry." Ad Francis, along with several other Hemingway characters, could have been used to illustrate the old count's point.[9]

As "The Battler" was coming to a close, Hemingway's Saturday mail produced another rejection as the *Dial* returned "The Undefeated." He sent it immediately to Ernest Walsh for the second issue of *This Quarter*, but continued rejection by American magazines was depressing. His mood was not bubbling when Hemingway put the signed Liveright contract back in the mail along with "The Battler" and a new table of contents, showing his revised arrangement of the stories. With the second story, "Up in Michigan," cut, he moved the following three stories up one position and slipped his new story into the fifth position without changing the sequence of the vignettes. Whatever relationship he once saw between sketches and following stories was arbitrarily changed, but the book was done. No more revisions. "If I at any time seem to repeat myself," he told Horace Liveright, "I have a good reason for doing so. . . . If cuts are made outside of possible necessary elimination of obscenities, if there are any, it will be shot to pieces as an organism." He had heard rumors that some editor wanted to eliminate parts that seemed to have nothing to do with the stories. "Probably," he said, "it was without foundation." The letter closed saying how pleased he was to be with the company and that he hoped to become a property, but that was up to both Liveright and himself. It was a cautious letter, filled with reservations and not a great deal of delight.[10]

If, when he returned his signed contract, Hemingway sounded less than enthusiastic, it was because he knew that he could have signed with Scribner's instead of Boni & Liveright. When he returned to Paris in March, Max Perkins' letter was waiting for him, a sore temptation. A telegram to New York could have cancelled the Liveright game, but Ernest felt committed. He had given his word, albeit a brief: "Delighted Accept." He might have used the excision of "Up in Michigan" as an excuse not to sign with Liveright, but his conscience would not let him. At the same time, he was angry with fate that kept Perkins' letter undelivered.

II

April in Paris began with the six-day bike races and ended with a new-found friend, Scott Fitzgerald and his strange wife, Zelda. In between there was the production of *This Quarter* and tennis games with Harold Loeb. Sometimes with Hadley, sometimes without her, Ernest was much on the boulevard, frequently in the Dôme, a young man about the Quarter loafing at his ease, doing everything but write the fiction his professional life depended upon. He was at Sylvia's one afternoon to listen to the new gramophone recording of Joyce reading a portion of *Ulysses*. Hearing the master's voice did not prick Ernest to his trade, for it was finally spring in Paris.[11]

Chestnuts blossomed in the Luxembourg, and suicides, a sure sign of the passing solstice, abounded. On Holy Saturday three depressed Parisians flung themselves into the Seine only to be rescued by spectators. Five days later an American medical man, suffering he thought from incurable angina, successfully cut his throat and bled to death in his hotel room. The next day twin sisters from Montparnasse, their wrists bound together, leapt into the Marne to drown. It was spring all right. Ford and Stella were back from the country, his new novel finished, he said. Ernest listened politely, his new novel not yet begun. That was a joke. He did not have the slightest idea for a novel. It had taken him six years to perfect his short-story form; how long would it take to learn the novel? That first week of April, Ernest was too busy watching the tactics of Brocco and MacNamarra in the bike races to worry about a novel. Ethel Moorhead's acceptance check for "The Undefeated" was large enough, he told her, to pay the rent, buy groceries, and tickets for the bike races. He and Hadley took enough wine and food to last them well into the night.[12]

Easter came warm and breezy and full of Ford, who popped into the Hemingway apartment unannounced as they were preparing a thank-you visit to Gertrude and Alice who had sent Bumby an elegant Easter egg. All three Fords arrived – himself, Stella and Jean Rhys – and, in Hadley's words, "stuck fast." "We were going driving in a fiacre," she wrote Gertrude in apology, "and wind up with you on the chance you'd not be in the country. When our fiacre man didn't turn up, Ford said, 'If he doesn't coooom, let us all take a taxi and drive in the Bois.' I wish you could have seen Hemingway! You can imagine him at any rate and it all happened just as planned by Ford. So that's why we didn't come Easter."[13]

The Wednesday following Easter, Hemingway finally made himself answer Max Perkins' letter. After explaining the delay in receiving Scribner's offer and his prior contract, he said Liveright had an option on his next two books. There was no way he could come to Scribner's unless Liveright should refuse to publish his next manuscript, thereby letting their option lapse. "You must know," he told Perkins, "how gladly I would have sent Charles Scribner's Sons the manuscript of the book that is to come out this fall." If he were ever in a position to approach another publisher, Scribner's would be the first to know. But there were only two books he wanted to write: one about bullfights and another volume of short stories. The novel seemed a worked out form, but as his stories were now getting longer, he might write a novel some day. The letter was not written by a happy man.[14]

One of the reasons for his unhappiness was his fiction stopped flowing. Although he managed to finish a version of "A Lack of Passion," little else was written between April and July. Instead he wrote thank-you letters. Thank you, Jane Heap, "You are a splendid woman to have kept after them to publish my book. Rest assured as we say that you have what I have dubbed my heartfelt thanks." Thank you, Don Stewart and Harold Loeb; thank you, John Dos Passos, "I never knew it was you trying to get the book over and did. . . . Christ knows I appreciate you and Sherwood jamming it through." Thank you, Sherwood Anderson, "I certainly do appreciate your having put my book over with Liveright." With so many friends pulling Horace Liveright's strings, Hemingway wondered if the quality of his fiction had anything to do with his contract.[15]

It was about this same time that Hemingway first met Scott Fitzgerald, whose early novel, *This Side of Paradise*, Ernest had read in Chicago. Fitzgerald, one of Scribner's prize authors, explained how his editor,

Max Perkins, became interested in Ernest. The previous October, not knowing Ernest but having read *in our time*, Fitzgerald wrote Perkins about "Ernest Hemminway," as he usually misspelled the name, who Scott thought was the real thing. Perhaps Hemingway and Fitzgerald first met at the Dingo American bar. That's how Ernest told it, and coming last, he could tell it his way. If not there, any of the Left Bank waterholes would have served as well. Where exactly was not important, but that they should meet was fundamental, for they complemented each other in strange ways. Both writers grew up in the Midwest, Scott with some money, Ernest with less. Each father failed his son's expectations; both mothers were strong, independent women. As high-school boys, neither was able to play football well enough for anyone to remember him. Both volunteered for the Great War, eager for something to happen. Scott, who got only as far as the troopship before the Armistice, always felt a bit guilty and a bit cheated that he'd missed front-line action. Ernest, at the front for less than a month, carried scars that Fitzgerald envied. After the war both quickly married women they wooed intensely by mail. Both writers created themselves in their own images, inventing destructive lives of epic proportions.[16]

Scott, with his delicate, blond features, handsome as a silent movie star, was that spring at the peak of his professional life. Ernest, rugged and darkly handsome, was only beginning his life as a writer. During the six years Hemingway spent learning to write short stories, Fitzgerald had published two best-selling novels and two collections of stories. In 1925, *Saturday Evening Post* paid Scott as much for a formula story as Hadley's diminished trust fund produced in a year. In 1924, the Fitzgeralds made and spent more money than the Hemingways lived on for their first five years. The two men appeared to be alter-egos: Scott, the overnight, precocious success; Ernest, the struggling artist, accepted only among the avant-garde. That year, despite good critical reviews, Scribner's could not sell out their 23,000 copies of *The Great Gatsby*; Scott hoped for at least 80,000 copies to pay off his debts and give him breathing room. In the fall when Boni & Liveright published Hemingway's *In Our Time*, they printed 1335 copies which satisfied reader demand for the next two years. Both wanted what the other had: Ernest wanted Scott's commercial sales; Scott wanted to write for the intellectuals. Both got what they wanted only to discover they had lost something in the process.[17]

As with so many of Hemingway's relationships, his friendship with Fitzgerald was brief but important. It was Scott who brought Hemingway to the attention of Max Perkins and Scott who always had time for literary advice. Disappointed with his *Gatsby* sales, Fitzgerald did not know he had passed his zenith on a curve heading down into professional and personal darkness. The party was almost over. Nor did Hemingway realize the approaching magnitude of his career whose curve was only beginning to move toward its peak. Hemingway was flattered with the attention paid him by Fitzgerald, who admired inordinately the physical and independent life Ernest led. All that May and June, they were frequently together, eating, drinking and talking the writing game. That spring and early summer the jokes were good, the laughter genuine, as each writer played to the other, an audience of one.

III

As his friendship with Fitzgerald opened, Hemingway's relations with Ernest Walsh and Ethel Moorhead began to close, damaged by Hemingway's pushing them too hard to hire Bill Smith. In Paris for the birthing of *This Quarter*, Walsh and Moorhead took the Hemingways to supper where Ernest talked enthusiastically about Bill who had only arrived in France the day before on the *Rochambeau*. As it turned out, Ernest talked too long and too hard about Smith's credentials and how no one, himself included, would do the job for free. Walsh became irritated with Hemingway's carping about his free work on the magazine. No one had asked Hemingway to do anything; he had volunteered. The evening ended unpleasantly with Walsh coughing up blood and with Hemingway feeling hurt. The next day he wrote Walsh a half apologetic, half angry letter:

> All right. Let it go at that. And don't worry about making me sensitive about accepting drinks because I don't panhandle so I'm not in the least sensitive. . . . I did worry a lot about your review, . . . But as you've explained that is none of my business. You seem suspicious that I'm just inventing some way to do you out of money. . . . Forget about the cost of wires, express, etc. I haven't kept any account. Buy a drink with it and drink to This Quarter.

There were other letters after that, but it was never the same. Bill Smith did not get his job, and eighteen months later Walsh hemorrhaged to death in the south of France.[18]

As spring burgeoned, Ernest tried to write a story about a revolution. The narrator, an outsider, tells us about seeing the plotters through the café window, but

> You could see them as easily and at greater leisure by going into the Rotonde and threading your way back through the long room full of tables to the alcove fronting on the Boulevard Raspail. You could not, however, get close enough to hear their talk for the two adjoining tables were occupied by the faithful.

It was the reporter's point of view: the fly on the wall. This fly, however, did not know enough about Spain or revolutions to carry the story off. He came back to it fifteen years later at the end of Spain's bloodiest revolution to write *For Whom the Bell Tolls*.[19]

That spring in Paris there were plenty of excuses for his fiction not working – interruptions, the weather, Walsh's magazine, Bill Smith – but the best reason of all was one for which he had no solution. He needed to write a novel, and he did not know how to do it. His only attempt at the form was the war novel begun in Chicago and stolen in Paris. In letters now he called the novel an artificial form, one that he might never pursue, but that was Ernest talking to himself. He knew at heart the next book had to be a novel. Doran told him in his rejection of *In Our Time*; Fitzgerald told him in the café: short story collections don't sell until you've made a reputation with a big book. How the hell do you start a novel?

Two and a half years after the train station theft of his unfinished novel, Hemingway returned to the war in Italy and his wounding, trying to reshape the lost material with tools developed for the short story. He talked about his war with Fitzgerald and also with Loeb – the big wound, the hospital in Milan, the nurse, her incredible body, nights together, and how she sent him home to jilt him. Tore him apart. Without the details of the wounding, this was the same story he'd told in three pages of "A Very Short Story." Always a fool for thwarted love, Scott listened, liked it and urged him on. Loeb was impressed: Ernest had suffered after all. Now all he had to do was start writing it, one word after another. First a verb. *Walking around the deck in the dark Nick passed the Polish officers in a row of deck chairs.* Nick was talking with the other men on the troop ship bound for France. Sure, he'd been with girls in whorehouses. Sure, he had a girl at home, engaged to her. She would have slept with him. They were going to get married. That was how the story began with the soldiers talking.

"It was a warm night in June" in the story but a cool spring morning in Paris. He worked with Gaby who was in the life boat with somebody. He did not know who. "Gaby was the only girl on the boat. She had blonde hair which was always coming down, a loud laugh, a good body, and a bad odor of some sort." But Gaby never got out of the life boat. Instead Nick and Leon talked about getting drunk, being scared and sleeping with women – the sort of stuff that young fictional soldiers are apt to discuss. Who has screwed the most women sort of talk. Who is still a virgin kind of questions. It came right out of evening camp fire bluster or Fitzgerald in the afternoon. One of the first questions he asked Ernest, as he asked many people that year, was had Ernest and Hadley slept together before their wedding.[20]

IV

Light snow fell across Paris, melting quickly but chilling the morning air on the first day of May. That was the month that Harold Stearns returned from a brief New York visit to report that despite his years in Paris he remained an American, but that he could never live there again happily. "Everybody was dissatisfied," he said, "everybody was hysterical."

> In New York nobody was happy, not even when a new case of gin was delivered. Everybody was hectic, making money furiously, working at the game of pretending to work, shameless and audacious in their heterogeneous love-making to a point where I, a quiet and respectable citizen of Paris, was actually embarrassed.[21]

Life in America, Stearns felt, was becoming too complicated and heartless. On rue Notre-Dame-des-Champs, Ernest's life was also becoming complicated, but not heartless. In fact complications of the heart made him unhappy and left the sentences dangling unfinished in his notebooks. That spring three new women – Zelda Fitzgerald, Pauline Pfeiffer and Duff Twysden – entered his life, changing it forever.

Zelda, for all her flirty southern charm and unpredictable behavior, was aging early, her face hardening and her eyes beginning to dull. Too many parties, too many drinks, too many nights without enough sleep were taking their toll on her looks and her nerves. The previous year, while Scott was working feverishly on *The Great Gatsby*, Zelda amused herself bewitching a French aviator and distracting Scott whenever possible. As Ernest watched her that spring, she seemed to confirm his worst fantasies about the destructiveness of wives. As she watched Ernest, he seemed an enormous fake, swearing too much and insisting too loudly on the beauty of killing bulls. Nobody, she thought, could be "as male as all that." Most women found Hemingway attractive, most men were drawn to Zelda, but together the two were bad chemistry from their first encounter. They met in the Fitzgeralds' expensive Right Bank apartment where the over-decorated stuffiness must have set off Hemingway's internal warning system: it was Oak Park revisited. Zelda was polite, Scott effusive, wanting so much to impress Hemingway that he trotted out his meticulous ledgers to show the year by year accounts of his writing and income.[22]

Forever after, Hemingway, first in private and later in his memoir, portrayed Fitzgerald as a talented writer who never understood his gift, a man with too much money and not enough confidence, a man driven to self-destruction by his wife. In 1950, when nothing he told strangers was to be trusted, Hemingway told Arthur Mizener that Zelda "was crazy all the time I knew them but not yet net-able. . . . Zelda really ruined Scott . . . she told him A.) That he had never given her physical satisfaction. B.) That it was because his sexual organ was too small." Ernest knew how to get in the counter-punches, knew well the most vulnerable spots. Maybe Zelda was crazy that first meeting in June, maybe not. Certainly Hemingway was becoming acutely attuned to mental problems, perhaps realizing that his own periodic ups and downs were not completely normal. Five years later Zelda was under treatment in Switzerland with a mind out of control, but before she came completely apart, she got to Hemingway at his softest point when she accused Scott and Ernest of having a homosexual affair. "Hawks," Hemingway said later of her, "Hawks do not share."[23]

Zelda Fitzgerald may have been crazy that year in Paris, but Pauline Pfeiffer was not. Independent, college-educated, rich and single, Pauline was having a wonderful time in Paris. Like so many of the women important in Hemingway's life, she came out of the Midwest with St. Louis connections, having attended a Catholic girls' school there. At the University of Missouri, where she majored in journalism, she became friends with Katherine Foster Smith, Katy of the green eyes. Small world, to become smaller still. In March, when Ernest and Hadley visited at Loeb's apartment, Pauline and her sister Jinny were there with Kitty Cannell. Small-boned and small-hipped, Pauline was a compelling woman in a boyish kind of way with close cropped hair and slim lines, looking much younger than the thirty she would turn in July. As an assistant working for the Paris *Vogue*, she not only knew her fashions, she wore them well. Her home town may have been Piggott, Arkansas, but she had worked on Cleveland and New York newspapers. She was well traveled and sophisticated without being a bore. Her Uncle Gus, part owner of the Richard Hudnut Corporation and New York City resident, was wealthy enough to keep a New England family compound, the "Old Homestead," and to keep Pauline's extraordinary bills paid. Not that she needed much help, for her own trust funds produced $3600 a year on top of her *Vogue* pay check. Some said Pauline was in Paris to find a husband; others said, to avoid marrying safely in New York. Pauline Pfeiffer looked over a lot of men that year, Hemingway and Harold Loeb included. She could afford to look them over carefully. Some called her spoiled, but no one ever called her stupid. What she wanted, Pauline usually got.[24]

Unimpressed with Pauline, Ernest said that Jinny was the prettier of the two sisters, not knowing that Jinny was more interested in women than men. Or maybe he did know. Like many men, Hemingway was attracted to lesbians. The stunning Margaret Anderson said that Ernest got so "gooey eyed" over her on first meeting, that she tried to avoid him in Paris. Jane Heap he treated as one of the boys; Janet Flanner, Sylvia Beach, Adrienne Monnier and Gertrude Stein were all his friends. If he thought Jinny the prettier of the two sisters, it was the safest response, for Jinny was not particularly interested in Hemingway. When Pauline returned the visit to the Hemingways' apartment, she found Ernest, sloppily dressed, expecting Hadley to do everything. Like Kitty Cannell before her, Pauline felt sorry for Hadley in her dowdy clothes. Ernest, unshaven and apparently uninterested, lay in bed reading, paying little attention to the women in the front room.[25]

If Zelda Fitzgerald irritated him and Pauline Pfeiffer did not interest him, it may have been because Duff Twysden entered his life that spring. Twice married, the last time to a British aristocrat, and twice divorced, Duff was a tall, slim, witty woman with a bawdy sense of humor and a great capacity for drink. Everyone remembered her grey eyes, but in the mid-to-late Twenties, grey eyes were everywhere. Some remembered her as a blonde. Loeb, who spent at least one week in bed with her, insisted her hair was brown. Her pictures are rare and not particularly stunning, not a face to turn a man's head more than a few degrees. Somewhere in England she had a son, and in Paris, she had her Scottish fiancé, Pat Guthrie, whom some thought her cousin. Usually broke, Duff Twysden used men like library books, checked them out, browsed through them and returned them late without paying the fine.[26]

George Seldes, working on the *Tribune* for small wages, never forgot the evening that Lady Twysden and Countess Modici invited him to join them at a Paris night club where they consumed several bottles of over-priced champagne. Late in the evening the two women excused themselves to the powder room and never returned. George, stuck with a fifty dollar tab (or was it forty-five), was neither the first nor the last American in Paris to pick up Duff's bill. Everyone remembered her throaty laugh, her ability to joke with the chaps, as she called everyone, and her legendary love life. Like most legends, it was mostly wistful thinking, but she created that sort of response in men whom she found generally eager to rescue her from her frequent financial crises.[27]

Duff Twysden's effect on Hemingway was instant and total. He brought her to the apartment where, like so many of the female visitors, she was charmed by his son and felt sorry for his wife. Like Kitty Cannell and Dossie Johnston, she gave Hadley dresses and other clothes. Duff was, in Hadley's words, "a man's woman, with delightful manners . . . and a great, broad sense of humor, and when she laughed, the whole of her went into that laughter." Her language was as broadly profane as Ernest's, a trait that endeared her to him. At late parties in the Quarter, he sometimes took Hadley home to disengage the babysitter and then returned alone to be with Duff. Eyes blinked. Was the Hemingway marriage going to come apart over this woman?[28]

Majority opinion says that Duff never let Ernest into her bed that spring or summer. Instead she used him to pick up bar tabs he could not afford, scrawling emergency messages:

> Please do come come at once to Jimmie's Bar – real trouble – Just rung up Parnass and find no word from you. S.O.S.   Duff[29]

She also used him as a foil to keep other men at a distance when that was desirable. At other times she surrounded herself with homosexuals, another perfectly safe way for an attractive woman to drink herself blind in the Quarter. When Hemingway told Loeb that Duff was joining them at Pamplona, he said, "As far as I know Duff is not bringing any fairies with her. You might arrange to have a local band of fairies meet her at the station carrying a daisy chain so that the transition from the quarter will not be too sudden."[30]

Listening to Duff's cadence and throaty lilt, Ernest made notes, trying to catch her voice on paper, for she was the stuff that stories were made of. A good many years have passed since Duff Twysden sat at the Select bar, turning heads on a spring evening. All we have of her now is a few soiled pictures, some late written memoirs from Quarterites, and this, her voice speaking.

"It is like living with fourteen men so no one will know there is some one you love."

"We can't do it. You can't hurt people. It's what we believe in place of God."

"I have to have it and I can't have what I want with you so I'm going to take this other thing."

"I have never been able to have anything I ever wanted."

"And I looked at you and I thought I wouldn't be able to stand it."

"What a shame he put the top thing down just as we came up."

"What are you so merry about? What were you so merry about the other day?"[31]

Maybe she said these things to Ernest or perhaps to someone else at the bar, but they sound too intimate for bar talk. Heard, overheard or invented, these fragments tell us something about Hemingway's relationship with Duff, which was more serious than friends realized or Hadley suspected. Duff was the married woman available for yencing without complications, or so he must have told himself. Only three months before he'd said: "Was I not married or was I married and not in love, I'd yence when yencing offered without entanglements."[32]

Years later Hadley said,

It was a very upsetting summer for me; I don't know why, because Ernest and I had not started to fall apart at that time. But everybody was drinking all the time, and everybody was having

290

affairs all the time. I found it sort of upsetting. [Duff was a] . . .
wonderfully attractive Englishwoman, a woman of the world with
no sexual inhibitions. . . . A lot of people thought Ernest had an
affair with Duff. He just adored her, but I'm sure they didn't have
an affair."[33]

That spring she was not so certain. Accustomed to Ernest's sexual
magnetism attracting women and equally accustomed to his need for a
small harem about him, she never doubted his fidelity, not since Chicago
days when there was a question of whether he would give up his local
girls to marry her. Then she asked him, "You don't have lots and lots
of 'infatuations' do you? What could I do if you did. Course if you do
I guess you can't help it." Maybe he could not help it in Chicago or
in Paris. Certainly he seemed to have no control of the situation, but
Hadley could have taken a less passive position on his "infatuations."
Not that it would have done much good, for she was watching the
onset of a behavior pattern that would haunt him all his life: an exciting
new woman apparently within reach and him with a wife in tow. Time
and again he would make his wife miserable with foolish and insulting
public behavior, trying to force her to set him free. It was the same
silly behavior that he first perfected on his mother the summer she
finally threw him out of Windemere cotttage. But Hadley was not
openly worried, not yet. Duff, whom Hadley liked and whose brass
she rather admired, assured her that she did not prey on husbands, and
Ernest probably had not shown his wife the letter to Bill about yencing
without consequences. Whatever the reasons, and there were many, that
Paris spring Ernest was distracted and less than attentive to his wife and
to his fiction.[34]

V

On May 11, Hemingway received a note from Max Perkins saying
rotten luck, remember us if ever the chance arises. Enclosed was a copy
of *in our time* to replace the one Ernest said he'd lost and could not
buy because it was sold out in Paris. A slight duplicity, for Sylvia Beach
was still selling copies in the fall of 1925. Feeling guilty about his lie,
Hemingway picked up a fresh copy at Shakespeare and Company which
he signed and sent to Perkins in June. From their cordial flow of letters,

it must have seemed to Hemingway that Max Perkins was more concerned about his future than was Horace Liveright. Hemingway wrote a huffy letter to Liveright wondering, six weeks after he'd signed their contract, where the hell his advance money was.[35]

On May 14, Liveright's letter arrived with the advance check, an apology, and the following:

> In one story, Mr. and Mrs. Eliot, I did my damndest to observe the sense without using some of your verbiage which would surely have made the book immediately suppressable. I suppose I've done a bad job. . . . galleys will be sent you very soon, and then you can change what I've done to suit yourself, bearing in mind, though, that it would be a pretty bad thing all around if your first book were brought into the court for obscenity.[36]

Ernest could just imagine what his story must look like. Goddamn editors rewriting his fiction. Stearns was right about America: no one could live there easily in repressive times.

About the same time the Liveright galleys arrived, Eugene Jolas reviewed *This Quarter*'s first issue, singling out Hemingway's "Big Two-Hearted River" for praise and adding that Hemingway

> told us recently that this story is the last of the cycle now under the press for fall publication . . . Hemingway always sees the object per se. Abstractions do not interest him. (We remember his joy, during a talk, when he noticed suddenly across the street the athletic ecstasy of a beautiful horse.)[37]

If Jolas could see the importance of the detail, why couldn't Horace Liveright take a chance on a few details? Reading through his galleys, Hemingway was disappointed. Liveright had so butchered the opening paragraph of "Mr. and Mrs. Elliot" that all its punch was gone, its rhythms ruined.

He sat down to repair the story as best he could. Apparently it was obscene in New York for a married couple to "try" to have a baby. The version first published by the *Little Review* began:

> Mr. and Mrs. Elliot tried very hard to have a baby. They tried as often as Mrs. Elliot could stand it. They tried in Boston after they

were married and they tried coming over on the boat. They did not try very often on the boat because Mrs. Elliot was quite sick.[38]

In Paris, that did not seem obscene. New York did not know what obscene meant. He should have given them real obscenity, maybe quoted some Shakespeare or Chaucer.

Nevertheless, he patched up his story as best he could, realizing that it was silly at this point to argue with Liveright. His revised opening now read:

Mr. and Mrs. Elliot tried very hard to have a baby. They were married in Boston and sailed for Europe on a boat. It was a very expensive boat and was supposed to get to Europe in six days. But on the boat Mrs. Elliot was quite sick.

He read it over slowly. It was shit. Stripped of its repetitions and bereft of babies, the opening lines sounded stupid and the essential humor of the story was dead. Oh brave publishers, oh lovely home of the brave publishers, where ladies may not "try" to have babies. But most amazingly no objections were raised to the ending: "Mrs. Elliot and the girl friend now slept together in the big medieval bed. They had many a good cry together." It was all right for a married lady to "sleep" with another woman so long as she did not "try" to have a baby. He told Liveright the story was still funny, but his heart was no longer in it. They'd cut his heart out of the story.[39]

The day after he returned the revised galleys, Hemingway wrote Sherwood Anderson, who had recently changed publishers from Heubsch to Boni & Liveright. It had been a long time between letters, and Anderson had seen the review of *A Story Teller's Story* in which Hemingway said the New York critics were responsible for Anderson's poorly written *Many Marriages*. Via Gertrude, Sherwood told Ernest that *Many Marriages* was a better book than he credited it. Ernest, a little chagrined that his own book might be reviewed by Sherwood, agreed, saying the problem was the paid critics, not writers like themselves. "Professional critics," he said, "make me sick; camp following eunuchs of literature. They won't even whore. They're all virtuous and sterile." His next book, he said, would contain a big part of the bullfights. Thanking Anderson doubly for helping push *In Our Time* with Liveright, Hemingway assured him that he and Hadley were "as fond of each other as ever and get along well."[40]

If his letter sounded less than sincere, it was because Hemingway was less than pleased with his Liveright relationship. First they cut "Up in Michigan," then they chopped up the Elliots and turned his "son of a bitch" into "bastard." Now they'd stolen Sherwood and his new novel for their fall list. Christ, what chance did he have against that competition. Loeb's book he could deal with, but not Sherwood, not if they weren't going to have more faith in his stuff.

VI

Then it was June, and Paris warmed quickly, absorbing record numbers of tourists uninterested in the Riffian war: French air planes and machine guns against native Moroccan cunning – the first guerrilla war of the century. Hemingway followed the news because war was his avocation to be studied at every opportunity. He was not as interested in the Catholic Holy Year, but it was irritating. Over three million tourists were flocking to Rome for special dispensations and religious events. It was the year the Pope canonized St. Teresa of the Little Flower and Bernadette of Lourdes – a good year for French virgins, but a bad summer to be on the road to Spain. The trains were already jammed with American pilgrims streaming southward from Paris. Back in the states a man named Scopes went on trial in Tennessee for mentioning Darwin's theory of evolution in the classroom, while the U.S. Coast Guard fought a losing war with rum-runners. It was the year the Charleston came to Paris with all its razzmatazz and exposed thighs. On both shores the jazz bands played on, and the dancers became the dance.

Depressed and angry with himself, Ernest moped, writing no fiction. Even his few letters turned terse and laconic. When the "Banal" issue of the *Little Review* appeared without his story in it, he wrote Jane Heap that he was pleased to see Amy Lowell declared officially dead, but he was a little hurt by his work's being cut without comment. "Listen, Jane," he told her, "while I appreciate your delicacy in keeping me out of such attractive company in the magazine was it because that piece you asked me to write wasn't considered good enough?" If that was the case she should tell him what was wrong with the story so he could fix it if he agreed with her. "Only for Christ sake don't be delicate."

Then he said that he was "all shot to hell inside and have lost 28 lbs.

in last 2 mos. Going down to Spain looking for something this month and if I find it do me a nice one like you did Amy Lowell." What Jane Heap had done for Amy Lowell was an obituary: Ernest was, for the first time since the summer of 1921, thinking about his own death. Was he serious, or was this merely looking for sympathy? If he had lost half the weight he claimed, he exhibited a major symptom of clinical depression. We also know he was not writing, sometimes for Hemingway another symptom of depression. After reading *The Great Gatsby* he buried "Along With Youth: A Novel" deep in his drawer of busted fiction never to be resurrected. Alongside Fitzgerald's poetry, Ernest's dialogue sounded childish, stilted and heavy handed.[41]

Wanting Duff and not being able to have her was depressing. Fitzgerald's talent was depressing. Liveright's revisions were doubly depressing. But these were symptoms, not causes. Ernest Hemingway needed no reasons to fall into despondency, for deep within himself he had all the genetic codes a man needed for depression. His symptoms and his behavior were the same ones that were already exaggerated in his father and which would push the Doctor to suicide before the decade was out. The worst part was that Ernest did not understand what was happening, for this was only the second or third time he'd fallen into the darkness of his mind. Hadley may have sensed a pattern, but there was nothing she could do to help; anything she said was wrong. It was frightening for both of them. Ernest did not know this was a cycle. He only knew that he could not write; there were no stories to tell. In his private midnight, he did not know if the stories would ever return. A few weeks earlier when the punchy boxer told Bugs that Nick had never been crazy, Bugs said, "He's got a lot coming to him."

On June 12, he and Hadley dressed up for Joan Miró's first one-man show at the Galerie Pierre. For a short time in a festive crowd, he could disguise the darkness within beneath a smiling face. Not that strange behavior would have attracted undue attention, for more than an art opening, the Miró exhibit was another public declaration by the French surrealists. Because Miró was now part of the surrealist revolt, card-carrying members were out in force. Hemingway's program was signed by Max Ernst, Louis Aragon and André Breton. (It must have been Hadley who asked for signatures. Even on his best day, one cannot imagine Ernest Hemingway asking anyone for his autograph, and this was far from his best day.)[42]

More important for Hemingway than the personages were the Miró paintings on the walls. Among them was "The Farm." Half way between cubism and surrealism, this large, detailed canvas captured for Hemingway the essence of rural Spain. Its muddy colors covered a farmscape strewn with objects become icons. If paintings had odors this one would smell of olive oil and garlic. It was a wonderful painting, one that Hemingway had long admired in Miró's studio, but, priced at 3500 francs, a painting he could not afford even at twenty francs to the dollar. So he bought it, putting down the next day a five hundred franc deposit with a promise to pay the remaining three thousand francs before October. Miró was delighted. The Galerie Pierre was delighted. Hadley was shocked. Ernest had promised to pay more for the painting than their normal month's expenses. He had Horace Liveright's $200 advance check in his pocket, but that was to pay for their summer in Spain. Without income other than her trust money, they would, in fact, be poor in Paris to pay for "The Farm," and she would wear last year's clothes to Pamplona. "Hadley's a perfect fool to take it," Kitty told Loeb. "Her clothes are falling off. She can't even show herself on the street. And it's her money." The exhibit catalogue said the painting belonged to Evan Shipman, who either had not yet paid for it or let Hemingway purchase it in his stead. Because the gallery bill was not completely settled until the end of September, Ernest called "The Farm" a birthday present for Hadley, but he bought it for himself. The purchase was one of those erratic, spontaneous acts of a depressed person, a momentary elation, artificial and unsustainable.[43]

When Ford Madox Ford tried to do Hemingway a favor by anthologizing Ernest's *transatlantic* stories, he did not anticipate Ernest's refusal, nor did he understand why his offer should depress the young man. Ford, who always had his next book in mind, would not have understood the emptiness of purpose Hemingway faced each day. With *In Our Time* finished, the emotional rush of its writing was gone, and Hemingway did not know what to write next. Finally he allowed Ford to reprint "The Doctor and the Doctor's Wife," but after his rejections from *Dial* magazine, Ernest resented the anthology being published by the Dial Press. To Horace Liveright, Hemingway wrote that it was better to let Ford have the story. "He dislikes me enough as it is," he said, "and it is only by a stern effort that he can like my work. I don't want him to stop making that effort." Only by reversing every element of his statement could Hemingway have approached the truth. Ford, long after Hemingway's worst insults, never ceased in his praise of Ernest's work.[44]

In truth, Ford's request was not really important to Hemingway except as an unpleasant reminder that he was not writing. However, the closer he came to departing for Pamplona, the better Ernest began to feel. Don Stewart, who had arrived from New York, was a welcome source of humor and a good companion for the fights. Earlier in the month, Ernest and Bill Smith watched Ledoux take a lesson from Kid Francis. The June 9th fight saw the ex-champion lose a twelve-round decision in a furious brawl with his younger opponent. The evening sustained Hemingway's view: champions never come back. Coming back and going back were, he knew, a fool's game. It was never the same when you got there. It was a lesson he learned in Italy and relearned periodically but never in time to prevent the disappointment.[45]

Everyone was leaving for Pamplona before Ernest and Hadley could slip out of town. Loeb left two weeks early without telling Ernest he was taking Duff Twysden to a coastal retreat at St. Jean-de-Luz. Loeb was as blinded as Hemingway by Duff's style and her casual, sensual approach to life; the only difference was that he had the money to act and no wife to inhibit him. Ernest did not know of their interlude, and Duff did not tell him when she returned to the Quarter alone, leaving Loeb at St. Jean. Hemingway wrote him there, saying that he would have Pauline Pfeiffer take care of Loeb's mail and what a swell time they would all have in Pamplona. Duff and Pat Guthrie were joining Loeb, Stewart, Bill Smith and the Hemingways for what was sure to be a memorable two weeks. He and Hadley, he said, had "been very tight and having a swell time. I haven't felt this good since we came back from Austria." Giving way to the prospect of fishing at Burguete and the bullfights of San Fermin, his depression was beginning to lift.[46]

The day before Hemingway's letter arrived, Loeb received the same news from Duff: "I am coming on the Pamplona trip with Hem and your lot. Can you bear it? With Pat of course. . . . I'm dying to come and feel that even seeing and being able to talk to you will be better than nothing." She was wrong about that. Not seeing her in Pamplona would have been much better for her brief lover. During the week of the bullfights, Harold Loeb lost Duff Twysden, lost Hemingway and lost his identity as he was transformed forever into a character of fiction, a rich Jew named Robert Cohn.[47]

Chapter Fifteen

SUMMER OF THE SUN
SUMMER, 1925

I

As soon as they crossed the border into Spain, time collapsed. In Paris one day methodically followed another. In Pamplona and Burguete, time twisted and days became interwoven and inseparable. There are few surviving documents: two letters, a couple of fishing licenses and some faded tickets to the bullfights. No one kept a diary, and no one forgot. Years later Don Stewart and Bill Smith remembered much of it clearly but differently. Almost thirty years after the last glass of Fundador, Harold Loeb wrote it down about Paris before and what happened at San Fermin. He got the dates wrong, not carelessly but sincerely, the way he remembered it. Memory is another country where an erratic compass does not matter, and the map scale is never stated.

There was something about that Pamplona summer that turned everyone's memory into a work of fiction. It began with Kitty Cannell. A week before the gang left for Spain, she and Bob McAlmon went by the Hemingways' flat to visit. McAlmon said, "I'm thinking of taking Kitty with me to Pamplona next week." That's when Ernest "turned a terrifying purple," Kitty said. "He lunged toward me, seized a lighted lamp from the table at my elbow and hurled it through the window into the yard piled high with boards and kindling." That's what she said forty-three years later. Sounds convincing until confronted with the calendar and a few facts.[1]

First, and by Cannell's own admission, there was no electricity in the Hemingway flat. Thus the lighted lamp must have been either coal oil or candle. Would Ernest have thrown a burning bomb into the woodyard below his own apartment? If he had, would not there have been some immediate consequences? Kitty doesn't mention any, and for good reason: she and McAlmon were both in London that week. At least that's what Hemingway's June 21 letter to Loeb said: "Bob McAlmon writes about going to the theater with Kitty in London." History becomes a quandary of bent memories and loose facts, iron filings on a white page that any magnet can rearrange.[2]

The confusion does not improve after the players reached Spain. Starting with the only benchmark available, we have Hemingway's letter to Fitzgerald written at Burguete and dated July 1. He says they've been fishing and are going into Pamplona early the next morning. The country, he told Scott, was wonderful and letters were "a swell way to keep from working and yet feel you've done something." Probably he did write that letter to Scott on July 1, but if he did, then we must play loose with calendar time.

We know that the Hemingway party left Paris the morning of June 25. On Saturday, June 27, Bill Smith bought a fishing license in Pamplona. For Ernest, Hadley and Bill Smith to have been fishing on the Irati by July 1, they must have gone to Burguete on June 28, which would have given them two days in which to fish before Ernest wrote his letter to Scott. The Irati river was a long hike from the inn at Burguete: starting early and returning late they could have made it in one day. However, the previous year Ernest had talked about hiking in to the river and camping out overnight. The calendar fits: they could have hiked in on June 29 and returned the next day, June 30, allowing Ernest to say on July 1 they had been fishing. It all fits nicely except for one small detail: Ernest Hemingway's fishing license purchased in Pamplona on June 30, 1925, the day before he wrote the letter to Fitzgerald. A date on a fishing license can be winked away: some clerk made a simple mistake, that's all. But wink as we will and sweep as we might, anomalies pile up beneath the pattern in the carpet until visitors notice their bulging presence and ask embarrassing questions. What happened that summer at Pamplona is multiple, self-contradictory and unknowable in absolute terms. But it did happen, and lives were changed.[3]

II

On the Irati, fishing was terrible. In the same pools where the summer before Hadley pulled out six fat trout, they all came up empty. Afterwards, Ernest told Gertrude that the stream was "ruined by logging and running logs down – all the pools cleaned out – trout dead." Years later Loeb remembered something about a reservoir's construction ruining the trout stream, but he was in St. Jean-de-Luz with Pat Guthrie and Duff and never saw the river. Hadley said, "What I remember as the prime cause of disturbed fishing conditions was the presence of rather rough-looking men in the beautiful stream, who cheated by standing in the water back of a large rock, then encircling the rock under water with arms and hands and pulling out the fish in that unsportsman-like fashion." Bill Smith remembered the country and fishing McGinty's and Yellow Sallies, worms and grasshoppers in the Rio della Fabrica and a larger river whose name he could not recall. Maybe that was the Pamplona summer. One fishing trip blends into another, he said. Don Stewart remembered nothing at all. The Pamplona whorehouse he remembered, but not the river.[4]

The fishing was poor, but Ernest was undaunted. His depression was lifting there in the high country among the beech forests of Roland. The simple food combined with the good humor of Smith and Stewart made a man feel whole again. For the first time in several weeks, his laughter was unforced, his own humor returning. It was not like turning on a light, not that quick. It was like a fog slowly lifting, dispersing, leaving patches in dank alleys, but still lifting. It was good to be drinking with the men again. On July 2 the fishing party took the rackety bus down the foothills to Pamplona to be at the station in time to meet the three stragglers coming in from St. Jean.

No one is certain when Ernest discovered that Duff had taken Loeb to bed. Loeb said only two people in the Quarter knew: Jimmy the barman and Flossie Martin, as if they could keep secrets. Maybe they did, but by the time the gang gathered in Pamplona, it was obvious to everyone that Loeb and Pat Guthrie were barely civil in Duff's presence. It was also obvious to all, including Hadley, that Ernest was treating Duff as if she belonged to him. She didn't, but Duff was in an uncomfortable situation. Not understanding the depth of Loeb's romantic soul, she had no idea he would behave like a love-sick loon in front of the chaps. Pat was miffed; Ernest felt betrayed; and Duff used them both to keep Harold at a distance. Hadley went to bed early, complaining of a headache. Usually the San Fermin poster featured bulls chasing runners up the street or blue-shirted musicians. But that summer, the poster ironically focused on a beautiful woman in a long blue dress with black lace and a black mantilla.[5]

The week was as insane as always, noisy, hot and strange. Drinking fraternities led outrageous, tipsy parades through the streets; some weaving about wearing huge heads of strange characters, others smirked behind stove-blacked faces and carnival noses. Always there was something happening, something rare, ribald and loud. On Thursday after the *Prueba*, a Spanish aviator performed stunts over the old fortress, looping, diving, thrilling the crowd. Then a parachute opened and his co-pilot came down in a billow of silk. The next night on the plaza, illuminated balloons rose into the sky laden with fireworks, and a mock battle was staged between a fortress and several ships while cornets and drums sounded. Early and late, brassy music played in the streets, and wine flowed as it had the year before.[6]

Pat bought a goatskin bota which he kept filled with rioja, and they all took turns squirting the wine into their throats. But Guthrie was a certified drunk, Duff not far behind him. Keeping up with those two required great capacity, particularly when they began ordering absinthe. No wonder the fiesta blurred for Don and Bill, later unable to tell one day from another. Stewart complained that too many English and Americans were there that summer. "My God," he said, "even the American ambassador was there in a big car. Things got cluttered and ordinary. I remember lining up with Pat Guthrie in front of a whore house and waiting an hour or so and then the whole thing being over in five minutes." But when it was suggested that Pat Guthrie "may have been some kind of latent homosexual," Stewart quickly allowed that maybe it was someone else waiting with him at the brothel. "These details," he explained, "get a bit fuzzy . . . You can't always tell about homos. Pat seemed a nice enough fellow for a drunk." But that was many Hollywood years and several brothels later when Stewart was able to entertain the idea that Hemingway might have been some kind of a homosexual as well. "Of course he did have these three sons which . . . is quite a lot for a pretender." For a man who once let a Pamplona cow crack his ribs, Don Stewart spent a lot of time worrying about homosexuality, which was hardly the problem that summer. Duff Twysden never had trouble with homosexuals.[7]

301

If Stewart, in fact, found a brothel in Pamplona that summer, the one person who was not with him was Harold Loeb. Harold was different, never getting truly drunk and always a little defensive for good reason. He understood Pat Guthrie's anger, but why was Ernest turning on him and making such mean remarks? Someone suggested that Harold might, if he were a gentleman, think of leaving Pamplona. Someone was wrong. Loeb was too much of an old-school gentleman to leave a woman in what might be distress. Duff's only problem was having two grown men behave like school boys in the presence of her fiancé. Duff Twysden, thirty-three years old and holding, was neither as confident nor as promiscuous as many thought her. What passed for confidence was frequently an alcoholic haze through which nothing touched her deeply. As for lovers, she had two husbands properly married and divorced; she had Pat Guthrie and a week with Harold. After that she married a Texas artist and lived out her brief remaining years without fanfare. There were lots of women in the Quarter who slept with more men than that in a single year, but Duff's flair for the dramatic made her appear more available than she ever was.[8]

As for Harold, she could not shake him, in fact, did not want to shake him. The week at St. Jean was past but not unpleasantly remembered. She told him things were over between them but she did not tell him to leave. So Loeb stayed on, love-sick and wallowing in his humiliation, for at every chance Pat Guthrie was making some needling remark. "Harold had a little genius," Hadley remarked, "for making a fool of himself. The other boys were rough and tough, and would catch him at these things." Each time Loeb looked at Duff, she looked away. To make matters worse, Loeb became that summer's darling when after challenging a young cow he somehow ended up seated between her horns to be carried about the sandy arena long enough for photographers to get their shots. Harold's brief moment in the bull ring combined with his knowing remarks about Duff to infuriate Hemingway.[9]

That a mean streak ran through Hemingway's character was no secret. Everyone who spent time with him in the Quarter saw it sooner or later. Loeb knew about it. He'd seen Ernest at the Select say really terrible things to strangers, but never to close friends like himself. That summer in Pamplona, Ernest made Loeb feel like a rich Jew who did not belong at the party. It was as if they had never shared a meal, played tennis, read each other's work or laughed together. It was as if Harold had no part in the Liveright contract. Stewart remembered the viciousness quite well. "The mean streak was a booby trap kind of thing. There's no explaining it. . . . he wasn't mean; he was charismatic; and it was for this very reason that the mean streak startled you so when it came to the surface. . . . he didn't have to have a reason to be mean. It was more of a mood thing."[10]

It was the same startling mood change of his father's that scared Ernest as a boy. It could take place in a moment's turn, the change over which he had little or no control, the bitter remark to be regretted later. That summer at San Fermin, Ernest was vulnerable. He felt sexually betrayed by Duff but at the same time knew he had no claim on her affections. Suppressing his anger and his desire, he continued to bend to her least wish, tutoring her on the bullfight's ritual and rhythms. Quite illogically, his anger turned on Harold Loeb. There were flimsy reasons, but Ernest needed no reason. Harold having taken Duff to bed when Ernest got only her sexy asides leaving him uncomfortable and unrequited was reason enough. Surfacing after a depressed period in which his writing failed him, Hemingway was mood tender and needed much coddling in Pamplona. Hadley, recognizing the signs but not the underlying cause, retreated, pulling into her protective shell. Duff, not understanding the game, played it anyway, half drunk, letting Ernest make as much a fool of himself as Loeb did. Pat Guthrie stayed drunk while Bill and Don, perplexed by Ernest's behavior toward Duff, tried to pretend it was not happening.

But it was happening. Once raised, Hemingway's mean mood did not subside quickly. The Pamplona madness seemed only to make it worse. Nothing – not fireworks, street dancers, brandy nor singing – nothing diverted his fixation on Duff and Loeb. Part of him wanted Duff to himself with the same instinct that governed a male lion's rights over his pride of females. That was part of it. Another part with Loeb was his hang-dog, long-suffering face, taking insults from Guthrie like a martyr taking well-placed arrows. Ernest would have respected him more if Harold had smacked Guthrie in the mouth.

Not even the spectacular performance of Niño de la Palma in the bull ring took Hemingway's mind off the matter for long. Born Cayetano Ordoñez, Niño was a young matador on his way up, fighting in the same ring with the famous Belmonte, now past his prime: two artists in the ring together – the older one with stylized moves patented in his name, doing nothing he had not done a thousand times before; the young one, surprising everyone, deft, cocky and very good. On the opening day, July 7, Niño did graceful, effortless things moving the bulls to his cape work with all the flow of a concert piece. On the last day, when he was awarded an ear, he gave it to Hadley, for Ernest had, in his broken Spanish, cultivated the young man all week. The fights were not uniformly excellent. The second fight on July 8 was called "extremely boring" by local observers; the *Prueba* was only ordinary. On Friday, July 10, there were no fights, and rain fell on the art festival in the plaza. But Saturday and Sunday gave *aficionados* their full money's worth.[11]

Loeb, unfortunately, did not much care about the bullfight as a work of art. Certainly he saw the grace of the matador, but his sympathies lay too often with the bull, and the messiness of the gored horses turned his head away. The bull's death seemed to him only shameful. The ritual, with its opening half-comic pomp and its closing blood, was interesting but not something to become religious about the way Ernest demanded. Ernest was a different man in Spain, a man Loeb never met in Paris. In Pamplona he became Spanish, wearing his black Basque boina and speaking as an insider with Quintana, the manager and owner of their hotel on the plaza. Loeb stayed Loeb, refusing to pretend to what he did not feel and irritating Ernest even more.[12]

As Loeb remembered it, the final break came after watching Niño and the famous Juan Belmonte perform brilliantly in the arena. After their evening hotel meal, the group moved to the plaza for after-dinner brandies. It was late on the sixth day of the fiesta. Nerves lay bare like frayed electric lines, as the male jousting recommenced. Pat said something to Loeb; Harold replied in kind. Bill and Don tried to look interested in the passing scene. Soon fireworks began to explode on the plaza, raining burning embers down on the milling throng. But nothing could interrupt the ugly conversation. Finally Ernest told Loeb to leave Pat alone. "You've already done enough to spoil this party," he said. Loeb did not reply. Pat, a little drunk as ever, agreed with Hemingway: "I don't want you here. Hem doesn't want you here. Nobody wants you here. . . . Get out!" Loeb turned to Duff. "I will," he said, "the instant Duff wants it." Duff quit pretending to talk to Hadley and said she did not want Harold to go. Ernest exploded. "You lousy bastard, running to a woman." That snapped the last thread keeping Loeb in check. Despite his smaller size, he challenged Hemingway to step down the alley with him to settle the matter. Once there, both tempers cooled, and they saw the comedy of their small-boy blustering. Ernest, grinning, offered to hold Harold's jacket; Loeb said only if he could hold Ernest's.

The fight was over, and both men laughed as they walked back to the party together.[13]

That's how Loeb remembered it, with himself as the victim and the chaps carping at him in front of Duff. The next day only Bill and Don were speaking to Harold as they went to the last and best bullfight of the fiesta. Niño de la Palma performed brilliantly, killing three Pablo Romero bulls and delighting the crowd with his grace. That night in his room, Hemingway wrote Loeb a note and left it for Harold to find in his box the next morning before leaving Pamplona.

Dear Harold,

I was terribly tight and nasty to you last night and I dont want you to go away with that nasty insulting lousiness as the last thing of the fiestas. I wish I could wipe out all the mean-ness and I suppose I cant but this is to let you know that I'm thoroly ashamed of the way I acted and the stinking, unjust uncalled for things I said.

So long and good luck to you and I hope we'll see you soon and well.

Yours, Ernest[14]

It was neither his first nor last letter of apology. If, at times, he lost control, he also had a keen and well-honed sense of remorse after behaving badly. As a child Ernest apologized in writing to his father for behavior at a church function; to Walsh, he sent a next-day retraction on his biographic note unnecessarily attacking Ford. Occasionally he caught himself in time; in his correspondence one finds incredible statements in unmailed letters – one a single, typed, page-long curse. That summer in Pamplona he was, at points, out of control, unable to keep his tongue in check.

On Monday morning, July 13, the players departed Pamplona, but not before one final unpleasantness. When the hotel bill arrived, Duff and Pat were completely broke, having come to Pamplona confident someone would pick up their tab. It was embarrassing, not to Pat or Duff, accustomed to using the money of others, but to the others. Don Stewart, always a soft touch, lent them money he would never see again. Don, Harold and Bill took the train for the coast and back to Paris; Pat and Duff disappeared with them. Ernest and Hadley went south to Madrid for another month of bullfights. Nothing turned out as Hemingway planned it, but as his train chugged across the open grasslands, the "lousy" feeling began to lift. In their compartment was a young man from Tafalla taking wine samples to Madrid which he began to open and share with his fellow travelers. By the time they reached the capital city, Ernest, Hadley, two priests, four *Guardia Civil* and one young man from Tafalla were pleasantly drunk, the sample jugs empty.[15]

III

In the early afternoon Madrid was quiet, no blaring bands or rowdy friends, only a few street noises coming through the heavy shutters. There, for the first time in almost four months, Hemingway began once more to write. Getting page proofs for *In Our Time* helped, because reading stories he could not remember writing gave him an emotional lift. Now the words returned to him, and Hadley was happy to have her husband back from whatever strange country he'd gone to when she was not looking. With the bad taste of Pamplona still in her mouth, she remembered too clearly his treatment of Harold Loeb and the moony way he looked at Duff Twysden. Undiscussed but unforgotten, the week of San Fermin lay there in the bed between them still as Ernest began to turn it into fiction.

The story began:

> I saw him for the first time in his room in the Hotel Quintana in Pamplona. We met Quintana on the stairs as Bill and I were comeing up to the room to get the wine bag to take to the bull fight. "Come on," said Quintana. "Would you like to meet Niño de la Palma?"[16]

Using real names, he was not sure where the story was headed, but the tensions of the previous week were there to be used. Belmonte's hemorrhoids and jutting jaw were in it; the American ambassador's sexy wife was there on the plaza trying to make the oldest kind of connection with Niño, but "Hem," the narrator, wouldn't deliver the message. He knew her like a book: "She took the husband she's got now away from his wife," he told Quintana.

The narrator is torn between two compulsions: his love of bullfighting and his desire to please Duff, who also wants to meet Niño. Finally in the dining room Quintana comes in to see "Niño with a big glass of cognac in his hand, laughing, between me and two women, one with bare shoulders and a table full of drunks. He did not even nod. All of a sudden I realized how funny it was." Only it wasn't funny, not at all. Maybe that was when the story jelled for him. He could almost see it: the Paris crowd comes to Pamplona and corrupts the young bullfighter with their Left Bank values. Duff seduces him, twisting him as she twisted Pat, Loeb and Ernest himself. In Madrid he wrote late mornings and early afternoons before going to the bullfights. The loose pages piled up slowly at first, then faster without obvious direction. "Well," the narrator tells us, "none of that has anything to do with the story and I suppose you think there isn't any story anyway but it sort of moves along in time. . . " Maybe he still thought of it as a story, but it was not going to be a short one.[17]

On his birthday, July 21, Ernest and Hadley followed the bullfight circuit to Valencia, but before packing his bags, he turned back to his first loose sheet of manuscript and wrote across the top:

Cayetano Ordonez
"Nino de la Palma"

Naming the story was his birthday present to himself. Once he put those words on paper, whatever remained of his depression vanished and he entered into the manic country of the truly blessed, the ecstatic high regions where he had been before but only for short visits. This cycle, which would last through the fall and into the winter, produced two books and three new stories in twenty weeks.

There was a great beach at Valencia, he wrote Bill Smith, where "the water is warm as pissing down your leg. Not your leg necessarily, anybody's leg. . . . I work from lunch until the bullfight starts. The story is fairly funny. Have Ford in it as Braddocks. The Master goes well as Braddocks." All the characters were going well, but most with new names. As soon as he saw what he was writing, Ernest knew he could not use real names, nor could he use all the people from Pamplona. Hadley disappeared completely; Bill Smith and Don Stewart melded into Bill Gorton. Pat Guthrie changed to Mike Campbell; Loeb to Gerald and then Robert Cohn, while Duff stayed Duff until the end of the first draft. The most significant change was the disappearance of "Hem" who metamorphosed into a new narrator, Jake Barnes.[18]

Jake was a newspaper man part of whose background belonged to

Bill Bird. Bill wouldn't mind. Jake was also a war veteran, an American aviator wounded while flying in Italy. A simple wound actually, small but effective: he'd lost his penis. We don't know how. In Hemingway's Milan hospital, some U.S. Navy pilots from Rimini were bedded down with wounds. Maybe he got the idea from them. It was an old pilot's joke: having the "joy stick" between one's legs change him into a soprano on crashing. Jake's problem was different: his testicles were intact, his penis missing. "What happened to me is supposed to be funny," Jake tells us in manuscript. "Scott Fitzgerald told me once it couldn't be treated except as a humorous subject."[19]

Apparently Ernest discussed the concept with Scott sometime in the spring, but it was not a new idea for Hemingway. In Chicago right after the war, he had discussed the maimed soldier story with a high-school friend, and the summer of 1924 he and Chink Dorman-Smith talked it over, remembering war wounds they'd seen and joking about others. At some point while writing it, Ernest told Chink a good deal about the book, for in December of 1925 Dorman-Smith wrote from England, "anxious to hear how the summer's book worked out. Having presided at a portion of its gestation I have kindly feeling for it quite apart from its originality. It's a damn queer theme when all is said and done. Damn queer. There is something attic about it. It would not take a great deal of effort to turn Pamplona to Olympus and the protagonists of your tale to the Gods who were equally lax in an equally masterless and regardless of consequences manner."[20]

In Valencia, Hemingway moved from the loose sheets of manuscript, now on page 37, into the blue notebooks he'd brought with him from Paris. He numbered the first page 38 and continued with what he thought was going to be a book about the bullfighter as his working title indicated. Without his completely realizing it, a number of ideas were coming together almost of their own accord. Harold Stearns' fabled but unwritten book about the different Latin Quarter types became part of the first six chapters. Hemingway put in the "fairies" and Flossie Martin's vulgar mouth. The reader, he said, had to understand about the Quarter to appreciate what happened in Pamplona, and he was going to put it all in, particularly the contempt. "There is a woman painter who has had seven abortions in the last year and she has great contempt, concealed in pity of course, for the wife of another painter who has had five miscarriages in an attempt to have a baby." Those who worked held those who did not in contempt; critics were contemptuous of writers, writers of critics. Later he had to take it out.

but on first draft all of his Oak Park revulsion with bohemian pretense boiled over, as it had when he first arrived in Paris. It was different now, for he had become a part of the Quarter, one of its local heroes. Some of the contempt of which he wrote so convincingly was self-contempt.[21]

It was tough keeping himself out of the story. Jake Barnes was like Nick, a day-dream of what might have been, a man with some of Hemingway's own problems but acted out in different ways. He tried to let Jake tell the story, but at the beginning, before he understood his narrator, Ernest kept intruding into the fiction with discursive asides, interrupting the narrative flow. At one point, he wrote:

> Now when my friends read this they will say it is awful. Gertrude Stein once told me that remarks are not literature. All right, let it go at that. Only this time all the remarks are going in and if it is not literature who claimed it was anyway.[22]

Statements like that came out later, for Jake Barnes was not the sort of person who visited Gertrude Stein's. Writing, as he was, on a euphoric, emotional high, Hemingway sometimes became Jake Barnes while the words were going down on the paper. Jake was a fictional ego, a man who lived without complications – no wife, no kid, no cat – a passive, laconic man to whom things happened. Jake could speak fluent Spanish, which gave him an edge on everyone, including Hemingway who relied mostly on English and his little French to get by. The more Ernest found out about Jake, the better he liked him, and each day he was living in the book as he had with Nick on the river.

IV

In Valencia, nothing got between Ernest and his fiction. In the mornings he and Hadley swam, enjoying the beach, but part of his mind kept the story going. For eleven days he wrote steadily, the black ink stain on his fingers a sign of his progress. While pages in the exercise book filled up, there was no time for letters. On August 3, when he reached the end of the first notebook, he wrote Sylvia what a swell trip they'd had: great bullfights and good weather. "I've written," he said, "six chapters on a novel and am going great about 15000 words done already." There it was on paper: "a novel." That's what he was writing.

He was sure of it now, certain enough to tell Sylvia who would tell everyone who came into the shop: Hemingway is in Spain writing a novel. He could see it all quite clearly.[23]

Shortly after writing Sylvia, he went back to the opening page of the loose manuscript and revised the statement at the top of the page:

Cayetano Ordonez
Nino de la Palma

Fiesta

A Novel

He still did not know precisely where the story was leading, but that did not matter. It was better not to know. If he knew everything about the story, it would be dead for him. This way each day was an adventure into the other country where he could be with Jake, watching him make his way through the Quarter with an ironic detachment.

Before leaving Valencia, he got all the characters but Niño set up: Duff, Cohn, Jake, Bill Gorton, Mike Campbell. He also got a couple of the Quarterites fixed to his page like rare specimens. He changed Ford and Stella Bowen into the bumbling Braddocks who could not recognize a whore when they met one. First, he let Jake pick up a *poule* for supper conversation and then take her to one of Ford's *bal musette* parties where he introduced her as Georgette Leblanc. It was Jake's joke. Georgette Leblanc was a singer and the loving friend for whom Margaret Anderson had left Jane Heap. Even better, no one at the *dancing* got the joke, only the reader.

Then Duff arrived in the company of homosexuals, which did not surprise Hemingway's Left Bank readers who recognized the *bal musette* in rue de la Montagne Sainte Geneviève as a homosexual bar. Hemingway had cut out most of Jake's remarks about the "fairies" who flitted about the Quarter in swarms, but this part would stand up. Taking in the white hands and wavy hair of Brett's entourage, the policeman at the door smiled at Jake: there was no need to say anything. And "with them was Duff." Inside, the two men immediately spotted Georgette.

"I do declare. There is an actual harlot. I'm going to dance with her, Lett. You watch me."

"The tall dark one called Lett said: "Now don't you be rash.""

That was enough: readers in the Quarter would recognize Arthur Lett-Haines, lover of Cedric Morris the painter, and Ernest's neighbors on

Notre-Dame-des-Champs. Jake arrived by taxi with a whore; Duff by taxi with homosexuals. Duff and Jake departed together by taxi, leaving the white-handed young man with wavy hair dancing with the *poule*.[24]

V

From Valencia they went back to Madrid for three days and then took the long train ride to San Sebastián and Hendaye on the border. The surf was weak, the sun bright, the living easy in cheap pensions. And every day he wrote. Nothing kept him from his time with Jake, not even a passing fever. On August 11, Hadley returned to Paris, leaving Ernest alone with his blue notebooks. Their summer sublet was over, and Marie and Bumby were back in Paris from Brittany. Hadley had not seen her child for six weeks, and she missed him. Ernest arranged by cable for Bill Smith to meet her at the station. With almost eleven chapters on paper, Hemingway wanted to write in solitude as long as he could afford it.[25]

He also needed time to digest the dustjacket for *In Our Time*, which, along with the Boni & Liveright fall catalogue, caught up with him at Hendaye. He looked at it a long time, put it away, trying not to let it get between him and Jake. It was no good. He took it out again. What the hell were they doing to him? There was the title in the middle of the jacket and his name, but the color was awful. Surrounding the title to the point where his name seemed irrelevant were blurbs by Dos Passos, Edward O'Brien, Waldo Frank and Gilbert Seldes for Christsake. Seldes was the sonofabitch who turned down his stuff at the *Dial* and now he's saying what a great story teller this Hemingway fellow is. Open it up and there is Sherwood saying the same thing on the flap. "They've got all my friends [on it]," he said, "and all my enemies, Seldes, Frank and the other bright Jews. God knows where they got them." The jacket told Hemingway that Liveright did not have much faith in his book, or they would have let it ride on its own merits. First it took half the literary men in New York to get *In Our Time* accepted and now they put the other half on the jacket with him.[26]

At Hendaye, despite the dustjacket, Hemingway filled up fifty pages of his third notebook in seven days. His writing was going smoothly, but not his sleep. Without Hadley beside him, the old problem of night fears and bad dreams returned. Some nights he wrote himself to exhaustion; others he woke in darkness and picked up his pen. He told Gertrude, "It certainly is funny how your head, I mean my head, can go most of the time like a frozen cabbage and then it can give you hell when it starts going. Have been so pleased to find it still functions." That's as close as he cared to describe the way his mind was racing faster than he could get the words down on paper.[27]

Maybe the money gave out, or maybe he was tired of not sleeping well; whatever the reason, on August 18, he, too, returned to Paris, where summer's madness had not yet abated. In the Bois de Boulogne, police, park attendants and soldiers of fortune, armed and scared, were tracking down an escaped Abyssinian leopard; while in French Morocco, his acquaintance from Constantinople, Charles Sweeney, was leading two squadrons of American bomber pilots against the Riffian rebels. With the franc fallen to twenty-one to the dollar, his landlord, M. Chautard, was threatening to raise his rent. Bumby wanted attention. Friends wanted favors. The days ran hot and muggy, and tourists filled the cafés. But none of it touched him. He lived in the book, making it up each day.[28]

It was a little difficult to eat supper with Bill Smith after being with Bill Gorton all afternoon in the book. But Smith left with Loeb on a bike trip for the Rhine soon after Hemingway got back in town, easing the confusion. In the manuscript Bill Gorton and Jake were past the pilgrims going to Lourdes, the ones who jammed the dining car. That was funny. Not a big laugh funny, but if you thought about it, you had to smile. Jake Barnes, the man without a cock, on his way to the bullfights where Ernest could not wait to hear Mike Campbell say, "Tell 'em the bulls have no balls!" Anyway, there was Jake off to a pagan fertility ritual crossing paths with pilgrims going to the shrine at Lourdes where the waters worked miraculous cures. If ever a man needed a miracle, it was Jake. Wrong man, wrong pilgrimage, wrong ritual. It was funny all right.

Two days after he was back, he filled the third notebook as Bill and Jake sat down to breakfast in Burguete and Bill was getting off some of Don Stewart's good lines. They'd been talking around Jake's wound without saying it, merely joking around the edges of it. Jake could do that with Bill. "Sex explains everything," Bill said. "You may think you're having fun. You're not having any fun. Everybody's frustrated. Abraham Lincoln was a fairy. He was in love with General Grant. So was Jefferson Davis. That's what the civil war was about. Will Rogers is unhappy. So is President Coolidge." He went on like that, making fun of the New York school of amateur freudianism that blossomed in *Vanity Fair*. Bill said, "And every literary bastard in New York never goes to bed at night not knowing but that he'll wake up in the morning and find himself a fairy." Then the notebook ran out and he stopped to catch his breath.[29]

On the inside backcover of his third notebook, Hemingway made a rough outline of what was to come:

Chap XII   Finishes work   Gerald [Cohn] not going
Chap XIV   Ride to Burgette [sic] – Fishing return to Pamplona
Chap XV   Duff Gerald [Cohn] and Mike thru the party out at the wine shop. When we get in. Mike's first outburst.
Chap XVI   Encierro, first corrida brings back to point where book starts; goes on with that night – the South American – the dancing place. Noel Murphy. Count shows up.
XVII   Duff sleeps with Nino de la Palma. Gerald [Cohn] fights with Nino.
XVIII   Corrida. Duff goes off with Nino. Count refuses Mike a job. Bill goes to Paris. Mike talks, goes to St. Jean de Luz to wait for Duff. Gerald talks, goes to San Sebastian afterwards Paris. I go on down into Spain to bring Duff back. Get her letter.[30]

It read like a travel agent's itinerary for a summer excursion, and like such itineraries did not go as planned. The Count, who appeared briefly in the Paris section, got lost in the shuffle, a casualty to an unplanned novel. Noel Murphy and the South American never did show up in Pamplona. But roughly the outline worked, giving Hemingway vague but sufficient parameters. It even had structure: start in the middle of the action, flash back to Paris and slowly return to the beginning.

Looking back over the page, he could not avoid those last lines: "I go on down into Spain to bring Duff back. Get her letter." Who the hell was telling this story? Did Jake write that or did he? It was all fiction. The Count was not in Pamplona, and the South American – the Gin Bottle King as he and Hadley called him – was there in 1923. The fishing came from 1924. And he was not Jake Barnes in the evening, but sometimes after writing all morning, he was not sure who he was.

What the hell difference did it make? Someone had to bring Duff back, but he needed to keep some distance between himself and Jake.

VI

He told Jane Heap that his book "was exciting as hell and no autobiographical first novel stuff." Sure life was a tragedy, but it was also very funny. That was the problem with all American writers. They didn't get the funny stuff into their books. Sherwood didn't. "He talks funny as hell. When he starts to write it's all wiped out." The English were worse, always "making delicate fun" of their characters. His book was getting the funny remarks in and no one was seeing it until it was finished. "I don't want all my great literary friends giving me good advice."

It was a strange letter: full of bragging but defensive, already imagining hostile critical responses. He wanted the critics to like his work, but he did not want it analyzed. And if they liked it too much, he took that also as an insult. In the recent *Criterion*, Eliot had said some nice things about him, but the new book, he told Jane, would put an end to that. He was already inventing defenses to protect his professional ego. He told Jane, "it is fun to write a hell of a really swell big book and know that you are definitely through with a hell of a lot of disappointed gents who instead of trying to push you because they think you were going to be one of them will now commence to knock you and hate you." It was the same phrasing he had used in his review of Anderson's *A Story Teller's Story*. Overly sensitive about his small books published in Paris, Hemingway called this one a "big book," and consistently in his letters over-estimated its length and its word count. But who were these people who had pushed him and would now turn on him? The list of his backers was impressive: Stein, Ford, Pound, Beach, Dos Passos, O'Brien, Anderson. Why would this novel make any of them hate him? Jane Heap must have been puzzled by the letter.

Realizing he was talking more to himself than to Jane, he said, "I ought to tear it up and start over again." But he didn't because the real purpose was to respond to Jane's question: was he happy with Liveright? Because if he were not, she had a publisher's representative who was eager to meet him, probably someone from Harcourt or Alfred Knopf. Ernest told her that Liveright had an option on his next three books –

"said option to lapse if they refuse any one book." Then he wrote something else which, when he read it over, he knew was going too far. He ripped the bottom half of the page off, continuing on a fresh sheet: "So I can't very well talk business yet." A paragraph later, he repeated it: "You see I can't talk business now but I would like very much to meet your friend and I wish you would bring him around. Because you can't ever tell what might happen."[31]

What "might happen" was perfectly obvious. Liveright might turn his book down, letting their option lapse. *In Our Time* was only six weeks from being released, and Hemingway was thinking seriously of ways to break his contract. He did not want to be in the same house with Anderson, his literary godfather. Tired of hearing himself compared with Sherwood, he wanted a place of his own. Horace Liveright's letters were full of business but no stroking of his fragile ego. He wanted to get letters from someone like Max Perkins, who knew how to make a writer feel secure. Perkins offered him a contract on the basis of his work, not the people he knew. Sure, Scott got his name in the door, but Max liked his stuff. At Liveright, they almost turned the book down, probably would have had it not been for so many friends carping at them. Then they cut one story and rewrote another. It would take another three months of working himself up to a frenzy before he acted on his gut response, but the idea was there in August. All it needed was a little time to fester, a few months of inventing excuses. Whenever he needed to break his word, he almost always found ways of forcing the other party to act for him. He might have felt better had he known that Tom Smith at Liveright was tempting Fitzgerald to switch publishers. Scott said, no, he was loyal to Scribner's, but would write any sort of review to help his friend "Hemminway."[32]

VII

Jake and Bill were hiking in through the old forest, just the two of them, to fish the Irati. Bill waded out into the river, fly fishing, leaving Jake to pin fish from the bank. That was Jake all right. He caught some small ones, but he wasn't going to bust his ass over trout. Ernest would, but not Jake, who preferred to read in the shade. As long as he kept Jake moving, talking, letting the action flow, the book went well. On August 20, Hemingway started his fourth exercise book, filling the last page ten days later. He stayed out of the Quarter as much as possible, and few people called at the apartment. Joyce and family had found yet another harbor town, this time Arcachon below Bordeaux, to spend August. Sylvia and Ernest Walsh were separately in Savoie until September; Gertrude was in Provence; Ezra in Rapallo; Scott in Antibes; McAlmon still in London. Loeb and Smith were biking eastward in the mud toward the Rhine, and the painters Hemingway knew had not yet returned from the country.[33]

The only person in town who bothered him was Pauline Pfeiffer, who looked better than she had in the spring. Bill Smith remembered her saying to Hemingway, "I was talking to someone about you." Ernest always rose to that bait. Pauline said she came by to talk to Hadley, but Ernest was the object of her visit. He must have sensed it but did nothing to discourage her. Ernest liked to have admiring women around him, Hadley and one or two others. So long as the game rules were clear, it could be fun as it was with Izzy at Chamby, the way it might have been with Duff if Loeb had not ruined Pamplona. No one stated the rules, but it was an old game, one they'd all played for years. At least that's what he thought if he thought about it at all. Hadley remembered Pauline as "very bright, very quick and shrewd, especially about money."[34]

Just how shrewd, Hadley did not begin to understand until that winter in Schruns. If she had seen Pauline's August letter to Harold Loeb, she might have been more worried. Before Loeb left with Smith on their bike trip, she wrote him:

My dear Harold,
    When you return from the Rhine, will you please look in all the more accessible pockets of the suit you had on the night you didn't take me to the Caveau (I think it was grey – in fact, KNOW it was grey) and see if you can find
        a lipstick
        a vanity
        a handkerchief (woman's) and
        2 gloves?
    And if you are able to find them, and you should be unless one of those Russians also found them, will you please (again please) devise some inexpensive yet expedient way of getting them to me? If I consulted my own happiness, I should say, of course, bring them yourself. But ANYWAY, do endeavor to get them back into

my life – what I call my life. For, though they may seem most incidental to you, it is by just such joyous trifles that I am enabled to endure, and be endured by this disinterested world.

Pauline
(the girl you left behind you in the Old Homestead)

What man could ignore such a letter? Pauline, whom no one remembered as a careless person, was having a wonderful time in Paris, leaving tokens behind to assure further connections with attractive men like Harold Loeb. Very soon Ernest and Hadley would be receiving similar letters from her.[35]

Pauline was small, like a bird, with nice eyes and delicate moves. When he was not lost in his book, Ernest began to notice her the way a man does without knowing it. There was much to notice in so small a version of the Twenties woman: trim, narrow-hipped, bobbed hair cropped close like a helmet, and small breasts that moved beneath her blouse. Compared to Pauline, Hadley was a matron whose ample hips and full breasts remained a strong attraction for Ernest. All along Montparnasse one could see "new women" like Pauline, the Twenties version of beauty. Hadley was the pre-war woman, built for bearing children. Both women had trust funds: Hadley's now provided only about $2000 a year. Pauline's trust sent her $3600 a year, and her Uncle Gus was always providing windfalls. She was also quite capable of earning her own way in journalism.

In his memoir, Ernest wrote of Pauline:

> We had already been infiltrated by another rich using the oldest trick there is. It is that an unmarried young woman becomes the temporary best friend of another young woman who is married, goes to live with the husband and wife and then unknowingly, innocently and unrelentingly sets out to marry the husband. When the husband is a writer and doing difficult work so that he is occupied much of the time and is not a good companion or partner to his wife for a big part of the day, the arrangement has advantages until you know how it works out. The husband has two attractive girls around when he has finished work. One is new and strange and if he has bad luck he gets to love them both.[36]

It was easier for him to remember the onset that way than to admit any responsibility on his part. Pauline moved in on Hadley and took

Ernest away as if he were a sack of potatoes to be stolen by any passing thief. He never did accept guilt that he could shuffle off on someone else.

Ernest was, in fact, ripe for an affair. Beginning with his last winter's advice to Bill Smith on "yencing," he spent too much idle time fantasizing about other women. That he was not in bed with Duff Twysden was not his fault, for she fulfilled his specifications for the ideal mistress: married and remarried, accustomed to sleeping with whomever she pleased and not likely to create complications. The only apparent reason he remained faithful to Hadley was Duff's disinclination to have him. She said she never slept with married men, and that she liked Hadley too much to upset her. True or not, Hadley saw how her husband behaved in Pamplona and continued to behave around Duff that fall, and she was hurt. Ernest had been unfaithful to her in everything but deed itself. All around them grand affairs and adulteries burgeoned; divorce broke out like hives. Far from the restraining values of Oak Park and St. Louis, the bonds of the Hemingway marriage were losing their meaning as Ernest looked long and long at dance hall girls and strange women on the street, wondering how they would be in bed.

Pauline Pfeiffer, however, was not a woman to be comfortable in an adulterous affair, for her deeply ingrained Catholicism controlled her life. Of course Catholic women had affairs, but they knew in doing so they were sinning so mortally their souls were in jeopardy. One could not remain a devout Catholic and an ardent adulteress. Pauline was thirty years old, attractive, moderately wealthy and a regular attendant at Mass. If that year she was looking for a husband, as many have said, then Ernest Hemingway was her least obvious choice. He was not Catholic; he was unemployed and making no money from his writing; he insisted on dressing sloppily; and he was married with a child. From Pauline's point of view, each of these attributes was a serious impediment to marriage. She was enough of a rebel to defy her family by marrying an artist: that she could explain. But no Catholic like Pauline could lightly wreck a marriage, steal the husband away from his wife and child, and then marry him when he was divorced. To do so would be not only to invite the damnation of her soul, but also the unforgiving wrath of her Catholic parents. Raised as she was in the Catholic Church before it began to liberalize its views, Pauline believed deeply that her soul would burn in hell for all eternity if she were to marry outside the Church. If she was going to take Ernest away from Hadley and marry him, she needed not merely encouragement but active collaboration. It was not a scheme she could have pursued of her own accord.

Chapter Sixteen

END GAME

FALL AND EARLY WINTER, 1925

I

As August ended, Hemingway completed his fourth notebook, chunks of which were scaffolding that had to be taken out by the page, but he was driving hard now, eager to finish. Almost everything he had to cut was Jake thinking, talking out loud to himself and the reader, useless talk that got pared away in the winter revisions. He did not worry about it now. Finally he had maneuvered the action back to Pamplona and the first *corrida* of the festival. But the story had changed since he left Niño in his hotel room dressing for the bull ring. Six weeks earlier, when he began the story, it was going to be about Niño's corruption by the Paris crowd.

The story, he finally saw, was Jake Barnes, just as Fitzgerald's *The Great Gatsby* was about its narrator, Nick Carraway. More than once in the manuscript, Hemingway had gotten into awkward interior discussions about who was the novel's central figure. In early August, Jake said,

> It looked as though I were trying to get to be the hero of this story. But that is all wrong. Gerald Cohn is the hero. When I bring myself in it is only to clear up something. Or maybe Duff is the hero. Or Niño de la Palma. He never really had a chance to be the hero. Or maybe there is not any hero at all. Maybe a story is better off without any hero.[1]

Jake got it right about heroes: they were over for this generation, no longer believable. Out of the trenches came anti-heroes like Nick Adams and Jake Barnes. But a book needed a central character upon whom the force of the action came to bear. By early September, Jake was telling us that "for a time" the bullfighter was going to be the hero. "Mr. Gerald Cohn is not the hero. He was the hero for a time but he has been chopped." All of which was so much wasted breath – Ernest talking to himself, trying to work out on paper what he had not wanted to plan – and it all got cut when he saw the real story he'd been writing.[2]

During the first week in September he changed Niño's name to Guerrita, indicating, without any markers, that his story had changed as well. Guerrita was the name of the legendary bullfighter, Rafael Guerra, who was alive in 1925 but retired from the bull ring. A few years later, Hemingway called him "another golden-age hero" whose retirement relieved everyone. The name stayed Guerrita through the first draft, but in revision was changed to that of an even more historical figure, Pedro Romero, who, between 1771 and 1779, killed 5600 bulls the most difficult way of all: *recibiendo* – standing perfectly still while the bull charged, impaling himself on the sword. Hemingway called it the "most difficult, dangerous and emotional way to kill bulls; rarely seen in modern times." Progressively changing his bullfighter's name to that of a more historical and classically pure matador, Hemingway made Pedro Romero the one idealized figure in the novel, but not the central character. That could only be Jake, for he alone understood what had happened at Pamplona, knew finally the enormity of his personal loss. It was a story about values and their corruption all right, but it was Jake who got corrupted. It was, Hemingway told Fitzgerald, "a hell of a sad story." It was also a story he could see in the mirror whenever he looked closely. He was not Jake Barnes, but like Jake, his values were not holding up very well under the pressures of the Quarter.[3]

Carefully now he got the story back to the Quintana dining room: Jake and the gang were sitting there at the table with Pedro Romero when Quintana walked in, saw them together and did not even nod. After his conversation with Jake about Pedro's needing to be protected from corrupting influences, Quintana could not believe what he saw. This special moment is buried in the blur of drunken talk, but Jake understands it. He is a member of the club, one who understands the bullfight and has the passion for it, *afición*. When the Paris gang first arrived at the hotel, Jake told us about the manager: "For one who had aficion he could forgive anything. At once he forgave me all my friends. Without his ever saying anything they were simply a little something shameful between us . . ." There at the table with Romero sitting next to Brett's bare shoulders, their cognac glasses full, Jake's friends are no longer forgiven him and he knows it.[4]

That's when Bill and Harold returned from their muddy bike trip on the Rhine, and Ernest stopped writing long enough to attend their farewell party: Loeb was going to New York for the publication of *Doodab*; Smith, having found no employment, was simply going home. Without ever saying anything, Bill took sides with Loeb in Pamplona and remained there in Paris. That hurt Hemingway a little, but it also let him put away his guilt for not finding Bill a Paris job. Loeb said Kitty gave the going away party; Kitty said Loeb and Smith got it up. Someone gave a dinner party: Loeb, Kitty, Bill, Ernest and Hadley were there. Loeb said it was at Lavenue's; Kitty said the Nègre de Toulouse. Maybe Loeb was served the duck breast and Hemingway "a helping of the lower anatomy." That's how Loeb remembered the evening, a bit strained but not a crisis.[5]

Kitty told a different story each time she remembered it. In 1963, she said that Hadley was walking ahead with Bill and Harold on their way to supper while Kitty and Ernest lagged behind. In 1968, Bill and Harold were walking ahead after supper, and Hadley was not there. Each time Ernest told Kitty essentially the same thing. In 1968, she remembered him saying,

"I'm writing a book with plot and everything. Everybody's in it. And I'm going to tear these two bastards apart. But not you, Kitty. I've always said you were a wonderful girl! I'm not going to put you in."

In 1963, she remembered Ernest saying,

"I'm writing a novel full of plot and drama. I'm tearing those bastards apart. I'm putting everyone in it and that kike Loeb is the villain. But you're a wonderful girl, Kitty, and I wouldn't do anything to annoy you."

Maybe he did say something. Maybe Kitty did remember it right most of the time. Or maybe she made it up, retelling it so often she got to believing it. Bill Gorton, Smith's fictional avatar, is not torn apart in the novel, and Cohn, *né* Loeb, behaves badly but not so badly as Jake Barnes. And Ernest had no reason to tell Kitty anything about his unfinished novel. So there the four of them go, walking down the boulevard, Hadley perhaps somewhere else. Try as we may, we cannot hear what they are saying to each other. We have only Kitty's word for it, and she never understood the novel.[6]

II

Within three weeks after Smith and Loeb sailed for New York, Hemingway was finished with the first draft of *Fiesta, A Novel*, as it was titled on each of his blue notebooks. There were lots of problems to clean up, names to straighten out, but it was done. The jokes were in it – some on the surface for anyone to get, others private – and the loss was there. When the gang was standing in the lobby, paying their bills, Jake said, "Quintana did not come near us. One of the maids brought the bill." The lovely bill that always came, but Jake's bill was reckoned in more than pesetas. By pimping for Brett, he'd torn up the only membership card he valued – the one that let him be an *aficionado* at Quintana's. Jake Barnes can never go back to Pamplona and expect it to be the same. He has permanently ruined it for himself. No one knows it that morning in the hotel lobby but Jake, Quintana and the reader if he's sensitive to nuances.[7]

There were lots of other things in the book, some of which, like the time joke, no one understood. He'd fixed it so none of the time references worked out right. Not a single one. He changed the date of the Kid Francis–Ledoux fight, moved the calendars around randomly, had William Jennings Bryan dying a month early and collapsed the days at Burguete. No matter what year you thought it might be in Pamplona, it would not fit the calendar. It was something he put in for other writers. When Jake took Georgette to supper they passed the New York *Herald* office with its window full of clocks.

"What are all the clocks for?" she asked.
"They show the hour all over America."
"Don't kid me."

Jake did not reply, but the time joke started there and continued all the way through. Pound and Joyce were playing time games in their fiction; Gertrude was writing in something she called "the continuous present" tense. Well, it did not take a college degree to turn the trick; even a high-school graduate from Oak Park could play time games if he put his mind to it.

He got in lots of good stuff: Brett's constant bathing, echoes of Eliot's *Waste Land* and the values no longer working. Money was the only thing left this bunch of emotional cripples. Jake, Mike and Brett were all war wounded one way or another; poor Cohn was trying to live by a romantic code that no longer worked. Jake, a Catholic, tried praying and confession, but neither was a great help. All they had was money: the profit and the loss. By the end Jake was quite sarcastic about it: "At the station I did not tip the porter more than I should because I did not think I would ever see him again." Jake was always paying bills, some with cash, some by compromising his few remaining values. That was it in a nutshell: put an American down in another country to see if his values were worth a damn. A boy and his dog: a man and his times – see how they run. See if they run.[8]

At the very end Jake had to run to Madrid to bring Brett back. She sent him this telegram: COULD YOU COME HOTEL MONTANA MADRID AM RATHER IN TROUBLE BRETT. Not real trouble, like money, for the bullfighter paid her bills. It was emotional trouble and a way to end the novel. Jake said to himself: "Send a girl off with one man. Introduce her to another to go off with him. Now go and bring her back. And sign the wire with love. That was it all right." But he did it anyway, unable to stop himself. That part was never quite clear, why Jake felt as he did about Brett. Certainly it was irrational and impossible. Ernest knew it. Jake knew it. But every time he let Jake explain it, the words did not help. Finally he cut out all the explanations: it was simply there, a given.

> "Oh Jake," Brett said, "we could have had such a damn good time together."
>
> "Yes," I said. "Isn't it pretty to think so."

Poor goddamn Jake was the loser. That's how it turned out and Ernest could do nothing to change it. No one else took Jake's emotional beating. No one else ended up so alone. It was not a pretty story at all, more like a morality play. After Pamplona, who is left to go down into the grave with Everyman Barnes? Not Faith, not Honor, and certainly not Hope, for Jake turned away from those three long ago. Charity, perhaps, will step down with Jake, for he did care about his fellow revelers. He got to feeling sorry for everyone, even Cohn. Humility, also, might go gravewards with the man who had lost what little pride he ever had. Outside, in the woodyard, a warm and erratic rain was falling out of grey, windy skies.[9]

III

The last page of the blue notebook left him empty, anxious, restless. For nine weeks he had lived so intensely in the book that all else was irrelevant. It was like returning from a long trip with a good friend. Now the friend was gone, and old acquaintances in the cafés began to see more of Hemingway. They all heard about his new novel, even Bob Wilson who was updating his *Paris on Parade* book. Before the year was out and ten months before Hemingway's novel was published, Wilson included Ernest among the Young Intellectuals, the "Bookshop Crowd" centered at Shakespeare and Company. Wilson said that Hemingway

> has recently finished a new novel which is said to break new ground. While an admirer of James Joyce, Hemingway is in no sense an imitator of him; he pursues his own ways, and his friends expect him to go far. He is a young man of vigorous health and physique who has been a soldier and war correspondent . . . and who when he is not writing in his quarters in the Rue Notre-Dame-des-Champs mingles democratically with the artist-writer crowd at the Café du Dôme.

Before anyone read *In Our Time* or saw his new novel, Ernest Hemingway had become a personage in Paris, a young writer to be mentioned early in case his talent paid off.[10]

Evenings at the Dôme, however, were not satisfying, for Hemingway was restless with no place to go. Most of his friends were still out of town, and there was no action in Paris: no bike races or boxing matches. He told Ernest Walsh that, hating to waste the autumn in town, he wanted to go on a walking trip but everything was against it. Hadley couldn't go because Bumby was back, and he himself had a torn ligament in his right foot.

There are no men in town I'd walk across the street with and am afraid to take any of my girls because I hate complications, illegitimate children and alimony. So will probably go by myself but I feel damned lonesome inside and wish to hell there were somebody to go with. . . . Would like to be in Venice and get a little romantic fucking . . . but you need to have a girl in Italy.

An ironic letter, for in the next few months, Walsh, while living on Ethel Moorhead's money, would become sexually entangled with Kay Boyle, married at the time, and leave her with an illegitimate child. A curious letter as well, for it is Hemingway's first mention of divorce, the implied corollary to alimony. As for Venice and "a little romantic fucking," there is no evidence Hemingway had yet been to Venice, much less with a woman.[11]

Writing to his father on almost the same day, he repeated his need to get out of town. "Not sure where yet," he said. "Will decide tomorrow. John Dos Passos and I may go down to the Riff together." The previous day, he read that Spanish troops were advancing on the Riffian rebels under Abd el Krim, and Charles Sweeney's mercenary airmen were getting lots of press. One voice for Walsh, another for Oak Park: Ernest was ever a correspondent of many guises. Nothing, of course, prevented him from taking wife and child with him, but maybe the fucking would not be so romantic then. As for the Riff, that was the day-dreamer speaking out loud. He could have gone to Antibes, which the *Tribune* told him was "athrob with the literary lights . . . assembled there. There's Scott Fitzgerald and wife, Floyd Dell, Max Eastman and wife, as well as a score of others." Dos Passos was there with his new rich friends, the Murphys. It sounded exactly like what he did not need. No literary men. He got out of town, alone but not far. Rather than the Moroccan war zone or an Italian bedroom, he went for a long weekend to visit the cathedral at Chartres.[12]

With the great wave of pilgrims going south to Lourdes and summer tourists departing, Chartres was a quiet place to clear his head, but his head refused. Beyond his control, it continued to work on *Fiesta*. At the great medieval cathedral, shrine of the Virgin and ancient point of pilgrimage, there was much simplicity but nothing simple. Every portal and nave was jammed with statues, allegories, faces of the dead. Whether he prayed or not we do not know, but Hemingway liked medieval cathedrals where prayer had efficacy. He liked the ritual, the mystery, the odors of age and incense. He liked its permanence in stone. Jake

Barnes, he told us, was a Catholic who prayed in the Pamplona cathedral and confessed himself in a foreign language. Unlike the secularized Congregational social activism of his youth, Catholicism held for Hemingway a strong emotional attraction. It was the religion of bullfighters and royalty, a religion of the streets and courts. At Chartres, every window told stories in stained glass. In the Ambulatory he saw the brightly colored tale of Charlemagne's military quest to free the Spanish tomb of St. James at Compostela. There was the king taking Pamplona; there was proud Roland at Roncesvalles dying from too many Saracens.

Later he said there were many places where one could not write. "Yet in nearly all of them you can re-write what you have already written, seeing what is not true and seeing the true that you have not put in and it is always much clearer and easier to re-write something in one of these places than where it was first written." Such a place was Chartres, a place to assay the metal of his summer's mining. It was not so much re-writing; that came later. He needed to wash the ore, let the dross float to the top for skimming. He needed to focus the novel and find a better title than *Fiesta*, which was misleading unless you had been to Pamplona. In Chartres, he turned to the Bible where many another had found a fine title. In his eighth notebook, he listed several possibilities and one epigraph. Four he found in Ecclesiastes, one in Paul's First Epistle to the Corinthians:

The Sun Also Rises
Rivers to the Sea
For in much wisdom is much grief and he that increases knowledge
    increaseth sorrow.
Two Lie Together
The Old Leaven

The last quote had its charm, for Paul said to the Corinthians, "It is reported commonly that there is fornication among you. . . . Purge out therefore the old leaven, that ye may make a new lump, as ye are unleavened." Good advice for Quarterites who, indeed, had fornication among them.[13]

Immediately following the biblical quotes, he wrote:

The Lost Generation

A Novel

Then he began his "Foreword," trying to focus the reader's attention. He started with a Stein anecdote about a garage owner in Aix who said the war generation out of the trenches was spoiled, no good: "C'est un génération perdu." A lost generation. Using this as his text, Hemingway, the preacher, drew a few conclusions:

> this generation that is lost has nothing to do with any Younger generation about whose outcome much literary speculation occurred in times past. This is not a question of what kind of mothers will flappers make or where is bobbed hair leading us. This is about something that is already finished. For whatever is going to happen to the generation of which I am a part has already happened.
>
> There will be more entanglements, there will be more complications, there will be successes and failures. There will be many new salvations brought forward. My generation in France for example in two years sought salvation in first the Catholic Church, 2nd DaDaism, third the movies, fourth Royalism, fifth the Catholic Church again. There may be another and better war. But none of it will matter particularly to this generation because to them the things that are given to people to happen have already happened.

The remark about bobbed hair and flappers-as-mothers was a snide reference to Scott Fitzgerald's early stories and novels that were said to have invented the flapper. As for salvations, his references to the Catholic Church were double edged: part of him resisted the kind of literary conversions which French writers seemed to have patented; another part of him needed ritual support in this game without winners called life. In Paris, Pauline Pfeiffer, once she saw this side of his character, began telling him more and more about her religion. Popes and bishops he could do without, for he was never one to admire hierarchies of authority. But, as is obvious from his list of titles and his place of retreat, religion and its substitutes were much on his mind since the Pamplona summer.[14]

IV

By September 30, Hemingway was back from Chartres and in the Galerie Pierre paying off the last 2000 francs on Miró's "The Farm." There was no place for the $100 to come from other than the Hemingway bank account, which was almost completely Hadley's trust money, for there were no windfalls that month. Two thousand francs would pay the rent and buy most of the groceries for two Paris months, but Hadley was pleased with her birthday present nonetheless. How could she not be? Ernest was sky high from finishing his novel and the coming October publication of *In Our Time*. They hung the large canvas over their bed where it reminded them always of Spain. If there were parts of the last summer Hadley did not want to remember, she did not mention them.[15]

On October 14, Sylvia Beach sold her first copy of Hemingway's *In Our Time*, published nine days earlier in New York. It cost 48 francs, about $2.25. Since June she'd sold eleven copies of *Three Stories & Ten Poems*, making Ernest not a best seller in Joyce's category, but a steady one. There in her window were both of his books, and with them was Sherwood Anderson's new novel, *Dark Laughter*, also published by Boni & Liveright. Ernest looked at the window with some pleasure and a little regret. Was Sherwood going to haunt him forever?[16]

As soon as his New York clipping service began sending him the reviews, he knew the answer to that rhetorical question. The boys liked the stories all right, but they could not refrain from mentioning literary debts.

> "There is something of Sherwood Anderson, of his fine bare effects and values coined from simplest words, in Hemingway's clear medium. There is Gertrude Stein equally obvious . . . Wanting some of the warmth of Anderson and some of the pathos of Gertrude Stein . . ." *New Republic*

> "With Sherwood Anderson and Ring Lardner this author shares a secret." Kansas City *Star*

> "There are obvious traces of Sherwood Anderson in Mr. Hemingway and there are subtler traces of Gertrude Stein." *Saturday Review of Literature*

"He shows the influence of Gertrude Stein very strongly, that of Joyce almost not at all; he is also very strongly under the influence of Sherwood Anderson." New York *Herald Tribune*

One goddamn race track story and he was "strongly under the influence of Sherwood." He knew he should have taken "My Old Man" out of the book. Without it what would they have said? And nothing from Joyce? Were they blind? Didn't they see the way the stories ended? They probably never read *Dubliners*, or Gertrude for that matter. They talked as if she wrote stories. She'd never written a real story in her life.[17]

In September, he had reminded his parents that his book would be out in October. Shortly after *In Our Time* reached Paris, he asked them anxiously if they had seen it yet. Two letters home in less than a month was a record for him of late, but it mattered deeply that Oak Parkers read his fiction. On November 20, having heard nothing from home, he wrote to tell them his book

> should be on sale in Chicago at various places. The name of the book is In Our Time. Am enclosing three reviews from the most influential N.Y. papers for you and mother to read. After you pass them around you might see that the Oak Leaves and the Oak Parker see them so they will hear that I'm not considered a bum in N.Y. at least . . . I wish the book would have a good sale in Chicago and Oak Park as I'd like the people I know to see what the stuff is that I am doing whether they happen to like it or not. I know that you, at least, will like the long fishing story called Big Two Hearted River and I think Mother may like the Cat in the Rain story.

He'd thought about it a good deal, looking over the stories, imagining his mother's reaction against most of them. He wondered if she would hear her own voice in "Soldier's Home"? The least offensive of the lot was "Cat in the Rain." Still, he wanted both parents to read his work, and he needed their approval just as he wanted Oak Park's approval. It was going to be a long wait.[18]

By the end of November, his euphoria was gone. With only a small printing and poor distribution, *In Our Time*, despite its excellent reviews, would have no great sales. Ernest wandered into the Right

Bank bookstores, casually glancing over the new releases, but his book was not among them. He saw now that he had been jobbed by Liveright, who never intended the book to have a chance. In October, he wrote Harold Loeb:

> Sorry to hear they are not making any attempt to sell In Our Time . . . Sylvia Beach orders 12, they send her 6. Sells them in one day and has to cable for more. It has been six weeks since Brentano's ordered theirs and they haven't come. Various people write me that they have read reviews and had to order the book. It not being on sale. Evidently they made up their minds in advance that it was not worth trying to sell a book of short stories.

Records show Sylvia selling only two copies of *In Our Time* in October and seven more in November. The most sold on one day was a single copy, not six. But Hemingway's exaggeration contained a truth: Liveright, despite the effusive reviews, was not distributing the book widely, and Ernest was hurt.[19]

He tried, in his letter to Loeb, to pretend that he was still happy with his Liveright contract, but his rancor would not stay down.

> So far I tell everybody I am very satisfied with Boni and Liveright, that they have treated me very decently, that I am very pleased, etc. It's up to them to keep me happy though and that means they've got to give In Our Time a good ride and that I must have a good advance on the novel. I'm not sore but I'm annoyed that they have done nothing in Chicago where hells own amount of books are sold and which is my home town and where I would have a certain amount of sale anyway.
>
> They are certainly putting Sherwood over big and will evidently make the boy a lot of money. I suppose it all takes time and they know what they are doing. They are evidently playing the book of stories as a sort of classic and then planning to splurge on the novel. I think they're damn good publishers.

It was not really a letter to Loeb but a warning to Horace Liveright, one which Ernest felt Harold would deliver without being asked. The contract was there, but as he told several people, a refused option on his next book would break that. Liveright printing so few copies was bad enough, not distributing or pushing the book with advertising was worse, but for Sherwood's *Dark Laughter* to turn up a best seller when no one in Oak Park saw a copy of *In Our Time* was the deepest wound of all.

Hemingway told Loeb he was working on a long boxing story called "Fifty Grand," which Fitzgerald thought he could sell for him. He did not mention the prospective buyer: *Scribner's Magazine*. The story, begun in October and finished in November, was a double-double cross, an O. Henry story in the manner of Charles Van Loan and Ring Lardner, a story like "My Old Man," easy for Hemingway to write because the genre was well established and the formula known. He used what he'd seen of the Siki–Carpentier fight: after Siki had beaten the favored champion to a bloody pulp, the referee tried to give the fight to Carp on a specious foul, but the crowd booed so loud, the ref quit trying to make it turn out right. Afterwards Siki claimed the fix was in for him to throw the match, but nothing was proven. In Hemingway's fiction, an old champion, reaching his limits, is determined to go out on his feet, beaten but undefeated. Knowing he cannot win, Brennan bets fifty thousand dollars against himself: "It's business," he says. The odds favor Walcott, but the fight, unknown to Brennan, is fixed: Walcott is scheduled by the gamblers to throw the match. In the late rounds when he has Brennan at his mercy, Walcott deliberately fouls the champion, hitting him in the groin. Through sheer will power Brennan gets to his feet, refuses the foul and then fouls Walcott deliberately, thereby losing the fight and his title. Thus the match works out as it should have if no fix were in: Walcott wins the title; Brennan adds a modest twenty-five thousand dollars to his fifty thousand investment. It was a neat double twist done with crisp dialogue, no profanities, no sex.[20]

"Fifty Grand" was also a story Horace Liveright might have read with some interest had he been given to speculation about Hemingway's capacity for duplicity. The contract called for two professionals to conduct their business without cheating. In the course of the bout, both men cheat. Walcott violates the contract first; Brennan retaliates in kind. Outsiders never know why the violations occurred. While writing this story, Hemingway's displeasure with Liveright's handling of *In Our Time* was growing daily. He felt that the publisher had not fulfilled his end of the bargain: printing only 1335 copies and never pushing the book. Maybe Hemingway's expectations were too high, but that did not change the bad taste in his mouth. After seven years of apprenticeship, he expected more. It did not take much rationalization to convince himself that Horace Liveright had not lived up to his side of their contract. Before October was out, Hemingway was working on an idea in his head, a literary foul to force Liveright to break their contract. It was, as Jack Brennan said, merely business.

V

"We've being seeing a lot of Pauline Pfeiffer," he told Loeb at the end of October. A month later, he wrote Bill Smith that Pauline was going to be part of the Schruns excursion for Christmas skiing. He bragged that "Pauline and I killed on a Sunday two bottles of Beaune, a bottle of Chambertin and a bottle of Pommard and with the aid of Dos Passos a q[uart] of Haig in the square bottle, and a quart of hot Kirsch." November was that kind of month: Hadley in bed sick much of the time, and Ernest still on his manic high, looking for company. A better drinker than Hadley, Pauline had another advantage: she could pay the bar bill. Through her sniffles, Hadley seemingly accepted the situation as another example of Ernest's magnetic attraction for stray women. They followed him home like lost kittens. She had seen it all before, but Pauline had not. For Pauline each step was a new one, tentative, testing the thickness of the ice. Smiling, charming and attentive, Ernest did much to encourage her.[21]

As Pauline became a part of his life, admiring his fiction and listening to his stories, he was writing "Fifty Grand" and "Ten Indians." In the second story, young Nick Adams learns from his father that Prudy, his Indian girl friend, was seen thrashing about in the bushes with another boy. Nick's heart is broken. That was one ending. In another rejected version, Prudy came to his window that night making everything all right. No matter how it ended, the story was the same: betrayal. "Fifty Grand" had been a different sort of betrayal. A third story, started but left unfinished, begins on a cold, snowy day with Nick entering George O'Neal's Harbor House café. As he eats his ham and egg sandwich and drinks whiskey from a coffee cup, two strangers enter and sit down. There the story breaks off, waiting for another day to become "The Killers," in which the hired guns are there to avenge a double cross by a boxer named Andreson.[22]

All of October, while Montparnasse twittered over the expatriate question, Ernest was writing fiction and reading European writers:

Flaubert's *Sentimental Education*, and Turgenev's *Torrents of Spring*. Somewhat detached, Ernest listened to the café talk, to those enraged by Sinclair Lewis' *American Mercury* blast at Left Bank phonies. Harold Stearns, attacked personally by Lewis, responded in the *Tribune*, calling the *Mercury* article

> chaotic, cheap, inaccurate, and absurd. He missed both the good points and the bad ones of the American Montparnasse colony – the good points, because he couldn't understand them, and the bad ones, because he so perfectly exemplifies them.

Playing kettle to Lewis' blackened pot, Stearns' retort fueled the controversy that would never end: do Americans in Paris work or are they all drunken loafers? Ernest was too busy working to care about it one way or another, using the pointless feud later in an important revision in his novel: at Burguete, Bill jokingly accuses Jake of being an expatriate, a man who never works and lives off women, an American who has lost touch with the soil. Jake, who values his job, is amused.[23]

Riding the crest of his emotional surge, Hemingway was charged with energy, unable to slow down. There were prize fights to see, gallery openings to attend, books to be read, stories to write, street life and night life coming and going. At Sylvia's, Paul Robeson was singing Negro spirituals; at Auteuil on a very good November day, "Light For Me" took the Prix Montgomery, paying 73.50 francs on a 10 franc bet. Eugene Jolas said "that we are on the threshold of a great literary epoch and . . . we today are merely witnessing a transition period of storm and stress." Hemingway was not particularly interested in having a great literary epoch. Writing was his trade, his business which must eventually pay his bills. If he turned out to be part of a great literary epoch that was fine too, but what he wanted was jam today, not jam tomorrow.[24]

The Monday morning after his good day at Auteuil, he stopped by Sylvia's lending library to check out Don Stewart's *Parody Outline of History* to see what a satire should look like. That afternoon he sat down at his typewriter with all the intensity of a reporter up against a deadline. In the adjoining room Hadley and Bumby were both sick with winter colds, the sort of distraction that normally broke his concentration, but not this time. For ten solid days he typed steadily, revising little as the draft spun off the rollers. Thursday was Thanksgiving, but the typing went on. Early snow falling in November rain chilled his upper rooms on Notre-Dame-des-Champs, reminding Ernest of the northern Michigan winter in which his story was set. The next day McAlmon's Contact Press issued the 925-page edition of *The Making of Americans*, and Hemingway included Gertrude in his story, calling the last chapter "The Passing of a Great Race and the Making and Marring of Americans."[25]

At one point during the writing, Fitzgerald showed up at Hemingway's apartment quite drunk and ended up in the text:

> It was at this point in the story, reader, that Mr. F. Scott Fitzgerald came to our home one afternoon, and after remaining for quite a while suddenly sat down in the fireplace and would not (or was it could not, reader?) get up and let the fire burn something else so as to keep the room warm. I know, reader, that these things sometimes do not show in a story, but, just the same, they are happening, and think what they mean to chaps like you and me in the literary game.

Two days later, November 30, Fitzgerald wrote Hemingway:

> I was quite ashamed the other morning. . . . However it is only fair to say that the deplorable man who entered your apartment Sat. morning *was not* me but a man named Johnston who has often been mistaken for me. . . . I'm crazy to read the comic novel. . . .
>
> > Best wishes to
> > Ernest M. Hemminway [sic]

Two days later and only ten days after it was begun, the book was finished: unplanned and unedited, *The Torrents of Spring* was ready for the typist.[26]

VI

The point was to write a short book that Liveright could not possibly accept and simultaneously make clear to critics that Sherwood Anderson was no longer his literary role model. With Anderson so recently signed to a contract and selling well, Liveright could not afford to offend him with Hemingway's slapstick. Ernest was counting on their choosing

Sherwood and setting himself free to find another publisher. With *Dark Laughter* as his main target, Ernest cudgeled Sherwood with heavy-handed parody. Setting his story around Petoskey, Michigan, Hemingway invented two Andersonian characters – Yogi Johnson and Scripps O'Neil – who blundered about in the winter night having absurd mystical experiences of the sort in which Sherwood specialized. Both characters were filled with the vague, inarticulate longings and pointless questions that Anderson's men always had.

> The long black train of Pullman cars passed Scripps as he stood beside the tracks. Who were in those cars? Were they Americans, piling up money while they slept? Were they mothers? Were they fathers? Were there lovers among them? Or were they Europeans, members of a worn-out civilization world-weary from the war? Scripps wondered.[27]

With his keen ear, Hemingway could imitate anyone's stuff, and Anderson was a particularly easy and vulnerable target whose maundering Whitmanianism Ernest found embarrassing.

Yogi Johnson was a war vet, and Scripps O'Neil a published short-story writer. Scripps, who lost or misplaced one wife, falls in love with and impulsively marries Diana, an older woman from the English lake district who happens to be a Petoskey waitress in Brown's Beanery. Their marriage, however, immediately flounders when Scripps' affection wanders to Mandy, another waitress who is full of literary anecdotes and gossip, like being able to quote the last words of Henry James. Mandy's stories were a satirical poke at the never-to-be-trusted anecdotes Ford Madox Ford was continually retelling to the point of dullness. As the new Mrs. O'Neil tells Mandy testily, "You don't always tell it the same way, dear." Scripps, however, says, "A chap could go far with a woman like that to help him!"[28]

Diana cannot compete with Mandy's store of literary gossip. She thinks: "She was no better than a slut, that Mandy. . . . Was that the thing to do? Go after another woman's man? Come between man and wife? Break up a home?" Hemingway was making fun of Anderson's several marriages and his book *Many Marriages* as well. However, writing in an almost automatic fashion, Ernest was also telling a prophetic story. Throughout the ten days of *Torrents'* creation, Pauline Pfeiffer dropped by his apartment regularly to visit with Hadley and to hear the latest chapter of the satire. She was a good listener with a wide

THE TORRENTS
OF SPRING

A ROMANTIC NOVEL
IN HONOR OF THE PASSING
OF A GREAT RACE
———
ERNEST HEMINGWAY
AUTHOR OF "IN OUR TIME"

Scribner dust jacket for Hemingway's contract-breaking satire published in 1926. (Stanford University Library)

interest in contemporary writers, able to hold her own in literary discussions and quick to encourage Ernest. Pauline, who looked and pretended to be younger than she was, and who thought *Torrents* wonderfully funny, was, in fact, a good deal like Mandy. Diana gorges herself on literary magazines in an effort to hold her husband, but nothing avails. In the last chapter Mandy takes Scripps away from Diana with another Ford Madox Ford story. It was all very funny there in the upper rented rooms and at the café table, but Hadley was not laughing.[29]

Later she said that she never approved of what Hemingway did to Sherwood in *Torrents*. Hadley was not given to judgements, but Anderson was a friend whose helping hand they'd used in Chicago and in Paris. He had opened literary doors and written a wonderful blurb for *In Our Time*. Hadley and Dos Passos both told Ernest that this was no way to treat a friend. Scott Fitzgerald and Pauline told him exactly the opposite: *Torrents* was a wonderfully funny book, and satire hurt no one.[30]

Toward the end of November, Fitzgerald wrote Horace Liveright that the new "Hemmingway" book was "about the best comic book ever written by an American. It is simply devastating to about seven-eighths of the work of imitation Andersons. . . . The thing is like a nightmare of literary pretensions behind which a certain hilarious order establishes itself before the end." It was a mendacious letter calculated to worry Horace Liveright. At the end, Fitzgerald said he hoped Horace would turn down this "extraordinary and unusual production," which would allow Hemingway to move to Scribner's. Hemingway, not wanting to say these things himself, either put Fitzgerald up to the letter, or Scott himself suggested writing it. Either way, they were in it together.[31]

Before sending the ten-day wonder to his typist, Hemingway added an author's preface in which he heaped bitter icing on his satirical cake. Reviewers, he said, having noted the resemblance between his short fiction and Anderson's work, would be happy to know that he had "resolved to write henceforth exclusively in the manner of Anderson." It was over-kill; Liveright would get the message without the preface which Hemingway cut. But Hemingway left the dedication intact: To H. L. MENCKEN AND S. STANWOOD MENCKEN IN ADMIRATION. The first H. L. Mencken was, of course, the influential essayist and editor whom Hemingway held responsible for the *American Mercury's* rejection of his fiction. S. Stanwood Menken was the president of the National Security League, one of the numerous right-wing groups spreading fear of bolsheviks and hate for pacifists. The latter Menken was exactly the sort of target the former Mencken loved to attack.[32]

On December 3, with *Torrents* finished and at the typist, Hemingway caught up on his correspondence, writing a note to his new acquaintance Archy MacLeish and long letters to Bill Smith and Izzy Simmons, now married to a man named Godolphin. To Smith, he said that *In Our Time* was "going well in the states. Had a report from Chicago it was selling very well. Have gotten over 50 good reviews from clipping bureau." He had to say that about Chicago because he wanted so much for it to be true. To Izzy, he wrote that he'd heard nothing from his parents since *In Our Time* was published. "Think the family are praying over what they should say to me about this last book. They'll have a lot to pray over in the funny one. Think they would be easier off just not to read them. What have your family written to you about it if anything? Oak Park re-actions are swell." It was his tough kid act, pretending that he did not want them to like his stuff back home. Now two months after his stories were published, it was as if no one in the Village had seen the book. This silence cut deeper than any negative response he had imagined.[33]

VII

Monday morning he carefully composed a long letter to accompany the *Torrents* manuscript. He assured his publisher that the thin sheaf of typescript would make a fine book, for it was longer than Don Stewart's *Parody Outline of History*. All it needed was wide margins, separate chapter headings and some illustrations. "If you take it," he said, "you've got to push it. I've made no kick about the In Our Time, the lack of advertising, the massing of all those blurbs on the cover . . . [which] simply put the reader on the defensive." To insure Liveright's interest, he wanted a $500 advance and should ask for $1000 because this book could go big. All the readers of *Dark Laughter* would be interested, and the book "should start plenty of rows too. And anybody who has ever read a word by Anderson will feel strongly about it — one way or the other."

He could not imagine them refusing the book, he said, unless they were worried about offending Anderson. No one "with any stuff" could be hurt by satire, and it was in Liveright's interest "to differentiate between Sherwood and myself in the eyes of the public." He'd never met Horace Liveright, which made it easier to write the letter, and by the time he finished, he almost believed it himself. Hadley kept saying don't do it; Sherwood's a friend. And Pauline kept saying how terrific the book was. At the end of the letter he asked Liveright to cable his decision to Schruns, "as in case you do not wish to publish it I have a number of propositions to consider." He hoped that made it clear: to refuse *Torrents* was to break their contract. His duplicity in writing *Torrents* loomed larger in his own mind than it, perhaps, should have. Liveright had stolen Anderson from Huebsch and tried to get Fitzgerald away from Scribner's. It was no more unusual for authors to change publishers than it was for them to change wives.[34]

The same day Hemingway put his manuscript into the mail, Scott Fitzgerald was splashed across the front page of the *Tribune*:

ELLIN MACKAY'S BORED DEBUTANTES
ARE SATIRIZED BY SCOTT FITZGERALD

F. Scott Fitzgerald . . . took occasion to attack Miss Ellin Mackay . . . the well known New York society girl . . . who in a recent number of *The New Yorker* . . . wrote that "the trouble with our elders is that they have swallowed too much of F. Scott Fitzgerald."[35]

Then, in the new "Who's Who Abroad" column, appeared the smiling Irish face of the writer "popularly credited with the discovery of the flapper. . . . no recent writer has exploited better than he the gin and jazz crazed milieu of modern New York."

Ernest probably was too tired to appreciate this coincidence: his contract-breaker going into the mail while the *Tribune* featured the man most responsible for his changing publishers. Nor did he add up the literary debts already accruing to him from his friendship with Scott, who first brought him to the attention of Max Perkins. Without telling Ernest, Scott kept Perkins continually informed of Hemingway's contractual condition. The previous May, shortly after meeting Ernest, Fitzgerald told Perkins, "Hemmingway [sic] is a fine, charming fellow and he appreciated your letter and the tone of it enormously. If Liveright doesn't please him he'll come to you, and he has a future."[36]

Then in November, when Ernest asked Scott to recommend "Fifty Grand" to *Scribner's Magazine*, Fitzgerald, with his eye acutely attuned to the market place, replied with a professional critique, suggesting substantial cuts to the story's opening. "Perhaps its conciseness makes it dull," he told Ernest. "You must know what I mean – the very impossibility of fixing attention for amount of time; the very leaving in only high spots may be why it seemed a slow starter." Hemingway, who earlier had cut the opening pages of "Indian Camp" and the end of "Big Two-Hearted River," recognized his tendency to inflate beginnings and write past natural conclusions; therefore, he took Scott's advice by cutting the opening two and a half typed pages. With the revised manuscript in hand, Fitzgerald wrote Perkins asking if the editor of *Scribner's Magazine* would look at Hemingway's new fiction. Knowing the nature of the *Torrents* manuscript, perhaps having had a hand in its inception, Fitzgerald was doing everything in his power to lure Hemingway into Scribner's fold.[37]

Fitzgerald's *Gatsby* had been there when Hemingway most needed a rough model for *The Sun Also Rises*. Now he owed Scott for changes to "Fifty Grand," as well as letters to Liveright and Perkins. It was also Scott and Dos Passos who recently introduced Hemingway to the pleasant, monied couple, Gerald and Sara Murphy, whose enthusiasm for his writing was matched only by their zest for life. They visited the Hemingway apartment one evening in early December to listen to Ernest read *Torrents* aloud. While Hadley kept her reservations to herself, the Murphys loved it. They and Dos Passos would be joining Ernest and Hadley at Schruns in the new year. Afterwards, in March, they might go down to Antibes where the Murphy's new Villa America could house everyone.[38]

His life was changing as his first line of Paris friends was being replaced. Since Ezra moved permanently to Rapallo, Ernest seldom saw him anymore. Gertrude, already becoming distant, would not be pleased with his attack on Anderson and herself. McAlmon, once his drinking buddy and publisher, was no longer on speaking terms with Ernest, who said:

> McAlmon is a son of a bitch with a mind like an ingrowing toe nail. I'm through defending that one. I still feel sorry for him but damned little. . . . I've defended the lousy little toe nail paring for 3 years . . . But am through now.[39]

Harold Loeb, who had no idea how Ernest had fictionalized his character in the Pamplona novel, would soon be alienated. Kitty Cannell, never much of a friend, turned shrill when the novel appeared. After Hemingway's unprovoked attack in the *transatlantic*, Lewis Galantière lost interest in their literary friendship. Ford saw little of his sub-editor now the review was dead. Sometimes Hadley dropped in for one of Ford's informal afternoons, but Ernest avoided the old duff. Bill Bird was still good for a free pass to the fights or an occasional drink, but he saw little of the Hemingways. Only Sylvia Beach remained as solid a friend as she was that first year in Paris. Some of the new friends, like Archy MacLeish and John Dos Passos, were hard-working, talented, literary men. But others like the Fitzgeralds, the Murphys and the Pfeiffer girls were richer than the first Paris group, richer and more dangerous.

VIII

On December 11, his sore throat on the verge of its usual winter infection, Ernest bundled Hadley and Bumby on the night train toward Schruns, Austria where they arrived late the next morning to find powder snow and crisp air. After checking into the Taube, Ernest went to bed sick, which gave him an undisturbed chance to start revisions on the novel he was now calling *The Sun Also Rises*. Hadley turned Bumby over to the *Kinderhaus* nursemaid and was out on the practice slopes recovering her ski legs. Now that they were back in the good place, everything was going to be all right. Snowy days, frosty nights and feather beds can cure more than a sore throat. This year they stocked up with enough books to last them three months: Thomas Mann, Knut Hamsen and Turgenev checked out from Sylvia's; Wilkie Collins, Captain Marryat and nine volumes of Trollope in paperback.[40]

By the second day, Ernest put aside his rough manuscript, unable to work on it. With his literary future in limbo, waiting for Liveright's decision, he could not face the summer's blue notebooks. For relief, he turned to letters, writing first a note to Sylvia and then a letter to his mother, who recently sent him MacLeish's review of *Dark Laughter* and several clippings concerning *In Our Time* without mentioning the contents of the book. Two days later a letter from his father came forwarded from Paris. "I bought 'In Our Time'," he told his son, "and have read it with interest." Ernest hurried on, but that was it: *with interest*. No other comments. Ernest stared at the signature on his father's ten dollar Christmas check. He had expected something more.[41]

The something more arrived shortly after Christmas. His father wrote him again:

> Many compliments every day viz "In Our Time"! Trust you will see and describe more of humanity of a different character in future Volumes. The brutal you have surely shown the world. Look for the joyous, uplifting and optimistic and spiritual in character. It is present if found. Remember God holds us each responsible to do our best.

A week earlier, his sister Sunny had written that "Dad's just about the same . . . much older looking – he's really not in such good shape physically." But his letter sounded as pious as ever if not as critical as his son had anticipated.[42]

For twelve days Ernest and Hadley skied, read, ate well and slept soundly. The weekly poker game continued as it had a year before, and Hadley's pool shooting improved rapidly. Then, the day before Christmas, warm winds blew and rain fell, ruining the snow and heralding the arrival of Pauline Pfeiffer. Later he remembered it as the winter of avalanches when rotten snow crashed down into the valley, but in the photographs they all seem so happy. Where before it was two, now it was three, a game they played with Izzy Simmons at Chamby: papa and his harem, his ladies in waiting. He was Drum, Hadley was Dulla, Pauline Doulbadulla. For a while it seemed that simple and that innocent: Hadley and Pauline dressing alike in white sweaters, laughing together in the snow, hugging each other like sisters. With them was Ernest, brother and protector, instructor on the slopes and scheduling officer. If his arms were sometimes around Pauline, showing her where to bend and how to shift her weight, they were brotherly arms. If Pauline needed considerable help, this was, after all, her first time on skis. That's what Hadley must have thought, for Pauline was her friend.[43]

No one can say when the relationship changed or who first noticed it. Probably it was no different than any other day. Her hand reached out touching his, as it had before, only this time it was different. There was no need to say anything. They both understood. Thereafter, Ernest began spending more time with Pauline, taking her for long evening walks up the valley while Hadley, who had seen this sort of behaviour in Pamplona, stayed behind. Pauline was still her friend, and if Ernest wanted to excite himself this way, it made for interesting evenings in bed. Like his other infatuations, Hadley was sure it would pass. She was wrong.[44]

With no way for either to know it, Hadley and Ernest were spending their last Christmas together. Months would pass before either acquiesced, but it ended that Christmas at Schruns. Later, fingers would point in all directions to place the blame, as if such an event were planned. It simply happened, an industrial accident, the risk one took living in Paris. Closer to home with its restraints and support, their marriage might have survived, but not in Paris. There was plenty of blame to go round: blame Ernest for being a romantic fool; Pauline for taking advantage of Hadley's friendship; Hadley for her passivity, for pretending it was not happening. Hemingway would say Pauline took him away from Hadley as if he were a prized toy to be struggled over. No one believed that fiction but himself, and then only sometimes.

When Ernest and Pauline were first in bed together – in Schruns immediately, or afterwards in Paris – does not matter. Their physical coupling was no more than working out the details of their silent message exchanged at the Taube. Once again he was in love with two women at once, thinking this time the game might be played by Paris rules learned from Ezra and Ford: a wife at home and a mistress on the side. It was all very French, very contemporary. But Ernest, who had never been in love with a Catholic girl, had much to learn about Pauline's moral code and her tenacity.

On the last day of the year, the cable came from New York, signaling the end of his first publishing contract.

REJECTING TORRENTS OF SPRING PATIENTLY AWAIT-
ING MANUSCRIPT SUN ALSO RISES WRITING FULLY
LIVERIGHT[45]

Immediately Hemingway wrote Fitzgerald the news:

> I have known all along that they could not and would not be able to publish it . . . I did not, however, have that in mind in any way when I wrote it. . . . So I am loose. No matter what Horace may think up in his letter to say.

With what seemed to be definite offers from Knopf and Harcourt in hand, Ernest felt bound to honor his earlier promise to Max Perkins that if he were ever free of Liveright he would come to Scribner's. What was the next move? He would wire Don Stewart to pick up the *Torrents* manuscript and deliver it to Perkins. But should Ernest wire Perkins? Or should Scott wire first?[46]

The next morning he added a postscript to Fitzgerald: maybe Ernest should go directly to New York and negotiate the deal face to face. Then there would be no delays with mails going back and forth. Only his new passport would not arrive for another two weeks. As he wrote those words, Horace Liveright's two letters – one to Ernest and one to Scott – were waiting for the next mail ship to Europe.

Chapter Seventeen

THE SECRET SHARERS
WINTER, 1926

I

The new year began with gale winds and rain sweeping across Europe, flooding rivers and ruining the snow of Schruns. The mails brought "Fifty Grand" back to Hemingway from the Hearst organization, but he, doubly in love, could not be upset. Mornings he worked steadily at revising *The Sun*; the rest of the day belonged to Pauline and Hadley. In their evening three-handed bridge games Hadley consistently lost. "Pauline," Ernest wrote Bill Smith, "is a swell girl. Anybody who goes big through seven consecutive rainy days when they expected skiing has got something in addition to the usual Christian virtues." Bumby was about, but always in the keep of his Austrian nanny, who dressed him in the jockey outfit the Fitzgeralds sent for Christmas. Silked and cropped, the sturdy child pounded away on his new wooden rocking horse, too young to understand the melodrama surrounding him.[1]

Not the least surprising turn of the new year was Hemingway's rediscovered Catholicity. In a response to Ernest Walsh, which he may never have mailed, Hemingway said,

> If I am anything I am a Catholic. Had extreme unction administered to me as such in July 1918 and recovered. So guess I am a super-catholic. . . . It is most certainly the most comfortable religion for anyone soldiering. Am not what is called a "good" catholic. . . . But cannot imagine taking any other religion seriously.

Later some found Hemingway's sudden return to the Church's bosom somewhat specious: Pauline was a devout Catholic, and Ernest's profession of faith seemed too convenient. But none of these doubters seriously thought of Hemingway as a Protestant, and he, himself, never looked back on his Congregational training which he associated with Oak Park hypocrisy, his father's unbearable piety and his mother's church politics of who would rule the choir loft. In Italy during his first war, he experienced a country where religion was woven into every facet of the culture, where men could make jokes about it without giving it up. That night in the battlefield dressing station, when the priest absolved him of all his sins, annointing his forehead with holy oil, was an intense moment. Coming back from death's kingdom, he found himself in the arms of the Church. Maybe he was kidding himself later. Maybe it was a bogus conversion. But when an eighteen-year-old kid thinks he's dying, a Catholic priest can make a lasting impression. Before Hemingway was involved with Pauline, the ritual, ceremony and mystery of the Catholic Church were a strong attraction for a man who needed all three. As became more obvious later in his life, Hemingway was deeply drawn to all things medieval, which is to say all things ancient and Catholic. Pauline Pfeiffer's presence in his life probably accelerated his profession of faith, just as it accelerated the dissolution of his marriage, but both would have happened without her.[2]

At Schruns, those first two weeks of the new year were steeped in natural disaster resulting from the spring-like thaws that swept Europe. Hundreds died as rivers flooded the low lands of Poland, Germany, Holland, Belgium and France. In the heart of the mountains, the group of three disappeared. On January 5, they took the electric train thirteen kilometers further up the valley to Hotel Rossle at Gaschurn where the snow was better. While Bumby stayed behind at the Taube's *Kinderhaus*, Ernest, Hadley and Pauline fared well on hearty meals from Herr Kessler's kitchen. A pine forest came almost down to the village on one side of the valley; on the other side there were steep, saw-toothed mountains blanketed in snow. Wherever they looked, the name Pfeiffer appeared, a prominent Gaschurn family. Daily climbs to ski the slopes left them bone tired at day's end. Then beneath coffered pine ceilings there was kirsch to warm them inside and a tall, green porcelain stove radiating warmth from without. From the walls stared faces of the old people, Kesslers and kin dating back to 1801 when the Rossle first opened. Each morning the skiers woke to church bells. Each evening they slept beneath down comforters.[3]

For two weeks Ernest apparently wrote no letters, which meant that he was once more working on *The Sun* revisions. Manuscripts and later letters indicate that, among other changes, he attempted to move the novel away from Jake telling the story to a more detached third-person point of view. He typed out five pages to see how it worked, revised a bit, and retyped it. The more distance he put between himself, Jake and the action, the worse the story read. By mid-January he gave up the experiment. It was Jake's story, first and last. In his critique of *This Quarter*, he said that when writing stories about actual people, which was not the best thing to do, "you should make them those people in everything except telephone addresses. Think that is only justification for writing stories about actual people." Ostensibly he was critiquing Djuna Barnes and Bob McAlmon, but he was speaking, as he frequently did in his letters, to himself, justifying his use of recognizable prototypes in *The Sun*.[4]

While Hemingway struggled with his manuscript, his literary future was being decided elsewhere and without his knowledge. Horace Liveright wrote Scott Fitzgerald, whose hand he rightly suspected helped stir this strange stew of events:

> You know we have a contract with Hemingway for three more books and you know too that we all, and I, especially, believe in Hemingway. I think he has a big future. And I'd hate you to get so hilariously enthusiastic about our rejection of Torrents of Spring that you would make yourself believe that we were in any way giving up on Hemingway. We're not, and we expect to absolutely go through with our contract with him.[5]

On January 8, Fitzgerald cabled Perkins: YOU CAN GET HEMM-INGWAYS FINISHED NOVEL PROVIDED YOU PUBLISH UN-PROMISING SATIRE HARCOURT HAS MADE DEFINITE OFFER WIRE IMMEDIATELY WITHOUT QUALIFICATIONS. Now *Torrents*, which Fitzgerald had encouraged Hemingway to complete, was "unpromising," indicating that perhaps Scott had more than a little to do with the whole scheme. Perkins wired back: PUBLISH NOVEL AT FIFTEEN PERCENT AND ADVANCE IF DESIRED ALSO SATIRE UNLESS OBJECTIONABLE OTHER THAN FINANCIALLY.[6]

Fitzgerald's wire was followed by a letter to Perkins explaining Liveright's refusal of *Torrents*: "Hemingway thinks, but isn't yet sure to my satisfaction, that their refusal sets him free from his three book (letter) agreement with them." Ernest, he said, was eager to come to Scribner's but was worried that they might find the satire too broad. Max should write, assuring Hemingway, but "Don't ever tell him I've discussed his Liveright & Harcourt relations with you."[7]

Having returned to Schruns, Hemingway waited, excited and a little impatient, for all the shoes to fall: the letters from Horace Liveright and Max Perkins. On an emotional high, he was delightful, keeping both women laughing. By January 14, with Pauline back in Paris and Schruns' skiing marginal, Ernest turned his energy to the ink-filled, blue notebooks, trying to make his novel jell. From Paris came almost daily letters from Pauline, written to himself and Hadley. The running motif was nightgowns. First, Pauline discovered she left her prized kimono at Gaschurn. "Do you think we drank enough there to get it back?" she asked. It was like her letter to Loeb, leaving intimate pieces of herself behind as mementos. "I trust the novel is settling well into the third person," she told Ernest, "and that the fingers [Hadley's] are tripping with abandon over the [piano] keys. I am proud to know two such great artists in such diverse fields." Two days later Pauline wrote in response to Ernest's account of his revisions. "The velocity with which The Sun Also Rises is being thrown off staggers me. At this rate . . . it should be finished before you start for N.Y., my dear Drum. . . . I miss you two men. How I miss you two men."[8]

Ernest also told Pauline about Liveright's letter which finally arrived, explaining that no one in his office found Torrents of Spring the least bit funny. The satire was vicious, bitter and uncommercial. Ernest spoke of selling 20,000 copies? Six or seven hundred was more like it. They were turning it down and waiting to see The Sun Also Rises. Nothing was said about lapsed options cancelling any contract. Pauline, being as supportive as possible, said, "There must be something rotten about a firm that hasn't anyone in it that thinks Torrents of Spring is funny. . . . Perhaps if Mr. and Mrs. Hemingway should go to America, or just Mr. Hemingway should go to America, I might go with them or just him and tell them a few things. . . . Damn it to hell, gentlemen, I could begin and go on from there." Her tone was light, the thrust funny, but beneath it lay her feelings for Ernest. She was sending two messages: one in ink and one between the lines.[9]

On January 19, Hemingway answered Liveright with a long, detailed argument for freedom from his contract, which stated clearly that unless Liveright accepted his second manuscript within sixty days their option would lapse not only on it, but also on his third book. Torrents, he said, was submitted in good faith, and he now felt free to go to the publisher who offered him the best terms. Boni & Liveright could not expect to reject his "books as they appear and waiting to cash in on the appearance of a best seller." As soon as his new passport arrived, he would come to New York to settle the matter.[10]

The same day that Ernest wrote to Horace Liveright, Pauline returned his borrowed books to Sylvia Beach's library, which she joined herself, checking out Maurice Baring's novel *C*. Whereas Hadley's reading interests tended toward nineteenth-century classic authors, Pauline was more experimental. That spring she read T. S. Eliot's essays *The Sacred Wood*, Virginia Woolf's *Mrs. Dalloway* and her *Common Reader*, as well as Defoe's *Moll Flanders*, the picaresque story of a determined woman's irregular and highly sexual adventures.[11]

On January 17 in response to a Hadley letter, Pauline said: "I'm overjoyed that Ernest will soon be here. I feel he should be warned that I'm going to cling to him like a millstone and old moss and winter ivy. You can't know how glad I'll be. I've missed you simply indecently ever since the return." She invited Hadley to stay with her in Paris when Ernest came down from the mountains, but suspected she would not accept the offer. At Hadley's request, Pauline promised to buy her some new "robes de nuit." It was an ironic exchange: nightgowns to Hadley, and Hadley's husband to Pauline. Four days later, when Hadley insisted she could not come to Paris, Pauline told her that she should seriously reconsider the offer, all the while knowing the Hemingways traveled on a joint passport: if Ernest went to New York, Hadley was stuck either in Schruns or in Paris until he returned. With the Hemingway apartment sublet, they could not afford for Hadley and Bumby to be in Paris. For a few days coming and going, Pauline would have Ernest to herself in a city large enough to hide their private life.[12]

II

Despite Pauline's anticipations, Ernest could not have arrived at a worse time for her *Vogue* job, for these were the days when all Paris fashion houses trotted out their new spring lines. Between January 28 when he arrived and February 3 when he left Paris, Pauline had to cover at least twenty designer openings, beginning early in the day and running late into the evening. When models disappeared, she typed up her rough notes while she could still make sense of them, for one day's experience tended to merge with the next. There was, in fact, little time for the two of them to enjoy the city or each other. She told Hadley, "I've seen your husband E. Hemingway several times – sandwiched in like good red meat between thick slices of soggy bread. I think he looks swell, and he has been splendid to me. . . . I had hoped to go with him to the Jeu de Paumes . . . this afternoon, but now Doucet has decided to open." Consciously or not, Pauline was sending coded messages into the mountains: she was devouring Hadley's husband.[13]

Although it seemed later that Hemingway took his sweet time in Paris arranging for Atlantic passage, there were only two ships he could book: one leaving February 1st, and the *Mauretania* two days later. The first ship, the *Berlin*, would not arrive in New York until February 10. The *Mauretania*, considerably faster, was due to dock a day earlier. All depended on the North Atlantic weather, just then boiling with killer storms. In a snow-driven blizzard, the *President Roosevelt* lost two men while rescuing the crew of a sinking British freighter. All across the dark and heaving waters radio appeals for help were going out.[14]

After checking into the Venetia Hotel on Montparnasse, Ernest attended to errands while Pauline covered fashion shows. He stopped by Sylvia's to check unforwarded mail and to buy another copy of *In Our Time*, probably to autograph for Max Perkins. He also browsed rapidly through a new book on bullfighting. The next day he found Elliot Paul mentioning his name in the same breath with Joyce's as writers featured in *This Quarter*, finally available from its Milan printers. He looked over Fanny Butcher's Chicago book review column, but still nothing about *In Our Time*. In his notebook he made a list of people to see and things to buy in New York. Among the polo shirts for Mike Ward, Ammolin for Hadley and Gem razor blades for himself was the reminder: "As soon as book [return] passage cable Hadley, Pauline, Murphys." At least he did not put Pauline's name ahead of his wife's, not yet. With Jinny Pfeiffer visiting in Arkansas, Ernest was quite probably spending his Paris evenings in Pauline's bed, for there was nothing to keep them apart except his conscience and her religion, neither of which was sufficient defense against desire.[15]

Wednesday morning, February 3, Ernest was up early to check out of his hotel and catch the 9:35 boat train to Cherbourg, where the *Mauretania* waited for the evening tide. As the grey, wet countryside went past his window, he read the morning papers: another disarmament conference at Geneva; Gene Tunney trying to embarrass Dempsey into a title defense; and two more ships gone down in the Atlantic storms. He did not want to be out there on another rough passage. He wanted to be in bed with Pauline. Or in bed with Hadley. In his vest pocket he carried his new fountain pen with the gold tip, a gift from Pauline.[16]

The next day, with the *Mauretania* heading into the open Atlantic, Pauline complained to Hadley how dull was her Paris life, just one fashion show after another. Ernest had been a delight to her. "I tried to see him as much as he would see me and was possible," she said. "I would give all I had in the world, including the new trust fund, if I could come to Schruns now. . . . I haven't even bought the nighties. Ernest said to get them and just send them by mail . . . Also I shall send you [a] blue kimona . . . It seems this kimona has been here a long time, since before Christmas, but I just found it a few days ago." At Schruns the two women had been in and out of each other's bedrooms like sisters, sharing girl talk. Hadley knew that Pauline aroused her husband; now she must have wondered how much of Pauline her husband saw in Paris. Pauline's conclusion did nothing to calm Hadley's nagging doubts: "Ernest said he wrote you that Bumbi is to be one of my heirs, that is, of course, if I die before he becomes a financial maggot thru his own efforts."[17]

III

After seven days of rough, stormy seas, the *Mauretania* docked late in New York in the midst of a fierce blizzard and foot-deep snow that stalled the night city almost completely. Trains ran erratically; cabs were impossible. By the time Hemingway checked through customs and made his way to the Brevoort Hotel, he was chilled to the bone, tired and dislocated. Everything that happened during his eleven-day visit was guaranteed to increase his geographic vertigo. New friends and old came armed with bootleg Scotch and shakers of martinis, determined to impress him with New York panache. There he was rubbing shoulders and sharing cabs with Dorothy Parker, Bob Benchley and Elinor Wylie on their way to Broadway shows and Greenwich Village parties. It was all very heady, fast-paced and flattering. He drank too much, slept too little and told more Paris stories than he should have.[18]

On Wednesday, February 10, he talked with Horace Liveright, repeating the thrust of his letter: their contract was cancelled when

Horace refused *Torrents*. A good lawyer could have kept Ernest in literary limbo for some time had Liveright been vindictive, but they parted on a handshake. In March, he said they'd had a couple of drinks together, but no one else remembered it that way. The only hard evidence remaining from that morning are Horace Liveright's notes scribbled across the top of Hemingway's Schruns letter:

> Hemingway was in and absolutely proved that our contract specified if we rejected his second book we relinquished our option on the third. Torrents of Spring a good honest delivery of second book. Everyone here had nice chat with H. who . . .[19]

Whatever else was said was recorded in unreadable shorthand, and Ernest walked out of Liveright's office a writer without a contract.

He felt fairly certain that Scribner's, Harcourt or Knopf would offer him favorable terms, but there was a catch. For the Liveright contract never to resurface, his new publisher had to accept *Torrents*. That was the deal that Hemingway insisted upon. Perkins' cable was a qualified yes: if there were no impediments other than financial. What if the book was unpublishable because of the kidding or the naked Indian woman or whatever else was immoral to print in New York where deeds themselves were winked away but not words on paper. Should he go to Harcourt first where Bromfield had paved his way, or should he go to Scribner's as he had promised Perkins a year earlier?

The next morning his sense of honor settled the matter: he had given his word to Perkins and he would keep it. Of course, he had given his word to Horace Liveright, but that water was already down river. When he appeared at Scribner's building on Fifth Avenue, Max Perkins met him with a firm handshake. Immediately Ernest relaxed. The calm, solid presence and pale, blue eyes of Perkins were assuring. Even better, he had read *Torrents*, delivered to him by Don Stewart, and found it publishable. They talked terms, reaching a deal: 15% royalty starting with the first sale and a $1500 advance on the two books, *Torrents* and *The Sun Also Rises*, the second of which Perkins accepted on faith alone, for Ernest did not bring the manuscript to New York. Perkins told Ernest that by early next week he could have an approved contract drawn up, the advance check written and a mock-up for *Torrents* ready to see. It could not have worked out better for Hemingway whose joy was matched only by his relief to have the thing settled. He told Bill Smith and Harold Loeb that he arrived in New York alone, accompanied only by his moral turpitude. "Scribner's say they will back me solidly and loyally," he told his two friends, "no matter how the books turn out financially. So now I don't have to worry, only to work."[20]

Shortly after his negotiations with Perkins, Hemingway booked return passage to France on the *President Roosevelt*, one of two ships leaving on February 20. Then he cabled both Hadley and Pauline the news and his arrival date. That weekend in New York, his business completed, Hemingway entered the flow of the city: a brief visit with Izzy Godolphin and a whirlwind of cabs taking him with newly met strangers into private literary corners of the city and a boxing match at the Garden. Monday morning at the Brevoort he received a note from Perkins: come by Tuesday, February 16, to see the plan for *Torrents*; "page cover and wrapper and the contract will be ready." Early that Tuesday morning, he signed the contract with his new Waterman fountain pen.[21]

The remainder of the week disappeared in a Scotch-filled haze. He partied and shopped; saw the stage version of *The Great Gatsby* and chummed about with Bob Benchley, the darling of New York urbane comedy. There were dinners and bootleggers, mixed in between nights with the room moving unless he put his hand on the floor to stop it. On the day of his departure, the Hotel Brevoort, indicted for selling liquor, was threatened with either a voluntary six-month padlocking of the front door, or a court trial that might shut it down permanently. Management was irritated; guests bemused: the curiosities of city life. Somehow that Saturday, Hemingway made it to the Hoboken pier before the *Roosevelt* sailed. Marc Connelly wanted everyone to see his new play, *The Wisdom Tooth*, but there was not enough time. Paris, for Hemingway, was crazy by degrees, but New York to him seemed permanently mad. An eight-day rest cure at sea was exactly what he needed: time to recover, time to think.[22]

They crossed New York harbor by ferry, huddled inside against the falling snow that obscured the Statue of Liberty. Dorothy Parker was nervous, edgy, worried about the voyage, for she had, unexpectedly, decided to join Hemingway to visit Paris. Bob Benchley, at the last moment, decided to accompany her. On board ship he joked about throwing the children's life preservers overboard. Given Parker's tendency toward suicidal depressions, it was well that she was in the company of the comedian, for Ernest was in no mood to be supportive. He had enough to say grace over. Once loose from the mainland, the *Roosevelt* made the trip in slow, rolling seas but not uncomfortably.

The food was decent, and the humor as contagious as the case of "crabs" Benchley somehow contracted in passage.[23]

Five days out Hemingway wrote a letter to Izzy in New York, apologizing for missing her on his last day and asking her not to mention his visit to his family in Oak Park as he had not told them of it. Then there was his fountain pen given him by Pauline. "I left a grand gold mounted Waterman fountain pen, large size in my room," he told her. "I wonder if you could go over and get it . . . before they padlock the Brevoort. . . . The pen has a gold band around part of the cap that screws down, it is a self filler and has a very hard sharp point." As if Izzy were going to test the point.[24]

On the same day Pauline was writing Hadley at Schruns as nightgowns continued to flutter between them. Refusing the guilt gift that Ernest asked Pauline to buy for her, Hadley wrote, saying not to buy her any gowns; she would simply hem up her old ones. "Darling," Pauline replied, "I was so overcome by your magnanimity in the matter of the gown that I won't even suggest my getting them now. But I have picked out of my own chorus girl array of night garments what I think is my most refined gown . . . and I hope you will wear it while you are hemming up the simple batiste. . . . don't pay any duty on it for it's old and you can tell them it's something I took away by mistake." The gown Pauline was sending would be obviously several sizes too small, reminding Hadley of what she did not need to think about.[25]

Stuck in Schruns without decent snow, no real friends and no ability to speak German, Hadley was really alone. At the piano she spent hours each day practicing her new Bach Busoni Chaconne to please Ernest on his return. For a month she had been without him, and his cables and letters, full of good fun elsewhere, did not help. Pauline's letters helped even less. She looked at the tiny nightgown briefly before giving it to one of the smaller girls at the Taube. Each day she read the Paris paper, watching for the *Roosevelt*'s progress. On March 1, she wrote Izzy, thanking her for a newsy New York letter, which

arrived this morning and roused me from a horrible feeling of despair I had succumbed to on discovering that the President Roosevelt which was due Saturday is still expected today. And me I'd thought to have my liebling here this very day. I hope storms aren't brewing – of course the P.R. has a way of encountering storms doggone it! — I don't see how I can live thru another few days! Because he'll surely have to stop in Paris for money and to do something about the apartment – please excuse me if [I] wail it's such a dark day, inside and out.[26]

Dark in Schruns and dark across the channel where the *Roosevelt*, that very moment, was making its way slowly toward a berth at Cherbourg. Ernest, watching the rolling swells from the railing, was less happy than he should have been. Like an Alger story, it was all coming true: hard-working kid rises in the world through pluck and luck. Add a few good friends. Add much talent and the ability to lie when he had to. It was contemporary Alger, where steps up the ladder were not without grave costs: burned bridges and broken promises which he preferred not to think about. At twenty-six, he had become the writer he set out to be, but the seven-year apprenticeship had changed him. Old friends saw it clearly. He was harder now, less simple, his moods deeper, their shifts more sudden. His genetic inheritance was beginning to expose itself, and his sexual needs left him either restless or guilty. He loved Hadley, and he loved Pauline, who was, in bed, a different, eager experience for him. He wanted them both: wifely mother and exciting lover. With a new contract in his valise, advance money in his pocket and two women waiting for him, he was a man riding dilemma's horns. As the lights of Cherbourg began to brighten in the night, he went back to his cabin; the face in the mirror seemed, for a moment, to be a stranger's.

NOTES

A biographer connects up the dots to draw the picture just as we did as children. First, of course, he must find the dots of data, leaving as little space between them as possible. These notes document as many dots as I thought the reader might possibly want to know about. Some familiar Hemingway stories do not appear, for I could find no supporting evidence to corroborate them. For example, there is no mention of his rented writing room in the hotel where Verlaine died. That story's only source is Hemingway himself in *A Moveable Feast*. I left the room out because I could not find a single letter or separate memoir from 1922 that spoke of it. Nothing in this book occurs at my convenience. Rain and snow fall as they once fell in another country. Boats and trains arrive and depart on schedule. My only fiction is the space between the dots.

The several references to my earlier books – *Hemingway's First War* (Princeton University Press, 1976), *Hemingway's Reading* (Princeton University Press, 1981) and *The Young Hemingway* (Basil Blackwell, 1986) – are a shorthand way of directing the reader to sources used in those works. To have repeated that documentation here would have made these notes unbearably long. References to other Hemingway biographies sometimes indicate my source of information. At other times they are meant to invite comparison. One work frequently cited, Paul Smith's *A Reader's Guide to the Short Stories of Ernest Hemingway* (Boston, Mass.: G. K. Hall, 1989), was available to me in manuscript. Without it and the help of its generous author this book would have been the less.

The following abbreviated forms are used in the notes.

NOTES

LIBRARIES

JFK	= John F. Kennedy Library, Boston, Mass.
Lilly	= Lilly Library, University of Indiana
NBL	= Newberry Library, Chicago
PUL	= Firestone Library, Princeton University
SUL	= Stanford University Library
UTex	= Humanities Research Center, University of Texas
UVa	= Alderman Library, University of Virginia
YUL	= Beinecke Library, Yale University

HEMINGWAY TEXTS

AMF	= Ernest Hemingway, *A Moveable Feast* (New York: Scribner's, 1964).
CSS	= *The Complete Short Stories of Ernest Hemingway* (New York: Scribner's, 1987).
DL:T	= William White (ed.), Ernest Hemingway, *Dateline: Toronto* (New York: Scribner's, 1985).
NAS	= Ernest Hemingway, *The Nick Adams Stories*, ed. Philip Young (New York: Scribner's, 1972).
SL	= Carlos Baker (ed.), *Ernest Hemingway, Selected Letters* (New York: Scribner's, 1981).

88 Poems, ed. Nicholas Gerogiannis (New York: Harcourt/Bruccoli Clark, 1979).
Death in the Afternoon (New York: Scribner's, 1932).
Green Hills of Africa (New York: Scribner's, 1935).
in our time (Paris: Three Mountains Press, 1924).
In Our Time (New York: Boni & Liveright, 1925).
The Dangerous Summer (New York: Scribner's, 1985).
The Sun Also Rises (New York: Scribner's, 1926).
The Torrents of Spring (New York: Scribner's, 1926).
Three Stories & Ten Poems (Paris: Contact Publishing Company, 1923).

NOTES

OTHER FREQUENTLY CITED TEXTS

Baker   = Carlos Baker, *Ernest Hemingway, A Life Story* (New York: Scribner's, 1969).

Brian   = Denis Brian, *The True Gen* (New York: Grove Press, 1988).

Bruccoli   = Matthew J. Bruccoli, *Scott and Ernest* (New York: Random House, 1978).

Fitch   = Noel Riley Fitch, *Sylvia Beach and the Lost Generation* (New York: Norton, 1983).

Kert   = Bernice Kert, *Hemingway's Women* (New York: Norton, 1983).

Knoll   = Robert E. Knoll, *McAlmon and the Lost Generation* (Lincoln: University of Nebraska Press, 1962).

Lynn   = Kenneth Lynn, *Hemingway* (New York: Simon & Schuster, 1987).

McAlmon   = Robert McAlmon, *Being Geniuses Together*, revised by Kay Boyle (London: Michael Joseph, 1968).

Mellow   = James R. Mellow, *Charmed Circle* (New York: Praeger, 1974).

Meyers   = Jeffrey Meyers, *Hemingway, A Biography* (New York: Harper & Row, 1985).

Poli   = Bernard Poli, *Ford Madox Ford and the Transatlantic Review* (Syracuse, NY: Syracuse University Press, 1967).

Sarason   = Bertram D. Sarason, *Hemingway and the Sun Set* (Washington, DC: Microcard Editions, 1972).

Smoller   = Sanford J. Smoller, *Adrift Among Geniuses* (Penn State Press, 1975).

Sokoloff   = Alice H. Sokoloff, *Hadley, the First Mrs. Hemingway* (New York: Dodd Mead, 1973).

Tribune   = The Chicago *Tribune*, Paris edition.

Chapter One: LOSSES

1. EH 1921–23 passport, JFK.
2. Gertrude Stein, *The Autobiography of Alice B. Toklas* (New York: Harcourt Brace, 1933); *Young Hemingway*, pp. 59, 240–1; "The Strange Country," *CSS*, pp. 645–50.
3. Greg Clark–EH, 21 Nov. 1922, JFK; Edmund Wilson, "Mr. Hemingway's Dry Points," *Dial*, 77 (October 1924), 340–1.
4. "A Divine Gesture," "Ultimately," *Double Dealer*, 3 (May 1922), 267–8; 3 (June 1922), 337.
5. "Living on $1,000 a Year in Paris," *DL:T*, pp. 88–9.
6. *Young Hemingway*, pp. 146, 154–5, 167–8, 203, 204; EH–Family, 2 Feb. 1922, Lilly; Anderson Collection, NBL. In 1927, Hadley's bank statement from St. Louis showed a balance on March 4 of $966.14, indicating that her trust fund remained solvent. Bank statement and cancelled checks at the Taube in Schruns, Austria (1988).
7. High-school notebook dated 1915, private collection, part of University of Virginia 1977 exhibit "In Their Time."
8. Hadley Hemingway–EH, letter of 16 Sept. 1926 misdated 16 Oct. 1926, JFK; Hadley Hemingway–EH, 17 Sept. 1926; *Young Hemingway*, pp. 37–9, 81–7.
9. John Bone–EH, 22 Mar. 1922, JFK.
10. "The Strange Country," *CSS*, p. 647; Baker, p. 103; *AMF*, p. 74.

Chapter Two: MAKING CONNECTIONS

1. EH 1921–23 passport, JFK; EH–Sherwood Anderson, c. 23 Dec. 1921, *SL*, p. 59.
2. *Young Hemingway*, pp. 149–50; Item 409, JFK.
3. EH–Sherwood Anderson, c. 23 Dec. 1921, *SL*, pp. 59–60; Hadley Hemingway–Grace Hemingway, 20 Feb. 1922, JFK.
4. "Tuna Fishing in Spain," *Toronto Star Weekly*, 18 Feb. 1922, *DL:T*, p. 93; Hadley interview, Baker file, PUL; Item 179, JFK.
5. *AMF*, p. 35.
6. *AMF*, p. 36; Fitch, pp. 115–16, 421–2; Beach records, Beach Collection, PUL.
7. Beach records, PUL.

8. Beach day books and records, PUL.

9. Fitch, pp. 77–9; Beach records, PUL.

10. Beach records, day books, inventories, PUL.

11. Beach records, PUL; EH Moving Inventory, 1928, JFK; Hadley Hemingway–Grace Hemingway, 20 Feb. 1922, JFK; *Hemingway's Reading*, pp. 15–28.

12. *Tender Buttons* in *Selected Writings of Gertrude Stein*, ed. Carl Van Vechten (New York: Modern Library, 1945), p. 476; Anderson, *France and Sherwood Anderson*, ed. Michael Fanning (Baton Rouge: Louisiana State University Press, 1976), p. 52: Richard Bridgman, *Gertrude Stein in Pieces* (New York: Oxford University Press, 1970), pp. 129–30.

13. *Tribune*, 6 Jan. 1922; *Baedeker's Paris and Its Environs* (Leipzig, 1924); Baker, p. 84.

14. *Baedeker's Paris*; Elliot Paul, *The Last Time I Saw Paris* (New York: Sun Dial Press, 1943), p. 49.

15. EH–Family, c. 15 Jan. 1922, Lilly.

16. EH–Katy Smith, c. 17 Jan. 1922, Dos Passos Collection, UVa.

17. Sokoloff, pp. 45–6; Hadley interview, Baker file, PUL.

18. Item 845, JFK.

19. Item 263, JFK.

20. Hadley Hemingway–Grace Hemingway, 12 Dec. 1922, JFK; EH 1921–23 passport, JFK; Hans Schmid, "The Switzerland of Fitzgerald and Hemingway," *Fitzgerald/Hemingway Annual 1978*, ed. Matthew J. Bruccoli and Richard Layman (Detroit: Gale Research Company, 1979), pp. 261–71; Baedeker's Switzerland (Leipzig, 1922); EH–Isabel Simmons, c. 1 Dec. 1922, *SL*, pp. 74–5.

21. EH–Katy Smith, c. 19 Jan. 1922, Dos Passos Collection, UVa; EH–Isabel Simmons, c. 1 Dec. 1922, *SL*, pp. 74–6; *Baedeker's Switzerland*; EH–Family, received 2 Feb. 1922, Lilly.

22. *DL:T*, pp. 101–2.

23. *Green Hills of Africa*, p. 109.

24. *DL:T*, p. 94.

25. EH–Howell Jenkins, 8 Jan. 1922, *SL*, p. 22; *Tribune*.

26. EH 1921–23 passport, JFK; *Tribune*; Fitch, p. 13.

27. Fitch, p. 59; Harold Loeb, *The Way It Was* (New York: Criterion Books, 1959), p. 61; Lynn, p. 163; Sokoloff, p. 49; Baker, p. 86; Nicholas Joost, *Scofield Thayer and the Dial* (Carbondale: Southern

Illinois University Press, 1964), pp. 166–7; Hadley interview, Baker file, PUL.

28. Baker interview with Galantière, Baker Collection, PUL.
29. *DL:T*, pp. 114–15.
30. "The Hotels of Switzerland," *DL:T*, p. 103.
31. High-school notebook, 21 Mar. 1915, JFK; *Young Hemingway*, pp. 23–5, 27–8.
32. EH–Anderson, 9 Mar. 1922, *SL*, p. 62.
33. "Homage to Ezra," *This Quarter*, 1, 1 (Spring 1925), 221–5.
34. Joost, *Scofield Thayer and the Dial*, pp. 166, 248; Baker, p. 86; *Young Hemingway*, pp. 246–7.
35. Hadley Hemingway–Grace Hemingway, 20 Feb. 1922, JFK; Nicholas Joost, *Ernest Hemingway and the Little Magazines* (Barre, Mass.: Barre Publishers, 1968), pp. 14–15; Joost, *Scofield Thayer and the Dial*; William Wasserstrom, *The Time of the Dial* (Syracuse, NY: Syracuse University Press, 1963); EH–Scott Fitzgerald, 1 July 1925, PUL, *SL*, p. 165.
36. John Peale Bishop, "Homage to Hemingway," *New Republic*, 11 Nov. 1936, p. 39.
37. *Literary Essays of Ezra Pound*, ed. T. S. Eliot (New York: New Directions, 1968), p. 9.
38. *Literary Essays of Ezra Pound*, pp. 4–5; Item 489, JFK; *The Autobiography of Lincoln Steffens* (New York: Harcourt, 1931), p. 835.
39. Ezra Pound, "How to Read," *Literary Essays of Ezra Pound*, pp. 25–38; *Hemingway's First War*, pp. 154–8; Robert O. Stephens, "Hemingway and Stendhal," *PMLA*, 88 (March 1973), 271–80; Harold M. Hurwitz, "Hemingway's Tutor, Ezra Pound," *Modern Fiction Studies*, 17 (1971–72), 469–82.
40. "The Serious Artist," *Literary Essays of Ezra Pound*, pp. 43–4; George Plimpton, "The Art of Fiction, XXI: Ernest Hemingway," *Paris Review*, 5 (Spring 1958), 85; Item 254, "The Ash-Heels Tendon," JFK.
41. *AMF*, p. 12; *Literary Essays of Ezra Pound*, pp. 3–9.

Chapter Three: RITES OF PASSAGE

1. Item 194, notebook 1: 10, JFK.
2. Hadley Hemingway–Gertrude Stein [7 Mar. 1922], YUL. Virgil Thompson in *Gertrude Stein: A Composite Portrait*, ed. Linda Simon (New York: Avon Books, 1974), p. 123.
3. Joost, *Scofield Thayer and the Dial*, pp. 167–8.
4. Knoll, pp. 201–7; Sisley Huddleston, *Paris Salons, Cafes, Studios* (Philadelphia: Lippincott, 1928), p. 315; Berenson quoted in Lynn, pp. 168–9.
5. See *Young Hemingway*, pp. 81–2.
6. *AMF*, p. 14. Paul Smith first identified the purple ink remarks as possibly coming from Stein.
7. Gertrude Stein–Sherwood Anderson, n.d., NBL; see also Linda Simon, *The Biography of Alice B. Toklas* (Garden City, NY: Doubleday, 1977) and Mellow, *Charmed Circle*; Bravig Imbs, *Confessions of Another Young Man*, in *Gertrude Stein: A Composite Portrait*, ed. Linda Simon, p. 159.
8. EH–Sherwood Anderson, 9 Mar. 1922, NBL; Shari Benstock, *Women of the Left Bank* (Austin: University of Texas Press, 1986), passim; *Young Hemingway*, pp. 78–81.
9. Baker, p. 87; Mellow, p. 316; typescript for "Up in Michigan," JFK; *AMF*, pp. 14–15.
10. Bravig Imbs in *Gertrude Stein: A Composite Portrait*, p. 163.
11. "Mildred's Thoughts," vol. 1 of *Previously Uncollected Writings of Gertrude Stein*, ed. R. B. Haas (Los Angeles: Black Sparrow Press, 1974), p. 83.
12. Item 247a, JFK.
13. Gertrude Stein, *Operas and Plays* (Paris, 1932), p. 108.
14. *Operas and Plays*, pp. 109, 110; this conjecture comes from Richard Bridgman's *Gertrude Stein in Pieces* (New York: Oxford University Press, 1970), pp. 165–6.
15. *Gertrude Stein: A Composite Portrait*, pp. 134–6; Mellow, p. 184; EH gallery bills, JFK.
16. "On Writing," *NAS*, pp. 239–40; Baker, p. 85; Louis Hourtico, *Guide to the Louvre* (Paris: Hachette, 1924), p. 159; Mellow, p. 94.
17. Mellow, pp. 306–8; *Hemingway's First War*, pp. 4–8; *Young Hemingway*, p. 224.

18. Ezra Pound–EH, 10 Apr. 1922, JFK.
19. *Tribune*; Carole Fink, *The Genoa Conference* (Chapel Hill: University of North Carolina Press, 1984), pp. 143–72.
20. "Genoa Conference," *DL:T*, p. 131; John Bone–EH, 12 Apr. 1922, JFK.
21. Seldes notes, Baker file, PUL.
22. "Russian Girls at Genoa," *DL:T*, p. 144.
23. *Tribune*, 11, 12 Apr. 1922; Fink, *The Genoa Conference*, pp. 150–5; Baker, p. 89.
24. Seldes notes, Baker file, PUL.
25. "Well Guarded Russian Delegation," *DL:T*, pp. 159–61.
26. Seldes notes, Baker file, PUL; George Seldes, *World Panorama*, (Boston, Mass.: Little, Brown, 1933), p. 199; Baker, p. 89.
27. *Tribune*, 14 Apr. 1922.
28. *Tribune*, 15–21 Apr. 1922; Seldes notes, Baker file, PUL.
29. *88 Poems*, p. 53.
30. Grace Hemingway scrap books, JFK; EH–Clarence Hemingway, 2 May 1922, JFK.
31. *Tribune*, 1 May 1922.
32. *Young Hemingway*, pp. 71–3.
33. *Tribune*, 2 May 1922.
34. *Tribune*; Beach records, day book 1922, PUL; EH 1921–23 passport, JFK.
35. *Tribune*; Baker file, PUL.
36. Dorman–O'Gowan memoir (1961), Baker file, PUL.
37. Hadley Richardson–EH, 3 June 1921, JFK; *Hemingway's First War*, pp. 4–5; *Young Hemingway*, p. 32.
38. Dorman–O'Gowan memoir, Baker file, PUL.
39. *Green Hills of Africa*, pp. 279–80.
40. *AMF*, pp. 15–16; Mellow, p. 317; EH–Ezra Pound, 6 Sept. 1923, *SL*, p. 93; Item 624.6, "Oh, Canada,", JFK; EH–Howell Jenkins, 8 Jan. 1922, *SL*, p. 61; EH–Family, received 2 Feb. 1922, Lilly; EH–Clarence Hemingway, 24 May 1922, *SL*, pp. 67–8; Hadley's Midnight Poem, Hadley Hemingway MS, JFK.
41. John Bone–EH, 8 Apr. 1922, JFK; EH–Clarence Hemingway, 24 May 1922, *SL*, p. 67.
42. Dorman–O'Gowan memoir, Baker file, PUL.
43. EH–Gertrude Stein, 11 June 1922, *SL*, p. 69.
44. *Baedeker's Switzerland* (1922), pp. 332–3.
45. Hadley interview, Baker file, PUL.

46. *DL:T*, pp. 172–3.
47. *DL:T*, pp. 176–80.
48. EH–James Gamble, 12 Dec. 1923, *SL*, pp. 106–8; Hadley Hemingway–EH [29 Mar. 1923], JFK; Ezra Pound, "Blandula, Tenulla, Vagula," *Selected Poems* (New York: New Directions, 1957), p. 13; *Canto III*, lines 12–16.
49. "A Veteran Visits the Old Front," *DL:T*, p. 176.

Chapter Four: FIRST BLOOD

1. Item 520, JFK.
2. *CSS*, p. 159.
3. *CSS*, p. 160.
4. *Young Hemingway*, pp. 30–1, 101–2; Baker, pp. 6–7, 11.
5. *Tribune*, 27 July 1922; London *Times*, 17 Aug. and 27 Sept. 1922; Greg Clark–EH, 2 Sept. 1922, JFK: "I shall watch for your Old Man story."
6. "On Writing," *NAS*, p. 237.
7. London *Times*, 18 Apr. 1923.
8. EH–Scott Fitzgerald, c. 24 Dec. 1925, *SL*, p. 180.
9. *Death in the Afternoon*, p. 122.
10. "Ultimately," *Double Dealer*, 3 (June 1922), 337.
11. John McClure–EH, August 1922, JFK.
12. EH–Harriet Monroe, 16 July 1922, *SL*, p. 70.
13. *Poetry*, 21 (January 1923), 193–5.
14. *Tribune*, 23 July 1922.
15. *88 Poems*, pp. 54–6.
16. EH 1921–23 passport, JFK.
17. *Tribune; DL:T*, p. 205.
18. *Tribune*, 18 July 1922; *DL:T*, p. 205; *Tribune*, 2 Aug. 1922; *DL:T*, pp. 206–7; Hadley's fur coat purchased before her wedding to Ernest.
19. *DL:T*, p.197.
20. *Tribune*, 24 Aug.–2 Sept. 1922.

Chapter Five: ON THE ROAD

1. *Tribune*, 8 Sept. 1922.
2. John Bone–EH, 25 Sept. 1922, JFK; Baker, p. 101; *Tribune*, 12 Sept. 1922; Scott Donaldson, "Hemingway of the Star," *Ernest Hemingway, the Papers of a Writer*, ed. Bernard Oldsey (New York: Garland, 1981), p. 93.
3. Baker interview with *Star* reporters, Baker file, PUL; Baker, p. 97.
4. EH–John Bone, c. 18 Sept. 1922, JFK; EH-John Bone, 27 Oct. 1922, JFK.
5. Hadley interview, Baker file, PUL; Kert, pp. 123–4; Sokoloff, pp. 56–7; Baker, p. 97.
6. EH–John Bone, 27 Oct. 1922, JFK.
7. EH–Bill Horne, 17–18 July 1923, JFK; *Tribune*, 24, 25 Sept. 1922; Item 773e, Miscl. Box, EH Collection, JFK.
8. Lincoln Steffens, *The World of Lincoln Steffens*, ed. Ella Winter and Herbert Shapiro (New York: Hill & Wang, 1962), "The Carpentier–Siki Fight," pp. 245–50; *Tribune*, 25 Sept. 1922.
9. *DL:T*, p. 225.
10. *Tribune*, 25–29 Sept. 1922.
11. Donaldson, "Hemingway of the Star," p. 94; EH Collection, various journalistic items, JFK; *DL:T*, pp. 237–8; EH–John Bone, 27 Oct. 1922, JFK; Frank Mason–EH, wire, 27 Nov. 1922, JFK.
12. EH–John Bone, 27 Oct. 1922, JFK.
13. EH–John Bone, 27 Oct. 1922, JFK; Black's Guide Books, *Constantinople* (London: Adam and Charles Black, 1910); *DL:T*, p. 229; *Tribune*, 1–3 Oct. 1922; Baker, pp. 97–9; Meyers, pp. 97–102.
14. EH expenses, JFK; *Tribune*, 4–16 Oct. 1922; "The Snows of Kilimanjaro," *CSS*, p. 48; EH 1921–23 passport, JFK.
15. *DL:T*, p. 232.
16. Hadley interview, Baker file, PUL; Sokoloff, p. 57; EH 1921–23 passport, JFK.
17. Frazier Hunt–EH, 21 Sept. 1922, JFK.
18. Greg Clark–EH, 21 Nov. 1922, JFK; EH–John Bone, 27 Oct. 1922, JFK; John Bone–EH, 8 Nov. 1922, JFK.
19. *Young Hemingway*, p. 134; Beach records, Beach Collection, PUL; John Bone–EH, 13 Dec. 1922, JFK.

20. Hugh Ford, *Published in Paris* (Yonkers, NY: Pushcart Press, 1975), pp. 96–9; Baker, pp. 100–1; Ezra Pound–F. M. Ford, 1 Aug. 1922, in *Pound/Ford*, ed. Brita Lindberg-Seyersted (New York: New Directions, 1971), pp. 68–9.

21. Greg Clark–EH, 21 Nov. 1922, JFK; Clarence Hemingway–Ezra Pound, n.d., Baker Collection, PUL; Grace Hemingway–Ezra Pound, 18 Nov. 1922, Lilly.

22. EH–Monroe, 16 Nov. 1922, *SL*, p. 72.

23. Alfred Kreymborg, "Bel Esprit," *Double Dealer*, 3 (June 1922), 326; William Carlos Williams–Ezra Pound, 29 Mar. 1922, Lilly.

24. Ezra Pound–EH [November 1922], Lilly. Hemingway habitually and willfully misspelled Eliot's name; Vivienne Eliot–Ezra Pound, 2 Nov. 1922, Lilly; T. S. Eliot–Ezra Pound, November 1922, Lilly.

25. *Post* article and Eliot's response clipped and part of the Pound Collection, Lilly; Pound solicitation in Ezra Pound–Kate Buss, March 1923, *The Selected Letters of Ezra Pound 1907–1941*, ed. D. D. Paige (New York: New Directions, 1971), p. 175.

26. *Tribune*, 5 and 7 Nov. 1922.

27. Donaldson, "Hemingway of the *Star*", pp. 93–6; Baker, pp. 102–3; EH 1921–23 passport, JFK; Mason–EH file, JFK; in spite of numerous statements about EH's duplicity at Lausanne, there is no evidence that he sent any telegrams to the *Star* or that he collected any expenses or pay from John Bone for the conference. He did sell the *Star* two feature stories, but no spot news.

28. *Tribune*, 22–24 Nov. 1922.

29. Mason–EH wires, 23, 24, 25, 27 Nov. 1922, JFK.

30. *Tribune*, 24–29 Nov. 1922; Mason–EH file, JFK.

31. *Tribune*, 29 Nov. 1922.

32. EH–Hadley Hemingway, 28 Nov. 1922, *SL*, pp. 73–4.

33. EH–Isabel Simmons, *SL*, pp. 74–6; Sokoloff, pp. 59–60; Baker, p. 103; Kert, pp. 127–8; EH 1921–23 passport, JFK.

Chapter Six: STARTING OVER

1. Hadley Hemingway–Gertrude Stein, 19 Dec. 1922 forwarded to St. Rémy, JFK; Bridgman, *Gertrude Stein in Pieces*, appendix; EH claimed in letter to Edmund Wilson (25 Nov. 1923) that he lunched with Gertrude the day after he returned to Paris, but that was Hemingway's fiction, dropping names to impress Wilson; dating of Hadley's arrival and EH's Paris trip confirmed by EH–Miriam Hapgood letter dated "Sunday," Lausanne, SUL.
2. Hadley interview, Baker file, PUL; Hadley Richardson Mowrer to author, 1972; Greg Clark–EH, 16 July 1922, JFK; see also "The Strange Country," *CSS*, for another version.
3. *88 Poems*, pp. 63–4.
4. L. Steffens–EH, 9 Dec. 1922, JFK.
5. Hadley Hemingway–Grace Hemingway, 12 Dec. 1922, JFK.
6. EH–Alice Langelier, 5 Dec. 1922, JFK.
7. *Baedeker's Switzerland*; Hadley Hemingway–Grace Hemingway, 12 Dec. 1922, JFK.
8. EH–Frank Mason, cable, n.d. [December 1922], JFK; Frank Mason–EH, 14 Dec. 1922, JFK; EH–Frank Mason, cable, JFK; EH–Frank Mason, 15 Dec. 1922, JFK.
9. Dorman–O'Gowan memoir, Baker file, PUL.
10. Silver cup in Princeton Library Hemingway Collection along with clipping from unnamed local paper in English; *Baedeker's Switzerland*.
11. *Tribune*, 2 Jan. 1923; Hadley Richardson–EH, 8 Jan. 1921, JFK; Hadley Hemingway–Isabel Simmons, c. 19 Jan. 1923, EH Collection, PUL.
12. EH–Ezra Pound, 23 Jan. 1923, *SL*, p. 77; Hadley Hemingway–Isabel Simmons, c. 19 Jan. 1923, EH Collection, PUL: Ezra Pound–EH, 27 Jan. 1923, JFK.
13. Items 647, 647a, JFK.
14. *Literary Essays of Ezra Pound*, pp. 3–4.
15. Item 647a, JFK.
16. Hadley Hemingway–Isabel Simmons, c. 19 Jan. 1923, JFK; EH–Ezra Pound, 23 Jan. 1923, Lilly, *SL*, p. 77.
17. EH–Ezra Pound, 29 Jan. 1923, *SL*, p. 79.
18. *Poetry*–EH, 15 Jan. 1923, JFK; Hadley Hemingway–Grace Hemingway [January 1923], JFK; Robert W. Chambers, "What is

Genius," in *Literature in the Making*, ed. Joyce Kilmer (New York: Harper Brothers, 1917), pp. 78–84.

19. *Literature in the Making*, p. 154; EH–Gertrude Stein, c. 18 Feb. 1923, YUL; Hadley Hemingway–Isabel Simmons, c. 19 Jan. 1923, PUL [misdated in *Hemingway's Reading*].

20. EH–Ezra Pound, 23 and 29 Jan. 1923, *SL*, pp. 76–9; Ezra Pound–EH, 27 Jan. 1923, JFK.

21. *Dial* (January 1923), 85; John Tytell, *Ezra Pound* (New York: Doubleday, 1987), pp. 178–80; *Nancy Cunard*, ed. Hugh Ford (New York: Chilton, 1968), pp. 38–97.

22. Items 299, 298, JFK.

23. Item 298, JFK; *Da Rapallo . . . con nostalgia* (Rapallo: Edizione a dura del comune di Rapallo, 1984); *Rapallo*, ed. Luigi Gravina (Rapallo: n.p., 1921 edn).

24. EH–Gertrude Stein, c. 18 Feb. 1923, JFK, *SL*, p. 79.

25. Hadley Hemingway Mowrer–Carlos Baker, 7 Aug. 1962, PUL.

26. Item 321, JFK.

27. EH–Edward O'Brien, 2 May 1924, *SL*, p. 117.

28. McAlmon, p. 257.

29. Baker, pp. 106, 118–19; EH–Edward O'Brien, 21 May 1923, *SL*, pp. 82–3; Item 670.4, JFK.

30. *The Complete Poems and Plays* (New York: Harcourt Brace, 1952), p. 43.

31. Nancy Cunard–Ezra Pound, 17 Mar. 1923, Lilly.

32. Stein, "Vacation in Britany," *Little Review* (Spring 1922), 6.

33. Ezra Pound–William Carlos Williams, 9 Feb. 1923, *Letters of Ezra Pound*, ed. D. D. Paige, p. 186; EH–Gertrude Stein, c. 18 Feb. 1923, *SL*, p. 79; EH–Ezra Pound, 10 Mar. 1923, *SL*, pp. 80–1; Ezra Pound–John Quinn, 17 Feb. 1923, quoted in Daniel Pearlman's *The Barb of Time* (New York: Oxford University Press, 1969), p. 303; Ezra Pound letter dated 24 Feb. 1923, YUL, Paige Collection (no. 628): "Expect to do a little cross country plunge next week"; Ezra Pound's Vatican Library call slips, YUL; Lawrence Rainey–Carlos Baker, 15 Nov. 1982, Baker Collection, PUL, containing Pound data at Yale; Hadley Mowrer–Carlos Baker, 7 Aug. 1962, Baker Collection, PUL.

34. See *Hemingway's Reading*; *Hemingway's First War*; James D. Brasch and Joseph Sigman, *Hemingway's Library* (New York: Garland, 1981).

35. EH–Scott Fitzgerald, c. 24 Dec. 1925, *SL*, p. 181; EH–Ezra

Pound, 10 Mar. 1923, *SL*, p. 80; McAlmon, p. 175.

36. Benstock, *Women of the Left Bank*, p. 361; see McAlmon's collections of short stories.
37. F. Scott Fitzgerald quote from notebooks reproduced in Bruccoli, p. 166; Benstock, *Women of the Left Bank*, pp. 312–13, 357–62; Smoller, p. 29.
38. Henry Strater interview in Brian, pp. 41–2.
39. *Der Querschnitt* (November 1924), reprinted in *88 Poems*, p. 77.
40. EH–Ezra Pound, 10 Mar. 1923, *SL*, p. 80; Joost, *Hemingway and the Little Magazines*, p. 138; Knoll, pp. 108ff.
41. "Recent Publications," *Tribune*, 5 Mar. 1923.
42. EH–Gertrude Stein, c. 18 Feb. 1923, *SL*, pp. 79–80.
43. Hadley Richardson letters to Ernest Hemingway, 1920–21, EH Collection, JFK.
44. Ezra Pound, "Mr. Nixon," in *Hugh Selwyn Mauberley, Selected Poems* (New York: New Directions, 1957), p. 67.
45. McAlmon, p. 255.
46. Item 529a, JFK.
47. Brian, pp. 41–2.
48. Item 670, JFK; since their baby was not born until October 10, Hadley would not have missed her second period until late February or early March, too late to color the month's activities.
49. Baker, p. 108; "In Our Time," *Little Review*, Exiles number, 9 (Spring 1923), 3–5, not published until fall of 1923. The confusion created by Hemingway's title is due to the three different versions of his vignettes printed under variations of the same title. The first six vignettes appeared as "In Our Time" in the 1923 *Little Review*. The second collection of eighteen vignettes were published in Paris in 1924 as *in our time*. In 1925, his first volume of short stories appeared as *In Our Time*, using most of the vignettes as divisions between stories.
50. Item 92, JFK.
51. *Little Review*, pp. 3–5.
52. *Tribune*, 29 Nov. 1922.
53. *Little Review*, pp. 3–5.
54. Item 94b, JFK.
55. Look at his depiction of artist-figures in his fiction and read Robert Fleming's forthcoming book on the subject.
56. Bone telegrams are in EH Collection, JFK; Hadley Hemingway–EH, 29 Mar. 1923, JFK, alludes to her pregnancy.

57. *Tribune*, 23–28 Mar. 1923.
58. *Tribune*, 23 Mar. 1923; EH–Clarence Hemingway, 23 Mar. 1923, JFK; telegram file, JFK; Hadley Hemingway letters to EH addressed in care of Guy Hickok, JFK.
59. Hadley Hemingway–EH, 29 Mar. 1923, JFK; see Gertrude Stein's account of this visit in *The Autobiography of Alice B. Toklas*.
60. "The Franco German Situation," "French Royalist Party" and "Government Pays for News," *DL:T*, pp. 260–70. These stories did not run until 14, 18, 21 April in the *Star*, for mail usually took two weeks by boat to reach Canada.
61. *Tribune*, 23–29 Mar. 1923; embassy letter, JFK; "Getting into Germany," *DL:T*, p. 277.
62. *Tribune*; Hadley Hemingway–EH, 29 Mar. 1923, JFK; Hadley Hemingway–EH, 31 Mar. 1923, JFK.
63. Safe conduct pass, JFK; John Bone–EH, 29 Apr. 1923, JFK; Hadley Hemingway–EH, 31 Mar. 1923, JFK; Press pass to fights, Miscl. Box, EH Collection, JFK.

Chapter Seven: FORM AND RITUAL

1. EH 1921–23 passport, JFK; *Tribune*.
2. John Bone–EH, 5 May 1923, JFK; *Little Review*, "Exiles Number," dated Spring 1923, did not appear until late in the fall. Ad appeared for *Two Stories & Ten Poems*.
3. Cable, c. 9 May in JFK, but telegram forms indicate it was sent on 11 May; Item 624, JFK.
4. *Tribune*, 7 May 1923, describing fight of 6 May; EH may have remembered the name Hobin when he named his Belgian prostitute Georgette Hobin in *The Sun Also Rises*; EH–Bill Horne, 17–18 July 1923, *SL*, p. 88; EH–Gertrude Stein, 20 June 1923, *SL*, p. 83; EH–Isabel Simmons, 24 June 1923, pp. 83–4.
5. See Kansas City *Star*, 19 Nov. 1917, and Reynolds, "Two Hemingway Sources for *in our time*," *SSF* (Winter 1972), 81–6; Item 94a, JFK.
6. "chapter 9," *in our time*, p. 17.
7. Versions in Items 671, 94 and 94a, JFK; "chapter 8," *in our time*, p. 16.
8. Item 94a, JFK.
9. See *Young Hemingway* for information on Nick Nerone; Item

633, JFK, found thanks to Paul Smith, part of the same pages as "One hot evening in Milan. . ."

10. Items 326, 326a, JFK.
11. EH–Edward O'Brien, 21 May 1923, *SL*, p. 82.
12. Baker, pp. 110–11; Meyers, p. 199; see also photographs in McAlmon, *Being Geniuses Together* and Smoller, *Adrift Among Geniuses; Young Hemingway*, on Jim Gamble, pp. 169–72, 189–90.
13. Baker, p. 110; Baker file and interviews, PUL.
14. McAlmon, pp. 178–80.
15. McAlmon, p. 179.
16. McAlmon, p. 179; Item 203b, p. 7, JFK. From the position in the notebook, it would appear this scene took place returning from Spain rather than on the way down; *Death in the Afternoon*, pp. 137–40.
17. Items 203b and 295, JFK; *88 Poems*, pp. 71–3.
18. Item 398, JFK; EH–Greg Clark, c. 20 June 1923, JFK; EH–Clarence Hemingway, 20 June 1923, JFK.
19. EH–Clarence Hemingway, 20 June 1923, JFK; EH–Isabel Simmons, 24 June 1923, JFK; *Tribune*, 17 June 1923.
20. *Tribune*, 18 June 1923; EH–Isabel Simmons, 24 June 1923, JFK.
21. EH–Gertrude Stein, 20 June 1923, YUL, *SL*, p. 83; EH–Greg Clark, c. June 1923, JFK; Linda Simon, *The Biography of Alice B. Toklas*, pp. 116–18.
22. See *Young Hemingway* for Oak Park background; Baker, p. 114; EH–Isabel Simmons, 24 June 1923, JFK; EH–Bill Horne, 17–18 July 1923, *SL*, pp. 85–9; Clarence Hemingway–EH, 22 Sept. 1923, UTex; Hadley interview, Baker file, PUL.
23. Item 414, JFK.
24. Item 645a, JFK.
25. Item 414, JFK; *DL:T*, pp. 347–50.
26. Item 414, JFK; EH–Bill Horne, 17–18 July 1923, *SL*, p. 88.
27. EH–Bill Horne, 17–18 July 1923, *SL*, p. 88; EH–Greg Clark, c. June/July 1923, JFK.
28. *El Sol* (Madrid newspaper), 11–13 July 1923.
29. *100 Años de Carteles de las Fiestas y Ferias de San Fermín 1882–1981*, textos: Ricardo Ollaquindia (Pamplona: Caja de Ahorros de Navarra, 1982), n.p., back of 1925 poster; "Pamplona in July," *DL:T*, pp. 351–4.
30. *Tribune*, 12–15 July 1923.
31. Item 409a, JFK.

32. *Tribune*, 16, 17 July 1923; EH–Bill Horne, 17–18 July 1923, *SL*, pp. 85–9.
33. EH–Ezra Pound, c. 5 Aug. 1923, *SL*, p. 91; *Death in the Afternoon*, pp. 2–3; "chapter 12," "chapter 14," *in our time*, pp. 22, 24.
34. "chapter 15," *in our time*, p. 25.
35. Items 564 and 564a, JFK.
36. "chapter 16," *in our time*, p. 27.
37. EH–Ezra Pound, 5 Aug. 1923, *SL*, p. 91.
38. *Tribune*, 29, 31 July, 4 Aug. 1923; "chapter 18," *in our time*, p. 30.
39. EH–Ezra Pound, c. 5 Aug. 1923, *SL*, pp. 91–2.
40. "chapter 17," *in our time*, p. 28.
41. See *Young Hemingway*, pp. 214–17.
42. EH–Robert McAlmon, 5 Aug. 1923, SL, p. 90; Ford, *Published in Paris*, pp. 95–8, 100, 105–6.
43. Contact Press journal, Beach Collection, PUL; Audre Hanneman, *Ernest Hemingway: A Comprehensive Bibliography*, vol. 1 (Princeton, NJ: Princeton University Press, 1967), p. 5.
44. *Tribune*, 16–26 Aug. 1923; EH 1921–23 passport stamped departing at Cherbourg 26 Aug. 1923, JFK.

Chapter Eight: RETURN TO TORONTO

1. EH–Ezra Pound, c. 6 Sept. 1923, *SL*, pp. 92–3; Charles Fenton, *The Apprenticeship of Ernest Hemingway* (New York: Farrar, Strauss & Young, 1954), pp. 242–6; EH–Ezra Pound, 9 Dec. 1923, Lilly.
2. Hadley Hemingway–Grace Hemingway, 15 Sept. 1923, Baker Collection, PUL; Pullman ticket in Item 682b, JFK.
3. Story dated 14 Sept. 1923, apparently unpublished, with note to Hindmarsh, typescript, Item 682a, JFK; see also Scott Donaldson's excellent article "Hemingway of the *Star*," in *Ernest Hemingway, the Papers of a Writer*, ed. Bernard Oldsey, pp. 89–107, used throughout this section.
4. EH–H. C. Hindmarsh, Item 682b, JFK; H. C. Hindmarsh–EH, undated, Item 682b, JFK.
5. Pullman ticket, Item 682b, JFK; "Search for Sudbury Coal," 25

Sept. 1923, *DL:T*, pp. 301–7; EH–Ezra Pound [23 Sept. 1923], Lilly.

6. Clarence Hemingway–EH, 22 Sept. 1923, UTex; Hadley Hemingway–Grace Hemingway, 27 Sept. 1923, JFK; Lease file, JFK; Hadley Hemingway–Grace Hemingway, 18 Oct. 1923, JFK; Hadley Hemingway MS, n.d., probably late 1924, JFK.

7. Fenton, *Apprenticeship*, p. 255; *DL:T*, pp. 318–39; *Little Review* (Spring 1923), 5; EH–Gertrude Stein, 11 Oct. 1923, *SL*, p. 94.

8. Hadley Hemingway–EH, n.d. [October 1923], JFK; Hadley Hemingway–EH, 8 Oct. 1923, JFK; Clarence Hemingway–EH/ Hadley Hemingway, 25, 30 Sept. 1923, UTex.

9. Kert, pp. 140–1; EH–Ezra Pound, 13 Oct. 1923, *SL*, pp. 95–7; Hadley Hemingway–Isabel Simmons Godolphin [October 1923], EH Collection, PUL.

10. Fenton, *Apprenticeship*, p. 255; EH–Ezra Pound, 13 Oct. 1923, *SL*, p. 96; Hadley Hemingway–Isabel Simmons Godolphin [October 1923], PUL.

11. Fenton, *Apprenticeship*, p. 256; Brian, p. 47.

12. *DL:T*, p. 354.

13. Ezra Pound–EH, 21 Sept. 1923, JFK.

14. William Bird–Ezra Pound, 17 Sept. 1923, PUL and JFK.

15. Edward O'Brien–EH [8 Oct. 1923; mailed to Paris and forwarded to Toronto], JFK.

16. EH–Edward O'Brien, c. 20 Nov. 1923, *SL*, pp. 103–4. This letter probably written earlier than it is dated. November 6 letter to SB, EH talks about O'Brien's request.

17. EH–Sylvia Beach, 6 Nov. 1923 [mailed sometime later], *SL*, p. 98; EH–Edmund Wilson, 11 and 25 Nov. 1923, *SL*, pp. 102–3, 104–6.

18. EH–Gertrude Stein, 9 Nov. 1923, *SL*, pp. 100–2; letter misdated, probably mid-December; *Tribune*, 27 Nov. 1923, p. 4; see Scott Donaldson, "Gertrude Stein Reviews Hemingway's *Three Stories and Ten Poems*," *American Literature*, 53 (March 1981), 114–15.

19. William Bird–EH, 8 and 11 Sept. 1923, JFK; EH–Ezra Pound, 13 Oct. 1923, *SL*, p. 96; Item 624.6, JFK; Ezra Pound–EH, 3 Dec. 1923, JFK.

20. *SL*, p. 97; EH–Clarence Hemingway, 7 Nov. 1923, *SL*, p. 100; EH–Gertrude Stein, 9 Nov. 1923, *SL*, pp. 100–1. Letter partially misdated. Begins on November 9, but breaks toward the end and finished sometime in December; *Tribune*, 9 Dec. 1923.

21. William Bird–EH, 24 Nov. 1923, JFK; EH–Clarence Hemingway, 7 Nov. 1923, *SL*, p. 99; William Bird–EH, 5 Dec. 1923, JFK.

22. William Bird–EH, 5 Dec. 1923, JFK; Beach record books, Beach Collection, PUL: *Tribune*, 10 Dec. 1923.

23. *Tribune*, 15 Dec. 1923.

24. Carol Hemingway–EH, November 1923, JFK; Hadley Hemingway–Isabel Simmons, c. 20 Oct. 1923, PUL; Clarence Hemingway–EH/Hadley Hemingway, 11 Oct. 1923, JFK; EH–Clarence Hemingway, 7 Nov. 1923, *SL*, p. 99; Hadley Hemingway–Grace Hemingway, 8 Dec. 1923, JFK.

25. Interview with *Star* reporters, Baker file, PUL.

26. EH–Ezra Pound, 9 Dec. 1923, Lilly; Hadley Hemingway–Isabel Simmons, 12 Dec. 1923, PUL.

27. Baker, p. 121; Grace Hemingway–EH, 26 Dec. 1923, JFK; Marcelline Hemingway Sanford, *At the Hemingways'* (Boston, Mass.: Little, Brown, 1961), pp. 215–16.

28. Hadley Hemingway–Grace Hemingway, 2 Jan. 1924, JFK; EH–John Bone, c. 26 Dec. 1923, *SL*, p. 108; EH–John Bone, c. 27 Dec. 1923, *SL*, p. 109; EH notebook 1923–24, JFK; William Bird–EH, 19 Dec. 1923, JFK.

Chapter Nine: TRANSATLANTIC PASSAGE

1. *Tribune*, 31 Jan. 1924; EH–Ezra Pound, 10 Feb. 1924, *SL*, p. 110.

2. EH–Ezra Pound, 10 Feb. 1924, *SL*, p. 110.

3. Lease agreement with P. Chautard, JFK; Baker, pp. 122–3; Hadley Hemingway–Grace Hemingway, 20 Feb. 1924, JFK.

4. *Tribune*, 12 Feb. 1924.

5. 10 Feb. 1924, *SL*, pp. 110–11; Contact Press records, Beach Collection, PUL: Marcelline Hemingway Sanford–EH, 20 Oct. 1923, JFK; EH–Scott Fitzgerald, 24 Dec. 1925, *SL*, p. 181.

6. EH–Gertrude Stein, 9 Nov. 1923, *SL*, p. 101; EH–Gertrude Stein, 17 Feb. 1924, *SL*, pp. 111–12.

7. Ticket stub, EH Collection, JFK; EH–Gertrude Stein, 9 Nov. 1923, *SL*, p. 101.

8. *Tribune*, 20 Feb. 1924.

9. Hadley Hemingway–Grace Hemingway, 20 Feb. 1924, JFK; "On Writing," *NAS*, p. 238.

10. "Indian Camp," *CSS*, pp. 67–70.
11. EH–Ezra Pound, 2 May 1924, *SL*, p. 115; EH–Ezra Pound, 17 Mar. 1924, *SL*, p. 113.
12. Poli, pp. 63–4; *Tribune*, 21 Feb. 1924.
13. *transatlantic*, nos 1, 2, 3 (Jan., Feb., Mar. 1924).
14. EH–Ezra Pound, c. 2 May 1924, *SL*, p. 116.
15. EH–Ezra Pound, 17 Mar. 1924, *SL*, p. 113; Arthur Mizener, *The Saddest Story* (New York: World Publishing, 1971), pp. 328–34.
16. "From a Paris Quay," *New York Evening Post Literary Review*, 3 Jan. 1925; McAlmon, pp. 127–8; Loeb, *The Way It Was*, pp. 188–9; Poli, *Ford and the Transatlantic Review*; Ezra Pound, "Hugh Selwyn Mauberley," *Selected Poems*, p. 61.
17. EH–Ezra Pound, 17 Mar. 1924, *SL*, p. 113; Mizener, *The Saddest Story*, pp. 281–93.
18. Poli, pp. 58–134; Mizener, *The Saddest Story*, pp. 328–42.
19. Baker, pp. 124–6; William Bird–Bernard Poli, 10 Nov. 1961, quoted in Poli, p. 26; Baker on rewriting stories, p. 123.
20. EH on Miró's boxing quoted in Carolyn Lanchner, "André Masson: Origins and Development," in her book *André Masson* (New York: Museum of Modern Art, 1976), p. 86; Lanchner quotes Masson on ego, p. 84.
21. Lanchner, *André Masson*, pp. 86–93; Emily Stipes Watts, *Ernest Hemingway and the Arts* (Urbana: University of Illinois Press, 1971), pp. 82–92; *Green Hills of Africa*, p. 96.
22. Program for Galerie Simon, EH Collection, JFK; *Tribune*; Lanchner, *André Masson*.
23. For reproductions of most of these paintings see E. S. Watts' *Hemingway and the Arts*. The only source for Stein's advice is Hemingway's own account in *A Moveable Feast*; Rudolph Levy, "Der Dome," *Der Querschnitt*, 6 (December 1921), 250.
24. Hadley interview, Baker file, PUL.
25. Kert, p. 144; Sokoloff, p. 71; William Carlos Williams, *Autobiography* (New York: Random House, 1951), pp. 226–7; Dr. Hemingway's baby food, family letters, UTex; see also Baker's footnotes on William Carlos Williams.
26. Paul Smith, *Reader's Guide* in MS; Hemingway MSS 321, 319, 320, JFK; "Cat in the Rain," *CSS*, p. 131.
27. Hadley Hemingway MS, EH Collection, JFK.
28. Although some have said the baptism took place on March 10, the baptismal certificate at JFK clearly says March 16. EH–Ezra Pound

letter, 17 Mar. 1924, *SL*, p. 113, says "We christened the baby . . . Sunday." The previous Sunday was March 16. March 10, 1924 fell on a Monday.

29. EH–Family, 7 May 1924, Lilly.

Chapter Ten: TWO-HEARTED PARIS

1. Hadley Hemingway–Mr. Cummings [late March 1924], JFK; Hadley Hemingway–Joseph White, 26 Mar. 1924, JFK; Hadley Hemingway–George Breaker, 11 May 1924, JFK; Hadley Hemingway–George Breaker, 20 May 1924, JFK. All wires drafted in EH's hand.

2. See Aaron E. Hotchner's *Papa Hemingway* (New York: Random House, 1966) for the invention of the pigeons and other rare birds; Baker, on boxing, p. 126; Hemingway day book, 1924, JFK.

3. Sarason, pp. 115–16, 147.

4. *Tribune*, 3 and 4 Apr. 1924.

5. *Tribune*, 6 Apr. 1924, "Literary Causeries," Sunday magazine, p. 3; *transatlantic*, 1,4 (Apr. 1924), 230–4, 247–8.

6. Three Mountains/Contact Press record books, Beach Collection, PUL; EH–O'Brien, 2 May 1924, *SL*, p. 117.

7. EH–Ernest Walsh, 2 June 1926, *SL*, p. 188; Ezra Pound–Ford Madox Ford, in *Pound/Ford*, ed. Brita Lindberg-Seyersted, pp. 68–9.

8. See Poli, p. 77.

9. "Ford Madox Ford," a talk taped by station KPFA in Berkeley, California, on 21 Nov. 1961 and printed in Poli, p. 82.

10. *transatlantic*, 1, 5 (May 1924), 355–7.

11. EH–Ezra Pound, c. 2 May 1924, *SL*, p. 115; the Galantière article refered to apparently appeared in the April 27, 1924 Sunday magazine, Paris edition, Chicago *Tribune*, missing on microfilm copy.

12. Dorothy Butler–Hadley Hemingway, c. 24 May 1924, JFK.

13. Copy kept by EH in JFK undated and maybe unsent.

14. EH–Ezra Pound, c. 2 May 1924, *SL*, p. 115.

15. *CSS*, p. 74.

16. *CSS*, p. 75.

17. Clarence Hemingway–EH, 8 Mar. 1925, JFK; see *Young Hemingway*, p. 27; EH–Bill Smith [August 1921], private collection; Paul

Smith has verified in the Charlevoix town records that Boulton's first name was Dick, not Nick.

18. Items 367, 368, EH Collection, JFK; see Paul Smith's chapter in his *Reader's Guide; Tribune*, 7 Apr. 1924.

19. My dating of the composition of the stories is highly dependent upon Paul Smith's *Reader's Guide*.

20. *CSS*, pp. 143–7; Paul Smith chapter; Items 344, 345, 346, 696, EH Collection, JFK.

21. "On Writing," *NAS*, pp. 237–8.

22. EH–Carlos Baker, 24 Feb. 1951, 11 June 1952, Field Collection, SUL; *CSS*, p. 111.

23. *CSS*, pp. 112–13.

24. *CSS*, pp. 114–16; Grace Hemingway–EH, 30 Mar. 1919, private collection.

25. Robert E. Gajdusek, *Hemingway's Paris* (New York: Scribner's, 1978), pp. 97–105; *Green Hills of Africa*, pp. 70–1.

26. Typescript with holograph corrections sent to Jane Heap for the *Little Review*: University of Wisconsin at Milwaukee.

27. *Contemporary Authors*, vol. 6/7, ed. Barbara Harte and Carolyn Riley (Detroit: Gale Research Company, 1969), p. 1064; Paul Smith, "From the Waste Land to the Garden with the Elliots," to be published in a UMI Research Press collection edited by Susan Beegel, 1989.

28. EH–Ezra Pound, 17 Mar. 1924, *SL*, p. 112.

29. Smith, "From the Waste Land to the Garden"; recent biographies have given conflicting dates for the death of Mrs. Smith. I am relying on Chard Powers Smith's own account of his wife's death, written probably in 1925 – "Dedication to O.C.M." – and intended as a forepiece to his first volume of poetry, *Along The Wind*, published by the Yale University Press. Holograph manuscript in the Bancroft Library, University of California, Berkeley.

30. Item 515, JFK.

31. EH–Ezra Pound, c. 2 May 1924, *SL*, p. 115; Brian, p. 49.

32. Item 719, JFK.

33. Item 582, JFK.

34. Item 515, JFK.

35. EH–Ezra Pound, c. 2 May 1924, *SL*, p. 116.

36. *Tribune*, 1, 2 May 1924.

37. EH–Bill Smith, 6 Dec. 1924, *SL*, p. 138; EH–Howell Jenkins, 9 Nov. 1924, *SL*, p. 130.

38. Poli, pp. 79–84, 92–7; EH–Ezra Pound, c. 2 May 1924, *SL*, p. 116.
39. EH–Family, 7 May 1924, Lilly.
40. Leicester's memoir *My Brother, Ernest Hemingway* (New York: World Publishing, 1962) does not mention any family scene, and he was living at home at the time. See Marcelline Hemingway Sanford, *At the Hemingways'*, pp. 218–19.
41. EH–Ezra Pound, 2 May 1924, *SL*, p. 116; Hadley Hemingway–Breaker, wire, 20 May 1924, JFK; Poli, p. 99; G. J. Nathan–EH, 20 May 1924, JFK.
42. *transatlantic*, 2, 1 (July 1924), 94–6.
43. *transatlantic*, 2, 1 (July 1924), 102–3.
44. Poli, p. 103.
45. EH–O'Brien, 2 May 1924, *SL*, pp. 116–17.
46. In 1929, EH, when asked about immortal books, named *Dubliners*, which he probably read early in Paris (EH–"Mr. Gud," October 1929, JFK); Sylvia Beach kept the book continuously in stock at Shakespeare and Company.
47. "In Their Time" exhibition at the Alderman Library, UVa (1977) had this map on exhibit. It was from a private collection.
48. "Trout Fishing" (10 Apr. 1920), *DL:T*, pp. 14–16; "Trout Fishing Hints" (24 Apr. 1920), pp. 22–4; "Camping Out" (26 June 1920), pp. 44–7; "Ted's Skeeters" (7 Aug. 1920), pp. 48–9; "The Best Rainbow Trout Fishing" (28 Aug. 1920), pp. 50–2; "Indoor Fishing" (20 Nov. 1920), pp. 62–4; Hadley Hemingway–EH on bad dreams [29 Mar. 1923], JFK.

Chapter Eleven: THE LITERARY GAME

1. Baker file, PUL.
2. *transatlantic*, 2, 2 (August 1924), 213.
3. See Poli, pp. 104–7.
4. June 1: *Tribune* Sunday magazine, Eugene Jolas, "Through Paris Bookland."
5. Paul Mariani, *William Carlos Williams* (New York: McGraw-Hill, 1981), pp. 237–9; Smoller, pp. 137–40.
6. Item 281, JFK.
7. Hadley Hemingway MS, JFK.
8. Hadley MS describing the 1924 Pamplona trip, JFK.

9. Lincoln Steffens–EH, 20 June 1924, JFK.
10. Hadley MS describing the arrival in Pamplona, EH Collection, JFK.
11. San Fermin program, 1924; EH 1924 notebook, JFK; *Death in the Afternoon*, glossary; EH letters to Gertrude Stein referenced in Baker, p. 129.
12. *El Sol* (Madrid), 14 July 1924.
13. Edward Dorman–Smith, "Il Encerrio," *R.M.C. Magazine and Record* (January 1925), 87–92.
14. Donald O. Stewart, *By a Stroke of Luck* (New York: Paddington Press, 1975), p. 132.
15. Dorman-Smith, "Il Encerrio."
16. Paul Augsburg, editor, to Clarence Hemingway, 29 July 1924, UTex.
17. Clarence Hemingway–Grace Hemingway, 6 Aug. 1924, UTex.
18. Knoll, p. 237.
19. EH–Ezra Pound, 19 July 1924, *SL*, p. 118.
20. Edward Dorman–Smith, "A Bull Fight at Pamplona,", *R.M.C. Magazine and Record* (1924), 20.
21. Ernest Hemingway, *The Dangerous Summer*, p. 135; Townsend Ludington, *John Dos Passos* (New York: E. P. Dutton, 1980), p. 232.
22. San Fermin program, 1924.
23. McAlmon, p. 274; San Fermin program, 1924.
24. San Fermin program, 1924.
25. McAlmon, p. 277; Baker, p. 130; EH–Dorman-Smith, 23 Dec. 1954, *SL*, p. 844.
26. EH day book, 1924, JFK.
27. McAlmon, p. 277; EH day book, 1924, JFK.
28. EH–Ezra Pound, 19 July 1924, *SL*, p. 119; EH day book, 1924, JFK.
29. EH–McAlmon, c. 15 Nov. 1924, *SL*, p. 133.
30. "On Writing," NAS, pp. 233–48.
31. *Tribune*, 27 July 1924.
32. EH–Gertrude Stein, 9 Aug. 1924, *SL*, pp. 120–1.
33. Poli, pp. 110–19; EH–Gertrude Stein, 9 Aug. 1924, *SL*, p. 120.
34. *transatlantic*, 2, 3 (September 1924), 300–2.
35. *Tribune*, 4 Aug. 1924.
36. *transatlantic*, 2, 3 (September 1924), 341–2.
37. EH–George Antheil, n.d., Beach Collection, PUL.

38. *Tribune*, 9 July 1924; see also Hugh Ford's *Four Lives in Paris*, "George Antheil" (San Francisco: North Point Press, 1987), pp. 3–81.

39. See Beach records, PUL, for Antheil "loans"; Antheil–Sylvia Beach, n.d., Beach Collection, PUL.

40. George Antheil–Sylvia Beach, n.d., Beach Collection, PUL.

41. George Antheil–Sylvia Beach, n.d., Beach Collection, PUL.

42. Ford, *Four Lives in Paris*, p. 115.

43. Robert McAlmon, "Truer Than Most Accounts," *The Exile*, 2 (Autumn 1927), 45–6, describing Bastille Day in 1923; EH, *The Sun Also Rises* manuscript, notebook I: 11–12, JFK.

44. *Tribune*, 5, 9 Aug. 1924.

45. "Summer People," *NAS*, p. 227.

46. *Tribune*, 10 Aug. 1924; EH–George Breaker, 27 Aug. 1924, JFK.

47. EH–Gertrude Stein, 15 Aug. 1924, *SL*, p. 122; see "Summer People," *CSS*, pp. 496–503; see Paul Smith, *Reader's Guide*.

48. Brian, pp. 48–9; by "blind eye" Hadley exaggerates Hemingway's poor vision in one eye. This was a genetic inheritance, not a wound.

49. Beach records and Beach postage book, PUL; *Hemingway's Reading*, Item 37, p. 79.

50. EH–George Breaker, 27 Aug. 1924, JFK; EH–Edward O'Brien, 12 Sept. 1924, *SL*, p. 123.

Chapter Twelve: IN THEIR TIME

1. EH–Edward O'Brien, 12 Sept. 1924, *SL*, p. 123.

2. EH–Edmund Wilson, 18 Oct. 1924, *SL*, p. 128.

3. See *Critical Essays on In Our Time*, ed. Michael S. Reynolds (New York: G. K. Hall, 1983) but most particularly Jackson Benson's article therein, "Patterns of Connection and Their Development in Hemingway's *In Our Time*," 103–19; *CSS*, p. 90; the Chaucer connection belongs to Robert Fleming; as will become apparent Hemingway cut the ending of "Big Two-Hearted River" before it was published, erasing what would have been his first metafiction.

4. George Jean Nathan–EH, 29 Aug. and 22 Sept. 1924, JFK; return mail envelopes with type drafts at JFK; keep in mind the two-week minimum delay between letters posted and their transatlantic delivery; Beach records, PUL; EH–Edmund Wilson, 18 Oct. 1924,

SL, p. 128; EH–William Smith, 4 Dec. 1924, *SL*, p. 138.

5. H. L. Mencken, "The Young Writer," *Tribune*, 23 Nov.1924.

6. EH–Gertrude Stein, 14 Sept. 1924, *SL*, p. 125; *Tribune*, 10 Sept. 1924.

7. EH–Gertrude Stein, 14 Sept. 1924, *SL*, p. 126; Hadley Hemingway–Gertrude Stein [19 Sept. 1924], on EH's bad dreams, YUL.

8. Sisley Huddleston, *Paris Salons, Cafes, Studios*, pp. 18–19.

9.. *Tribune*, 17 Sept. 1924.

10. *Tribune*, 26 Sept. 1924.

11. *transatlantic*, 2, 5 (November 1924), 550–1.

12. *transatlantic*, 2, 5, 559–60.

13. Ezra Pound–EH, 6 Oct. 1924, Baker file, PUL; EH–William Smith [9 Jan. 1925], W. B. Smith Collection, PUL.

14. "The Soul of Spain with McAlmon and Bird the Publishers," *Der Querschnitt*, 4 (Autumn 1924), 229.

15. Sarason, pp. 117, 147–8; Loeb, *The Way It Was*, pp. 226–8.

16. "Mr. Hemingway's Dry Points," *Dial*, 77 (October 1924), 340–1; EH–Edmund Wilson, 18 Oct. 1924, *SL*, p. 129.

17. 10 Oct. 1924, *SL*, pp. 127–8.

18. *transatlantic*, 2, 6 (December 1924), 682; Poli, pp. 125–32.

19. *Tribune*, 16 Nov. 1924.

20. *Tribune*, 23 Nov. 1924; Hemingway's comment about being mistaken for a Canadian bears no reference to the Jolas column.

21. See Scott McDonald, "Implications of Narrative Perspective in Hemingway's 'The Undefeated',"*Journal of Narrative Technique*, 2 (January 1972), 1–15.

22. "On Writing," *NAS*, p. 240; Lynn, p. 268.

23. *Selected Writings of Gertrude Stein*, ed. Carl Van Vechten, p. 207.

24. EH manuscript notes originally misfiled with Hadley Hemingway materials at JFK.

25. c. 15 Nov. 1924, *SL*, p. 133.

26. EH–McAlmon, 15 and 20 Nov. 1924, *SL*, pp. 133, 135.

27. Enclosed in a Lewis Galantière–EH letter, 30 Nov. 1924, JFK.

28. EH–McAlmon, 15 Nov. 1924, *SL*, p. 133; *Hemingway's Reading*, pp. 163, 187. Note the 1925 date for his reading of these explorers should be changed to 1924; *Tribune*, 14 Nov. 1924.

29. *Tribune*, 19 Nov., 16 Dec. 1924; EH sent a copy of Van Loan book to a friend, signed copy in a private collection; Lardner book reviewed by *transatlantic*, EH likely read it.

30. EH–McAlmon, 10 Dec. 1924, *SL*, p. 139; McAlmon–EH, c. Christmas 1924, JFK. Without access to the McAlmon letter, Baker misidentified the story in his footnote. See Paul Smith, *Reader's Guide*.

31. *Tribune*, 7 Dec. 1924; EH–Wilson, 18 Oct. 1924, *SL*, p. 129; "The Poppy," *transatlantic*, 2, 5 (November 1924), 483.

32. EH–McAlmon, 20 Nov. 1924, *SL*, p. 135; EH blue notebook #2, JFK.

33. EH–William Smith, 6 Dec. 1924, *SL*, pp. 136–7.

34. Baker, p. 88; see also *Young Hemingway* on "Cross Roads" sketches.

35. EH–William Smith, 6 Dec. 1924, *SL*, p. 137. William Smith–EH, 8 Apr. 1920, JFK.

36. Paul Smith pointed out this usage in Item 384, discarded portion of "Fathers and Sons," JFK.

37. *Tribune*, 22 Dec. 1924, "Notes on Books." *Mal entouré* means "badly surrounded" as associating with the wrong friends. Hemingway was of two minds about the New York crowd. He wanted their acceptance and their praise, but he feared their rejection. It was easier to attack them first, for then when the rejection came, he could take comfort in his expectations fulfilled. At heart, he never learned to take criticism lightly or instructively.

Chapter Thirteen: WAITING IN SCHRUNS

1. *A Moveable Feast*, pp. 198–211.

2. Baker, p. 587; EH–Harold Loeb, 29 Dec. 1924, *SL*, p. 142; EH–Ernest Walsh, c. 27 Dec. 1924, JFK; Herbert Ruhm, "Hemingway in Schruns," *Commonweal*, 99 (28 Dec. 1973), 344–5.

3. Items 298 and 538, Schruns notebook, JFK.

4. EH–Harold Loeb, 29 Dec. 1924, *SL*, p. 141; *AMF*, pp. 201–3; *Fitzgerald/Hemingway Annual 1971*, ed. Matthew J. Bruccoli and C. E. Frazer Clark (Washington, DC: NCR Microcard Editions, 1972), p. 195.

5. Item 553b, Schruns notebook, JFK.

6. EH–Harold Loeb, 5 Jan. 1924, *SL*, p. 142.

7. EH–Harold Loeb, 5 Jan. 1924, *SL*, p. 142; Item 298, blue notebook (Schruns), JFK; EH–George Horace Lorimer, 21 Jan. 1925, *SL*, p. 148.

8. EH–Walsh and Moorhead, c. 12 Jan. 1925, *SL*, p. 144.
9. Item 553b, JFK; see Baker, p. 135.
10. EH–Miriam Hapgood, 12 Jan. 1925, SUL.
11. *AMF*, pp. 198–201; Edward Hattam, "Treks Through Hemingway's Vorarlberg," MS in Baker Collection, PUL; see also Gunter Salzmann, "Hemingway's Schruns," *Bodensee Hefte*, 6 (June 1988), 60–5.
12. EH–Gertrude Stein, 20 Jan. 1925, *SL*, p. 147; I am indebted to Don Junkins for research and details of this paragraph.
13. EH–McAlmon, n.d., Fenton Papers, YUL.
14. EH–Ernest Walsh, 29 and 30 Jan. 1925, JFK.
15. *Der Querschnitt*, 1 (Spring 1924), 86.
16. EH–Jane Heap, 30 Jan. 1925, Baker Collection, PUL; EH notebook, JFK; *CSS*, p. 275; the "farts" were suppressed then and now. See Paul Smith's *Reader's Guide*. EH–William Smith, 30 Jan. 1925, private collection.
17. *Tribune*, 28 Jan. 1925; EH–Jane Heap, 30 Jan. 1925, PUL.
18. Item 291, Schruns notebook, JFK.
19. EH–William Smith, 30 Jan. and 4 Mar. 1924, private collection.
20. EH–William Smith, 17 Feb. 1924, Baker Collection, PUL; EH–William Smith, 28 Feb. 1924, Field Collection, SUL.
21. Meyers, p. 154; EH–William Smith, 18 Jan. [1925], W. B. Smith Collection, PUL; W. B. Smith interview with Carlos Baker, Baker file, PUL.
22. EH–William Smith, 17 Feb. 1925, W. B. Smith Collection, PUL.
23. Schruns notebook, JFK; Frank Crowninshield–EH, 22 Jan. 1925, JFK; *In Our Time*, p. 66. Because the rejection letter does not mention the title of the rejected story, it is my speculation that it was "A Very Short Story." It was the only story he had that was short enough for the *Vanity Fair* format and that could be called "clever and amusing." Paul Smith disagrees.
24. Max Perkins–EH, 21 Feb. 1925, Scribner's Author file, PUL.
25. Scribner's Author file, PUL; EH–William Smith, 26 Feb. 1925, W. B. Smith Collection, PUL. Loeb's telegram only said, "BOOK ACCEPTED." (22 Jan. 1925, JFK).
26. EH–Harold Loeb, 27 Feb. 1925, *SL*, p. 151; EH–Leon Fleischman, 2 Mar. 1925, *In Their Time* catalog, Item 38, UVa.
27. EH–Ernest Walsh, 28 Feb. 1925, JFK; EH–Jane Heap, 4 Mar. 1925, Baker Collection, PUL; telegram, *In Their Time*, Item 37; EH–Ernest Walsh, 9 Mar. 1925, *SL*, p. 152.

28. "Homage to Ezra," *This Quarter*, 1 (Spring [May] 1925), 221–5.
29. "Rambles Through Literary Paris," 17 Feb. 1924.
30. See Kenneth Lynn's suppositions on this animosity, pp. 246–8.

Chapter Fourteen: PARIS DOLDRUMS

1. 15 Feb. 1925.
2. Biographers have misdated this sequence on the basis of a February 13, 1924 EH letter. Evidence shows he could not have gotten the Liveright contract and letter until March 16.
3. *Tribune*, 14 Mar. 1924; EH–Walsh, 18 Mar. 1925, Baker Collection, PUL; Robert F. Wilson, *Paris on Parade* (Indianapolis, Ind.: Bobbs Merrill, 1925), p. 220.
4. EH–Walsh, 18 Mar. 1925, Baker Collection, PUL.
5. Clarence Hemingway–EH, 8 Mar. 1925, JFK. Dr. Hemingway calls the Indian "Nic" but records have his name as Dick.
6. EH–Clarence Hemingway, 20 Mar. 1925, *SL*, p. 153.
7. *Tribune*, 27 Jan. 1925.
8. *In Our Time*, pp. 55–7.
9. Item 773e, JFK: this is Count Guiseppi Greppi who reappears in *A Farewell to Arms* (1929) as Count Greffi. When EH made these notes is not known. Greppi died in 1921 at 102.
10. EH–Ernest Walsh and Ethel Moorhead, March 1925, JFK; EH–Liveright, 31 Mar. 1925, *SL*, pp. 154–5; EH–Ernest Walsh, 27 Mar. 1925, JFK.
11. *Tribune*, 2 Apr. 1925.
12. EH–Walsh and Moorhead, n.d. 1925, JFK; EH–Jane Heap [April 1925], Baker Collection, PUL.
13. Hadley Hemingway–Dear Godmothers, n.d., YUL.
14. EH–Max Perkins, 15 Apr. 1925, *SL*, p. 156.
15. EH–Jane Heap, c. April 1925, Baker Collection, PUL; EH–John Dos Passos, 22 Apr. 1925, *SL*, p. 157; EH–Sherwood Anderson, 23 May 1925, *SL*, p. 161.
16. Scribner's Author file, PUL; Bruccoli, p. 7; James R. Mellow, *Invented Lives* (Boston, Mass.: Houghton Mifflin, 1984), pp. 230–2. *AMF*, pp. 149–54, 179; Mellow, *Invented Lives*, pp. 235–7; Bruccoli, pp. 17–19.
17. Bruccoli, p. 26; Mellow, *Invented Lives*, pp. 233, 261.
18. EH–Ernest Walsh, 19 Apr. 1925, JFK, original at UVa. Smith

arrival: W. B. Smith interview with Carlos Baker, Baker file, PUL; and *Tribune*, 17 Apr. 1925.

19. Item 239a, JFK; EH–Ernest Walsh, March 1925, JFK.
20. "Night Before Landing," *NAS*, pp. 137–42.
21. *Tribune*, 3 May 1925.
22. Mellow, *Invented Lives*, pp. 242–3; Baker, pp. 144–9; *AMF*, p. 179; Scott Donaldson, *Fool for Love* (New York: Congdon & Weed, 1983), pp. 69–72.
23. EH–Arthur Mizener, 22 Apr. 1950, Baker Collection, PUL; Mellow, *Invented Lives*, pp. 358–60; Donaldson, *Fool for Love*, pp. 74–5; *AMF*, p. 186.
24. Meyers, p. 174; Baker, pp. 142, 592.
25. Baker, p. 142; Margaret Anderson, *My Thirty Years War* (New York: Covici, Friede, 1930).
26. Harold Loeb, "Ernest Hemingway: A Life Story," *Southern Review*, n.s. 5 (Autumn 1969), 1214–25. See also his book, *The Way It Was*, and his comments in Sarason's book.
27. Brian, p. 60; Hadley interview, Baker file, PUL.
28. Hadley interview, Baker file, PUL.
29. Undated note, JFK.
30. Baker, pp. 142–5; Meyers, pp. 155–9; Lynn, pp. 291–9; Kert, pp. 157–9; EH–Harold Loeb, 21 June 1925, *SL*, p. 164.
31. Item 202b, JFK.
32. EH–William Smith, 17 Feb. 1925, W. B. Smith Collection, PUL.
33. Brian, pp. 55–6.
34. Hadley Richardson–EH, 8 Jan. 1921, JFK.
35. Max Perkins–EH, 28 Apr. 1925, Scribner's Author file, PUL; EH–Horace Liveright, 11 May 1925; *SL*, p. 159; Three Mountains records, Beach Collection, PUL: she sold nine copies between May 13 and September 4; EH–Max Perkins, 9 June 1925, *SL*, p. 162.
36. Horace Liveright–EH, 1 May 1925, PUL.
37. *Tribune*, 17 May 1925.
38. EH manuscript, Jane Heap Collection, University of Wisconsin at Milwaukee.
39. EH–Horace Liveright, 22 May 1925, *SL*, pp. 160–1; *In Our Time*, pp. 109–15.
40. EH–Sherwood Anderson, 23 May 1925, *SL*, pp. 161–2.
41. EH–Jane Heap, n.d., Jane Heap Collection, copy in Baker

Collection, PUL: internal reference to going to Spain "this month" dates letter in June 1925.

42. Miró program and announcement of the opening, JFK.

43. Galerie Pierre bills and catalog, JFK; Loeb, *The Way It Was*, p. 207. Baker, p. 158; Meyers, p. 166; Lynn, p. 302; see Hemingway's version in Clement Greenberg, *Joan Miró* (New York: Quadrangle Press, 1948), p. 5; see Hadley's comments in Brian, pp. 41, 71.

44. EH–Horace Liveright, 18, 21 June 1925, JFK.

45. *Tribune*, 9, 10 June 1925.

46. EH–Harold Loeb, 21 June 1925, *SL*, p. 164; Loeb, *The Way It Was*, pp. 255–77.

47. Loeb, *The Way It Was*, p. 280.

Chapter Fifteen: SUMMER OF THE SUN

1. Kathleen Cannell, "Scenes with a Hero," reprinted in Sarason, p. 149.

2. *SL*, p. 164; Sylvia Beach's postage record books appear to corroborate Hemingway's letter.

3. *SL*, pp. 165–6; all licenses are in EH Collection, JFK.

4. EH–Gertrude Stein, 15 July 1925, *SL*, p. 167; Loeb, *The Way It Was*, p. 285; Hadley interview, Baker file, PUL; "Interview with Hemingway's 'Bill Gorton'," Donald St. John in Sarason, p. 183; Baker interview with W. B. Smith, 3 Apr. 1964, Baker file, PUL; "Interview with Donald Ogden Stewart," Donald St. John in Sarason, pp. 189–206; Bernice Kert files.

5. See Baker, pp. 149–51; Lynn, pp. 293–6; Loeb, *The Way It Was*, pp. 284–98; Sarason, throughout the book; Meyers, pp. 156–9.

6. *100 Años de Carteles de las Fiestas y Ferias de San Fermín 1882–1981*, textos: Ricardo Ollaquindia (Pamplona: Caja de Ahorros de Navarra, 1982), n.p., back of 1925 poster. The parachute was a recent invention.

7. Sarason, pp. 195–205.

8. Duff Stirling King's certificate of death filed in Santa Fe, New Mexico, on June 27, 1938 listed her occupation as housewife. She died of pulmonary and intestinal tuberculosis. She was cremated in Albuquerque the following day.

9. Brian, p. 57; Loeb, *The Way It Was*, pp. 291–2.

10. Sarason, p. 199.

11. *100 Años de Carteles de las Fiestas y Ferias de San Fermin.*
12. Loeb, *The Way It Was*, pp. 286–8.
13. Loeb, *The Way It Was*, pp. 294–7.
14. *SL*, p. 166.
15. EH–Gertrude Stein, 15 July 1925, *SL*, pp. 167–8.
16. Item 193, p. 1, JFK.
17. Item 193, pp. 16, 18, 27, JFK.
18. EH–William Smith, 27 July 1925, W. B. Smith Collection, PUL.
19. Item 194, notebook I: 39, JFK.
20. Morris Musselman–EH, 8 Nov. 1926, JFK: speaks of "the idea you had . . . the love story of a guy that's had 'em shot away." Musselman had not seen Hemingway since 1919–21; Dorman-Smith–EH, 16 Dec. 1925, JFK.
21. Item 194, notebook I: 11, JFK.
22. Item 194, notebook I: 9, JFK.
23. EH–Sylvia Beach, c. 3 Aug. 1925, Beach Collection, PUL.
24. The bar is identified in *The Secret Paris of the 30's* by Brassai (trans. Richard Miller, New York: Pantheon Books, 1976) in the "Bal Musette" chapter. This was pointed out to me by both Jerry Kennedy and Jim Hinkle. Item 194, notebook I: 32–3, JFK. Cedric Morris and Arthur Lett-Haines identified in letter from Richard Morphet to Carlos Baker, 20 Sept. 1983, Baker Collection, PUL.
25. EH–William Smith, 5 Aug. 1925, W. B. Smith Collection, PUL; EH–Barklie Henry, 12 Aug. 1925, JFK.
26. EH–Barklie Henry, 12 Aug. 1925, JFK.
27. EH–Gertrude Stein, misdated letter 20 Aug. 1925, Gertrude Stein Collection, YUL.
28. EH–Clarence Hemingway, 20 Aug. 1925, *SL*, pp. 168–9.
29. Item 194, notebook III: 51, JFK.
30. Item 194, notebook III: 53, JFK.
31. EH–Jane Heap, c. 20 Aug. 1925, copy in Baker file, PUL, original probably in Jane Heap Collection, University of Wisconsin at Milwaukee.
32. Scott Fitzgerald–Tom [Smith], n.d., private collection.
33. Beach postage book records, 1925, Beach Collection, PUL; *Tribune*; numerous letters.
34. W. B. Smith interview with Carlos Baker, Baker file, PUL; Hadley interview, Baker file, PUL.

35. Pauline Pfeiffer–Harold Loeb [August 1925], Loeb Collection, PUL.
36. *AMF*, pp. 209–10.

Chapter Sixteen: End Game

1. Item 194, notebook II: 7, JFK.
2. Item 194, notebook V: 15, JFK.
3. *Death in the Afternoon*, pp. 239–40, "Glossary"; see also my essay, "False Dawn," in Don Noble's *Hemingway: A Revaluation* (Troy, NY: Whitston Publishing Company, 1983), pp. 115–34; EH–Scott Fitzgerald, c. 20 May 1926, *SL*, p. 204.
4. *The Sun Also Rises*, p. 132.
5. Loeb, *The Way It Was*, p. 300; Baker, pp. 154, 589.
6. Cannell, in Sarason, p. 149; Baker, pp. 154, 589.
7. *The Sun Also Rises*, p. 228.
8. *The Sun Also Rises*, p. 233.
9. *The Sun Also Rises*, p. 239, 247.
10. Wilson, *Paris on Parade*, p. 249.
11. EH–Ernest Walsh, *SL*, pp. 169–70, dated c. 15 Sept. 1925 but must have been at least a week later for he says the novel is finished. Also makes same complaints in letter of September 25.
12. EH–Clarence Hemingway, 25 Sept. 1925, JFK; *Tribune*, 24 Sept. 1925; "Latin Quarter Notes," *Tribune*, 25 Sept. 1925.
13. Item 630, "On Cathedrals," JFK; Item 202c, dated Chartres, September 27, 1925, JFK.
14. Item 202c, JFK, quoted from Noble, *Hemingway: A Revaluation*, p. 117.
15. Galerie Pierre bill marked paid, JFK.
16. Beach day books, 1925, Beach Collection, PUL.
17. Hemingway clipping file, JFK.
18. EH–Family, 25 Sept. 1925, JFK; EH–Family, 19 Oct. 1925, Baker file, PUL; EH–Clarence Hemingway, 20 Nov. 1925, JFK.
19. EH–Harold Loeb, c. late October or early November 1925, JFK; Beach day books, 1925, PUL.
20. *CSS*, pp. 231–49; see James J. Martine, "Hemingway's 'Fifty Grand': The Other Fight(s)," *Journal of Modern Literature*, 2 (September 1971), 123–7; see also *Tribune* for month following the Siki–Carpentier fight.

21. EH–Harold Loeb [c. October 1925], JFK; EH–William Smith, 3 Dec. 1925, Field Collection, SUL.
22. Item 535, JFK.
23. Beach check out records, PUL; *Tribune*, 10 Oct. 1925.
24. Galerie Druet catalog for Exposition Annuelle du 4ᵉ Groupe (3–13 Nov. 1925), JFK; Robeson: *Tribune*, 13 Nov. 1925; Auteuil: *Tribune*, 23 Nov. 1925; Jolas: *Tribune*, 15 Nov. 1925. As Paul Smith remembered, Hemingway used Light For Me in *A Farewell to Arms* and in 1949, on another Auteuil afternoon, Hemingway remembered the six-year-old steeplechaser in his poem "Across the Board," *88 Poems*, p. 120:

    But light she was and light for me
    And who slept with eternity?
    Eternity is scarcely found
    Until we're underneath the ground
    Where thudding hooves will seldom sound.

25. Beach check out records, PUL; Stein: "Latin Quarter Notes," *Tribune*, 27 Nov. 1925.
26. *The Torrents of Spring*, p. 76; Fitzgerald letter quoted from Bruccoli, pp. 24–6.
27. *The Torrents of Spring*, p. 10.
28. *The Torrents of Spring*, p. 39.
29. *The Torrents of Spring*, p. 42.
30. Brian, p. 57; Hadley interview, Baker file, PUL; Baker, p. 159; Ludington, *John Dos Passos*, p. 241; Virginia Spencer Carr, *Dos Passos: A Life* (Garden City, NY: Doubleday, 1984), p. 224.
31. Fitzgerald letter quoted in Bruccoli, pp. 29–30.
32. The dedication has been removed from the Scribner's reissue of *Torrents*. See *New York Times*, 27, 28 Oct., 7 Nov. 1924.
33. Hemingway Collection, PUL; EH–MacLeish, *SL*, pp. 140–1, misdated 11 Dec. 1924. EH–William Smith, 3 Dec. 1925, Field Collection, SUL; EH–Isabel Simmons Godolphin, 3 Dec. 1925, *SL*, pp. 171–2.
34. EH–Horace Liveright, 7 Dec. 1925, *SL*, pp. 172–4.
35. *Tribune*, 7 Dec. 1925.
36. Scott Fitzgerald–Max Perkins, c. 22 May 1925, *Dear Scott/Dear Max*, ed. John Kuehl and Jackson Bryer (New York: Scribner's, 1971), p. 106; best discussion of this period on Hemingway's relationship with Fitzgerald is in Bruccoli's *Scott and Ernest* and in Scott Donaldson's article "The Wooing of Ernest Hemingway,"

American Literature, 53 (March 1981), 691–710. I have relied heavily on both accounts in this paragraph and those that follow.

37. Scott Fitzgerald–EH, c. 15 Oct. 1925, quoted by Donaldson, "The Wooing of Ernest Hemingway," p. 694; Items 387, 388, JFK; Scott Fitzgerald–Max Perkins, *The Letters of F. Scott Fitzgerald*, ed. Andrew Turnbull (New York: Scribner's, 1963), p. 182.

38. EH–Grace Hemingway, 14 Dec. 1925, *SL*, p. 174; EH–Scott Fitzgerald, 15 Dec. 1925, *SL*, p. 176.

39. EH–Scott Fitzgerald, 24 Dec. 1925, *SL*, p. 181.

40. EH passport, JFK; EH/Hadley Hemingway–Sylvia Beach, c. 14 Dec. 1925, *SL*, p. 175; Hadley Hemingway's part of letter in EH collection, PUL; Beach check out records, Beach Collection, PUL; EH–Archibald MacLeish, 20 Dec. 1925, *SL*, p. 179.

41. EH–Grace Hemingway, 14 Dec. 1925, *SL*, pp. 174–5; Clarence Hemingway–EH, 2 Dec. 1925, Baker file, PUL.

42. Clarence Hemingway–EH, 9 Dec. 1925, JFK; Madelaine Hemingway–EH, 6 Dec. 1925, JFK.

43. EH–Scott Fitzgerald, c. 24 Dec. 1925, *SL*, p. 182; Kert, pp. 172–3; Baker, p. 162; Pauline Pfeiffer–Hadley Hemingway, 29 Jan. 1926, JFK. In fact there were no avalanches according to Gunter Salzmann who has checked the records of the Montafon valley on this point.

44. Kert, p. 173.

45. Horace Liveright–EH, 30 Dec. 1925, EH Collection, PUL.

46. EH–Scott Fitzgerald, 31 Dec. 1925, *SL*, pp. 183–5.

Chapter Seventeen: THE SECRET SHARERS

1. EH–Ernest Walsh, 2 Jan. 1926, JFK; their bridge scores are recorded on the backs of letters in the Hemingway Collection, JFK; EH–William Smith, 2 Jan. 1926, private collection; EH–Scott Fitzgerald, on rocking horse and jockey outfit, 21 Dec. 1925, JFK.

2. EH–Ernest Walsh, 2 Jan. 1926, JFK; Baker, pp. 183–5; Meyers, pp. 184–6, 321, 594; Lynn, pp. 249, 269, 312–14; see also H. R. Stoneback's several excellent articles on the validity of Hemingway's religious belief.

3. Register of Arnold Kessler, Hotel Rossle, Gaschurn, Austria.

4. Pauline Pfeiffer–EH, 14 Jan. 1926, JFK; Items 197a, 197, JFK; EH–Ernest Walsh, 2 Jan. 1926, *SL*, p. 186. This letter is misdated.

More likely mid-January. EH refers to *This Quarter* which he probably did not see until then.

5. Horace Liveright–Scott Fitzgerald, 30 Dec. 1925, EH Collection, PUL.

6. Cables between Fitzgerald and Max Perkins, 8 Jan. 1926, quoted in Bruccoli, p. 34.

7. Scott Fitzgerald–Max Perkins, dated December 1925, in Bruccoli, pp. 32–3, but could not have been written until Fitzgerald received the EH letter mailed January 1, 1926.

8. Pauline Pfeiffer–EH/Hadley Hemingway, 14 and 16 Jan. 1926, JFK.

9. Baker, p. 163, based on Liveright–EH, 30 Dec. 1925; Pauline Pfeiffer–EH/Hadley Hemingway, 16 Jan. 1926, JFK.

10. EH–Horace Liveright, 19 Jan. 1926, *SL*, pp. 191–2.

11. Beach library records, Beach Collection, PUL; Pauline Pfeiffer–EH/Hadley Hemingway, 19 Jan. 1926, JFK.

12. Pauline Pfeiffer–Hadley Hemingway, 17 and 21 Jan. 1926, JFK.

13. *Tribune*, 25 Jan. 1926; Pauline Pfeiffer–Hadley Hemingway, 29 Jan. 1926, JFK.

14. *Tribune*, 25–30 Jan. 1926.

15. Baker, p. 164; Beach records, 30 Jan. 1926, PUL; *Tribune*, 31 Jan. 1926; EH notebook, JFK.

16. *Tribune*, 3 Feb. 1926; EH passport, JFK.

17. Pauline Pfeiffer–Hadley Hemingway, 4 Feb. 1926, JFK.

18. EH–Isabel Simmons Godolphin, 25 Feb. 1926, *SL*, p. 193: note that others have Hemingway staying as long as a month in New York. He arrived very late on February 9 and departed the night of February 20 on the first boat sailing after his Scribner's contract was signed.

19. Letter with note reproduced in catalog, *In Their Time*, Item 41, UVa.

20. EH–William Smith and Harold Loeb [n.d. February 1926], private collection.

21. Max Perkins–EH, carbon in Scribner's Hemingway file first read in Scribner's offices, now at Princeton in Scribner's Author file.

22. EH–Isabel Simmons Godolphin, 25 Feb. 1926, *SL*, pp. 193–4; *Tribune*, 21 Feb. 1926.

23. Marion Meade, *Dorothy Parker* (New York: Villard Books, 1988), pp. 164–6.

24. EH–Isabel Simmons Godolphin, 25 Feb. 1926, *SL*, pp. 193–4.

25. Pauline Pfeiffer–Hadley Hemingway, 25 Feb. 1925, JFK.

26. Hadley Hemingway–Isabel Simmons Godolphin, 1 Mar. 1926, EH Collection, PUL.

INDEX

400